FAITH AND HISTORY
Essays in Honor of Paul W. Meyer

Paul William Meyer

FAITH AND HISTORY
ESSAYS IN HONOR OF PAUL W. MEYER

edited by

John T. Carroll
Charles H. Cosgrove
E. Elizabeth Johnson

PUBLISHERS
Eugene, Oregon

Wipf and Stock Publishers
199 W 8th Ave, Suite 3
Eugene, OR 97401

Faith and History
Essays in Honor of Paul W. Meyer
Edited by Carroll, John T., Cosgrove, Charles H., and Johnson, E. E.
Copyright©1990 by Carroll, John T., Cosgrove, Charles H., and Paulsen, Elizabeth J.
ISBN: 1-59752-001-2
Publication date 11/18/2004
Previously published by Scholars Press, 1990

Preface

A *Festschrift* is inevitably the product of many people's labors. We are deeply indebted to the contributors who so willingly shared with us in honoring our teacher, particularly Professors J. Louis Martyn and Wayne A. Meeks, themselves seasoned editors who advised and encouraged us from the beginning of the project. The Rev. Dr. David R. Adams served as a wise and trusted guide throughout. We are most grateful to Dr. Harry Gilmer for his willingness to publish the volume in the Homage Series of Scholars Press.

President Thomas W. Gillespie of Princeton Theological Seminary provided substantial financial as well as moral support, Ms. Donna Musso and Ms. Joan Ferguson of his office graciously supervised much of the correspondence and hospitality, and Ms. Ellen Myers of the Dean's Office compiled the list of Princeton dissertations. The library staffs of Yale Divinity School and Vanderbilt Divinity School compiled the lists of Yale and Vanderbilt dissertations.

Our own institutions, New Brunswick Theological Seminary, Northern Baptist Theological Seminary, and Louisiana State University, generously provided us with copying, mailing, and telephone service; library support; and encouragement of our own writing and editing. We are particularly indebted to our student assistants, Mr. Thomas M. Jordan, Ms. Sherri C. Smith, Ms. Cynthia M. Bunch, and Ms. Patricia A. Fraser, who efficiently and cheerfully typed essays, hunted missing footnotes, kept track of our editing, and frequently suggested editorial improvements.

Dr. Michael J. Gorman translated Professor Cullmann's essay from the French. Mr. Dennis Ford of Scholars Press advised and assisted us with the production of the volume. Mr. Russell Gasero, Archivist of the Reformed Church in America, prepared the camera-ready manuscript for publication. Our families patiently endured our various absences from home, long telephone calls, and even longer hours at the computer.

Ms. Mary Louise Meyer helped us from the very beginning, assisting us with the composition of the guest list and faithfully keeping the secret from Paul until the time of presentation.

We are grateful to them all.

> John T. Carroll
> > Louisiana State University
>
> Charles H. Cosgrove
> > Northern Baptist Theological Seminary
>
> E. Elizabeth Johnson
> > New Brunswick Theological Seminary

CONTENTS

Frontispiece: Paul William Meyer
Preface   v
Introduction   1
Tabula Gratulatoria   14

PART ONE
FAITH AND HISTORY: STUDIES IN THE GOSPELS

1. Jesus and Early Christian Eschatology
   John T. Carroll   18
2. The Birth of the Reader in Matthew
   Bernard Brandon Scott   35
3. The Human Face of Otherness: Reflections on Joseph and Mary (Matthew 1:18-25)
   Karl A. Plank   55
4. John and the Synoptics in Light of the Question of Faith and History
   D. Moody Smith   74

PART TWO
FAITH AND HISTORY: STUDIES IN PAUL

5. Conversations with a Friend about Romans
   J. Christiaan Beker   90
6. Paul's Midrash: Reflections on Romans 4
   Lou H. Silberman   99
7. On Trusting an Unpredictable God: A Hermeneutical Meditation on Romans 9-11
   Wayne A. Meeks   105
8. Romans 15:4: An Interpolation?
   Leander E. Keck   125
9. The Wisdom of God as Apocalyptic Power
   E. Elizabeth Johnson   137
10. Death and Victory in 1 Corinthians 15:51-57: The Transformation of a Prophetic Theme
    Walter J. Harrelson   149
11. The Covenants of Hagar and Sarah
    J. Louis Martyn   160

12	Apostles as Babes and Nurses in 1 Thessalonians 2:7 *Beverly R. Gaventa*	193
13	Job and the Problem of Doubt in Paul *David M. Hay*	208
14	Faith and Its Moral Life: Individuation in the Thought World of the Apostle Paul *J. Paul Sampley*	223
15	Romans 8:1-11: Pauline Theology in Medieval Interpretation *Karlfried Froehlich*	239

PART THREE
FAITH AND HISTORY: THEOLOGICAL STUDIES

16	Christian Faith's Partnership with History *John D. Godsey*	261
17	The Salvation of Jesus: A Theological Reflection on the Destiny of the Kingdom in History *Charles H. Cosgrove*	279
18	What Do We Really Mean When We Say, "God Sent His Son"? *Eduard Schweizer*	298
19	Revelation as Our Knowledge of God: An Essay in Biblical Theology *C. P. Price*	313
20	Inclusive Language and Biblical Authority *Paul S. Minear*	335
21	Pluralism and Unity in the New Testament *Oscar Cullmann*	352
22	Calvin's Scriptural Ethical Monotheism: Interpretation, Moral Conscience, and Religious System *Wendell Dietrich*	360

Introduction

Charles H. Cosgrove

Paul William Meyer was born May 31, 1924 in Raipur, India, to the Reverend Armin F. and Hulda K. Meyer, missionaries of the Evangelical Synod of North America (part of what later became the Evangelical and Reformed Church). He received his undergraduate education at Elmhurst College in Elmhurst, Illinois (1945), and then went on, after World War II, to complete a B.D. (1949) and Th.D. (1955) in New Testament at Union Theological Seminary in New York. He is married to the former Mary Louise Yonker and they are the parents of two daughters.

During a year of graduate work in Switzerland from 1949 to 1950, while studying with Oscar Cullmann and Eduard Schweizer, Meyer became acquainted with Karl Barth, whose writings have served him as a constant partner in theological dialogue over the years. He did postgraduate study at the University of Göttingen as a Fulbright Research Fellow in 1961-62 and was the same year named a Morse Fellow at Yale University. Over the course of a distinguished career in theological education, Paul Meyer has taught at Union Theological Seminary, The Divinity School of Yale University, Colgate Rochester Divinity School, Vanderbilt University Divinity School, and Princeton Theological Seminary, from which he retired in 1989.[1] He has also been an active member of the American Theological Society, serving as its president in 1987-88, a founding member of the Biblical Theologians, and an active

---

[1] Union Theological Seminary (1951-54), Yale University Divinity School (1954-64), Colgate-Rochester Divinity School (1964-70), Vanderbilt University Divinity School (1970-78), Princeton Theological Seminary (1978-89).

member of both the Society of Biblical Literature and Studiorum Novi Testamenti Societas.

At a dinner given in his honor on the occasion of the production of this *Festschrift* Meyer announced to his colleagues and former students, "You are my letters of recommendation." His invocation of the Apostle Paul's statement to the Corinthians is a characteristic gesture of humility. It points, however, to the fact that one of Meyer's greatest contributions to both the academy and the church has been his teaching, which has taken place both in classrooms and informally in hundreds of conversations over forty years' service in theological education.[2]

The title of this volume of essays points to Meyer's own deep commitment to the twin tasks of promoting rigorous theological reflection in the service of the church and keeping theology in constant conversation with history, especially the irreplaceable history of the Crucified. These essays are divided into three groupings, and one might be tempted to regard the first two sets as a series of exegetical and historical studies in the Gospels and Paul's letters and the final set as a collection of theological pieces. This impression is welcomed at one level since it suggests the division of Meyer's own labors throughout his career between the disciplines of both New Testament and theology. But at another level the essays themselves reveal that explicitly theological questions animate the exegetical and historical studies, while questions of exegesis and history enliven the theological studies.

The relationship between "faith and history" has been the recurring theme of Meyer's teaching, lecturing, and writing. Over the years he has focused this problem in a variety of ways, expressed in questions such as the following. What is the relationship between theology and exegesis? What is the relationship between the Christ of faith and the Jesus of history? What is the relationship between the cross and the resurrection? A close reading of Meyer's published writings reveals a preoccupation with the meaning of Jesus' death, a concern motivated by the unswerving conviction that the kerygma marks the crucified Jesus of history as the clue to authentic Christian faith. The kerygma itself binds faith to history, which means that it binds faith to responsible historical existence carried out in the light of the history of the crucified Jesus of Nazareth.

The content of the kerygma is the "public" Jesus of history, whose execution came about because of the things he said and the way he lived. Meyer presented a breathtaking defense of this thesis in his 1976 Shaffer Lectures at Yale Divinity School. The title of these lectures,

---

[2] See the list of dissertations following this Introduction.

"The Justification of Jesus," refers to the meaning of the resurrection as God's vindication of the discredited Jesus of Nazareth. The resurrection marks *this* Jesus as both the "warrant" and "criterion" of Christian faith.[3]

Meyer's understanding of the relation between the cross and the resurrection leads him to put the cross—the historical *event* of the crucifixion—rather than a *theology* of the cross at the heart of Christian faith.[4] But this center cannot stand on its own. It is made central to Christian self-understanding by God's vindication of the crucified Jesus at Easter.

The vindication of the crucified Jesus of Nazareth makes Christian faith irreversibly "this-worldly," to use Meyer's own term for the historicality of faith implied by the historical referent of the kerygma. He employs the "clumsy" expression "this-worldly" for the simple reason that "it has no substitute as the opposite of 'otherworldliness'."[5] One may recall here Dietrich Bonhoeffer's insistence that the Christian hope of resurrection, unlike the promise of "redemption myths", makes "no last line of escape available from earthly tasks and difficulties" but "sends a man back to his life on earth in a wholly new way."[6] Nevertheless, the accent in Meyer's work is not on the resurrection as "hope" but on its meaning as *disclosure*. In this respect Meyer stands very close to Rudolf Bultmann; it is also the point where he departs most radically from him. Where Bultmann grants "continuities" between the historical Jesus and the kerygma but denies that knowledge about the historical Jesus ought to be made a criterion of faith, Meyer stresses

---

[3] A copy of the typescript of these lectures is housed in Speer Library at Princeton Theological Seminary.

[4] See "The 'This-Worldliness' of the New Testament," *The Princeton Seminary Bulletin* 2 N.S. (1979) 228-230.

[5] Ibid., 221. "By the phrase 'The "This-Worldliness" of the New Testament' I am *not* in the first instance thinking of the historically conditioned character of the New Testament writings or their situation-bound particularity, even though the proper recognition of both these features is today utterly indispensable for the work of honest exegesis. And I certainly do not mean to convey the notion that the New Testament belongs without remainder to the everyday world of the secular and the profane. Part of our problem is that the *mundane* so often connotes the *profane*, the earthly has become God-forsaken, and we can no longer tell the difference. And the last thing I mean to suggest is a hermeneutic of the New Testament that would deny the deliberate preoccupation of its writers with the actions and presence of the living God. No, clumsy as it may be, the term 'this-worldliness' has been chosen simply because it has no substitute as the opposite of 'otherworldliness.' Otherworldliness is our problem, a problem of our religion and our theology, a problem of our ways of reading the New Testament."

[6] *Letters and Papers from Prison* (enlarged edition; ed. E. Bethge; New York: Macmillan, 1971) 336-337.

that the kerygma refers faith to none other than the Jesus of history, for he is the one "in need of" that vindication by God about which the earliest proclamation of the resurrection speaks. The reference of the kerygma to Jesus of Nazareth does not imply that the relation of faith to history is to be established by discerning "continuities" between Jesus and the post-Easter witness of the church. Instead, the public execution of Jesus of Nazareth is the fundamental criterion of Christian faith.

One of Meyer's ongoing concerns in emphasizing the "this-worldliness" of Christian faith is the nature of Christian eschatology. Here again, the meaning of Jesus' death proves to be decisive, signifying at once a crisis for all traditional eschatological hopes and the clue to the true nature of God's presence and work in history:

> The [Jewish] eschatological tradition has not continued unbroken; it has passed through a crucible fired by a public act not only available but also inevasible to every onlooker and inquirer, the crucifixion of Jesus of Nazareth. It has become irreversibly "this-worldly."[7]

Meyer likes to frame his understanding of the relationship between the crucifixion and eschatology by citing comments by Martin Buber regarding the difference between Jews and Christians in their attitudes toward Jesus as the Messiah. In a speech to Dutch pastors Buber remarked:

> To the Christian the Jew is the stubborn fellow who in a redeemed world is still waiting for the Messiah. For the Jew the Christian is a heedless fellow who in an unredeemed world affirms that somehow or other redemption has taken place.[8]

Meyer's starting point in responding to what he calls "the withering force of that elemental refutation" is once again the meaning of the resurrection as the vindication of the crucified Jesus. A right understanding of the resurrection leads Christians to affirm not that the world has "somehow or other" been redeemed but that "the Messiah *has* come in an *un*redeemed world."[9] There is a significant echo of this

---

[7] "The 'This-Worldliness' of the New Testament," 222.

[8] As cited by Reinhold Niebuhr, "Martin Buber: 1878-1965," *Christianity and Crisis* 25 (July 12, 1965) 146. See Meyer, "The 'This-Worldliness' of the New Testament," 221, with note 1.

[9] "The 'This-Worldliness' of the New Testament," 222.

Introduction 5

affirmation in some comments by Meyer on Rom 8:18-30 in his commentary on Romans[10] under the heading, "Justification as the Gift of Hope in a Still Unredeemed World." Here Meyer epitomizes the Apostle Paul's own understanding of Christian existence in the world as follows:

> Paul now returns [at Rom 8:18] to the afflicted and precarious quality of life mentioned in 5:3-4. The credibility of his many intervening affirmations is threatened by the falsifying power of the actual experience of transiency and suffering, the footprints of death's continuing presence. Careful readers will have noted that Paul has never denied that presence, even in the last section (8:10a). Death is still "the last enemy" (1 Cor 15:26). This is exactly why the death of Jesus remains so central to Paul's gospel. The indisputable reality of death in human life is also the most public feature of Jesus' life.[11]

The early church's (and *our own*) appropriation of the Hebrew scriptures, Jewish tradition, the life and witness of the Jewish Jesus—all indispensable resources of faith's ongoing reflection—"become distinctively *Christian*...when they are all altered under the impact of the brutal historical reality of the crucifixion of Jesus of Nazareth and the reflections that reality set in motion."[12] One example of this alteration is Paul's "hard realism," which "reinforces the correspondence between Christ's life and those who are 'in him,' so that present affliction verifies the truth of the gospel instead of refuting it."[13]

In his Shaffer Lectures Meyer speaks about the way in which the brutal reality of the crucifixion alters the story of the Messiah as told in the Gospels. Meyer characterizes this transformation as "history intruding into myth"[14] in contrast to the view that sees the creation of Christian faith as a mythologization of history. To this extent Meyer agrees with Karl Barth that a particular historical reality is the referent of the Christian witness to Christ. But where Barth locates that reality,

---

[10] "Romans" in *Harper's Bible Commentary* (ed. James L. Mays; San Francisco: Harper and Row, 1988) 1130-1167.

[11] Ibid., 1152.

[12] "Faith and History Revisited," *The Princeton Seminary Bulletin* 10 N.S. (1989) 82-83.

[13] "Romans," 1152-1153.

[14] "The Justification of Jesus," 76.

at least for our knowledge, exclusively in the New Testament witness,[15] Meyer locates it first and foremost in the public history of Jesus of Nazareth which lies "behind" that witness. It is interesting to note in this connection that Barth once declared in an exchange with Paul Tillich that "even if all is myth, the myth also describes the revelation as inseparably bound to an 'empirical fact'."[16] For Meyer God's vindication of the one who is this "empirical fact" makes that "fact" itself the criterion by which any mythological speech about God is to be judged.

The crucified Jesus of Nazareth, vindicated by God, is the ground of faith; faith is not the ground of believing in Jesus. It is interesting to see how Meyer finds support for this theological judgment even in the Gospel of John, where the history of Jesus of Nazareth barely peeks through faith's portrait of the incarnate Lord and where Jesus is authenticated for faith, according to Meyer, as much by his death as by his resurrection. Meyer defends this interpretation in a short article on John 10,[17] in which he argues that the "door" through which the good shepherd enters, so that the sheep might know that it is he and not one of the thieves or robbers, is his death: that he lays down his life for the sheep. Meyer comments at the close of his essay that "John 10:1-18 thus finds Jesus' messianic claim confirmed and vindicated rather than contradicted by his death upon the cross."[18] Meyer makes no further comment on this observation, but many years later he would refer to John 10 in discussing his own view of the center of New Testament theology. That center, according to Meyer, is not a particular theology within the New Testament but rather the historical event of the crucifixion "that has left its mark on every theology, every narrative, every interpretation of Jesus and every memory of Jesus, every admonition to Christian living, every exhortation and every consolation in the New Testament."[19] In the course of illustrating this point, Meyer poses the following rhetorical questions about the Gospel of John:

> Or who will claim that the Gospel of John could have come to the notion that the one who genuinely claims to be a shepherd

---

[15] See *CD* IV/2, 154-155. Meyer takes up Barth's views on the question of the historical Jesus in an extensive footnote in the typescript of his Shaffer Lectures (110-113, note 24).

[16] Karl Barth, "Von der Paradoxie des 'positiven Paradoxes': Antworten und Fragen an Paul Tillich," in *Anfänge der dialektischen Theologie*, Part 1 (2nd ed.; ed. Jürgen Moltmann; München: Chr. Kaiser, 1966) 185.

[17] "A Note on John 10:1-18," *JBL* 75 (1956) 232-235.

[18] Ibid., 235.

[19] "The 'This-Worldliness' of the New Testament," 230.

Introduction

of God's people is the one who distinguishes himself from every hireling and every fraudulent claimer of that title by laying his life down for the sheep—if it had not been for that event [the crucifixion]?

In other words, the Fourth Gospel is indebted to a kerygma to which it accords little, if any, explicit witness—namely, to the earliest preaching about how God vindicated the crucified Jesus of Nazareth and thus made this one and his *cross* definitive for faith.

Among Meyer's unpublished but widely circulated manuscripts is an address entitled, "Seeing, Signs, and Sources in the Fourth Gospel,"[20] in which he argues that in John "faith" is not—as prevailing and more or less Bultmannian interpretations would have it—the *presupposition* of "seeing" signs but rather the *consequence* of having seen them. Although Meyer does not develop the theological significance of this exegetical conclusion in his paper, its implications become clear in the Shaffer Lectures. There Meyer points out that Bultmann's teacher Wilhelm Herrmann reasserted, against Martin Kähler, "a distinction between [the historical Jesus] and the kerygma and the need for both faith and preaching to have a ground that is antecedent to and independent of all productions and creations of the believing mind and heart."[21] By the end of the Shaffer Lectures Meyer's own agreement with Herrmann on this point is clear. The justification of the crucified Jesus establishes a warrant and criterion of faith that is "antecedent to and independent of" human faith. The sign, namely the justified Jesus himself, evokes faith and provides its ground.

The resurrection "makes the crucifixion (or, more exactly, the One who was crucified) normative for Christian faith."[22] Meyer expresses the broader significance of this insight for the relation of faith to history as follows:

> ...the resurrection makes the cross the paradigm, the clue, the source of the disclosing impact that is sedimented in various ways in the New Testament. Indeed, it is only an understanding of the New Testament as tradition that enables us to trace the functioning presence of this paradigm and to appreciate the truly historic (in the sense of history-creating) character of this

---

[20] Presented at the annual meeting of the Society of Biblical Literature in Dallas, October 18, 1968.
[21] "The Justification of Jesus," 7.
[22] "The 'This-Worldliness' of the New Testament," 230.

event and then of the Scriptures in which it comes to us. When it functions in that way in our time, the New Testament can reshape our Christian consciousness and provide again the reliable index we so urgently need to authentic Christian speaking about God and his presence and care in an unredeemed world.

These words are from the conclusion of Meyer's Inaugural Lecture at Princeton in February of 1979.[23] Upon his retirement ten years later, his students and friends wish to express their gratitude for his own illumination of the New Testament tradition in which the witness to Jesus of Nazareth is found. We also wish to honor his insistent pointing to that witness and its referent, the One who was crucified, as the "right clue and the criterion"[24] for defining Christian obedience and discerning the care of God in an unredeemed world.

Publications by Paul W. Meyer

"A Note on John 10:1-18," *JBL* 75 (1956) 232-235.

"Judgment and Forgiveness in the Synoptic Gospels," *Children's Religion* (Congregational Teacher's Guide; May, 1958) 10-11.

"The Person of Christ in New Testament Teaching, by Vincent Taylor." Lead review in *Religion in Life* 29 (1959-60) 135-138.

"The Problem of the Messianic Self-Consciousness of Jesus," *NovT* 4 (1960) 122-138.

---

[23] Ibid., 230-231.

[24] Ibid., 227. The earliest missionaries "were proclaiming neither a new God nor an unknown Jesus. Instead, they were declaring that the God of their fathers had made of the discredited Jesus of Nazareth the right clue and the criterion for discerning God's true intentions; the measure of the right way to talk about salvation and God's kingship and their obedience; the way to face what was for them a clear and self-evident part of their future, namely the coming judgment of God."

"Trinität. II. Im NT" in *Die Religion in Geschichte und Gegenwart*, 3. Aufl., Band VI (Tübingen: J. C. B. Mohr [Paul Siebeck], 1962) cols 1024-1025.

"The Polarity of Faith: A Johannine Paradigm for our Time," *USQR* 21 (1965-66) 51-61.

Translation of Martin Stallmann, "Contemporary Interpretation of the Gospels as a Challenge to Preaching and Religious Education," in *The Theology of Rudolf Bultmann* (ed. Charles W. Kegley; New York: Harper and Row, 1966) 236-253.

"John 2:10," *JBL* 86 (1967) 191-197.

"A Response to Professor Ogletree" in "The Davis Cup Controversy at Vanderbilt University," NICM (National Institute for Campus Ministries) *Journal* 3 (Fall, 1978) 108-113.

"The Holy Spirit in the Pauline Letters: A Contextual Exploration," *Int* 33 (1979) 3-18.

"The Door That Closes," *The Princeton Seminary Bulletin* 2 N.S. (1979) 121-123.

"The 'This-Worldliness' of the New Testament," *The Princeton Seminary Bulletin* 2 N.S. (1979) 219-231.

A Review Essay on Hans Dieter Betz, *Galatians: A Commentary on Paul's Letter to the Churches of Galatia* (Hermeneia; Philadelphia: Fortress, 1979) in *RSR* 7 (1981) 310-318.

"Romans 10:4 and the 'End' of the Law" in *The Divine Helmsman: Studies on God's Control of Human Events, Presented to Lou H. Silberman* (ed. James L. Crenshaw and Samuel Sandmel; New York: KTAV, 1980) 59-78.

"The Parable of Responsibility," *The Princeton Seminary Bulletin* 6 N.S. (1985) 131-134.

"Matthew 21:1-11," *Int* 40 (1986) 180-185.

"Context as a Bearer of Meaning in Matthew," *USQR* 42 (1988) 69-72.

"Romans" in *Harper's Bible Commentary* (ed. James L. Mays; San Francisco: Harper and Row, 1988) 1130-1167.

"The Worm at the Core of the Apple: Exegetical Reflections on Romans 7" in *The Conversation Continues: Studies in Paul and John in Honor of J. Louis Martyn* (ed. Robert T. Fortna and Beverly R. Gaventa; Nashville: Abingdon, 1990).

"Faith and History Revisited," Princeton Seminary Bulletin 10 n.s. (1989) 75-83

Dissertations Directed by Paul W. Meyer

Wayne Gilbert Rollins, "The Christology of Colossians" (Yale University, 1960).

D. Moody Smith, "The Composition and Order of the Fourth Gospel" (Yale University, 1961). Published as *The Composition and Order of the Fourth Gospel: Bultmann's Literary Theory* (New Haven: Yale University, 1965).

Kenneth Bruce Welliver, "Pentecost and the Early Church: Patristic Interpretation of Acts 2" (Yale University, 1961).

Lee Herbert Reiff, "Paul's Damascus Experience and His Theology: A Study of the Recent History of the Interpretation of Paul" (Yale University, 1963).

David M. Hay, "The Use of Psalm 110 in the Early Church" (Yale University, 1964). Published as *Glory at the Right Hand: Psalm 110 in Early Christianity* (SBLMS 18; Nashville: Abingdon, 1973).

Wayne A. Meeks, "Jesus As King and Prophet in the Fourth Gospel" (Yale University, 1964). Published as *The Prophet King: Moses Tradition and Johannine Christology* (Leiden: E. J. Brill, 1967).

John H. Schütz, "Soteriology and Apostolic Authority in the Pauline Homolougomena" (Yale University, 1964). Published as *Paul and the Anatomy of Apostolic Authority* (Cambridge: University, 1975).

Fred O. Francis, "A Reexamination of the Colossian Controversy" (Yale University, 1965).

Bernard Brandon Scott, "Adolf von Harnack and Alfred Loisy: A Debate on the Historical Methodology of Christian Origins" (Vanderbilt University, 1971).

Harold E. Littleton, "The Function of Apocalyptic in 2 Thessalonians as a Criterion for Its Authorship" (Vanderbilt University, 1973).

Allan J. McNicol, "The Relationship of the Image of the Highest Angel to the High Priest Concept in Hebrews" (Vanderbilt University, 1974).

James W. Thompson, "'That Which Abides': Some Metaphysical Assumptions in the Epistle to the Hebrews" (Vanderbilt University, 1974).

F. Harry Daniel, "The Transfiguration (Mark 9:2-13 and Parallels): A Redaction-Critical and Traditio-Historical Study" (Vanderbilt University, 1976).

Eugene C. Kreider, "Matthew's Contribution to the Eschatological-Ethical Perspective in the Life of the Early Church: A Redaction-Critical Study of Matthew 18" (Vanderbilt University, 1976).

John S. Lown, "Toward A Morphology of Repentance: A Study of Conversion Terminology in the Pauline Epistles Against the Background of the Book of Acts and Selected Graeco-Roman Literature" (Vanderbilt University, 1977).

James J. H. Price, "Submission-Humility in I Peter: An Exegetical Study" (Vanderbilt University, 1977).

Charles H. Cosgrove, "The Law and the Spirit: An Investigation into the Theology of Galatians" (Princeton Theological Seminary, 1985). Revised and published as *The Cross and the Spirit: A Study in the*

Argument and Theology of Galatians (Macon, GA: Mercer University, 1988).

Benhardt Y. Quarshie, "Paul and the Culture of the Gentiles: First Corinthians and Some Methodological Issues" (Princeton Theological Seminary, 1987).

Michael J. Gorman, "The Self, the Lord, and the Other: The Significance of Reflexive Pronoun Constructions in the Letters of Paul, With a Comparison to the Discourses of Epictetus" (Princeton Theological Seminary, 1989).

Stanley P. Saunders, "'No One Dared Ask Him Anything More': Contextual Readings of the Controversy Stories in Matthew" (Princeton Theological Seminary, 1990).

Dissertations Advised By Paul W. Meyer as Second Reader

Robert C. Tannehill, "Dying and Rising With Christ: A Study in Pauline Eschatology" (Yale University, 1963). Published as *Dying and Rising with Christ: A Study in Pauline Theology* (Berlin: Töpelmann, 1967).

G. Byrns Coleman, "The Phenomenon of Christian Interpolations Into Jewish Apocalyptic Texts: A Bibliographical Survey and Methodological Analysis" (Vanderbilt University, 1976).

Barry S. Crawford, "Near Expectation in the Sayings of Jesus" (Vanderbilt University, 1978).

Ivan Thomas Blazen, "Death to Sin According to Romans 6:1-14 and Related New Testament Texts: An Exegetical-Theological Study With a Critique of Views" (Princeton Theological Seminary, 1979).

Takeshi Nagata, "Philippians 2:5-11: A Case Study in the Contextual Shaping of Early Christology" (Princeton Theological Seminary, 1981).

Douglas K. Fletcher, "The Singular Argument of Paul's Letter to the Galatians" (Princeton Theological Seminary, 1982).

John W. L. Hoad, "A Perspectival Understanding of Faith in the Light of the Synoptic Gospels and of George Kelly's Psychology of Personal Constructs and in the Context of Pastoral Counseling" (Princeton Theological Seminary, 1984).

Michael W. Holmes, "Early Editorial Activity and the Text of Codex Bezae in Matthew" (Princeton Theological Seminary, 1984).

Charles D. Myers, Jr., "The Place of Romans 5:1-11 Within the Argument of the Epistle" (Princeton Theological Seminary, 1985).

G. Franklin Shirbroun, "The Giving of the Name of God to Jesus in John 17:11-12" (Princeton Theological Seminary, 1985).

John T. Carroll, "Eschatology and Situation in Luke-Acts" (Princeton Theological Seminary, 1986). Published as *Response to the End of History: Eschatology and Situation in Luke-Acts* (SBLDS 92; Atlanta: Scholars Press, 1988).

Paul F. Feiler, "Jesus the Prophet: The Lukan Portrayal of Jesus as the Prophet Like Moses" (Princeton Theological Seminary, 1986).

Larry L. Bethune, "Abraham, Father of Faith: The Interpretation of Genesis 15:6 from Genesis to Paul" (Princeton Theological Seminary, 1987).

E. Elizabeth Johnson, "The Function of Apocalyptic and Wisdom Traditions in Romans 9-11" (Princeton Theological Seminary, 1987). Published as *The Function of Apocalyptic and Wisdom Traditions in Romans 9-11* (SBLDS 109; Atlanta: Scholars Press, 1989).

R. Neil Elliott, "The Rhetoric of Romans: Argumentative Strategy and Constraint, and Paul's 'Dialogue with Judaism'" (Princeton Theological Seminary, 1989). Published as *The Rhetoric of Romans: Argumentative Strategy and Constraint, and Paul's 'Dialogue with Judaism'* (JSNTSupp; Sheffield: Academic, 1990).

Tabula Gratulatoria

Paul J. Achtemeier
David R. Adams
Diogenes Allen
Bernhard W. Anderson
Richard S. Armstrong

William Baird
David L. Balch
C. K. Barrett
Jouette M. Bassler
J. Christiaan Beker
Hans Dieter Betz
James Bibza
Hendrikus Boers
Peder Borgen
M. Eugene Boring
Günther Bornkamm
Robert L. Brawley
Raymond E. Brown, S.S.
Schuyler Brown
James V. Brownson

Donald Capps
John T. Carroll
David R. Catchpole
Edmond LaB. Cherbonnier
G. Byrns Coleman
J. -F. Collange
Carsten Colpe
Charles H. Cosgrove

Charles B. Cousar
Barry S. Crawford
Oscar Cullmann
R. Alan Culpepper

Nils A. Dahl
F. Harry Daniel
Martinus C. de Boer
Marinus de Jonge
Wendell S. Dietrich
Karl Paul Donfried
Jane Dempsey Douglass
Edward A. Dowey
James D. G. Dunn
Craig Dykstra

Elizabeth G. Edwards
Bart D. Ehrman
Neil Elliott
E. Earle Ellis
Eldon Jay Epp

William R. Farmer
Paul F. Feiler
Joseph A. Fitzmyer, S.J.
Douglas K. Fletcher
Robert T. Fortna
†Hans W. Frei
Lawrence E. Frizzell
Karlfried Froehlich

Tabula Gratulatoria

Reginald H. Fuller
Robert W. Funk
Victor Paul Furnish

John G. Gager
Harry Y. Gamble
Freda A. Gardner
Beverly R. Gaventa
Thomas W. Gillespie
John D. Godsey
Michael J. Gorman
Erich Grässer
James M. Gustafson

Ferdinand Hahn
Barbara Hall
Charles Arthur Mann Hall
Robert G. Hamerton-Kelly
Paul L. Hammer
Geddes W. Hanson
Stanley Samuel Harakas
Douglas R. A. Hare
Walter J. Harrelson
Lars Hartman
David M. Hay
S. Mark Heim
Martin Hengel
Carl L. Holladay
Michael W. Holmes
John C. Hurd

Robert Jewett
E. Elizabeth Johnson
Luke Timothy Johnson

Ernst Käsemann
James F. Kay
Leander E. Keck
Howard Clark Kee
David H. Kelsey
Karl Kertelge
Jack Dean Kingsbury

Eugene M. Klaaren
William Klassen
John Knox
John Koenig
Helmut Koester
Steven J. Kraftchick
Eugene C. Kreider
Edgar M. Krentz
Robert Kysar

X. Léon-Dufour, S.J.
Herbert Leroy
George A. Lindbeck
Eduard Lohse
Thomas G. Long
John S. Lown
Gerd Lüdemann
Dieter Lührmann
Ulrich Luz

Donald Macleod
†James I. McCord
Elsie McKee
Allan James McNicol
Kathleen E. McVey
Abraham J. Malherbe
Joel Marcus
Clarice J. Martin
Dale B. Martin
J. Louis Martyn
Conrad Massa
Theodor M. Mauch
Wayne A. Meeks
Bruce M. Metzger
J. Ramsey Michaels
Daniel L. Migliore
Patrick D. Miller, Jr.
Paul S. Minear
Samuel Hugh Moffett
James H. Moorhead
Robert Morgan
Christopher Morse

C. F. D. Moule
Lucetta Mowry

Takeshi Nagata
Alan Neely
Murray L. Newman
Charles M. Nielsen
J. Randall Nichols
Richard A. Norris, Jr.

Dennis T. Olson
Douglas F. Ottati

John Painter
Peter J. Paris
Daniel Patte
Pheme Perkins
Karl A. Plank
Mark A. Plunkett
Petr Pokorný
Thomas Evan Pollard
Charles P. Price
James J. H. Price
James L. Price

Lee H. Reiff
John Reumann
George A. Riggan
Mathias Rissi
J. J. M. Roberts
James M. Robinson
William C. Robinson, Jr.
Calvin J. Roetzel
Wayne G. Rollins

Katharine Doob Sakenfeld
J. Paul Sampley
E. P. Sanders
James A. Sanders
Judith E. Sanderson
Stanley Paul Saunders
Margaret A. Schatkin

Hans-Martin Schenke
Wolfgang Schrage
John H. Schütz
Eduard Schweizer
Bernard B. Scott
Robin Scroggs
Jean-Loup Seban
Mark A. Seifrid
C. L. Seow
Gerald T. Sheppard
G. Franklin Shirbroun
Jeffrey S. Siker
Lou H. Silberman
Gerard S. Sloyan
Christine M. Smith
D. Moody Smith
Graydon F. Snyder
Gerhard Spiegler
Robert A. Spivey
Max L. Stackhouse
Cullen I K Story
Georg Strecker
Peter Stuhlmacher
M. Jack Suggs

Robert C. Tannehill
Mark Kline Taylor
James W. Thompson
W. Sibley Towner
Phyllis Trible
Kiyoshi Tsuchido
Joseph B. Tyson

Dan O. Via
Burton L. Visotzky

Robert D. Webber
Michael Welker
Kenneth B. Welliver
Charles C. West
Ulrich Wilckens
Amos N. Wilder

Tabula Gratulatoria

Gibson Winter
Sara C. Winter
Wilhelm Wuellner
D. Campbell Wyckoff

John H. Yoder
Franklin W. Young

Gordon Zerbe

1

Jesus and Early Christian Eschatology

John T. Carroll [1]

Nowhere is the nexus of faith and history more evident, and nowhere more problematic, than in reflection on the role to be played by the Jesus of history in Christian theology.[2] Günther Bornkamm's classic statement poses the issue sharply:

> We possess no single word of Jesus and no single story of Jesus, no matter how incontestably genuine they may be, which do not contain at the same time the confession of the believing congregation or at least are embedded therein. This makes the search after the bare facts of history difficult and to a large extent futile.[3]

This awareness that the Jesus of history is accessible to critical inquiry—and to the Christian theologian—only in and through the believing proclamation of the first Christians did not, of course, deter

---

[1] John T. Carroll is Assistant Professor of Religious Studies at Louisiana State University, Baton Rouge, Louisiana.

[2] Those of us privileged to have studied with Paul W. Meyer know how important this complex inter-relationship of faith and history has been in his own exegetical and theological work, and how carefully and perceptively he has always treated it. Although keenly aware that this essay will not develop the theme with the nuanced, informed judgment that Paul Meyer would give it—another of his legacies to his students!—I offer it nonetheless in tribute to an esteemed mentor and colleague.

[3] Bornkamm, *Jesus of Nazareth* (New York: Harper & Brothers, 1960) 14.

Bornkamm from reconstructing the historical career and message of Jesus, even as it did not prevent other students of Rudolf Bultmann from assigning to the Jesus of history a constructive role in theological reflection as the fruit of their somewhat chastened "new quest" for the historical Jesus.[4]

Early Christian assent to God's disclosure in the person of Jesus was bound to history, yet it continually took that history up into itself, reinterpreting Jesus' public ministry in the light of its τέλος (crucifixion, resurrection, and the emergence of the Christian movement). This interaction of faith and history in the gospels makes the problem of the Jesus of history perpetually acute. This remains true despite the accelerating pace of recent studies of Jesus, which cannot camouflage the limitations imposed on all such inquiry by the nature of our sources.[5] The diversity in recent accounts of Jesus and his message is therefore neither surprising nor novel. At this point one may be tempted to join ranks with Bultmann, refusing to ground faith in the historical Jesus at all. Moreover, the validity of early Christian claims about Jesus could not rest entirely on Jesus' own public career and teaching even if they were available to us in a form both unambiguous and precise, for the resurrection, understood as God's validation of Jesus, assigns to Jesus a significance beyond what he had claimed for himself. Nevertheless, the resurrection, construed precisely as God's "justification of Jesus," serves to validate Jesus "as he actually was," for no other Jesus than the Jesus of history required such legitimation. This point was made persuasively

---

[4] For an insider's account of this development, see James M. Robinson, *A New Quest of the Historical Jesus and Other Essays* (Philadelphia: Fortress, 1983) esp. 153-71.

[5] For a sampling of recent contributions (monographs only), see James H. Charlesworth, *Jesus within Judaism* (Garden City: Doubleday, 1988); Marcus J. Borg, *Jesus: A New Vision* (San Francisco: Harper & Row, 1987); Ragnar Leivestad, *Jesus in His Own Perspective* (Minneapolis: Augsburg, 1987); E. P. Sanders, *Jesus and Judaism* (Philadelphia: Fortress, 1985); Walter Simonis, *Jesus von Nazareth: Seine Botschaft vom Reich Gottes und der Glaube der Urgemeinde* (Düsseldorf: Patmos, 1985); Marcus J. Borg, *Conflict, Holiness and Politics in the Teaching of Jesus* (Toronto/New York: Edwin Mellen, 1984); Bernard Brandon Scott, *Jesus, Symbol-Maker for the Kingdom* (Philadelphia: Fortress, 1983); Heinz Schürmann, *Gottes Reich—Jesu Geschick: Jesu ureigener Tod im Licht seiner Basileia-Verkündigung* (Freiburg: Herder, 1983); Gerard S. Sloyan, *Jesus in Focus* (Mystic, CT: Twenty-Third, 1983); James Breech, *The Silence of Jesus: The Authentic Voice of the Historical Man* (Philadelphia: Fortress, 1983); A. E. Harvey, *Jesus and the Constraints of History* (Philadelphia: Westminster, 1982); Ben F. Meyer, *The Aims of Jesus* (London: SCM, 1979); Morton Smith, *Jesus the Magician* (San Francisco: Harper & Row, 1978). The work of Robert Funk's "Jesus Seminar" and the Society of Biblical Literature's "Historical Jesus" section confirms that at least in some circles inquiry into the Jesus of history is being pursued as vigorously as ever. One recent study that goes against the grain by holding to a thoroughly skeptical stance, with regard to the sayings tradition at least, is that of E. P. Sanders (*Jesus*; see esp. the discussion of method, pp. 3-18).

by the honoree of this volume in his 1976 Shaffer Lectures at Yale Divinity School.[6]

The question, posed already by Meyer, is whether the Jesus of history, however elusive, has a significant part to play not only as presupposition but also as norm of faith.[7] Where recoverable with some probability, should not the structure and character of Jesus' own faith in the God of Israel serve at least as corrective, and perhaps also as warrant, for Christian theology? Certainly, given the almost unavoidable tendency, beginning with the New Testament writings themselves, to turn theology toward christology—and often enough with an anti-Jewish bent—one would be justified in insisting that christological developments be evaluated, to the limited extent possible, in the light of the teachings of Jesus himself.[8]

1. The Eschatological Message of Jesus

Particularly in the area of early Christian eschatological thinking these questions loom large. On any reading of the evidence, early Christian claims for Jesus and his role in the eschatological drama far outdistanced the claims he had made for himself. Is the relationship between early Christian eschatology and Jesus' own message one of utter discontinuity? Did the watershed of Easter so transform the perception of Jesus and his role that one must posit a radical disjunction between his understanding of the βασιλεία τοῦ θεοῦ ("sovereign rule of God," or "sphere of God's sovereign rule") and the eschatological beliefs that motivated and energized the Christian movement? Or were early Christian eschatological views informed, at least in part, by what Jesus had said and done? Further, does the message of Jesus about God's future in relation to humanity's present provide a basis for surveying, perhaps even assessing, subsequent eschatological developments?

---

[6] Paul W. Meyer, "The Justification of Jesus" (unpublished manuscript, 1976). See also Simonis, *Jesus*, 15-16.

[7] Leander E. Keck has also endeavored to reserve a role for Jesus in the theological reflection and preaching of the church, in his book *A Future for the Historical Jesus* (Nashville: Abingdon, 1971).

[8] Robert Morgan makes a similar suggestion in his essay, "The Historical Jesus and the Theology of the New Testament," in *The Glory of Christ in the New Testament: Studies in Christology in Memory of George Bradford Caird* (ed. L.D. Hurst and N.T. Wright; Oxford: Oxford University Press, 1987) 186-206. See also the provocative remarks of Paul Hollenbach ("The Historical Jesus Question in North America Today," *BTB* 19 [1989] 11-22, esp. 19-20).

Jesus and Early Eschatology

Of course, satisfactory treatment of such questions is too large a project for this modest essay. Moreover, the undertaking is rendered all the more precarious by the widely diverse accounts of Jesus' eschatological (or non-eschatological) message presently competing for a hearing in the academic arena. Which Jesus concerns us? Richard Hiers, perpetuating Albert Schweitzer's thoroughly apocalyptic Jesus, insists that the announcement of the imminent kingdom of God dominated Jesus' proclamation and activity.[9] Yet Marcus J. Borg counters with an image of Jesus as holy sage and prophet who proclaimed not the imminent end of the world but the "nearness of the other world."[10] Meanwhile, Dale C. Allison traces back to Jesus himself what he believes to be the primitive eschatological conviction that with the death and resurrection of Jesus the new age had already dawned.[11] Unlike Borg, both Hiers and Allison discern a high degree of continuity between early Christian eschatology and the message of Jesus. Nevertheless, the views of the future attributed to Jesus by Hiers and Allison are incompatible. Bruce Chilton and J. I. H. McDonald[12] seek to hold together the seemingly uneschatological moral teaching of Jesus[13] and his announcement that the divine kingdom had drawn near.[14] They

---

[9] See most recently *Jesus and the Future* (Atlanta: John Knox, 1981); cf. Johannes Weiss, *Jesus' Proclamation of the Kingdom of God* (Philadelphia: Fortress, 1971; German 1st ed., 1892); Bultmann, *The Theology of the New Testament* (2 vol.; London: SCM, 1952-55) 1.4-6; Werner G. Kümmel, "Eschatological Expectation in the Proclamation of Jesus" in *The Kingdom of God in the Teaching of Jesus* (ed. Bruce Chilton; IRT 5; Philadelphia: Fortress, 1984) 36-51; E. P. Sanders, *Jesus*, esp. pp. 152-55; and, of course, a host of others.

[10] Borg, "An Orthodoxy Reconsidered: The 'End-of-the-World Jesus,'" in *The Glory of Christ in the New Testament: Studies in Christology in Memory of George Bradford Caird* (Oxford: Oxford University Press, 1987) 207-17. Borg develops his alternative image of Jesus in *Jesus*. Another scholar who has recently questioned the presence of imminent eschatological expectation in the message of Jesus is Barry S. Crawford (*Near Expectation in the Sayings of Jesus* [Ann Arbor: University Microfilms, 1981]; *idem.*, "Near Expectation in the Sayings of Jesus," *JBL* 101 [1982] 225-244). Crawford, applying stringently the criterion of dissimilarity and analyzing the form of the sayings in Mark 9:1; 13:30; and Matt 10:23, concludes that these sayings likely derive from early Christian prophets.

[11] Allison, *The End of the Ages Has Come* (Philadelphia: Fortress, 1985) esp. 115-41.

[12] Like W. G. Kümmel before them, though in a different fashion. Kümmel's classic defense of the authenticity of both imminent hope and presence of the divine kingdom appears in *Promise and Fulfillment* (SBT 23; London: SCM, 1957).

[13] Hiers, by contrast, reaffirms and strengthens Schweitzer's view that Jesus offers an *interim* ethic (see *Future*, esp. 50-61).

[14] *Jesus and the Ethics of the Kingdom* (Grand Rapids: Eerdmans, 1987) esp. 1-23. A survey of the eschatological teachings ascribed to Jesus leads Chilton and McDonald to conclude that "any attempt to bracket a radical claim in respect of the future from Jesus' preaching, as—for example—a subsidiary element of his Jewish background which he himself dispensed with, is critically untenable" (p. 5). For further discussion of the relation

suggest that the kingdom of God in Jesus' teaching is "God's decision for salvation, which he has taken and will effect in the future."[15] So in their view present and future, ethical and eschatological stand together in the message of Jesus.

Inevitably, a rounded presentation of Jesus' message about the divine future and the way it impinges upon the human present becomes highly speculative.[16] Even the cursory survey above shows how a controlling image of Jesus—as sage or eschatological prophet, for example—both arises from and substantially affects judgments of authenticity or inauthenticity concerning eschatological sayings attributed to Jesus in the gospel tradition. We cannot settle the issue here, although a plea may be registered for cautious assessment of individual units of the Jesus tradition as a control for the more ambitious, rounded pictures of Jesus presently being sketched. Our task here, however, will not be to define in general terms the continuity between early Christian eschatological beliefs and the teaching of Jesus. Rather, we narrow the focus to a consideration of two themes important to early Christian eschatological faith, themes about which the question can be put whether they are grounded in the message and activity of the Jesus of history.

The problem of a disjunction between Jesus' own view of things and later claims made for him is most acute in our interpretation of the Gospel of John. The eschatological orientation of early Christianity—and presumably of Jesus as well[17]—undergoes in the hands of John a radical reinterpretation.[18] Johannine eschatological statements shift

---

of eschatology to moral injunction in the teaching of Jesus, see Wolfgang Schrage, *The Ethics of the New Testament* (Philadelphia: Fortress, 1988) 18-40; Hans Bald, "Eschatological or Theocentric Ethics? Notes on the Relationship between Eschatology and Ethics in Jesus' Preaching," in *The Kingdom of God in the Teaching of Jesus* (ed. Bruce Chilton; Philadelphia: Fortress, 1984) 133-53.

[15] *Jesus*, 9.

[16] On the other hand, to present as a *rounded* picture of Jesus a reconstruction based only on materials judged to be authentic after stringent use of the criterion of dissimilarity is to distort the historical reality. Such a procedure leads James Breech, for example, to depict a strikingly original, unique figure, which the method employed has generated (*Silence*, see esp. 218).

[17] Naturally, C. H. Dodd would disagree. See, e.g., *The Parables of the Kingdom* (New York: Scribner's, 1961); cf. Eta Linnemann, *Gleichnisse Jesu: Einführung und Auslegung* (6th ed.; Göttingen: Vandenhoeck & Ruprecht) 138-42.

[18] Still one of the best treatments of Johannine eschatology remains Paul Meyer's Union Seminary doctoral dissertation, "The Eschatology of the Fourth Gospel: A Study in Early Christian Reinterpretation" (New York, 1955). For a brief analysis, with reference to secondary literature since 1955, see John T. Carroll, "Present and Future in Fourth Gospel 'Eschatology,'" *BTB* 19 (1989) 63-69.

attention from the future to the present, and also transfer to Jesus eschatological prerogatives evidently assigned to God in Jesus' own teaching. Does such a radical recasting of Jesus' perception of his own eschatological role have any warrant in the Jesus of history?

We begin by considering two divine eschatological functions given by John to Jesus, judgment (κρίσις) and life (ζωή), and then turn to the temporal shift from future to present.

2. Jesus as God's Eschatological Agent

"The Father has given all judgment to the Son": The Eschatological Role of the Johannine Jesus

The Fourth Gospel gives to Jesus the decisive eschatological prerogatives of judgment and resurrection. This is perhaps not surprising in a narrative so thoroughly dominated by christological claims, yet it is remarkable nonetheless. The Johannine Jesus announces that God has conveyed to him the divine prerogative of judgment: "For the Father does not judge anyone, but has given all judgment to the Son" (5:22; cf. v 27). Why? Jesus receives the authority to judge, according to verse 23, in order that he may be accorded the same honor granted to God. Reverence for God must now express itself in reverence for the Son, who reveals him to the world. Jesus exercises judgment on behalf of God. Nevertheless, John's Jesus also expressly disavows any intent to judge (3:17; 8:15). God sent the Son into the world with the purpose not of condemning but of eliciting belief, and therefore of giving life (3:16-17; 12:47). Yet some turn away from the one who reveals God, who grants light and life, and judgment therefore does ensue. Moreover, it is Jesus as light of the world who exposes their evil (3:19-20); it is Jesus' own word that pronounces verdict on their unbelief (12:48). John's Jesus, however, does not arrogate judgment to himself. It is only by virtue of his function as revealer *of God* that he judges. That is, he pronounces only that judgment which the Father has already spoken (5:30; 12:49-50). Accordingly, when John assigns eschatological judgment to Jesus, it must be construed in terms of this peculiar Johannine understanding of Jesus' relation to God.

John also presents Jesus as giver of life—both eternal life now and resurrection life in the eschatological future. Indeed, the gift of life for believers involves a deliverance from judgment:

> For as the Father raises the dead and makes alive, so also the
> Son makes alive those whom he wishes....Truly, truly I tell you,

one who hears my word and believes the one who sent me has eternal life and does not come into judgment but has crossed over from death to life. Truly, truly I tell you, an hour is coming and now is when those who are dead will hear the voice of the Son of God and those who have heard will live. For as the Father has life in himself, so also he has granted that the Son have life in himself.... an hour is coming in which all who are in the tombs will hear his voice and will come out, [some] to a resurrection of life, but [others] to a resurrection of judgment (5:21, 24-26, 28-29).

As "Bread of Life," Jesus provides the food of eternal life, not as future prospect but as present reality, for those who believe him (6:40,47). Yet, in order to validate the abiding faith of disciples, Jesus will also give resurrection life at the end-time (6:39,40,44,54).[19] John narrates the raising of Lazarus to give dramatic substance to both claims (see especially 11:24-26). Jesus, the "Resurrection and the Life," grants eternal life now to believers and will crown their persevering faith with resurrection life beyond the experience of physical death. Once again, however, Jesus bestows life because that is the design of God (5:19-21; 6:37-40): God purposes the eternal life of all who believe, and Jesus is faithful to the charge given him to preserve their life.

This brief sketch indicates the extent to which christological convictions govern the presentation of eschatological themes in the Fourth Gospel. To be sure, eschatology is not *reduced* to christology, for we have seen that Jesus is the "eschaton"—that is, the eschatological judge and life-giver—only by virtue of his unity with God in mind and purpose. He effects *God's* eschatological purpose, namely, provision of eternal life for faith and, on the other hand, confrontation with the consequences of repudiating divine disclosure ("judgment"). Nevertheless, the lofty eschatological role ascribed by John to Jesus is noteworthy. Did the message of the historical Jesus prepare for such claims? Does it provide any warrant for them?[20]

---

[19] For development of this view, see Carroll, "Present and Future."

[20] It should be emphasized that, while the Johannine presentation of Jesus poses this issue in its sharpest form, it is not confined to the Fourth Gospel. The allegorical parable of final judgment in Matt 25:31-46 revolves around the definitive pronouncement of judgment by Jesus, the King/Son of man. Moreover, Luke has Peter declare that God has ordained Jesus "judge of the living and the dead" (Acts 10:42), a formulation echoed in Paul's Areopagus speech (Acts 17:31), although in this latter text Jesus appears as the agent or instrument of *God's* activity judging the world on an appointed day. The identification of Jesus as source of life likewise is not restricted to the Johannine corpus. To be sure, Paul speaks explicitly of *God* as the one who gives life (e.g., Rom 4:17; 8:11), yet he also binds

One may first ask whether the Jewish milieu of Jesus could have nourished pretensions of this nature. Although God's exercise of judgment is axiomatic in Jewish thought,[21] early Jewish literature does offer occasional examples of eschatological judgment being attributed to an individual. In one text, Abel is cast in the role of judge, with Enoch as court clerk (*Testament of Abraham* 11); nevertheless, it is God who actually issues the sentence (11:7). The Septuagint text of Dan 7:22 awards judgment (κρῖμα) to the saints of the Most High.[22] Yet by far the most striking example comes from the Similitudes of *1 Enoch*, where the Elect One (= the son of man) repeatedly assumes the position of eschatological judge (see *1 Enoch* 45:3; 49:4; 61:8-9; 62-63).[23] Further, Proverbs 8 pictures personified wisdom as the source of life for human beings (8:35).[24] Therefore, if one could make a case for Jesus'

---

the experience of life to participation "in Christ" (1 Cor 15:22; Rom 6:23), or to the agency of Jesus' death and resurrection (Rom 5:10,17,18,21), and he even characterizes the risen Jesus as a "life-giving Spirit" (1 Cor 15:45). Colossians, too, links life to participation "with Christ" (3:3) but takes this one step farther: "When Christ, your life, is manifested, at that time you also will be manifested with him in glory" (v. 4). This is not too far removed from the Johannine claims on which we have focused attention. This sampling of texts confirms that other early Christian writings also enhance Jesus' eschatological role (e.g., in decreeing judgment and bestowing life) and so raise, while perhaps not so acutely as John's gospel, the problem of continuity between the historical career of Jesus and early Christian eschatological convictions.

[21] See, e.g., Pss 94:1-2; 96:10; 98:9; Isa 2:4; 3:13-14; 24:21-23; Jer 25:30-31; Ezek 28:22; 30:19; 39:21; Dan 7:9-14,21-22 (differently, LXX); Joel 3; *Jub.* 23:31; *T. Judah* 20:1-5; *T. Benj.* 10:8-10; *Pss. Sol.* 15:12-13; 4 Ezra 7:32-44; *Sib. Or.* 4:183-84. Of course, the twin themes of judgment and resurrection are, as in the Fourth Gospel, often intertwined in the literature of early Judaism. God raises some or all of the dead in order to effect appropriate judgment; resurrection, then, is a means of judgment, that is, of vindication and punishment, respectively, for the righteous and wicked (often in compensation for the absence of appropriate retributive justice before death).

[22] Cf. the depiction of the oppressed "righteous" ones as judges in *1 Enoch* 48:9; 95:2-3; 96:1; 98:12; cf. Wis 3:7-8. In Wisdom of Solomon 4-5, the "righteous one," persecuted but now vindicated (after death), becomes judge of his persecutors (Wis 4:16). Yet the scene does not concern final, eschatological judgment; rather, it remedies a specific instance of unwarranted persecution (so correctly George W. E. Nickelsburg, *Resurrection, Immortality, and Eternal Life in Intertestamental Judaism* [HTS 26; Cambridge: Harvard University Press, 1972] 68; against Joachim Jeremias, "παῖς θεοῦ," *TDNT* 5.688 n. 254).

[23] Mention may also be made here of the exercise of the function of judgment by the messianic king (as in Isa 11:3-4 and *Pss. Sol.* 17:26,29), which appears, however, to lack the finality of eschatological judgment present in the other texts cited.

[24] Cf. *T. Levi* 18:11, where the messianic priest, by giving access to paradise, enables individuals to enjoy the fruit of the tree of life. Needless to say, *God* is the author of *resurrection* in Jewish writings (see, e.g., 2 Macc 7:9,14,23; *Jub.* 23:30; *Pss. Sol.* 15:12-13; *Sib. Or.* 4:179-91). Note, however, the close connection between the activity of Israel's patron angel Michael and the resurrection of "many" in Dan 12:1-2.

self-understanding as Messiah or Son of man, or for his identification with divine wisdom, the plausibility of Jesus' laying claim to these kinds of eschatological prerogatives would be significantly strengthened. The nature of our sources, however, precludes precisely this kind of argument. In light of early Christian convictions about Jesus, the question of whether Jesus viewed himself as Messiah or as Son of man, and if so in what sense, remains a matter for debate. We cannot answer our question about Jesus' perception of his own eschatological role—as distinct from later convictions—by making such precarious assumptions.[25] Can one find within the Jesus tradition, sifted through stringent use of the criterion of dissimilarity, any other basis for accepting the kinds of claims made for Jesus by John? Or does Jesus' own response to a request that he play the judge (at least if we are to believe Luke) suggest, rather, that John's picture has no basis whatever in the public career of Jesus? "Man, who made me a judge or divider over you?" (Luke 12:14).

"Friend of Sinners"

Our point of entry into the Jesus tradition comes by way of a series of texts focusing on Jesus' posture toward "sinners," that is, unrepentant transgressors of Torah.[26] There is little doubt that Jesus' behavior provoked the accusation, preserved by both Matthew and Luke on the lips of Jesus, that he was a "glutton and a drunkard, a friend of tax collectors and sinners" (Matt 11:19; Luke 7:34). He evidently numbered a tax collector among his circle of disciples, and his practice of offering meal fellowship to sinners earned him contempt. Both the accusation and the conduct prompting it meet the test of dissimilarity; indeed, it would be difficult to account for the present shape of the Jesus tradition on any other basis. Several texts elaborate this distinctive feature of

---

[25] So, e.g., we are unable to draw firm conclusions from the saying of Jesus reported in Mark 8:38 and Luke 9:26: "Whoever is ashamed of me and my words, of him the Son of man will be ashamed...." This logion links one's eschatological fortunes to his or her present response to Jesus, whether the Son of man is taken as Jesus or another party; accordingly, Jesus assumes an important, though perhaps indirect place, in eschatological judgment. Matthew's treatment of this material heightens the initiative of the Son of man in judgment, and is clearly secondary: "[The Son of man] will repay each according to his [or her] deeds" (Matt 16:27).

[26] See the characteristically provocative, and helpful, treatment by E. P. Sanders (*Jesus*, 174-211). Although Sanders finds reason to doubt the authenticity of much of the sayings material concerning Jesus' acceptance of sinners, he observes that "the one distinctive note which we may be certain marked Jesus' teaching about the kingdom is that it would include the 'sinners'" (p. 174).

Jesus' ministry, notably the healing/forgiveness of a lame man (Mark 2:1-12 par.), the forgiveness of a sinful woman (Luke 7:36-50), the forgiveness of an adulteress (John 7:53-8:11 in some manuscripts), and such parables as the lost sheep (Matt 18:10-14; Luke 15:3-7), the unmerciful servant (Matt 18:23-35), and the lost son (Luke 15:11-32).

Although it is likely that this rich array of passages reflects considerable early Christian embellishment of the theme, they contain extensive authentic Jesus tradition as well. If any of these texts put us in touch with the Jesus of history, then we have a clear indication that in associating with sinners, Jesus assessed the character and conduct of Torah transgressors in an unexpected way. He offered them forgiveness, and inclusion in the company of those people who belonged to the rule of God. The pronouncement of forgiveness this side of the eschatological judgment suggests that Jesus anticipated a favorable outcome for these sinners. While not presenting himself as the eschatological judge, he certainly acted as if he were privy to the divine verdict awaiting in the near future.

The logion asserting wholesale forgiveness of human sins (Mark 3:28-29 par.), if authentic, leads to the same conclusion. The first half of this saying is consistent with the picture of Jesus' attitude toward sinners that has been sketched above, and, in view of its radical thrust, it seems safe to ascribe it to Jesus himself: "Every sin and blasphemy will be forgiven human beings..." (Matt 12:31). Once again, Jesus speaks confidently of divine forgiveness (in the case of blasphemy against the Holy Spirit, of divine judgment[27]), though he does not expressly assume the position of judge. It seems probable, therefore, that the historical Jesus anticipated the eschatological judgment when he extended forgiveness and a place in the divine βασιλεία to sinners. While the conceptuality and the terminology differ from John's, the claim is nearly as forceful. The Fourth Gospel would have made the same point this way: these [sinners] "have crossed over from death to life... they do not enter into judgment." Within the public ministry and proclamation of Jesus, there is, it would seem, preparation for the more sweeping declarations of John, yet with no hint of Jesus' usurping the divine prerogative to pronounce final judgment. John's Jesus, we recall, had received that prerogative from God, but only as one who himself executed the very wishes of the Father. It is this christological

---

[27] The accent falls on the prospect of condemnation in a series of oracles of judgment aimed at Galilean cities that failed to respond to Jesus' mission (Matt 11:21-24 // Luke 10:12-15; Matt 12:41-42 // Luke 11:31-32). If these oracles stem from Jesus, they too speak with (a prophet's) confidence about the course of eschatological judgment.

conception that moves the Johannine reflection on Jesus' eschatological role to a quite different plane from the self-perception of Jesus himself.

The Narrow Path to Life

Jesus' raising of Lazarus is not without parallel in the synoptic tradition (Mark 5:21-24, 35-43 par.; Luke 7:11-17), the synoptic Jesus opens up (or closes) access to the βασιλεία τοῦ θεοῦ (hence, to "eternal life"; see, e.g., Luke 6:20 // Matt 5:3; Matt 7:21-23; Matt 8:11-13; Luke 13:25-27; Matt 22:1-14; Luke 14:15-24), and his healings and exorcisms can be construed as flowing from the life-giving power of the new age that is dawning (cf. Luke 11:20 // Matt 12:28). Nevertheless, the radical Johannine claim that Jesus is himself Life, and as such the source of eternal life and resurrection, finds no analogy within the synoptic gospels. Here, Jesus speaks of the narrow, arduous path that leads to life (Matt 7:13-14), and he advocates Torah observance as the avenue to eternal life (Mark 10:17-22 par.; Luke 10:25-28). Yet while he is able to point the direction to life, he does not appear as one who bestows it. In any case, the authenticity of much of this material, including the miracles restoring life (Mark 5 and Luke 7), is open to serious question. Is there complete discontinuity between the Johannine Jesus who authors eternal life and the Jesus of history? An affirmative answer to the question would seem to commend itself, for certainly this is one point at which the resurrection faith of early Christians (that is, the conviction that Jesus had been raised from the dead) significantly altered perceptions of Jesus.

Yet it is perhaps unwise to dismiss the question so abruptly. One might make the case that Jesus viewed the fellowship enjoyed by his circle of followers, particularly their shared meals, as an anticipation of the communion of the divine βασιλεία.[28] If so, the life to be experienced in the future by those who participate in the sovereign rule of God is tangibly linked to Jesus himself, although, of course, that life does not derive from him.

Also of interest is the saying preserved in Matt 10:39 (cf. Luke 17:33): "One who finds his life [ψυχήν] will lose it, and one who loses it... will

---

[28] The parable of the banquet (Luke 14:16-24; Matt 22:1-10; *Gos. Thom.* 64) suggests this interpretation, although it must be acknowledged that each extant version of the parable shows signs of significant reshaping by early Christians. Moreover, the parable of the prodigal son, especially with its feast celebrating the prodigal's return (Luke 15:23), seems to point in a similar direction. Luke 22:30 and 13:29 // Matt 8:11, if authentic, would lend additional plausibility to this view. See the treatment by Norman Perrin (*Rediscovering the Teaching of Jesus* [New York: Harper & Row, 1976] 102-08).

find it." Mark 8:34-35 par. attaches a similar saying to another which summons hearers to hazardous discipleship: "If anyone wishes to come after me, let him deny himself and take up [his] cross and follow me. For whoever wishes to save his life [ψυχήν] will lose it, but whoever loses his life for my sake... will save it." At the root of these sayings almost certainly lies an authentic logion of Jesus warning that life comes only to those willing to relinquish it. In my judgment, it is also likely, though not certain, that Jesus associated that giving up of one's life with his cause, that is, the cause of the divine βασιλεία. Once again, although Jesus does not appear as the author of life here, the nature of one's response to his activity seems to have a significant bearing on the question whether he or she will have (future) life, the life of God's eternal rule.

In the Fourth Gospel, Jesus so dominates the eschatological stage that, by virtue of his functional identity with God, he is the eschaton. By contrast, the Jesus of history probably acted out of the conviction that the βασιλεία of God was pressing into the world, bringing with it the blessings of the new age; that is, Jesus was God's eschatological agent. As such, he offered forgiveness, healing, and exorcism, harbingers of the advancing rule of God. Jesus played, then, a pivotal role in the entry of human beings into the life of the βασιλεία, yet without making his own relation to God the central issue, as it is in John. Moreover, if for Jesus, one must follow a treacherous path leading to the life of God's βασιλεία *in the future*, for John one enters eternal life *in the present* through belief in the one who is Resurrection and Life. We need to examine more closely now the relationship between these two perspectives on present and future.

3. Present and Future

The Johannine Accent on the Present

Our discussion of the themes of judgment and life in the Fourth Gospel drew attention to the christological cast given them by John. Jesus is here the determinative figure in the working out of God's purpose (intending and granting life, yet resulting also in judgment). In large measure because of this christological focus, we discover in John a thoroughgoing transformation of the temporal structure of Christian eschatology. What others fervently hope to receive in the future, John brings into the present as already realized. The present life of Jesus— and that means both his historical career and his subsequent activity through the Spirit/Paraclete—mediates possession of eternal life. As revealer of divine glory (1:14; 11:4,40; 13:31-32; 14:8-9; 17:1-5), as judge, as vanquisher of the world ruler (12:31; cf. 16:11,33), and as one who returns in the form of a second Paraclete (14:16-18; 16:5-7,12-22), Jesus accomplishes fully in the present what early Christians generally anticipated in the eschatological future.

This is not to say that the future fades from view altogether in the Fourth Gospel, for that is clearly not the case. Future resurrection and future judgment retain a place in the Johannine symbolic universe, although the future serves now to confirm the ultimate decisions reached already in one's present response to Jesus, rather than as a powerful new reality invading and radically qualifying the present.[29] The present of God's disclosure ("incarnation") determines the future, in the Johannine perspective. The future can only ratify the effects produced by that disclosure. Did the activity of the Jesus of history anticipate—and can it provide a warrant for—this temporal shift in eschatological proclamation?

The Present and Eschatology in the Message of Jesus

Marcus Borg and Barry Crawford attack what they term a consensus view that Jesus expected the βασιλεία τοῦ θεοῦ in the imminent future.[30] On the other hand, E. P. Sanders seeks to undermine a widely held opinion that the distinctive thrust of Jesus' proclamation was the βασιλεία τοῦ θεοῦ as already present.[31] It would appear that we have stepped into a mine field! Without pretending to be able to solve this conundrum with respect to the eschatological proclamation of Jesus as a whole, we are able to point here to a number of texts which indicate that there does exist a measure of continuity between John's accent on present fulfillment and the message of the historical Jesus.[32]

Luke 17:20-21 appears to offer unambiguous evidence that Jesus announced the presence of God's sovereign rule: "The rule of God is not coming with observation, nor will they say, 'Look, here!' or 'There!' For

---

[29] On the relation of present to future in Johannine eschatology, see Carroll, "Present and Future", and the studies noted there.

[30] See Borg, "Orthodoxy;" Crawford, "Expectation."

[31] See *Jesus*, 153-54. Note the response by James D. G. Dunn, "Matthew 12:28/Luke 11:20—A Word of Jesus?," *Eschatology and the New Testament: Essays in Honor of George Raymond Beasley-Murray* (ed. W. Hulitt Gloer; Peabody, MA: Hendrickson, 1988) 29-49.

[32] In speaking of continuity, here as elsewhere in this essay, I am not seeking to explain the origins of the Johannine perspective (did John's view develop out of the expectation held by Jesus himself?), but exploring possible areas of convergence between two distinct theological points of view.

see! the rule of God is in your midst [and you do not see it]."³³ It is not unlikely that this logion transmitted by Luke and the *Gospel of Thomas* stems from a genuine saying of Jesus, which interprets his activity as a sign of a larger, world transforming event—the intervention of God in sovereign power.³⁴ Nevertheless, it will be prudent to proceed with extreme caution, in light of the confusion still reigning in this area of Jesus research. Let it be granted that further evidence is needed before the attribution of this logion to Jesus is accepted.

Such data are not wanting. Especially illuminating are two sayings of Jesus which, at least in the synoptic tradition, serve to interpret his exorcisms. According to Mark 3:27, the exorcisms point to the binding of Satan: "No one can enter the strong man's house and plunder his goods unless he first binds the strong man."³⁵ There is no reason to question the link between this declaration and Jesus' activity as exorcist, a feature of his public ministry which satisfies the most stringent application of the criterion of dissimilarity.³⁶ And if that is the original setting of the logion, then its allusion to Satan (the "strong man") and to his demon-possessed "instruments" (σκεύη) is unmistakable.³⁷ Since the expectation that Satan's activity would cease in the eschatological era is well attested in early Jewish literature (occasionally with the image of "binding"),³⁸ it appears likely that Jesus associated his activity as exorcist with both the defeat of Satan and its correlate, the dawn of the new age.

We encounter the obverse of this claim in the saying transmitted in Matt 12:28 and Luke 11:20.³⁹ Jesus asserts: "If it is by the Spirit [or finger] of God that I cast out demons, then the rule of God has reached you [ἔφθασεν ἐφ' ὑμᾶς]." The syntax of this verse places stress not on Jesus as an exorcist who is without parallel, but on the divine

---

³³ Cf. *Gos. Thom.* 3, 113. On the interpretation of Luke 17:20-21, see John T. Carroll, *Response to the End of History: Eschatology and Situation in Luke-Acts* (SBLDS 92; Atlanta: Scholars Press, 1988) 76-80, 87, and the literature cited there.

³⁴ For further discussion, see Perrin, *Rediscovering*, 68-74.

³⁵ Cf. the parallel in Matt 12:29. Luke 11:21-22 preserves the essential idea, though in a substantially altered formulation.

³⁶ See the discussion in Dunn, "Matthew 12:28," 31-33, 42-43.

³⁷ For the image of human "instruments" or servants of Satan, see, e.g., *T. Naph.* 8:6; *Mart. Isa.* 1:9; 2:1-4; 5:15.

³⁸ See Isa 24:21-22; *1 Enoch* 10:1-7; *Jub.* 23:29; *T. Mos.* 10:1; *T. Levi* 18:12; *T. Judah* 25:3; Rev 20:2-3.

³⁹ For a forceful defense of the authenticity of this logion, against Sanders (*Jesus*, 133-41), see Dunn ("Matthew 12:28"). For the original form of the saying, Dunn prefers (p. 39, n. 24) the Matthean version ("by the Spirit of God") to the Lukan ("by the finger of God").

instrumentality of the exorcisms (whether by the Spirit or the finger of God), and on the arrival of the rule of God.[40] Therefore, the logion may well stem from Jesus himself.[41] If so, we have three closely related sayings, Luke 17:20-21, Mark 3:27, and Matt 12:28, each of which associates Jesus' activity (notably the exorcisms) with the eschatological power of God, already making itself felt in the present.[42]

It would be rash to conclude from this survey of texts that Jesus' proclamation of the βασιλεία τοῦ θεοῦ highlighted the present operation of God's sovereign rule at the expense of its futurity. Rather, what God has begun to effect through Jesus, his eschatological agent, will come to full flower in the imminent future. Our analysis suggests, therefore, that when Jesus prayed for the coming of the βασιλεία of God (Matt 6:10 // Luke 11:2), he petitioned a God whose sovereign reign was already exerting itself, as evidenced by Jesus' own ministry of healing and exorcism.

The public ministry of Jesus represented, then, a frontal assault of the divine βασιλεία in the world, both pointing to and itself already expressing the power of that approaching mighty rule of God. It was a vehicle of that transformation by which the βασιλεία of God overturned present conditions,[43] most visibly for the benefit of the poor, the oppressed, the sick, and the sinner. As in the Fourth Gospel, the present is here the arena of the decisive activity of God, yet the present flows from the future reality of God's sovereign rule—the new age—in a way quite different from the pattern we find in John. For John, the future flows inexorably from the present of Jesus, who as God's incarnation in the human sphere releases people (of faith) from judgment and gives them life even now. The fundamental transformation of the human world, still waiting on the horizon from Jesus' vantage point, has already

---

[40] Rightly emphasized by Dunn, "Matthew 12:28," 38-39. On the force of ἔφθασεν, see esp. p. 47, n. 45 (with bibliographical notes).

[41] Dunn ("Matthew 12:28," 42) concludes that it is difficult to explain this logion "as originating either from the Jewish context of Jesus' ministry or from the theological concerns of the first Christians. Matthew 12:28/Luke 11:20 is one of the relatively few sayings within the Jesus-tradition which comes strongly through the criterion of double dissimilarity—generally acknowledged to be overly stringent as a criterion for recognizing words of the historical Jesus."

[42] Matt 11:12 (cf. Luke 16:16), too, seems to presuppose the present operation of the βασιλεία of God, although that saying accents the crisis and opposition provoked by the rule of God since the time of the Baptizer. The logion appearing in Matt 13:16-17 // Luke 10:23-24 implies that the present ministry of Jesus is the long awaited time of fulfillment, a claim consistent with the interpretation being advanced here.

[43] Cf. the parables of the mustard seed (Mark 4:30-32 par.), the seed growing in a hidden way (Mark 4:26-29), and the leaven (Matt 13:33 // Luke 13:20-21).

occurred for John's community. Perhaps, that is in no small measure the product of its sectarian mode of being in the world. Those who remain outside the Johannine cosmos, rejecting its vision of God and its testimony to Jesus, are beyond transformation in any future, even God's. They are lost. At just such a juncture as this, the voice and actions of the Jesus of history—however faintly discerned—can and must divert Christian theology from its own worst tendencies, even though they originate in a desire to honor God by honoring the one who came to make him known.

4. Concluding Reflections

The line of inquiry being pursued here points to the way in which the message and activity of the Jesus of history should play a crucial role as corrective in Christian theology. From the vantage point provided by Jesus' acceptance of sinners, one can assess the sharply dualistic orientation of the Johannine literature (although such theological evaluation must take seriously the socio-historical matrix out of which this Johannine posture emerged). Moreover, for all Jesus' celebration of the present activity of the divine βασιλεία, his enactment of that divine drama in cures, meals, and stories remains tantalizingly elusive— "unconsummated"—and this view of the sovereign rule of God counters any theological program of fully "realized eschatology" which one might seek to ground in John's gospel.

So much for the historical Jesus as negative criterion or corrective in Christian theological reflection. But what of the question, raised by Meyer's Shaffer Lectures, whether Jesus (in view of his justification by God in the resurrection) should not serve also as a positive criterion, as a warrant for theology? Constructively, I would wish to assert that Jesus, in his conduct among sinners and in his recognition of the presence of the divine rule among the "unholy," offers a paradigm for contemporary theological reflection and praxis. Moreover, while the Jesus of history— that is, Jesus prior to and apart from his vindication by God—is not a sufficient basis for theological construction,[44] Christian claims for Jesus' eschatological activity that have no connection whatever to Jesus as he actually was would seem to me suspect. Yet our analysis suggests that certain eschatological claims advanced by early Christians, even by such a creative reinterpreter of eschatological traditions as the author of

---

[44] See the provocative remarks of Charles H. Cosgrove in his essay in this volume, "The Salvation of Jesus: A Theological Reflection on the Destiny of the Kingdom in History."

John's gospel, can after all be grounded, with important qualifications, in the activity of Jesus himself.

It is a distinct pleasure to offer these reflections in tribute to Paul W. Meyer, esteemed teacher and scholar, whose own commitment to truth, to honest faith, and to a life consonant with that faith exemplifies the very *best* in Christian theology.

2

The Birth of the Reader: Matthew 1:1-4:16

Bernard Brandon Scott [1]

Raymond Brown once remarked, "If the first two chapters had been lost and the Matthean Gospel came down to us beginning with 3:1, no one would have ever suspected the existence of the missing chapters."[2] This may be so, but I contend that the loss of the first two chapters should affect the way we read the text and even more that the non-use of these two chapters in determining how to read has led to a misreading. Redaction criticism, the recent apex of Matthean studies, has abetted the ignoring of the first two chapters and has left a problematic residue because it determined the parameters for the study of Matthew by comparison with Mark. This comparative reading subtly has defined the point of view from which we read Matthew. I would suggest that we set these parameters aside, since they establish the significance of Matthew by its relation to and difference from Mark.[3]

---

[1] Bernard Brandon Scott is Darbeth Distinguished Professor of New Testament at the Phillips Graduate Seminary, Tulsa, Oklahoma.

[2] *The Birth of the Messiah* (New York: Doubleday, 1977) 49.

[3] This remark reflects no rejection of the dependence of Matthew on Mark. Actually, I think Matthew is at times a shrewd reader of Mark, and literary work on Matthew as a performer of Mark needs attention.

Of the five gospels from the first century,[4] all begin in quite different ways. There is no obvious ἀρχή ("beginning"), despite Mark's attempt to create one. Even the two gospels that have narratives of Jesus' birth begin in distinctive fashions. Matthew begins with a genealogy while Luke, following a formal introduction, begins with the foretelling of John the Baptist's birth.

The five different beginnings suggest that the way in which a gospel begins affords clues as to how the story is to be viewed. The initial narrative unit provides the story's first instance of point of view. Genette uses the term "focalization" for this process by which the narrative shapes the perspective from which it will be viewed.[5] The focalizing agent is the narrator, who in Matthew's gospel is an external and omniscient focalizer. The focalizer is an agent whose perception orientates the presentation, and the object of the focalization is what the narrator focuses for the narratee. A primary aspect of focalization is the ideological plane. These are the "norms of the text" supported by the narrator. It is "a general system of viewing the world conceptually."[6] The ideological level represents the values or norms by which the narrator judges and orientates the narration. Insofar as that ideology is transmitted to the narratee-implied reader,[7] it should be observable in the introduction to the narrative. To test this, I propose a reading of the narrative at the ideological level and, to confirm that reading, an inquiry

---

[4] Thomas is probably to be dated in the first century between 50 and 100 CE. See Bentley Layton, *The Gnostic Scriptures* (Garden City, NY: Doubleday, 1987) 377; Francis T. Fallon and Ron Cameron, "The Gospel of Thomas: A Forschungsbericht and Analysis," *ANRW* 25.6 (1988) 4224-26; Helmut Koester, *Introduction to the New Testament*, vol. 2: *History and Literature of Early Christianity* (2 vols.; FFNT; Philadelphia: Fortress, 1982) 2.152.

[5] Gérard Genette, *Narrative Discourse: An Essay in Method* (Ithaca, NY: Cornell University Press, 1980) 189-94. The value of this term over the more common "point of view" or "perspective" is that it is more abstract and less visually dominated. See the helpful remarks of Shlomith Rimmon-Kenan, *Narrative Fiction: Contemporary Poetics* (New York: Methuen, 1983) 71-72.

[6] Boris Uspensky, *A Poetics of Composition* (Berkeley: University of California Press, 1973) 81.

[7] In the narrative of Matthew there is no distinction between the narratee and the implied reader. Some literary theorists have disputed the distinction of Seymour Chatman (*Story and Discourse: Narrative Structure in Fiction and Film* [Ithaca, NY: Cornell University Press, 1978] 148-51) between narratee and implied reader. I am inclined to agree with Rimmon-Kenan (Narrative Fiction, 89) that "the narratee is the agent which is at the very least implicitly addressed by the narrator," and the implied reader is the implementation of the role of the narratee. Thus neither is a "person" but an "it," a textual function.

The Birth of the Reader: Matthew 1:1-4:16

into whether such a reading opens up other aspects of the Matthean narrative.

Extent of Beginning

Unit 1 of Matthew extends through 4:16.[8] This initial unit has three sections, each with its own principles of internal organization. Further, each section has two sub-sections. Section 1 (chapter 1) consists of a genealogy and the birth of Jesus from the point of view of the character Joseph. Section 2 (chapter 2) consists of events after Jesus' birth. The primary story here is that of Herod, with Joseph's story interwoven into the narrative. The final section (3:1-4:16) is the story of John and Jesus.[9]

The theme of unit 1 is γένεσις, origins. Γένεσις is used in the broad sense that the name of a person determines meaning. A genealogy is a list of names by which the ascribed honor of the lineage is bestowed upon the descendent whose genealogy it is, and the name given at birth portends a future fate. Every section of unit 1 is concerned with proper names, those of the genealogy, the birth names of Jesus, and the designation of him as Son of God and Nazarene.[10]

Γένεσις I: The Genealogy

Section 1 contains two sub-sections, the first of which is a genealogy (γένεσις). The sub-section bears a title which, although not technically a title for the whole book, does create a sense of beginning for the whole gospel. The phrase βίβλος γενέσεως is the same phrase that begins the genealogy in Gen 5:1, a genealogy from Adam to Noah.[11] The use of γένεσις ties the genealogy to the story of Jesus' birth (1:18), and the occurrence of the same word in 1:1 and 1:18 indicates that these

---

[8] Jack D. Kingsbury, *Matthew: Structure, Christology, Kingdom* (Philadelphia: Fortress, 1975) 7-17. Nevertheless, Matt 4:17 should not be envisioned as a break or a chapter heading; rather, 4:12-25 is a transition from unit 1 to unit 2. That is, the hearer of the story needs narrative time to shift from one unit to another.

[9] Because of considerations of space and because it is dependent on Mark, I have set aside this third section of unit 1.

[10] Uspensky (*Poetics of Composition*, 20-43) shows the importance of names in focalization.

[11] It is not clear whether βίβλος γενέσεως is also meant to echo the title of the Book of Genesis, since it is not evident that the LXX book had that title in the first century.

two narratives are closely related and explicate the same theme of origin.[12]

The title in 1:1 also evinces the genealogy's initial organization. The expression "son of David, son of Abraham" structures in a chiasma the first two movements of the genealogy. With these two figures the narrator orientates the implied reader to a very focused reading of Hebrew history. In comparison with the genealogy in Genesis 5, this genealogy begins with Abraham, not with Adam.[13] The expression "son of David, son of Abraham" not only marks the first two movements of the genealogy but also defines the focalization. David is given prominence by being placed first in the title, and even greater prominence will emerge later in the narrative. Similarly, by singling out Abraham, the narrator also gives him a prominence that subtly announces a theme that achieves its climax at the end of Matthew. Abraham is the father not only of Israel but also of the Gentiles in the figure of his first son (Gen 17:5). The final command of the gospel orders the community to turn its attention to the Gentiles, the nations (Matt 28:19; see Gen 22:18 LXX). For a largely Jewish community that has been expelled from the synagogue, this use of Abraham constructs a bridge between the church as true Israel and the nations.[14]

The genealogy is extremely stylized and maintains a repetitive rhythm in comparison with other genealogies. The constant repetition makes the phrases sound the same. This stylized, repetitive character means that a reader/hearer tends to slide or skip through it. Put another way, variances in the stylized rhythm will capture a reader/hearer's attention. Certain features break the stylized rhythm. The first is the naming of four women.[15] Three are mentioned in the genealogy's first

---

[12] See Krister Stendahl, "Quis et Unde? An Analysis of Matthew 1-2," in *The Interpretation of Matthew* (ed. Graham Stanton; IRT 3; Philadelphia: Fortress, 1983) 60-61.

[13] By way of contrast, Luke's genealogy ends with Adam. It is normal to begin a genealogy with the last descendent.

[14] Wolfgang Trilling (*Das wahre Israel* [SANT 10; Munich: Kösel, 1964]) deals with this theme, but not in connection with the birth narratives.

[15] Str-B 1.15 notes that references to women are rare in Jewish genealogies. Exceptions occur where there is irregularity of descent or the woman's name is noteworthy. The study of Marshall D. Johnson (*The Purpose of the Biblical Genealogies with Special Reference to the Setting of the Genealogies of Jesus* [SNTSMS 8; Cambridge: Cambridge University Press, 1969]) contains a wealth of information about the genealogy. While his interests are quite different from mine, I have found his study most thorough and useful.

movement, while the fourth occurs at the beginning of the second movement.[16]

Tamar is the mother of the twins Perez and Zerah. Two elements in this reference break the stylized form. Not only is the mention of the mother unusual, but so also is that of the twins. The twins are an important note, since the genealogy only picks up on Perez and the mention of twins is superfluous. By mentioning the twins, the narrator focuses upon a particular part of the Tamar story.[17] Tamar was the wife of Judah's firstborn son, Er, but he was evil and the Lord killed him (Gen 38:7). Judah then sent his second son Onan to Tamar to fulfill the levirate law which obligates the brother-in-law to father a male heir for the deceased brother (cf. Deut 25:5-10). Onan did not wish to do this so he spilled his seed on the ground. As a result, the Lord likewise killed him. Judah then refused to send his youngest son Shelah to Tamar and instead sent her back to her father's house until the boy should grow up. When Tamar realized that Judah had no intention ever to send Shelah to her, she dressed up as a prostitute. When Judah approached her,[18] she bargained for a kid in payment for services rendered. Tamar took as a pledge for payment Judah's signet and staff. When he subsequently discovered that Tamar was pregnant, he demanded that she be burnt as punishment, but she sent him his own signet and staff to prove who had shamed her. Judah concluded: "She is more righteous than I, inasmuch as I did not give her to my son Shelah" (Gen 38:26). The Genesis narrative judges Tamar not as guilty but as righteous, even though what she had done was unrighteous. Although the impregnation was a transgression according to the law, Perez, the firstborn of the twins, became an ancestor of David.[19]

The second woman in the genealogy is Rahab, a prostitute in Jericho. When Israel was preparing to invade Jericho, two spies were sent into

---

[16] There are actually five women; the fifth woman, Mary, is mentioned only at the genealogy's end.

[17] The triangulation of Judah, Tamar, and the twins indicates, of course, that this is not David's daughter Tamar, who was raped by her half-brother Amon (2 Sam 13:1-29).

[18] There is no question of adultery since Judah's own wife is dead.

[19] This became more problematic in the later tradition and there was a tendency, by no means universal, to exonerate Tamar and even to deny the embarrassing story. Philo, for example, says the impregnation was divine and she bore virtue and noble actions (*Quod Deus* 136-37). Johnson (*Purpose of the Biblical Genealogies*, 159-62) provides a detailed summary of the evidence concerning Tamar. While the Hebrew Bible does not explicitly state Tamar's ancestry, Genesis 38 probably portrays her as a Canaanite, and that was generally accepted in the Rabbinic tradition (see Johnson, *Purpose of the Biblical Genealogies*, 270-72).

the city and Rahab hid them. In return they promised that when Israel attacked the city, she and her family would be protected (Josh 2:14).[20] When Joshua prepared to attack the city, he told the two spies to go into the city and bring out Rahab and her family. The story concludes, "But Rahab the harlot, and her father's household, and all who belonged to her, Joshua saved alive; and she dwelt in Israel to this day, because she hid the messengers whom Joshua sent to spy out Jericho" (Josh 6:25).[21] There is no mention in the Hebrew Bible of Rahab's marriage, nor is there any evidence in the Rabbinic literature of her standing in David's lineage.[22] Indeed, to put her in the lineage creates problems, for she is both a prostitute, i.e., unclean, and a Gentile. Nevertheless, because she hid the spies, she has a permanent place in Israel.

Ruth the Moabite, the third woman in the genealogy, is not someone whose virtue can in any way be doubted, for she is described as a woman of worth (Ruth 3:11). Following the death of her husband, an Israelite, Ruth returned with her mother-in-law, Naomi, to Bethlehem rather than to her own father's home. Since Naomi is both a widow and childless, she is unable to provide Ruth a husband to produce offspring. At Bethlehem Boaz claims Ruth from her next of kin and marries her. In the final blessing upon Ruth, Boaz compares her to Rachel and Leah and prays that "your house be like the house of Perez, whom Tamar bore to Judah" (Ruth 4:12). The mention of Rachel is significant in light of the role she will play in the second section of unit 1, where upon Herod's slaughter of the innocents she weeps for her children. The reference to Tamar clearly binds her fate and that of Ruth. Both were Gentiles and had to have a husband provided for them, although the joining of Ruth and Boaz is irreproachable, unlike that of Tamar and Judah. But Ruth the Moabite, the ancestress of David, flies in the face of the post-exilic demands for pure marriages.[23] Finally, the Book of Ruth closes with a short genealogy which the author of Matthew has obviously employed (Ruth 4:18-22).

---

[20] The spies gave her a scarlet cord as a sign for the attackers to recognize her family during the attack. Zerah, the second born of Tamar, was born holding a scarlet cord.

[21] Heb 11:31 mentions Rahab the harlot as an example of faith, and Jas 2:25 employs Rahab the harlot as an example of justification by works. In both cases "harlot" is part of the stereotyped reference to her.

[22] Johnson, *Purpose of the Biblical Genealogies*, 162.

[23] The fact that Ruth is a Moabite was problematic for the later Rabbinic tradition, which found a number of ways to explain it. See Johnson, *Purpose of the Biblical Genealogies*, 165-70.

The final woman is not introduced directly but is rather referred to as ἐκ τῆς τοῦ Οὐρίου ("the wife of Uriah"). By invoking the name of her husband, the narrator clearly focuses on a particular aspect of Bathsheba's story. Uriah was a Hittite[24] who fought in David's army. While a campaign was underway, David seduced his wife and she became pregnant. He tried unsuccessfully to entice Uriah to have relations with his wife so that Uriah would claim the child as his own. But failing this, David instructed the commander of his army to place Uriah in the forefront of the fighting where he would be killed. After his death, David took Bathsheba as his wife and she gave birth to a son. "But the thing that David had done displeased the Lord" (2 Sam 11:27). Following Nathan's rebuke, the child died (12:15) and she bore another son, Solomon. "And the Lord loved him" (12:24). Through a word of the prophet Nathan he was called Jedidiah, beloved of the Lord. In Bathsheba's story, the activity of David is clearly judged as unrighteous, but in the end the union between David and Bathsheba is blessed by the Lord with the birth of Solomon.

What do these women have in common?[25] The narrator simply mentions each woman without comment, but surely this is not merely random or fortuitous. Other women without the problems associated with these four could have been selected—for example, the four ancestral mothers mentioned several times in Rabbinic literature, Sarah, Rebekah, Rachel, and Leah.[26] Two of the four women in Matthew's genealogy are clearly Gentiles, and the other two (Tamar and Bathsheba) are probably Gentiles. Second, the women are all tied to David. Ruth is his great-grandmother and dwells in his hometown of Bethlehem. Tamar is compared to Ruth in the Book of Ruth and mentioned in the genealogy that concludes that book. Although Rahab does not figure in David's lineage in the Hebrew Bible, the narrator of Matthew makes her the mother of Boaz, his great-grandfather. Finally, Bathsheba is directly tied to David as his wife and the mother of

---

[24] By implication so was Bathsheba. Thus all four women in the genealogy were Gentiles.

[25] Johnson (*Purpose of the Biblical Genealogies*, 154-59) provides a thorough summary of various opinions. He divides commentators into four groups: (1) the women foreshadow the concern in Matthew with sinners and Gentiles; (2) they demonstrate that God can use the humble and despised; (3) they are types of Mary and prepare for the virgin birth; (4) their mention refutes attacks on the legitimacy of Jesus' birth. Jane Schaberg (*The Illegitimacy of Jesus* [San Francisco: Harper & Row, 1987] chap. 2) has turned these arguments on their head, demonstrating the difficulties in moving from fictional narrative to historical conclusions.

[26] Str-B 1.29-30.

Solomon. Both of these elements, Gentile status and the linkage to David, are part of the reason the narrator focuses on these women. Indeed, the title of the genealogy already makes this clear. "Son of Abraham" corresponds to the Gentile aspect, and "son of David," of course, corresponds to the Davidic connection.

There is an even more important aspect that the women have in common, however. In a patriarchal society lineage is traced through the male, as with this genealogy, and the function of a genealogy is to illustrate the honor to be ascribed to the final descendent.[27] Insofar as Jesus stands in the lineage of David and Abraham, he has a great deal of ascribed honor. But all four women, from the point of view of a shame/honor system, are tainted sexually—Tamar through prostitution with Judah, Rahab because she was a prostitute, Ruth because she was a foreigner, and Bathsheba because David seduced her and killed her husband. Yet despite this shame, these women all have the honor ascribed to them by the Lord. Even though on the surface they have shame, in truth they possess honor.

The final woman mentioned in the genealogy is Mary. Her insertion into the genealogy claims attention. Joseph is the next to last male in the lineage but he is the only male in the genealogy who does not father (ἐγέννησεν) offspring. He is "the husband of Mary out of whom Jesus who is called the Anointed was born"[28] (Matt 1:16). The stylized formula's breakdown when applied to Joseph and Mary forewarns the implied reader that something is amiss with them. Further, Mary's inclusion in the list of women sets up a pattern of anticipation that there is something shameful, yet ultimately honorable, about the birth. This is reinforced by the fact that she is not a Gentile. So the aspect common to the women on which the narrator must be focusing is that of sexual taint.

Two other features of the genealogy's narration need comment. Unlike the first two movements of the genealogy, the third does not begin with a person's name, but with an event, the return from the Babylonian exile. This use of an event and a geographical reference to introduce the third movement breaks the genealogy's formalistic and stylized character. As such it calls attention to itself, but the genealogy offers no clues as to its significance and so it is a gap[29] that the implied reader

---

[27] Bruce Malina, *The New Testament World: Insights from Cultural Anthropology* (Atlanta: John Knox, 1981) 29.

[28] "Was born" (ἐγεννήθη) is the passive voice of the same verb used to describe the "fathering" (ἐγέννησεν) activity of the men.

[29] "Gap" is a technical term from Wolfgang Iser, *The Act of Reading: A Theory of Aesthetic Response* (Baltimore: Johns Hopkins University Press, 1978) 163-79. It represents

will fill in later. It breaks the consistency of the genealogy and demands explanation.

The other aspect of the genealogy requiring comment also occurs in the third section. In the summary of the genealogy (1:17), the narrator reports that there are fourteen[30] generations in each of the three movements, but there are only thirteen in the final one. Various ingenious explanations have been offered to explain why the author apparently cannot count.[31] But at the level of narration, the missing number is significant only because it calls attention to a section whose beginning and ending are odd—it begins with the return from the Babylonian exile and ends with Mary, again calling attention to Mary and her child's place in her husband's genealogy.

The narrator focuses the story by what is selected for narration, but how to form that into a *Gestalt* that makes sense is the role of the implied reader. The narrator requires the implied reader to recall specific elements of these women's stories in order to complete the focalization provided by the elements selected for narration.

Γένεσις II: The Birth

The second sub-section of section one has a title that resonates with the title of the first sub-section. Each is a γένεσις. Even more, the titles of the two sub-sections form a chiasm.

βίβλος γενέσεως // 'Ιησοῦ Χριστοῦ
'Ιησοῦ Χριστοῦ // ἡ γένεσις

the book of origin // of Jesus the Anointed (1:1)
of Jesus the Anointed // the origin (1:17)

In both cases γένεσις means origin, but in the elaborated sense of genealogy in the first case, and birth in the latter. This chiastic relating

---

an indeterminacy in a narrative discourse which creates asymmetry between the text and the implied reader, demanding interpretation.

[30] The division of three units of fourteen each is artificial. The number fourteen may well be based on the Hebrew spelling of David (*dahleth-waw-dahleth:* $4 + 6 + 4 = 14$), as F. W. Beare (*The Gospel according to Matthew* [New York: Harper & Row, 1981] 63) and others have suggested.

[31] Brown (*Birth of the Messiah*, 81-84), after surveying the evidence, suggests that Matthew implicitly is counting the missing generation of Jehoiakim at the beginning of the third section. He admits, "With ingenuity, then, one can salvage Matthew's reputation as a mathematician" (84).

of the title for both sub-sections indicates that they are closely tied together.

The title of the second sub-section inaugurates as the goal of this narrative the origin/birth of Jesus the Anointed. Thus Jesus' story is the main story line. But immediately the narrator introduces an intersecting story line, that of Jesus' mother Mary. This is the narrative line the genealogy leads one to expect, since it ends with Mary. When Mary had been engaged to Joseph but before they had come together,[32] "she was found to be with child by the Holy Spirit" (1:18). This complicated sentence shifts narrative time from the main story of Jesus' birth to the events prior to his birth, and it changes the subject of the narrative from Jesus to Mary. Thus narration and focalization shift from the main story, Jesus' story, to a sub-narrative, Mary's story.

The narrator also furnishes the implied reader with two elements that disturb the narration. First, the child is by the Holy Spirit, i.e., of divine origin. The narration is not interested in the mechanics of the divine origin, only in the statement of it. Second, "she was found to be pregnant." The use of the passive voice indicates the public character of her situation; there are other unnamed actors witnessing this drama. Thus the implied reader knows that Mary is both potentially publicly shamed and yet divinely honored. These two disturbing details are a technique for focalizing the textual ideology. This disturbance is often overlooked by contemporary real readers who approach the text with the pre-determined dogmatic ideology of the virgin birth, with the result that these two items are no longer perceived as disturbing.

As soon as this second narrative is launched the narrator once again shifts narrative perspective and introduces Joseph's story as a third narrative, a sub-sub-narrative. The potentially shameful aspect of Jesus' birth is the threat to this narrative completion. The narrative's tension is driven initially by the distance between Joseph's knowledge and that of the reader, since Joseph does not know that the child is of the Holy Spirit.

The narrator states Joseph's dilemma: he is righteous and does not wish to shame Mary.[33] The mentioning of shame in this context

---

[32] According to *BAGD* (2nd ed., 788), one denotation of συνέρχομαι is coming together in a sexual sense. The word is used in the papyri to mean "to marry," and that probably is the appropriate sense here. Ernst Lohmeyer and W. Schmauch (*Das Evangelium des Matthaus* [MeyerK; 2nd ed.; Göttingen: Vandenhoeck & Ruprecht, 1958] 13) warn against such a reading, but the evidence seems clearly to point to a meaning of sexual relations.

[33] The verb δειγματίζω is used of publicly exposing an adulteress. It is a negative term. See *BAGD*, 2nd ed., 172.

indicates that the story draws upon the shame/honor repertoire.³⁴ Mary has already shamed herself since "she was found" to be pregnant. Joseph does not wish to add to her shame by a public denunciation. The narrator also notes that Joseph is righteous. One need not be precise at this point about the meaning of "righteous," but simply indicate that δίκαιος represents the Hebrew ṣadiq, and that in the narrator's symbolic world it is the highest virtue.³⁵ Joseph's righteousness and his not wishing to shame Mary create for him a dilemma. Because he is righteous he cannot ignore what has happened, but also because he is righteous he does not want to shame her any more than has already occurred. His solution to this dilemma is to put her away quietly,³⁶ rather than to proclaim her publicly as shameful.

The narrator has already revealed that God is involved in Mary's story of Jesus' birth. Now an angel in a dream provides Joseph with the same information that the narrator has previously provided. This cements the narrator's and the text's ultimate ideological authority, God. The angel goes even further. Joseph is to claim Mary as his wife and to name the child. The angel's command fills in one of many gaps created by the genealogy. Why was it Joseph's genealogy when the genealogy explicitly omits any notice of his fathering the child? The answer is now clear; he is to adopt the child as his own, and so Jesus is an adopted son of David.³⁷ This creates an irony involving narrated knowledge and public knowledge. Only the narrator, the implied reader and Joseph³⁸ know that Jesus is adopted. But from the public perspective, Joseph is the real father. This disjunction between narrated reality and the public perception has gone unnoticed in the understanding of this text, yet it forms an important aspect of the narrator's ideological focalization. From the narrated perspective, Joseph remains righteous, but from the public perspective he must forfeit his righteousness, because by claiming Mary as his wife and naming the child he is implicitly

---

³⁴ "Repertoire" is all those conventions necessary for the establishment of the textual situation. The repertoire is extratextual since it is cultural in origin, but it is drawn into the text and undergoes a fictional transformation. See Iser, *Act of Reading*, 68-69.

³⁵ The term δίκαιος and its cognates are prominent in Matthew. See Benno Przybylski, *Righteousness in Matthew and His World of Thought* (Cambridge/New York: Cambridge University Press, 1980).

³⁶ Probably this means she will return to her father's home. The command of Deut 22:21 that the woman who engages in premarital intercourse be stoned at her father's door was no longer in effect in the first century.

³⁷ Verses 24-25 make clear that Joseph does as the angel commands.

³⁸ The narrator provides no insight into Mary's knowledge.

admitting that they "came together" before they were married.[39] Thus in order to maintain his (narrated) ascribed righteousness, he will be publicly shamed. Mary's case is like that of the women mentioned in the genealogy. The birth may be divinely sanctioned, but there is about it, as with those other women, an element of shame.

Joseph, too, is drawn into this pattern of narrated honor and public shame. In the five examples the narrator provides, the public shame involves a violation of the law. The focalization employs an ideology in which true righteousness opposes the expected law. For Joseph to maintain his true righteousness he must suffer public shame (forfeit his public righteousness), because he must admit that he violated the law. This perspectival model is built upon the paradox that true righteousness is contrary to the expectations of the law. For the narrator-focalizer, public shame implies narrated honor, and contrariwise public honor implies true shame. But there is also implied a counter-focalization. For the counter-focalizer, the narrator's righteousness is shame because it violates the law. This same pattern is true of the women in the genealogy.[40]

It might be objected that this model of ideological focalization cannot make any sense of other aspects of Matthew. For example, in the sermon on the mount, in a statement with which the narrator obviously agrees, Jesus says that he has not come to abolish the law and the prophets but to fulfill them (5:17). If this is true, how can righteousness be the contrary of the law? Yet the pericope's final line warns: "For I tell you, unless your righteousness exceeds that of the scribes and Pharisees, you will never enter the kingdom of heaven" (5:20). The Pharisees, as those who sit on Moses' seat (23:2), obviously know the law and possess public honor. Yet it does not in their case lead to righteousness, because they do not produce fruits of righteousness. The narrator's and Jesus' favorite epithet for them—hypocrite, impostor—represents in miniature the ideological phalanx drawn against them. They know the law, and they are publicly clean, but inside they are unclean (23:24-28). True righteousness must go beyond the law into what is apparent lawlessness in order to be righteous.

---

[39] Much is often made of Jewish marriage practices, where a betrothal is in our terms a marriage. But it is clear that the actual coming together, not the betrothal, marks the point where sexual intercourse is permitted. See *m. Ketub.* 1.5 and *b. Ketub.* 9b, 12a; Brown, *Birth of the Messiah*, 123-24; Schaberg, *Illegitimacy*, 42-62.

[40] For example, Tamar's seduction of Judah is unlawful and thus shameful, but the narrator judges it righteous.

The "mixed community" motif so prominent in Matthew belongs to the same ideology. In the parable of the wheat and the tares, the master forbids the uprooting of the weeds because in so doing "you root up the wheat along with them" (13:29). Because the ideology is dynamic, perspectival, and built upon a paradox, the wheat and tares are indistinguishable without the judge's insight. Therefore the community should not risk judgment (13:41).

Since from the perspective of the counter-focalizer (i.e., normally) righteousness and law imply each other, by paradoxically correlating them as contraries the narrator makes judgment impossible.

Similarly, in the Sermon on the Mount Jesus proclaims, "Not everyone who says to me, 'Lord, Lord,' shall enter the kingdom of heaven, but the one who does the will of my Father who is in heaven" (7:21).[41] The same paradoxical perspective is at work, only its effects are even more radical.

Those who make the Christian confession, prophesy, and cast out demons are denied, even though they are obviously righteous. There is, then, more to doing the will of the Father. Unfortunately, Jesus does not state why these 'believers' are rejected. But the vivid scene of the last judgment goes to the heart of the matter. The king tells those included in the kingdom that "I was hungry and you gave me food, I was thirsty and you gave me drink..." (25:35). They ask when they did these things, and he replies, "Whatever you did for one of these insignificant ones, my brothers, you did it for me" (25:40). Those who were hungry, thirsty, foreigners, naked, sick, and prisoners are persons who have shame and are unclean. The identification of Jesus as king-judge with the insignificant, the least, as his brothers completes the paradigm of the shameful.

Joseph is the first fully sketched model of doing the will of the Father: narrated righteousness, true or hidden righteousness, involves public shame or uncleanness. By the end of the first section, this basic ideological focalization is in place, yet it will be greatly elaborated and complicated as the narrative progresses. Several elements of that complexity are yet to emerge in the gospel's first unit.

The conclusion of the Joseph story deals with the naming of the child. The angel announces that the child is to be named Jesus and then gives an explanation of the name: "He will save his people from their sins" (1:21). The implied reader already knows the name of his story's hero from the genealogy, as well as his title, the Anointed. Here there is no

---

[41] The speech continues with a similar warning against those who prophesy and cast out demons.

mention of the Anointed and instead the angel provides an interpretation of the name Jesus. This interpretation is based upon a Hebrew word play. The Greek name 'Ιησοῦς is derived from the Hebrew yēšûa', which in turn is derived from yāšā', meaning to help or save.[42] Given the importance of names in the ancient world and even more the importance of names in this first unit of the gospel, the fate and mission of the hero Jesus now become clearer.

Following the angel's pronouncement, the narrator quotes God as having spoken through the prophet Isaiah. This activity of the narrator is important to observe because of his authority. The narrator of Matthew is an omniscient (panoramic) narrator whose focalization is external to the narrative. Now the narrator calls as a witness to the narrator's ideology the ultimate external authority, God. So there is to be a divine focalization of the story as well as the narrator's focalization. This allows the narrator to reevaluate the law. Previously, law has been opposed to righteousness; now law is the repository of the divine focalizer. Law is reclaimed by being refocused by the narrator's ideology. The law will paradoxically turn upon itself.

The quotation has two parts. First, a virgin shall conceive. This, of course, is paradoxical. Normally, for a virgin to conceive would be unrighteous and shameful. But in the ideology of the narrator it is righteous, honorable, and divinely foretold in prophecy. Here the law deconstructs itself: it is shown to approve of an apparently unrighteous activity, a virgin conceiving.

The narrator elaborates the second segment of the quotation, thereby underlining it. The child "shall be called Emmanuel." Like the angel who explained the meaning of the name Jesus, the narrator translates Emmanuel for the Greek-speaking implied reader as "God with us." Significantly, this new name for the child disagrees with that prescribed by the angel. Is the implied reader to decide that the narrator is unreliable? Not only can the narrator not count, but now the narrator seems mistaken about the name! Kingsbury has suggested that the new name Emmanuel forms an inclusio with the gospel's conclusion, where Jesus says, "Behold, I am with you all the days until the completion of the age" (28:20).[43] The phrase μεθ' ἡμῶν ὁ θεός is parallel to ἐγὼ μεθ' ὑμῶν εἰμι. This argument is very suggestive and may be correct, but it is a long way for a reader/hearer to remember the phrase without

---

[42] W. Foerster, "'Ιησοῦς," *TDNT* 3.289. The angel does not explicitly state that it is providing a translation of the name. The interpretation of the name may be traditional and the wordplay and derivation forgotten.

[43] Kingsbury, *Matthew* (Proclamation Commentaries; Philadelphia: Fortress, 1977) 27.

The Birth of the Reader: Matthew 1:1-4:16

significant reinforcement. Many[44] have also pointed to 18:19-20, where there is a firm identification between "my Father in heaven," who ratifies whatever two members of the community have agreed upon, and the reason given for that ratification: "For where two or three are gathered in my name, there I am in their midst" (18:20).[45] But the immediately unfulfilled status of the name in 1:23 and the compounded conflict with the angel's command creates for the implied reader a gap that cannot be dealt with by recourse to an unreliable narrator. Rather, the quotation from scripture is actually God's voice, just as the angel is God's voice. Thus both names are true. The first, Jesus, is immediately fulfilled by the action of Joseph and is the public name. The reader must then find some way to fill in the gap created by the name Emmanuel. I would suggest that Emmanuel is the presiding image or metaphor[46] of the narrative, and the function of the gospel narrative is to form a consistency or *Gestalt* in which Jesus is the presence of God with us. To fill in this gap is the way in which the implied reader will make sense (form a consistency) of the narrative.

Section 2: After the Birth

Section 1 of unit 1 of Matthew is composed of two sub-sections, a genealogy and a story of naming and adoption. Section 2 reports events after the birth, and again narration is by indirection, by means of a series of sub-narratives. The primary actor in this section is Herod, and his story, his response to the news of the birth of a king of the Jews, organizes the other sub-narratives. The three main parts of the section are all introduced by (1) a genitive absolute, (2) ἰδού ("behold") introducing the main clause, (3) a participle of λέγω ("say") and (4) direct speech.[47]

> 2:1 After Jesus was born...
>   behold, magi from the east came
>   saying,

---

[44] Kingsbury (*Structure, Christology, Kingdom*, 69-70) provides an excellent summary of the arguments. Trilling (*Das wahre Israel*, 42) is the only significant interpreter who denies a relationship among these three texts.

[45] The Greek is not as closely parallel here as in 28:20: ἐκεῖ εἰμι ἐν μέσῳ αὐτῶν.

[46] See Philip Wheelwright, *Metaphor and Reality* (Midland ed.; Bloomington: Indiana University Press, 1968) 95.

[47] In the first two sub-sections (2:7,16) a shift in narrative action is indicated in an identical fashion: τότε Ἡρῴδης and a participle.

"Where is he who is born king of the Jews?"
2:13 When they had departed
   behold, an angel of the Lord appeared in a dream to Joseph
      saying,
         "Rise, take the child and his mother...."
2:19 When Herod died
   behold, an angel of the Lord appeared in a dream to Joseph
   ... saying,
         "Rise, take the child and his mother...."[48]

In the first section there was only one geographical reference, the exile to Babylon, and this is as much an event as a place. In Joseph's story there was no mention of place. By contrast, this second section has a surfeit of geographical references. In fact geography plays an important symbolic function in this section.

The section begins with a density of geographical references. The narrator reports after the fact that Jesus was born in Bethlehem of Judea. In Matthew Jesus is a Judean, not a Galilean as in Luke. This is clearly implied in the genealogy with the multiple references to David and Bethlehem, and no trip to Bethlehem is narrated. The magi visit the child at his house (2:11). At the section's end, when the angel instructs Joseph to return to the land of Israel, Joseph chooses Galilee after initially considering Judea.

There are also other geographical references. The magi from the east come to Jerusalem. Herod is in Jerusalem, since the magi speak to him there. Following their question the chief priests and scribes (not the narrator) quote the prophecy[49] that Bethlehem is not the least among the leaders of Judah. There is a double irony in the quotation. The chief priests and scribes who report the divine forecast are identified with Herod as among those in Jerusalem who are troubled at the magi's report. Likewise, the quotation itself is ironic because Bethlehem is an insignificant village in comparison with Jerusalem, but in the divine scheme it is significant. This ironic twist on the significance of

---

[48] In 2:13 the verb in the genitive absolute is the same verb (ἀναχωρέω) that ends the previous narrative (2:12), and the participle τελευτήσαντος in the third section (2:19) picks up on the death or murder of the infants which concludes the previous sub-section.

[49] This formula quotation is very different from the others in the first two chapters. It is the only quotation that is part of the story and not the narrator's discourse. Its introduction does not conform to the formula quotations; it states, "It is written," rather than "in order to fulfill." Finally, this text is an extremely free form even for the formula quotations. See George M. Soares Prabhu, *The Formula Quotations in the Infancy Narrative of Matthew* (AnBib 63; Rome: Biblical Institute, 1976) 37-40.

Bethlehem is clearly intended because the quotation in Matthew, "not at all are you least among the leaders of Judah," is the exact opposite of what the Masoretic and LXX texts state.[50] Thus the true king's birthplace is on the surface insignificant, while in the divine view it is significant. This pattern replicates the ideology from the first section.

The narrator warns that the magi's question has thrown Herod and all Jerusalem into consternation (2:3). Further, when the magi find the child they are warned in a dream not to return to Herod (2:12). Even though this dream is only narrated and no angelic voice is recorded, the implied reader clearly is to understand the dream as a divine command.

These various geographical references endow Judea with a symbolic, ideological interpretation. Judea is divided into two parts, one represented by Jerusalem, the holy city, the holy mountain, the center of the universe, and the other represented by Bethlehem, one of the unimportant villages of Judea. All of this is at the surface level, while at the ideological level everything is reversed. The prophecy indicates that Bethlehem is a place of blessing from which will come a leader who will shepherd the people of Israel. On the other hand, Jerusalem is a place of Herod and threat. This threat escalates throughout the narrative.

At first Herod is shaken (2:3); then in secret he seeks the time of the star's first appearance; next the magi are warned not to return to Herod (2:12); and finally Herod strikes out in rage (2:16). Even Jerusalem is implicated with Herod in the threat (2:3). The narrative sets up a conflict within Judea. Jerusalem, the magnificent holy city, is a place of threat and intrigue, the home of a murdering king. Bethlehem, the insignificant village, is a place of blessing and leadership, the home of the true king.

This symbolic reorganization even extends beyond Judea. The east is also a place of revelation, the place of the star. The magi, of course, are Gentiles, and in the narration they are the first to do obeisance (προσκυνῆσαι)[51] to Jesus (2:2,11). This exaltation of the east is a reversal of its expected symbolic value and causes retrospection on the part of the reader. The third movement of the genealogy stood out for a variety of reasons, but one of the first markers of its distinctiveness was that it began with an event, the exile in Babylon, rather than an appellation. The last birth in the section beginning after the exile to

---

[50] Ibid., 262.

[51] This is a favorite Matthean word. It occurs thirteen times in Matthew, twice in Mark, and three times in Luke. The gospel concludes with the eleven doing obeisance to Jesus, "but some doubted" (28:16). This last note about doubt is part of the paradoxical reversal that I am arguing is characteristic of the narrator's ideology.

Babylon is that of the Messiah. Thus the narration reverses the symbolism of the place of exile, and by implication the place of the Gentiles as well. It is a place of true obeisance. This symbolic reversal receives its fulfillment in the gospel's final speech, when the resurrected Jesus commands, "Go and make disciples of all nations [ἔθνη]" (28:19). The reorganization of the expected symbolic structure creates an ideology of paradoxical reversal.

A second outside place is symbolically and ideologically reevaluated. After the angel commands Joseph to take the child to Egypt, the narrator quotes the prophet, "Out of Egypt have I called my son" (2:15). Egypt, formerly the place of exile and enslavement, will protect the child Jesus much in the same way it protected Moses.[52] This symbolic reversal of both the east and Egypt is part of the ideological focalization. From the perspective of the law, these places are unclean and shameful. But in narrative organization and divine focalization they are warranted as places of true righteousness—paradoxically by quotations from the law. Furthermore, the Messiah to whom Gentiles first do obeisance will appear to come out of Gentile territory.

Now abandoned by the Messiah because it lacks Emmanuel, Judea becomes a place of murder. Herod seeks to destroy the child whom he knows to be divinely attested as the king of Israel. This negative death symbol for Judea is confirmed by the story of the slaughter of the infants. Once again the narrator refers to the prophet, the divine focalizer of these events: "A voice in Ramah was heard, weeping and much lamenting, Rachel weeping for her children; and she did not wish to be comforted, because they were not" (2:18). Rachel is associated with Bethlehem, and traditionally it was the site of her burial.[53] This powerfully disturbing quotation seals the fate of Judea. In the narrative it is now a place of death. Even after Herod's death it retains its negative value, since Joseph is afraid to return there. In the end it will be the place of Jesus' betrayal, Judas' suicide, and Jesus' death.

The ideology of the narrative affects even the narration of Jesus' return from Egypt. Even though Jesus was born in Judea, it was in the least of the Judean towns (Bethlehem), and he becomes a foreigner from Egypt. Upon his return he does not go home to Judea, but to a city

---

[52] The extent of the Moses typology in Matthew is a matter of considerable debate. Brown (*Birth of the Messiah*, 112-16) sees a strong influence from the Joseph and Moses cycle, while W. D. Davies (*The Setting of the Sermon on the Mount* [Cambridge: Cambridge University Press, 1964] 61-83) concludes that the Davidic motif is more prominent than the Mosaic.

[53] See Gen 35:19; 48:7.

in Galilee called Nazareth. Once again the narrator quotes the prophets: "He shall be called a Nazarene" (2:23). Regardless of what one does with the derivation of this quotation,[54] its intention is clear. The surface narrative assumes that the Messiah, the son of David, will come from Bethlehem. But Jesus is a Nazarean. The narrator has clearly instructed the reader in a complex allegorical reading in which all of these things are true, but at different levels. Jesus is from Galilee (which the divine focalizer will soon refer to as "Galilee of the Gentiles" [4:15]), and Gentiles first recognize him. Thus as a son of Abraham he will finally instruct his disciples to go to all the nations. He is also from Bethlehem, but a Bethlehem of tragedy, a place of the slaughter of the innocents.

These same themes are picked up in the final section of the first unit (3:1-4:16), which concerns the story of John the Baptist and the initial scenes of Jesus before his preaching of the gospel of the kingdom (4:23). I will not undertake here a comparable analysis of this section, but would like to indicate briefly how the ideology undergirding sections one and two is carried forward.

The introduction of John the Baptist describes him as preaching "in the desert of Judea" (3:1).[55] This description of Judea confirms the ideological structure—Judea is a desert, a place of death. Those who come to hear John's preaching are from Jerusalem, all of Judea, and the region about the Jordan (v. 5). The Pharisees and Sadducees are rejected by John and characterized as sterile; "the axe is laid to the root," reinforcing the image of desert.

Jesus then comes from Galilee (3:13), which sets him apart from the others who are from Judea. When John hesitates to baptize him, Jesus replies, "It is fitting for us to fulfill all righteousness" (3:15). First Joseph and now Jesus are presented as righteous, and the sense is the same. For Jesus to be truly righteous, he must publicly appear to be in need of repentance, i.e., to be shameful. Yet John and Jesus know that he has no such need. That paradox will fulfill righteousness. In the testing story which follows, Jesus is tested in the desert by the devil. The second test takes place in "the holy city," a deliberate irony, for it is not holy at all.[56]

The transitional quotation in 4:15-16 forms the conclusion to part one of the gospel and the opening of part two. This quotation is introduced by the narrator with the comment that after John had been handed over,

---

[54] See Prabhu, *Formula Quotations*, 215.

[55] Mark 1:4 reads simply "in the desert."

[56] The Q story of this test is preserved almost verbatim in Matthew and Luke. The Lukan text reads simply "Jerusalem," whereas Matthew has "the holy city."

Jesus departed for Galilee. The verb ἀναχωρέω (depart) recalls the activity of the magi following their obeisance to the child. The verb had concluded 2:12 and introduced 2:13.[57] The narrator concludes by calling on the divine focalizer by means of a reworking of Isa 9:1-2 (LXX).[58] The reference to "across the Jordan," missing from the Isaiah text, excludes Judea, and the quotation climaxes with "Galilee of the Gentiles." This brings to a head the Gentile theme of the birth narratives and introduces the next unit, in which Jesus will go only to the house of Israel.[59] Thus it prepares the reader for the long wait until the promise of the magi is fulfilled in the risen Lord's final command (28:19).[60]

In the quotation's conclusion, the people of Galilee are those who sat in darkness and have seen a great light, a reference to the star and metaphorically to Jesus as light. For those in the shadow of death a light has dawned. Thus the divine focalizer has warranted the narrator's ideological paradox. Judea and the holy city are now a place of murder, death, and darkness, while Galilee of the Gentiles, once a place of darkness, is now a place of light and life.

Matthew's birth narrative never describes the birth of Jesus. Rather, it reports the events before and after that birth. The birth in this first unit of the gospel is that of the reader, for the narrator constructs an ideological map by which the reader is to make sense of the story that follows.

---

[57] See above, n. 48. In Mark Jesus "goes" (1:14), and in Luke he "returns" (4:14). The verb ἀναχωρέω is a favorite transition word in the gospel. It occurs ten times in Matthew, once in Mark, and not at all in Luke.

[58] See Prabhu, *Formula Quotations* 86-104.

[59] See Matt 10:5-6 and 15:24, texts with no synoptic parallels.

[60] This final command to preach to all nations takes place on a mountain in Galilee.

3

The Human Face of Otherness: Reflections on Joseph and Mary (Matthew 1:18-25)

Karl A. Plank[1]

Is not the human face a living mixture of mystery and meaning?
Abraham Joshua Heschel[2]

The Silent Question and the Seeking of Otherness

Questions stir the spirit of those in whom they dwell. Quietly, they may steal upon us and veil familiar certainties. Or, with the force of a black night's thunder, they may jolt us to an awareness of portentous reality. Such questions may fill us with wonder or simply terrify but, in every instance, they incite within us a rhythm of quest or of flight.

The question which animates us may remain inarticulate, nesting in the noise of other askings. Martin Buber speaks of this as "the silent

---

[1] Karl A. Plank is Associate Professor of Religion at Davidson College, Davidson, North Carolina.

[2] Heschel, *Who Is Man?* (Stanford, CA: Stanford University Press, 1965) 38.

question" inflected repeatedly, yet unknowingly, in our various instances of speech. That question, a testament of desire as well as deep need, asks: "'Are you, perhaps, the power that can help me? Can you teach me to believe? ... Teach me to have faith in reality, in the verities of existence, so that life will afford some aim for me and existence will have some meaning. Who, indeed, can help me if you cannot?'"[3]

As we seek in our silent asking a presence that confirms, we know the question itself will not leave us alone. In need, we seek the presence of an other.

Modern theology, in its persistent wrestling with faith's relation to history, gives voice to the silent question. Already, in its attempt to explore faith and history as a relation, theology acknowledges our quest for a presence that both confirms human existence and transcends its contingency. Indeed, observation of history not only challenges the claims of faith, it also goads one to pursue meaning within history, a seeking for God that denies not history, but history's autonomy.[4] If in our time—now some four decades after Hashoah and Hiroshima—theology cannot presume to answer the silent question, it can at least guard and interpret the meaningfulness of the asking.

Although theology identifies the silent question as a seeking for God, the actual asking of that question remains hidden in our speech. Rarely do we hear the silent question, even as we pose it. But should we, in a moment of unusual stillness, become aware of our asking, we would sense as well that we do not really know what we are asking for. The object of our tacit prayer eludes us, varying from moment to moment with the context of our asking and escaping our firm grasp. In times of chaos, fearing overwhelming change, we seek constancy, a presence on which to rely. In times of stultifying tedium, fearing the impossibility of change, we seek novelty, a presence to surprise and quicken us. Superficially, the elusiveness of our asking—now for this, now for that, now for simply something—may derive from uncertainty or *ressentiment*. Still, in its deeper expression, it reflects a fundamental yearning for that

---

[3] Martin Buber, "The Silent Question," in *On Judaism* (ed. N. Glatzer; New York: Schocken, 1967) 202. Buber's reflections here give echo to a poignant encounter earlier in his life in which he understands himself to have missed precisely this silent question in the speech of another. He later reflects, "What do we expect when we are in despair and yet go to a man? Surely a presence by means of which we are told that nevertheless there is meaning." See "Autobiographical Fragments," in *The Philosophy of Martin Buber* (ed. P. Schilpp and M. Friedman; LaSalle, IL: Open Court, 1967) 25-26.

[4] On the theologically necessary dialectic between faith and its contemporary critiques, see Emil Fackenheim, *God's Presence in History. Jewish Affirmations and Philosophical Reflections* (New York: New York University Press, 1970).

which is always other: a yearning to stand in relation to that other who, unlike ourselves, can confirm the meaning of our precarious and dull existence. Fragile and weary, we would embrace an otherness whose presence restores belief in the durability and possibility of our condition.

The Face of the Human Other

Ever situated in time and place, we cannot fulfill a quest for absolute otherness any more than we can live in a pure present or float indefinitely in mid-air.[5] A spiritual gravity holds us to the world and resists any attempt to flee our human condition.[6] Absolute otherness, if somehow attained, could only mean that we had ceased to be the human beings that we are. No simple expression of human limitation, spiritual gravity reminds us that the god whom we would find would not be the God whom we really sought, the absolutely other. As the silent question itself indicates, we do not have the power to transcend ourselves or to confirm our own existence. The silent question is ours only to ask; and though that question stirs us deeply, the advent of any answer is one upon which we must finally wait.[7]

Were we able to defy gravity, our quest for absolute otherness would still leave us with a troubling ambiguity. Pure transcendence, in and of itself, cannot answer the silent question, for its onset would only intensify the plight which generates that question. No less than death would unbroken otherness remove us from the world of common life, the fear of which creates an anxiety over life's meaning and our ability to trust it with confidence.[8] We ask the silent question in the face of a

---

[5] On the constraints that limit our encounter with otherness and fix its presence as an object in the world, see Martin Buber, *I and Thou* (tr. W. Kaufmann; New York: Scribners, 1970) 82-85.

[6] On gravity see the writings of Simone Weil. For her, God-seeking falls to the force of gravity: "all the natural movements of the soul are controlled by laws analogous to those of physical gravity" (*Gravity and Grace* [tr. A. Wills; New York: Putnam's, 1952; reprinted, Octagon, 1979] 45). Thus, as she writes elsewhere, futile are those "whose manner of seeking God is like a man making leaps into the air in the hope that if he jumps a little higher each time, he will end up staying there and rising into heaven" ("Some Reflections on the Love of God," in *Gateway to God* [ed. D. Raper; New York: Crossroad, 1982] 74).

[7] For amplification of this point, see Larry E. Carden, "Waiting: Spiritual Transformation and the Absence of God," *St. Luke's Journal of Theology* 31 (1988) 189-203.

[8] Cf. Kierkegaard's depiction of the radical singularity of the knight of faith who renounces the finite for the infinite and, though he does not doubt, yet faces a sleepless ordeal. In its moment, the transcendence of his faith has separated him decisively from the world in which he could speak and pursue common life. See *Fear and Trembling* (ed. and tr. H. Hong and E. Hong; Princeton: Princeton University Press, 1983) 70, 76. Note also

mortality that is at once the condition for life and the assurance of its loss. Where transcendence may defy the mortal condition for life, it cannot do so without also robbing me of the life which I would preserve and whose meaning I would guard.[9] The otherness which meets the silent question cannot be otherworldly or simply so. It must be an otherness to which we can stand in relation and know within our worldly condition.[10]

If we cannot endure the journey that is always "Away-From-Here,"[11] we yet confront a relative otherness in selves who share our world and condition, albeit uniquely.[12] Otherness comes to us first in the person of the stranger whose speech voices words not of our making, whose memory knows echoes beyond our hearing, whose spirit springs from sources outside our reach. That stranger may come to us from afar or lie as near as an intimate's breathing, accompanying us through night's slumber. It does not matter. The human condition we share is to be stranger to one another, to bring to each a difference that familiarity cannot exhaust. No twin's resemblance can mask what our faces would reveal: lines of countenance formed in the singularity of experience; the irreducible gaze of eyes whose mystery reflects what they alone have seen.[13] This stranger, this human face, emerges in the world of stirring questions and silent askings, bearing a presence of infinity. If we have

---

Martin Buber's critique of mysticism as a form of self-annihilation that preempts the possibility of standing in relation to either a human or a divine other. See *I and Thou*, 128-43. Although they value it differently, both Kierkegaard and Buber recognize that absolute otherness, like death itself, brings meaningful life in the world to a halt.

[9] See the comparable point which sets the stage for Franz Rosenzweig's seminal work, *The Star of Redemption* (tr. W. Hallo; New York: Holt, Rinehart & Winston, 1971) 3-5.

[10] Note Paul W. Meyer's contending with the problem of other-worldliness—"a problem of our religion and our theology, a problem in our ways of reading the New Testament"—in his 1979 Princeton inaugural. See "The This-Worldliness of the New Testament," *Princeton Seminary Bulletin* N.S. 2 (1979) 219-31. See also Karl A. Plank, "Confronting the Unredeemed World: A Paradoxical Paul and His Modern Critics," *ATR* 67 (1985) 127-36.

[11] See the important imagery of Franz Kafka, "My Destination," in *Parables and Paradoxes* (New York: Schocken, 1961) 189.

[12] In addition to the writings of Martin Buber generally, one should also note the development of this insight in Hannah Arendt (*The Human Condition* [Chicago: University of Chicago Press, 1958] 175-247) and in Emmanuel Levinas (*Totality and Infinity* [tr. A. Lingis; Pittsburgh: Duquesne University Press, 1969]).

[13] The notion of "face" is central to the writings of Levinas on exteriority and otherness. See, e.g., *Totality and Infinity*, 187-247. Note also Stephen D. Crites' sensitive reflection, "Myth, Story, History," in *Parable, Myth, and Language* (ed. T. Stoneburner; Cambridge, MA: Church Society for College Work, 1968) 66-73.

sought another, we could not have sought this other, for him or her we do not fully know. Yet to this stranger we may entrust the silent question: "'Are you, perhaps, the power that can help me? ... Who, indeed, can help me if you cannot?'"

The silent question invites relation between human selves who seek in each other the trace of a larger Other. No single person can bear the burden of the silent question or alone provide its answer. Still, as Elie Wiesel's haunting messenger, Gavriel, insists, "The struggle to survive will begin here, in this room, where we are sitting."[14] Here, where we glimpse the mysterious countenance of intimate and stranger, the signs of transcendence freight human encounter. Here, where we meet the gaze of another or avert the searching eye, something of infinity is won or lost. As we ask the silent question of another we, in turn, are claimed by his or her own otherness. Our response to this other may allow a certain presence—a reality which confirms existence—to come into view, or may eclipse its reality before our searching stare.

Seeking an otherness that would arrest our fragility and weariness, we find no vessel of pure transcendence but the near claim of other persons whose lives partake of our condition and yet bring mystery to it. We do not come to infinity, but infinity comes to us in the human other. If to that other we entrust our silent asking, we too are called into question as we stand before a presence—human and yet eternally freighted—that asks us for a basic justice, for an honoring of the mystery that dwells therein. The desire for God never escapes its essentially human context. As absolute Other, the God of our desire transcends this context, but human life does not and ever bears the signs of its creation. Apart from gravity, we might encounter God in untold ways; but we encounter human selves in one way only and that as persons whose lives claim us with an otherness bearing divine mystery. Our welcome of that mystery may open us to the presence we had sought but could never have expected to find in the window of another's eyes. Our inhospitality to the near stranger, however, sends away one who might enable us to hear the silent question's tacit answer.

As we confront the stranger, we encounter a certain ambivalence in ourselves. On the one hand, we are attracted to those persons with whom, in relation, we may know a greater constancy and renewal of life. But, on the other hand, we may recognize those same persons to be both more and less other than we want: in their infinity they lie beyond our prediction and control and may limit our autonomy; in their common humanity, which infinity can scarcely mask, they may remind us of our

---

[14] Elie Wiesel, *The Gates of the Forest* (tr. F. Frenaye; New York: Schocken, 1982) 225.

own fears and needs and make us acutely aware of mutual reliance.[15] In this ambivalence we will be tempted to compromise, if not annihilate, the otherness of the stranger, to objectify that person so as to tame the threat of his or her mystery.[16] But to do so only scars the face of the other, for what is most essential to it is precisely that mystery whose preciousness summons our protection and whose infinity holds us accountable. Moreover, such objectification finally turns and attacks us in our own lonely fears: when we banish the mysterious face of other selves, we render ourselves incapable of perceiving what that mystery might disclose to us, a presence that addresses decisively our haunting, silent question. The encounter with strangers, always and deeply a moral situation, occasions the demand to do justice to the mystery of the other, even in the midst of our own resistance to it. No less is it a situation of faith, for strangers bear a mystery not their own. If, in the world, we would seek the presence of God, we must open ourselves to the presence of that other who comes near with face unveiled, vulnerable, and infinitely precious.

Joseph's Justice: Honoring the Mystery of Mary

Sensitivity to the phenomenon of otherness affords a certain entree into the workings of biblical narrative. As with any conceptuality used in biblical interpretation, the usefulness of speaking about "otherness" does not depend upon the biblical author's familiarity with it, but upon its ability to illumine aspects of the ancient text, to pose the question which enables the text to disclose its meaning and implication. Though the language is not theirs, the dynamics of otherness mark a fundamental feature of human relatedness that the biblical authors could scarcely escape if they wanted to. And they do not seem to want to, for the underlying concern of "otherness"—the mysteriousness of human

---

[15] Note Levinas's parallel point that, as other, strangers always confront me as being both higher and lower than I am: lower, because their need places them in a situation of some reliance upon me; higher, because their need indicts me and obligates my freedom. Thus, one might fear or resent in the stranger the implied bonds of dependence and of mastery. See *Totality and Infinity*, 75, 251. See also James Breech's interesting reflections on the offense of the actual other in *The Silence of Jesus* (Philadelphia: Fortress, 1983) 13-20.

[16] Thus, Levinas observes that the primordial expression of the other's infinity is the unrelenting imperative: "You shall not commit murder" (199). Because the other "is the sole being I can wish to kill" (198), and because the infinitely precious face of the other ever resists that wish, the encounter with the stranger is ever a moral one. To deny the otherness of the stranger is to kill in the name of my own fear; to welcome that otherness is to do justice that brings life to both host and guest.

life and the justice due it—shares too nearly the impulse of biblical narrative to situate human life in the context of a divine image and responsibility.

Such a case occurs in the Matthean birth narrative (Matt 1:18-25) in its depiction of Joseph's confrontation of Mary, a character filled with an extraordinary otherness. Here, as a just Joseph responds to the pregnant Mary, the story exposes a situation of otherness. The features of otherness that concern us most directly in the reading of this story are as follows: (1) the embodiment of otherness in the person of Mary; (2) the moral dimension of the relation which asks for Joseph's justice amid the temptation to banish Mary's otherness; and (3) the theological context which freights this human relation with a larger significance.

The Otherness of Mary

Matthew tells the story of Jesus' birth as being, in most respects, Joseph's story. Joseph's actions singularly cause the narrative to progress and, indeed, along with the Lord's angel, he is the only real actor in the story.[17] The narrator situates other characters, namely Mary and the infant Jesus, relative to Joseph: Mary appears as the one betrothed to Joseph (1:18), the one whom he resolves to divorce quietly (1:19), and the one whom he subsequently takes as his wife (1:24); Jesus, although borne by Mary (1:25), assumes significance in the story through Joseph's act of naming him in accordance with the angel's command (1:21,25). The role of the remaining character, the angel of the Lord, does not depend upon Joseph in the same way—the angel has its own agency—yet focuses attention upon him as the lone recipient of the speech (1:20-21). The angel's word brings about a crisis that is clearly Joseph's own.

If Joseph appears as the central character in the story, he must still act within a setting that he does not control, a setting that constrains and challenges his intentions. More than a simple backdrop for a character's actions, setting can become an effective force within a story by creating an environment that frustrates or summons those actions.

---

[17] Not only does the story's moment of crisis revolve around Joseph's decision to take Mary as wife, but he appears as the one character, along with the Lord's angel, who acts in the present of the story. By contrast, the narrator consistently depicts Mary as one who is acted upon, rather than herself acting. The only place where she is neither the object of another's actions nor has her situation rendered inactive through the passive voice is Matt 1:25, when she bears (ἔτεκεν) her son. But note that, even here, the narrator subordinates her action to a preoccupation with Joseph. The narrator reports her action as the temporal marker before which Joseph had not known his wife (1:25).

Certain characters, though they do not act significantly within a story, may become elements of its setting and thereby shape the narrative's progress in a more subtle way than by doing this or that deed. For example, Mary, who seemingly does not act in this birth story, exists as a crucial part of its setting. Through Mary's circumstance, the situation of her enigmatic pregnancy, a climate of otherness comes into the story. No neutral foil to set off Joseph's action, the otherness of Mary exists forcefully in the story as a reality with which Joseph must contend.[18]

Matthew has prepared his reader to discern the otherness of Mary through the striking pattern of the genealogy (1:1-17) that immediately precedes the birth narrative. There the reader finds the conspicuous presence of four women—Tamar (1:3), Rahab (1:5), Ruth (1:5), and the wife of Uriah (1:6)—whose mention suggests continuity with the genealogy's fifth woman, "Mary of whom Jesus was born" (1:16). Attempts to understand what the women from Israel's history may hold in common with each other and, as a group, with Mary, have tended to emphasize two features: (1) their status as foreigners; and (2) actions of sexual irregularity that render them vulnerable to scandal.[19]

The foreign status of the group of women is relatively clear within Hebrew scripture: Tamar and Rahab are Canaanites (Gen 38:1-6 and Joshua 2); Ruth, a Moabitess (Ruth 1:4); and Bathsheba, the wife of Uriah, most likely a Hittite (2 Sam 11:3). Alien identity marks them as "outsiders" whose purity was ever suspect and whose existence within the family or society precariously depended upon the protection of "insiders" (i.e., of those who shared neither their ethnicity nor their gender).[20] While Mary, herself no alien, cannot be linked to the women

---

[18] Mary's pregnancy, of course, presupposes certain actions and itself might be narrated as a story. Here, however, the narrator refers to Mary's being with child simply as a given circumstance, an item in a sequence of earlier events, that provides the background for Joseph's quandary. In Joseph's story Mary functions less as a character than as what Hitchcock referred to as a "MacGuffin," a prop of sorts, such as a poisoned coffee cup or the plans for the fort, whose role in a narrative is to place certain characters in jeopardy. The MacGuffin itself undertakes no action, but characters care a great deal about it, for its presence in the setting requires their action and gives to it an aspect of urgency. On the "MacGuffin" and setting, see Seymour Chatman, *Story and Discourse. Narrative Structure in Fiction and Film* (Ithaca: Cornell University Press, 1978) 140.

[19] For a review of these interpretations, see Raymond E. Brown, *The Birth of the Messiah* (Garden City, NY: Doubleday, 1977) 71-74; and Jane Schaberg, *The Illegitimacy of Jesus* (San Francisco: Harper & Row, 1987) 20-36. Note also L. William Countryman, *Dirt, Greed, and Sex* (Philadelphia: Fortress, 1988) 90-91.

[20] On the plight of alien existence in ancient Israel, see John B. Mathews, "Hospitality and the New Testament Church: An Historical and Exegetical Study" (Th.D. dissertation, Princeton Theological Seminary, 1965) 105-18. For a discernment of the sociological

as foreigners, her circumstance, which potentially subjects her to public disgrace (1:19), threatens no less to estrange her from the structures of protection and community. Otherness, be it ethnic or biological, marks Mary and her predecessors as in need of a certain hospitality, but thereby also vulnerable to the discriminating norms and whims of the communities within which they stand as outsiders.

The association of the genealogy's women with sexual irregularity provides a more direct link to the otherness of Mary. Though the genealogy affirms the maternities of Tamar, Rahab, Ruth, and Bathsheba—through them the Messianic line was preserved—their grouping intends no less to convey, if not justify, the sexual scandal embedded in their stories. All four deviate from certain aspects of Israel's sexual codes: though Judah, her father-in-law, has been deficient in meeting levirate obligations, Tamar seduces him as a prostitute in order to perpetuate a family line (Genesis 38); Rahab, praised for her rescue of Israelite spies, does so as a harlot (Joshua 2); Ruth undertakes sexual relations with Boaz before he properly had rights to respond to her (Ruth 3); and Bathsheba, clearly designated in the genealogy as the "wife of Uriah" (1:6), suffers an adultery with David (2 Samuel 11). Outside the norms of sexual conduct, their otherness manifests itself as a difference from the habits of household and community designed to maintain boundaries of social order and purity.[21] When reckoned as deviation, otherness invites not only scandal, but condemnation.[22] Mary, pregnant, but not by her husband (1:18), shares this difference from the social norms of purity and thus, also, its vulnerability.

If the genealogy prepares the reader to see in Mary's circumstance an otherness comparable to that of the four women from Israel's history, the dynamics of that otherness manifest themselves in relation to Joseph's vantage in the story. The fact of Mary's scandalous pregnancy brings into Joseph's world a reality that he can neither predict nor control and whose presence will tempt him to fear. In these verses he contends with

---

situation, see Susan Niditch, "The Wronged Woman Righted: An Analysis of Genesis 38," *HTR* 72 (1979) 143-49. On purity and foreigners, see Countryman, *Dirt, Greed, and Sex*, 39-42.

[21] On sexual conduct as related to social order and purity, see Countryman, *Dirt, Greed, and Sex*, 11-65; more generally, note Mary Douglas, *Purity and Danger: An Analysis of Concepts of Pollution and Taboo* (London: Routledge & Kegan Paul, 1966).

[22] Schaberg rightly notes that all four are vulnerable to condemning accusations: "Accusation of improper sexual conduct is actually made in the case of Tamar, implicit in the case of Rahab, avoided in Ruth's case by the secrecy of Boaz, and leveled in Bathsheba's case against her partner" (*Illegitimacy*, 33).

an otherness that overturns expectations, makes a claim upon the one who stands in relation to it, and cannot itself be fully known.

By providing the reader with certain details of setting, the narrator allows us to know something of Joseph's intention and likely expectation. For example, the context of betrothal which the narrator establishes at the story's outset calls for the reader to envision through the eyes of Joseph a given sequence of events and maintain a certain willful expectation of them. Betrothal, a formal exchange of consent, begins a process of marriage that culminates in the subsequent step (usually a year later) of the groom's taking the bride to his own family home. Betrothal legally constitutes marriage—the terms "husband" (1:19) and "wife" (1:20) are appropriate—and implies certain rights and obligations, not the least of which is the prohibition of the woman's adultery.[23] Yet this very sequence of events and obligations Joseph can only expect, not ensure. Expectation, desire, and intention on his part do not suffice to fulfill the sequence, for in its progress another self participates whose intentions or situation may run counter and surprise. Though Joseph has expectations of her, Mary's otherness cannot be assimilated to them; her pregnancy thwarts his intention with a reality he cannot avert. Surprised, he must respond to a crisis not of his own making, yet one which claims his situation decisively.

If in no other way, Mary's situation claims Joseph out of the common context of betrothal. He has no power to ignore this fact for, within that context, Mary's pregnancy is his situation as well, a circumstance which he can change only by initiating some form of divorce (1:19). Indeed, even to continue the sequence of marriage requires a new act of overcoming fear (1:20) and the implicit scandal of Mary's situation, an act different from what the sequence originally entailed. Thus, Joseph can complete the sequence or not—acts tantamount to accepting or rejecting Mary's situation as his own—but he cannot refuse to contend with this changed reality that alters even the option of completing the original intention. Mary's otherness requires of Joseph a new decision. If he controls his own actions, he does not control the world which he shares with the other, the context within which he must act anew.

Not only does Mary's otherness resist Joseph's intention and compel response to a changed situation, but it also suffuses that situation with a degree of unknowing and mystery. It is striking, given the lengthy genealogy, that the narrator not once mentions the father of Jesus—a feature that does not imply the non-existence of a father, but simply the

---

[23] On betrothal, note *m. Ketub.* 4:4-5; also see Joachim Jeremias, *Jerusalem in the Time of Jesus* (tr. F. H. and C. H. Cave; Philadelphia: Fortress, 1969) 364-68.

undisclosed nature of Mary's story. That the narrator twice identifies the child as being "of the holy spirit" (ἐκ πνεύματος ἁγίου [1:18]; ἐκ πνεύματός ἐστιν ἁγίου [1:20]) drapes Mary's pregnancy with otherness.[24] Leaving Jesus' father unnamed, the language of the spirit does emphasize divine begetting, but in a metaphorical way: the birth of Jesus does not occur apart from God's intention and creative power, the ultimate source of all human life and generation.[25] Scandalous origin notwithstanding, the child's life is holy—it is to this claim, embodied within the person of Mary, that Joseph must finally respond.

Joseph's response, however, as Auden put it, must occur "alone in the dark."[26] The unnamed father, no less than the presence of the spirit, becomes a strong marker of Mary's otherness, for it leaves undisclosed the character of her pregnancy and thus obscures features of her identity. In one sense, the unnamed father is beside the point: as betrothed, Joseph needs to know only that he himself is not the father in order to bring sanctions against Mary (thus, 1:19). In another sense, however, the silence around the paternity masks whether Mary's situation derives from adultery or violence inflicted upon her—a matter which not only shapes the legal context for Joseph's response to Mary, but also affects

---

[24] See Eduard Schweizer's discussion of spirit as "stranger," an understanding that accents the spirit as a sign of God's surprising and uncontrollable activity (*The Holy Spirit* [tr. R. and I. Fuller; Philadelphia: Fortress, 1980] 46-57). The revelation of spirit occurs in no definite form that can be received or contained as knowledge; as alien, it shows itself to be other. Associated with the spirit, the birth of Jesus, like the condition of natality itself, is freighted with the mystery of new beginnings which cannot be predicted nor comprehended. If in no other way, the simple fact of Mary's maternity, here understood with the language of spirit, testifies to her otherness. On natality, see Hannah Arendt, *Human Condition*, 177-78.

[25] Thus, e.g., Eduard Schweizer: "Certainly the Holy Spirit is not involved in any sexual relationship between God and a human being. It is the Spirit of God's creative power as in Genesis 1:2, once more at work at the beginning of the new creation" (*Holy Spirit*, 54). On the metaphorical understanding of divine begetting, see Schaberg (*Illegitimacy*, 62-68); for another view, see Brown (*Birth of the Messiah*, 124-25, 137-43). Much depends upon how one reads Mary's relation to the other women in the genealogy. If the genealogy indicates a vindication of the scandalous activity of the women (i.e., through their scandalous activity God has acted to bring his Messiah), and Mary stands in continuity with them, then one must allow Mary's scandal—her implied adultery—full play. From this angle, any notion of virgin birth would be a domestication of Mary that undercuts the theological affirmation of the genealogy and, in my view, the birth story proper.

[26] W. H. Auden, "For the Time Being. A Christmas Oratorio," in *The Collected Poetry of W. H. Auden* (New York: Random House, 1945) 423.

the status of the child she bears.[27] Joseph, no less than the reader, faces an opacity in the story that renders Mary and her situation enigmatic. The paternity—that which has so contributed to Mary's condition and, thus, the context of Joseph's response—remains inaccessible. Joseph must respond to Mary's world as a world of difference from his intention and expectation; and, moreover, a difference whose origin and character he cannot fully know. Little wonder that the angel's speech recognizes this temptation as one of fear (1:20).

The Moral Demand of Otherness

The advent of otherness brings with it a moral crisis that is double-edged. On the one hand, one faces the demand to do justice to the otherness of the stranger, to honor the need of his or her difference as a natural right, if not an inevitable feature of human plurality. On the other hand, one faces the temptation to deny or banish the otherness of that self at the point at which it compromises one's own autonomy and intention.[28] Joseph's crisis is of this sort. Before the otherness of Mary

---

[27] Drawing from biblical and Mishnaic sources, interpreters of the legal context face a veritable *tohu we bohu*. The legal situation is complex and, even when clarified theoretically, leaves open the problematic question of what sanctions apply to and/or were in fact carried out in the first century CE. Biblical law distinguished between the acts of a betrothed virgin's seduction (adultery) and her rape (Deut 22:23-27). The former case requires "purging the evil" through the death of both parties; the latter holds only the man accountable. Mishnaic law recognizes a similar distinction: a woman violated against her will, as in the case of a captive, may retain her sanctity and knows certain rights (*m. Ketub.* 3:2-3); an adulteress, even and especially in the case of a priest's daughter, was vulnerable to the death penalty (*m. Sanh.* 7:2; 9:1), though it is doubtful that the actual penalty would have been executed. Regarding offspring, it is at least a source of contention in the Mishnah as to what constitutes a *mamzer*, one view being the offspring of a union whose penalty was punishable by death, e.g., incest or adultery (*m. Yebam.* 4:13). In that case, the offspring of a rape, while vulnerable with the mother to certain social forms of ostracism, would potentially occupy a less disadvantaged position that encouraged the husband's adoption of the child. On these matters generally, see Jeremias, *Jerusalem*, 337-42; Schaberg, *Illegitimacy*, 42-62; J. D. M. Derrett, *Law in the New Testament* (London: Darton, Longman & Todd, 1970) 166-70; and Louis M. Epstein, *Sex Laws and Customs in Judaism* (New York: Bloch, 1948) 179-215.

[28] In this respect we may experience the nearness of the other as a form of suffering. Note, e.g., H. Richard Niebuhr's definition of suffering as "that which cuts athwart our purposive movements. It represents the denial from beyond ourselves of our movement toward pleasure; or it is the frustration of our movement toward self-realization or toward the actualization of our potentialities. *Because suffering is the exhibition of the presence in our existence of that which is not under our control, or of the intrusion into our self-legislating existence of an activity operating under another law than ours*, it cannot be brought adequately within the spheres of teleological and deontological ethics [i.e., within the

he knows the fear of a just man, but also the demand to affirm the strangeness of what she now embodies.

At the outset of the story, the narrator juxtaposes a description of Mary's circumstance with an identification of Joseph as a just person (1:19), resolved to divorce his betrothed. If Mary's pregnancy, a situation of scandal, sets her at odds with the codes of sexual purity, Joseph's initial intent to divorce her shows his desire to reinforce precisely such a purity. His justice, though tempered with a kindly concern to avoid Mary's public humiliation, would manifest itself in the act of divorce, an act tantamount to declaring himself separate from the origin and implication of the scandal. Not completing the sequence of marriage, he would deny Mary's situation to be his own and maintain a righteousness that honors a distance between purity and impurity.[29]

The pressure for Joseph to divorce Mary may derive from a sensitivity to tendencies in the Law, but no less from the fear of impurity itself. Indeed, the angel's imperative for Joseph to complete the marriage has as its condition an abolition of fear (1:20), a fear that cannot easily be reduced to worry over the legal consequences of accepting his wife.[30] Joseph's fear—a sense of taboo that would estrange him from the suspected adulteress and make of their union a source of horror—

---

domains of our intention or concern for lawful obedience]" (*The Responsible Self* [New York: Harper & Row, 1963] 60; emphasis mine). The other self is precisely that person whom we cannot control or assume to take seriously the laws governing our own existence.

[29] Some exegetical controversy exists over the nature of Joseph's "justice." In particular, does that justice show itself in his unwillingness to disgrace Mary, or in his resolve to divorce her in the first place (which he has simply qualified with a more merciful form)? I assume the latter to be the case, reading the story to indicate that Joseph understands it to be legally appropriate—permitted, if not required—to separate himself from Mary's scandal. Again, the legal situation is difficult to recover, but the burden of its obscurity is eased if one looks to the story as presupposing not the obligation to divorce—an obligation which presses the known evidence too far—but the appropriateness of doing so. Thus, Joseph's justice would take the form of divorcing Mary, an act not obliged, but allowed and encouraged in recognition of the inherent difficulty in making a union with one suspected of violating the Law, especially in the case of adultery. Granting the permission to divorce, Joseph's resolve shows him forsaking the ordeal of a public trial for suspected adultery (see *m. Sota*) and divorcing Mary instead on more trivial grounds available to him (e.g., as noted in *m. Git.* 9:10). On the problem of identifying Joseph's legal obligation, see Myles Bourke's review of Brown's *Birth of the Messiah, CBQ* 40 (1978) 121-22; and the reply of A. Tosato, "Joseph, Being a Just Man (Matt 1:19)," *CBQ* 41 (1979) 547-51.

[30] Note that the forgiveness of an adulterous wife, though likely uncommon, may also have been permitted under the Law; at least, no evidence exists to indicate that such an act would have been strictly forbidden. See Bourke's review of *Birth of the Messiah*, 121-22; and Schaberg, *Illegitimacy*, 50-53.

involves his confrontation with Mary's otherness and the experience of that otherness as offense and threat.

The perception of impurity frightens. As Joseph faces the choice to divorce Mary, he stands in danger. Were he to complete the marriage, Mary's plight would become his, rendering his world precarious with an intrusion of impurity. Such impurity would not strike first at Joseph's concern for legal righteousness, but at his sense of well-being and belonging to a particular human community. Though often immediate in experience, the fear of impurity does not occur in a vacuum. Whether in terms of an explicit legal demand or through a less formal influence, Joseph perceives his danger relative to some system of purity that ties him to a community and its norms of justice.

Systems of purity, the ways human cultures distinguish between "dirty" and "clean," seek to keep "matter in place" and thereby preserve the boundaries that order human interaction.[31] An order of purity, in its narrow focus upon the regulation of eating and sexual activity, yet expresses fundamental values of a group. When a system of purity preoccupies itself with the boundaries of the human body, it creates a metaphor for the particular human community, its principles of order, and the boundaries that make its society human. Accordingly, to transgress the limits of purity violates the bonds that relate selves to each other and impart a human quality to those relations. Impurity then coincides with an estrangement from the society of one's fellows and from the customary expectations of common life in an orderly world.

If we understand purity in this way, Joseph's danger appears to be twofold. First, in making Mary's impure situation his own, he risks isolation from the group that maintains purity, and thereby also a certain dehumanization. Here Joseph would share in Mary's difference and himself become estranged from the righteous or pure community. Insofar as the freedom to participate in that community reflects a certain conferral of human status, Joseph's estrangement would approximate a dehumanization that renders him, along with Mary, vulnerable to ostracism and discrimination.[32] Second, in standing outside the boundaries of order he would leave behind a context wherein his intention and control could be meaningfully exerted. As chaos, impurity subverts familiar expectations of human activity and introduces a

---

[31] I paraphrase Mary Douglas's well-known conclusion that dirt is matter out of place and thus a symbol of disorder (*Purity*, 2).

[32] W. H. Auden, in "For the Time Being," has given particularly strong expression to the mocking isolation of Joseph. See within that lengthy poem the section entitled "The Temptation of St. Joseph" (pp. 421-28).

seemingly alien character—a sense of different rules of play—to the world in which action occurs. Acting in relation to Mary, Joseph must leave behind the illusion that the world conforms to his just intentions and thus is subject to his control. In sum, Mary's otherness, as impurity, offends. It looms before Joseph as a reality of uncertain human quality that would separate him from his community and, potentially, his own humanity. And that otherness threatens, for in relation to Mary his world itself has become strangely other—resisting his expectation and control, and intensifying insecurity.

Joseph's resolve to divorce Mary allows us to see his intent not only to reinforce purity, but also to diminish the fearful danger which her otherness has created. Threatened by a perceived loss of humanity and effective intention, Joseph seeks to secure both by a legal action that would relocate him in a context of purity and order. Though he cannot deny Mary's scandal, he can control its implications for himself by the separation of divorce. Such an act, however, would also banish the otherness of Mary from the world of his responsibility and concern. Here Joseph's moral crisis thickens. The plan to divorce, reasonable within the isolated logic of purity, becomes a dilemma as he hears the competing demand of the Lord's angel: "Do not fear to take Mary your wife" (1:20).

The angel's speech does not eradicate Mary's scandal before Joseph and his community. Nothing in the angel's words denies what Joseph has suspected—the adultery of his betrothed. Rather, the speech places Mary's impurity in a larger context that vindicates the scandal by pointing to its salvific effect: the child born of this Mary, out of divine intention, will save his people (1:20-21). In Joseph's eyes, Mary may remain suspect and his own danger real, but the angel's speech claims him with a challenge to befriend precisely those fears. The impurity which frightens, though it may offend, estrange, and threaten, does not warrant a taboo that requires separation from Mary. Scandal notwithstanding, Mary's otherness embodies no sign of God's absence, but of his presence—"Emmanuel" (1:23), a sign that calls Joseph to draw near and challenges the ground of his fear.

Between the intent to divorce and the hearing of the angel's speech lies Joseph's moral dilemma. On the one hand, he must contend with the understandable resolve to diminish the perceived threat of impurity's chaos. On the other hand, he confronts the angel's counter-demand to complete the marriage (1:20), an act which requires his embracing the scandal of Mary as his own. Where the resolve to divorce would banish Mary's otherness, the completion of the marriage would affirm its presence, recognizing the holiness of what occurs in its midst. Where

Joseph's resolve would separate him from Mary's scandal, the angel's declaration compels a justice that honors her otherness, scandal notwithstanding, with welcome and openness. Joseph's dilemma is this: if he takes Mary as his wife, he invites danger; but he can separate from her only through an action which denies her otherness, the very otherness the angel has called him to affirm.

The dilemma reflects a deep tension between two different modes of justice: the justice of Joseph, here manifest in the intent to preserve a social order—a purity—within which one can safely pursue life with intention and control; and the justice of the angel, here manifest in the concern to uphold the otherness of the stranger, even at the expense of the social order and its gains of freedom from danger. Though they may each have their appropriate moment,[33] the two directions cannot be assimilated to each other, at least not in terms of Joseph's situation, for at every point at which he would defend himself from the threat of Mary's impurity, he becomes involved in a denial of her otherness.[34] Joseph's dilemma makes clear that the moral demand to honor the other is incommensurate with any concern for purity that protects the autonomy of one's own intention or the norms of one's own group. The face of the other calls for a justice that does not flee from the scandal of impurity, but embraces it with an openness to the world of the other.[35] Yet, how does one move from defensiveness to trust? How does Joseph move from fear to acceptance and responsibility?

---

[33] Note, e.g., James E. Crouch's reflections on the tension between the radical demand for co-humanity and the persistent need to preserve a social order within which that co-humanity can be expressed. See *The Origin and Intention of the Colossian Haustafel* (*FRLANT* 109; Göttingen: Vandenhoeck & Ruprecht, 1972) 158-61.

[34] In particular, for Joseph to divorce Mary out of a perceived impurity would be to proceed on the assumption that he can sufficiently know her situation to judge its value. But precisely in its otherness—dramatized in the silent paternity—Mary's situation cannot be so known. In still another way the divorce potentially compromises Mary's otherness by rendering her the object of Joseph's justification. At the point at which Joseph might justify himself at her expense—his purity being served by her impurity—Mary ceases to be other and becomes simply an item within his resolve and intent.

[35] Thus, the angel's justice seems to recognize what Levinas has claimed as the "asymmetry" of the moral relation (*Totality and Infinity*, 215). Those who enact such justice cannot proceed out of simple integrity with their own intentions or the objective norms of their group, but must in a real sense bow before the other as the one whose need obligates and whose freedom judges.

Otherness and the Presence of God

Moral issues inevitably bear theological freight. If Joseph's dilemma reflects a tension between two modes of justice, it no less opposes conflicting perceptions of divine presence. The logic of purity assumes that God withdraws from human impurity. Accordingly, to draw near to impurity risks harm, for therein one is vulnerable to the simple chaos of human experience, unprotected against its seemingly strange powers whose ways may or may not sustain life. Joseph's fear, seen in this light, grows from a perception of divine absence, a lurking doubt that Mary's circumstance can do anything other than drive away God's presence. In the resolve to divorce, Joseph would separate himself from Mary not simply because of who she was, but because of whom he understood God to be—namely a God who could not be trusted to be present within human plight or to protect the one who ventures near its impurity. Though one may sympathize with Joseph's plan, it comes with a theological cost: a basic defensiveness that suspects the otherness not only of persons, but also of God; a distrust of God's freedom to be present in the human situation in a way that differs from moral, religious, or social expectation.

Over against the fear of divine absence stands the angel's affirmation of divine presence. Appearing to Joseph in a dream, the angel countermands his fear by proclaiming Mary's child to be of a holy spirit; in short, that Mary's pregnancy accords with God's intention and does not corrupt.[36] The narrator reinforces the point by breaking into the story with the citation of Isa 7:14 (1:23), a verse which indicates that in Mary's child—a child who will be called Emmanuel—God is "with us."[37] Where God is "with us," Joseph must not be frightened of any human reality; where human otherness, even in scandalous form, does

---

[36] Again, "spirit" here indicates the presence of God's creative activity and intention, though not a peculiar agency of that presence. The power which gives life to the child Jesus derives from no unholy force, but is God's. See above, n. 25.

[37] The Isaiah citation, often taken as a prooftext for the doctrine of virgin birth, does not in its own context presuppose this notion, nor does such seem necessary in its Matthean use. The verse's emphasis, in both contexts, falls upon the name Emmanuel as a sign of God's presence, which Matthew confirms through the narrational aside and through the framing of the citation with references to the naming of Jesus. The problematic παρθένος—the LXX rendering of the Hebrew *alma*—may be taken to imply that a woman, presently a virgin, will naturally conceive a child at some point in the future; or the word itself may share the vagueness of *alma*, indicating simply a young woman, though not necessarily a virgin (e.g., Gen 34:3 LXX). Note also Schaberg's contention (*Illegitimacy*, 71) that Matthew's interest in the Isaiah text reflects an association of parthenos with the betrothed woman (LXX: parthenos) whose rape is discussed in Deut 22:23-27.

not banish divine presence, the ground for defensiveness collapses. Within the angel's perspective the scandal of otherness remains, but forfeits its defilement, its warrant to estrange. Thus, Joseph heeds the command to accept Mary because, at the least, he can no longer assume God's absence and, moreover, he can anticipate divine presence.[38] The angel calls for a trust in God's surprising presence that issues in an openness to Mary's difference. Joseph moves from defensiveness to openness out of no ordinary altruism or new affinity for scandal, but out of the perception that God takes no offense, that God has met Mary in her otherness and identified himself with the child she bears. God's presence summons Joseph to draw near to Mary's world.

As the story concludes, Joseph completes the turn away from his initial resolve (1:19) and toward a new acceptance of Mary's situation. He does so as the Lord's angel had commanded, fulfilling the marriage and naming the child Jesus (1:24-25). In doing so he enacts a mode of justice that upholds the life of the other, that refuses to let the scandal of difference estrange, that trusts God's presence to be unfettered by human expectation or desire for purity. Joseph's acceptance of Mary responds to the vulnerability of her otherness, yet without robbing that otherness of its integrity: in Mary's situation he finds not the dependent claim of simple need, but the challenging claim of God's presence.[39] The naming of the child, an act which legally acknowledges the child as his own (*m. B. Bat.* 8:6), similarly exceeds the charity of adoption to express a still deeper hospitality. In the naming of Jesus, Joseph establishes kinship with one not his own. No mere protection of the suspected *mamzer*, his act bows to the reality of the given name that the child brings near—the claim that in the stranger-child Jesus, Yahweh saves.[40]

Matthew's birth narrative never doubts Joseph's intent to be just. Neither in his resolve to divorce nor subsequently in his acceptance of Mary does Joseph act arbitrarily, cruelly, or out of simple self-interest. Within the story, his seeking of justice reflects a concern to be rightly related to Mary and her child, but also to the presence of God which

---

[38] The inability to assume God's absence makes it impossible for Joseph to judge or condemn Mary's otherness. Already implicit in the inexhaustibility or unknowability of that otherness, the stifling of human judgment finds here its strongest theological warrant. Cf. Matt 7:1-5.

[39] One should recall here the insistence of Levinas (*Totality and Infinity*, 75, 251) that the other always confronts one as both higher and lower than oneself, i.e., from a vantage point of power and need.

[40] On the etymology of the name "Jesus," see Brown, *Birth of the Messiah*, 130-31.

decisively shapes the features of that right relation. Joseph's righteousness, at the outset freighted with the theological load of purity, undergoes a transformation as the angel's word encourages a new perception of God's presence. The justice of Joseph which the story finally sustains is that action which honors Mary as other and, refusing offense at the scandal of difference, seeks to stand in relation with her.

The reason for Joseph's deference to the other—and why such is just—should by now be clear. Joseph abandons purity's self-defense not out of a love of otherness itself, but for what occurs in its midst. Mary, in her difference, brings to the world of Joseph the surprising presence of God. Remaining estranged from her, Joseph would stand alone in his purity, joined perhaps by moral peers but alienated from the God whose presence he would protect. As he hosts Mary's otherness, however, Joseph is related to the larger Other whose spirit shocks yet nurtures the birth of his people's salvation. Embodied in Mary's scandalous condition, divine presence comes near to Joseph. His hospitality recognizes that it is the stranger, Mary, and the spirit she manifests that bless him as host. As such, this hospitality of otherness is ever just for, in their gift, strangers are due the honor that divine presence accords. In the stranger's face the silent question finds response—the glimmer of God's own gaze.

4

John and the Synoptics in Light of the Problem of Faith and History

D. Moody Smith [1]

Paul W. Meyer has always directed his students' attention to longstanding and fundamental questions of New Testament criticism and interpretation. Appropriately, the relationship of John to the synoptic gospels is probably the oldest historical-critical problem in the history of the church. Already at the end of the second century, if not earlier, it was proving troublesome. Very likely, the rejection of the Fourth Gospel in some Christian circles had to do not only with its association with gnostics but also with its obvious divergences from the synoptics.[2] The acceptance of John in the church, and in the emerging canon, went hand in hand with its attribution to the Apostle John and with a developing formula or mode of reconciling its differences with the synoptics.

Thus John was thought to have been written to supplement the other gospels or to provide a more spiritual perspective on the ministry of

---

[1] D. Moody Smith is George Washington Ivey Professor of New Testament at the Divinity School, Duke University, Durham, North Carolina.

[2] See J. J. Gunther, "Early Identifications of Authorship of the Johannine Writings," *JEH* 31 (1981) 413-15; and especially Joseph Daniel Smith, Jr., "Gaius and the Controversy over the Johannine Literature" (Ph.D. dissertation, Yale University, 1979) 289-92, 384-91. Smith argues that Gaius' opposition to the Fourth Gospel was motivated by its use among the Montanists whom he opposed (p. 426).

John and the Synoptics

Jesus. Some such way of reading the Gospel of John not only survived but was dominant, also among critical scholars, into the twentieth century. Even as acute a scholar as B. W. Bacon did not break with the ancient consensus in this respect.[3] Obviously, the question of John and the synoptics has important implications for broader questions of faith and history, a fact that has been recognized from antiquity. Ancient efforts to reconcile John with the synoptics had as their presupposition that it was intolerable for authoritative witnesses to the earthly ministry of Jesus to contradict one another about matters of historical fact. Gaius of Rome and any *alogi* who rejected the Gospel of John may have found the contradictions intolerable. On the other hand, Origen acknowledged them gladly, and goaded the "conservative" church exegetes who were attempting to assimilate John to the synoptics on the historical level.[4] While himself not committed to the view that history must undergird faith in such a prosaic way, Origen was a sufficiently sharp critic to see that the developing modes of reconciling John to the synoptics were fundamentally suspect historically.

After Origen, however, churchly exegesis generally took the position that John was written in light of the other, synoptic, gospels in order to interpret them theologically and/or supplement them historically. The earlier modern criticism for the most part accepted this view, but not necessarily the traditional assumption that John was an historically accurate account, if, indeed, it was an historical account at all. The purpose of this essay is to sketch the course of later, twentieth-century investigations of the relation of John to the synoptics and to reflect upon the problem of faith and history in the light of the issues thereby raised.

The Twentieth-Century Consensus

The brief but important monograph of Hans Windisch, *Johannes und die Synoptiker* (1926), broke with the ancient and traditional view of their relationship in that the author argued that John wrote with the purpose of displacing the other gospels, which he took to be dangerously inadequate theologically.[5] Since Windisch, the problem has come full

---

[3] See my article, "B. W. Bacon on John and Mark," *Johannine Christianity: Essays on its Setting, Sources, and Theology* (Columbia: University of South Carolina Press, 1984) 106-27, where Bacon's position, as represented in a number of his works, is set forth in some detail.

[4] *Commentary on the Gospel of John* 10.2.15.

[5] Hans Windisch, *Johannes und die Synoptiker: Wollte der vierte Evangelist die älteren Evangelien ergänzen oder ersetzen?* (UNT 12; Leipzig: J. C. Hinrichs, 1926).

circle, so to speak: John's knowledge of the synoptics has been forthrightly denied (Percival Gardner-Smith), but is now strongly reaffirmed with more thorough consideration of the consequences than were entertained in antiquity (Frans Neirynck).

Windisch proceeded on the traditional view that John knew and was familiar with all the synoptic gospels, but because they were inadequate representations of the gospel as John understood it, he wrote a gospel to supersede them and in doing so found most of their content useless. This explains why John, while knowing the other gospels, differed so sharply from them. Although Windisch's solution to the problem of John and the synoptics seems radical, there is a sense in which it is entirely reasonable, given the seriousness of the problem. That is, if the differences between John and the synoptics are really not amenable to solution on the basis of the traditional view that John intended only to supplement, interpret, or mildly correct the other three—and Windisch argued vigorously and persuasively that they were not—the problem of explaining their relationship assumes a considerable magnitude. Why did John write such a different gospel without accommodating his narrative to the others? A profound problem that was more or less swept under the rug in antiquity demands a thoroughgoing and searching answer.

Gardner-Smith's thesis begins from and argues for a contrary working hypothesis, maintaining that there is no convincing evidence that the Fourth Evangelist knew and used the other gospels at all.[6] If one considers the large amount of disparity and the relatively small amount of agreement, particularly verbatim agreement, it is not at all obvious that John must have known any or all of the synoptics. Once it is conceded that oral tradition was an important factor in early Christian tradition, the relatively small areas of agreement, even the word-for-word agreements, are rather easily accounted for. The extensive departures are—if John did not know the synoptics—no problem to be explained. As it stands they represent a conundrum. The fact that they have not been seen as a problem, as exegetes have fixed upon the agreements, does not make them less so. Gardner-Smith and Windisch really agree in one central respect: conventional and traditional exegesis has not adequately taken account of, and accounted for, the differences between John and the synoptics.

Gardner-Smith did not deal with Windisch or even mention his book. His work stands on its own as an alternative way of coming to grips with the same perceived problem. It had no immediate impact on the

---

[6] *St. John and the Synoptic Gospels* (Cambridge: Cambridge University Press, 1938).

John and the Synoptics

Continent, largely because of the onset of World War II only a year after its publication. But a compatible thesis was soon set forth in Germany. Shortly after the outbreak of war, which was to put an end to scholarly interchange between English-and German-speaking scholars for nearly a decade, Rudolf Bultmann's enormously influential commentary on the Fourth Gospel appeared.[7] Although the explanation of Johannine-synoptic relations was not a central concern of the commentary, it had a significant impact on the discussion of that problem in subsequent scholarship. Bultmann did not find John's dependence on the synoptics a necessary presupposition for exegesis. Instead, his literary, source-critical analysis led repeatedly to the conclusion that John was not based upon the synoptics, but rather analogous tradition which had already been fixed in written sources, principally the *semeia* and passion sources. Bultmann's developed position on this issue had, however, already been adumbrated a decade and a half earlier, when in a review of Windisch he had expressed doubts as to whether John knew the synoptic gospels at all.[8] His subsequent exegesis obviously confirmed this sense of doubt. Certainly Bultmann's view of John's independence was not advanced in the service of any attempt to defend the historicity of the Fourth Gospel. (Interestingly, Windisch frequently refers to earlier espousals of John's independence as "conservative.") Only in a highly distinctive and rarefied sense is Bultmann's John interested in history's relation to faith. Revelation intersects history, but is not contained in it so that revelation could be obtained or clarified through historical study or research. Nevertheless, this intersection was important for Bultmann, in whose view John represents what has become a classic understanding of incarnation as the presence of God in fully historical, fully human existence in Jesus.

Meanwhile in England particularly, Gardner-Smith's influence and impact were being felt directly, but also indirectly through the subsequent work of C. H. Dodd.[9] Dodd's own studies of the Fourth Gospel confirmed in his mind the correctness of Gardner-Smith's insights. In North America the appearance of Raymond Brown's widely used commentary had a similar effect. For in his own exegetical study

---

[7] Bultmann's *Das Evangelium des Johannes* (Göttingen: Vandenhoeck & Ruprecht), completed in 1941, is available in English translation (by G. Beasley-Murray *et al.*) as *The Gospel of John: A Commentary* (Philadelphia: Westminster, 1971).

[8] *TLZ* 52 (1927) 198.

[9] Especially *Historical Tradition in the Fourth Gospel* (Cambridge: Cambridge University Press, 1963).

Brown found little reason to think that John had drawn on the synoptics directly, and certainly not in the gospel's originative stages.[10] Of course, unlike Bultmann, both Dodd and Brown found the Fourth Gospel a potentially valuable source of historical tradition about Jesus, at the same time recognizing the considerable extent to which that tradition is refracted through the gospel's theological interests and, particularly in the case of Brown, its traditional and literary stages. Thus, in the mid-1960's there was already forming in diverse quarters a considerable body of scholarly opinion at odds with the traditional view that John had known and used the other gospels.

The Re-emergence of the Problem

I had observed this consensus in 1964.[11] About a year later Josef Blinzler contested the accuracy of my observation.[12] A decade after the appearance of Blinzler's *Johannes und die Synoptiker*, Frans Neirynck corroborated my judgment about the consensus but expressed a strong demurral from it, signaling his own program of demonstrating John's use of the synoptic gospels, which is still very much in progress.[13]

Passion Narratives

A number of North American scholars, particularly those associated with the late Norman Perrin of Chicago, have expressed their doubts that John was independent of the synoptics. To a large extent their contention grew out of the redaction criticism of the Markan passion narrative.[14] John Donahue, one of Perrin's foremost students, showed the extent of Markan redactional activity in the trial scene (Mark 14) and

---

[10] *The Gospel according to John* (AB 29/29A; Garden City, NY: Doubleday, 1966-70).

[11] D. Moody Smith, "The Sources of the Gospel of John: An Assessment of the Present State of the Problem," *NTS* 10 (1963-64) 336-51, esp. p. 349; reprinted in *Johannine Christianity*, 39-61.

[12] Josef Blinzler, *Johannes und die Synoptiker: Ein Forschungsbericht* (SBS 5; Stuttgart: Katholisches Bibelwerk, 1965) 31-32 and *passim*.

[13] Frans Neirynck, "John and the Synoptics," in *L'évangile de Jean: Sources, rédaction, théologie* (ed. M. de Jonge; BETL 44; Louvain: Louvain University Press, 1977) 73-106, esp. pp. 73-74. See also n. 23 below.

[14] See Werner H. Kelber, ed., *The Passion in Mark: Studies in Mark 14-16* (Philadelphia: Fortress, 1976). Cf. Kelber's *The Oral and Written Gospel: The Hermeneutics of Speaking and Writing in the Synoptic Tradition, Mark, Paul, and Q* (Philadelphia: Fortress, 1983) 185-99. In the latter work Kelber advances exegetical and theoretical arguments against a pre-Markan narrative.

raised the possibility that in the passion narrative as well as in the narrative of Jesus' public ministry Mark had worked with independent units of tradition which he was the first to incorporate into an extended narrative.[15] A similar questioning of the existence of a pre-Markan passion narrative had already found expression on the Continent in the work of Eta Linnemann.[16]

Whether Mark had such a passion narrative before him is a question still debated. The outcome has implications for research into Johannine-synoptic relations, but is probably not as decisive as is sometimes assumed. If Mark knew no earlier passion narrative, but composed his own, it is reasonable, but actually not imperative, to think that John must have relied on Mark's gospel for his own account. John's account still differs from Mark's in ways that are not so easily explained, and it is not inconceivable that John and Mark should have independently constructed continuous accounts of Jesus' passion out of individual elements of tradition. Thus the finding that Mark had no earlier continuous passion narrative—if correct—does not *eo ipso* mean that John must have relied on Mark. But whether individual units of passion tradition would have existed apart from some general narrative framework is on the face of it doubtful. If there were traditions of Jesus' arrest, trial, etc., their preservation and transmission would have presupposed some narrative sense of how they fit together. This consideration speaks on the side of some sort of pre-gospel tradition of the passion as a whole (cf. Paul's reference to the institution of the Lord's supper on the night Jesus was betrayed in 1 Cor 11:23-25).

John and Mark

The question of John's relation to the synoptics is not simply interchangeable with that of John's relation to Mark, although there is a great overlap between them, and for good reason. A survey of scholarly opinion would doubtless show that of the scholars who think that John knew the synoptics the largest number would agree that the Fourth Evangelist knew Mark. The reasons for this are clear enough. First of all, since most still adhere to the Markan hypothesis, Mark figures as the earliest of the synoptics and, for whatever reason, the gospel known to Matthew and Luke independently. Moreover, the pattern of agreements

---

[15] *Are You the Christ? The Trial Narrative in the Gospel of Mark* (*SBLDS* 10; Missoula, MT: Scholars Press, 1973).

[16] *Studien zur Passionsgeschichte* (FRLANT 102; Göttingen: Vandenhoeck & Ruprecht, 1970).

between John and the other gospels comports with a fundamental or primary agreement with Mark. Those episodes or pericopes which John has in common with Mark he has, by and large, in the same order as Mark. John does not agree in order with Matthew or Luke against Mark. The verbatim agreements between John and the synoptics are basically agreements with Mark. There are few verbatim agreements of several successive words with Matthew or Luke that are not also verbatim agreements with Mark.

John and Luke

Strangely, many of the more prominent verbatim agreements between John and Mark are not found in Luke. This is particularly puzzling because of the rather extensive agreements of other sorts between Luke and John. For example, Luke refrains from describing explicitly Jesus' baptism by John, contains no account of a nocturnal trial of Jesus before the Sanhedrin, has the risen Jesus appear to his disciples together in Jerusalem, portrays Jesus as interested in Samaria and Samaritans, and in many other respects shows affinities with John rather than Matthew and Mark. Not surprisingly, a major and to some extent separate aspect of the question of John and the synoptics has been the relationship of John and Luke.

Interestingly enough, some seventy years ago Julius Schniewind argued that their affinities were based on the use of common traditions rather than John's use of Luke, although at the same time he continued to assume that John wrote with an awareness of the other gospels.[17] Subsequent scholarship has tended to move along similar lines, emphasizing common tradition rather than a direct relationship. This is true, for example, even of J. A. Bailey, who nevertheless contends that John also knew Luke directly.[18] For obvious reasons the hypothesis that Luke knew John has not attracted many adherents. Yet Lamar Cribbs was able to point to a fair number of instances in which Luke seems to follow John, or at least to waffle a bit, precisely where John contradicts or departs from the Matthean-Markan line.[19] Even Cribbs did not go so far as to suggest that Luke knew John—a possible logical implication of this state of affairs—but contented himself with the reasonable

---

[17] Schniewind, *Die Parallelperikopen bei Lukas und Johannes* (2nd ed.; Darmstadt: Wissenschaftliche Buchgesellschaft, 1958), first published in 1914.

[18] *The Traditions Common to the Gospels of Luke and John* (NovTSup 7; Leiden: Brill, 1963).

[19] "St. Luke and the Fourth Gospel," *JBL* 90 (1971) 422-50.

hypothesis that among Luke's sources was an earlier stage of the Johannine narrative.

In any event, John's affinities with Luke remain a major and distinct factor to be understood and explained, differing as they do from the Fourth Gospel's direct parallels in wording and order with Mark. Probably because Luke so often lacks verbatim parallels with John, often precisely those that are found in Mark (and usually also in Matthew), few scholars have thought that John knew only Luke. Just because Luke's distinctive affinities with John seem diffuse and indirect—although quite real—in comparison with Mark's, attempts to explain the relationship as mediated through tradition rather than based on John's use of Luke have flourished.

Thus the latest of such attempts, that of Anton Dauer, extends to the distinctive relationships between Luke and John a thesis he had first applied to the gospel passion narratives.[20] Because he finds some Johannine parallels to Lukan redaction (i.e., parts of Luke which on other grounds are judged to be from the Third Evangelist's own hand), but cannot derive other basic aspects of the Johannine reports from Luke (or Mark), Dauer proposes a new kind of resolution of this seemingly contradictory situation. Luke has influenced John via the continuing oral tradition (just as Matthew and Luke have both influenced John in the passion—the point made in his earlier work). Because by and large the evidences of Lukan influence fall within material which Dauer, in agreement with a number of other scholars, would assign not to the evangelist but to the pre-Johannine tradition or source, Dauer theorizes that this oral influence must have already affected that pre-gospel level of development. That is, Luke's gospel has influenced the oral tradition that shaped John's sources.

Developing Complexity

Dauer's position typifies a development in Johannine-synoptic investigations which began to appear during the 1970's. Increasingly, the relationship is seen to be more complex than was once thought. Possibly the most elaborate theory of Johannine-synoptic and other gospel relationships has been advanced by M.-E. Boismard.[21] Boismard's

---

[20] *Johannes und Lukas: Untersuchungen zu den johanneisch-lukanischen Parallelperikopen Joh 4,46-54/Lk 7,1-10--Joh 12,1-8/Lk 7,36-50; 10,38-42--Joh 20,19-29/Lk 24,36-49 (FB* 50; Würzburg: Echter, 1984).

[21] M.-E. Boismard and A. Lamouille, *L'évangile de Jean,* vol. 3: *Synopse des quatre évangiles en Français* (Paris: Les Editions du Cerf, 1977).

complex interweaving of ancient traditions and other, earlier modern theories of gospel origins is at the very least a masterpiece of scholarly ingenuity. For example, the ancient opinion that Matthew was the first gospel is preserved in the thesis of a Document A (which might be called primal, as distinguished from both intermediate and final, Matthew). Document A has influenced Document B (primal Mark) as well as intermediate Mark. Intermediate Mark was then a primary source of both final Matthew and final Luke (Markan hypothesis). Each gospel except Luke has a primary, intermediate, and final (canonical) recension. Luke begins, so to speak, at the intermediate level with Proto-Luke, composed under the influence of Q (also used by intermediate Matthew), Document B, and Document C. With Document C we arrive at the primary source of John's Gospel (John I), which underwent two redactions at the hands of the Fourth Evangelist (John II-A and II-B) before being subjected to a final redaction (John III) by a later editor. At the level of the second redaction by the evangelist (II-B) elements from the synoptic gospels were incorporated. Thus John the evangelist, not just the final, later redactor, knew all the synoptics in the form in which we have them.

But as complexities are introduced, either in method or in result, agreement or consensus among scholars declines. Windisch proposed that John knew but rejected the synoptics; Gardner-Smith, that he never knew them at all. Brown, like Bultmann, allowed for John's betraying some knowledge of the synoptic gospels at the final redactional stage.[22] Boismard's theory posits gospel sources with various interrelationships lying behind our canonical gospels, including the Gospel of John. Moreover, the Fourth Evangelist at the point of his own final redaction of the gospel knew and made use of the synoptics. Neirynck counters with an application of Occam's razor to source criticism: if John is parallel to the synoptics at points, it is better to explain these parallels on the basis of a direct literary relationship than to multiply source-and tradition-critical hypotheses unnecessarily. The positions of Windisch, Gardner-Smith, and Neirynck have the advantage of simplicity, clarity, and forthrightness. This does not mean that one or more of them must be true. Indeed, they all could not be, although it would be possible to combine Windisch's position with a version of Neirynck's. We shall in due course consider how that may be so.

---

[22] *The Gospel according to John*, 1.xxxviii.

Neirynck's response to Boismard is as understandable as it is clear.[23] If at the final redactional stage John knew all the synoptic gospels, is such an intricate theory of sources necessary in order to explain the Fourth Gospel? Inasmuch as Boismard's stylistic, contextual, and other evidence and arguments for the existence of earlier literary strata are not unambiguous, why not begin with the hypothesis that those other gospels, which we have and know, and which Boismard agrees John finally knew, are the basis for the Fourth Gospel? Then the exegetical, redaction-critical task is to explain how John understood and altered his sources to produce the canonical Fourth Gospel. Over against Boismard, whose thesis is a kind of synthesis of all plausible hypotheses combined into one, Neirynck's desire to restore simplicity comes as a breath of fresh air, in character if not in content similar to Gardner-Smith.

Neirynck's proposal carries with it the strengths of both simplicity and tradition. There is no airtight argument that can prevail against it. What may count against it, however, are, first, the vast differences of content and structure of the Fourth Gospel from the others, unless they can be made intelligible; and, second, the problem of understanding the small differences between John and the synoptics where, in fact, they run parallel. But there is another consideration, one that bears upon the question of faith and history, as it has been traditionally understood. On such terms as Neirynck has proposed, the Gospel of John is, by implication, an embellishment or midrash, however extensive and sophisticated, upon the synoptic gospels. It ceases to be an original source of historical tradition, as much as the evangelist may insist on the importance of the events of Jesus' ministry and his (or someone's) own witness (or eyewitness testimony).

John's Setting

As we earlier observed, the major differences between John and the other gospels have traditionally been understood in terms of supplementation. Either John was to supplement the other gospels, or vice versa, or both. Windisch has shown the difficulties of that perspective once the protective aura of canonicity is allowed to fall away. (By "aura of canonicity" I mean the implication, tacitly drawn from the canonical status of the other gospels, that John would have accepted their adequacy and authority.) In light of recent research, however, it is not too much to imagine within the Johannine community,

---

[23] Frans Neirynck *et al.*, *Jean et les synoptiques: Examen critique de l'exégèse de M.-E. Boismard* (BETL 49; Louvain: Louvain University Press, 1979).

or at its boundaries, the need for a gospel very different from the synoptics to underscore the divine origin of Jesus or to set him in opposition to Judaism, or both.[24] In such a setting, if the synoptics were known, they likely would not have been regarded as sufficient or definitive, whether or not John sought to displace them. ("Supplementation" is too weak a term to describe the relationship, although "displacement" may be too strong.) Such a position carries with it at least two significant, and related, implications.

First, if John regarded the other, synoptic, gospels in this way, Windisch's description of his purpose and intention will not have missed the mark entirely. It should be observed, of course, that such affinities of recent research with Windisch's view are not arguments against Neirynck's general position on John's dependence. One would have to ascribe to John neither the negative assessment of the synoptics entailed in Windisch's approach nor, obviously, ignorance of the synoptics in order to subscribe to the view that for the evangelist and the Johannine community they were inadequate and incomplete. John could have known the synoptics but for good reason departed from them to go his own way. A further implication perhaps carries with it more troublesome consequences, perhaps particularly for Neirynck's approach. If John does not reject the three other gospels, but knows them and largely leaves them on one side, it then becomes problematic to interpret the Gospel of John, or even to analyze individual passages, with the synoptics primarily in view. In other words, it becomes less than a safe assumption that the synoptics provide the base line against which the Fourth Gospel is to be measured and understood. Therefore, interpretation so based loses persuasiveness, however deftly and diligently it may be pursued.

Patterns of Agreement

Another consideration relevant to the assessment of the problem of John and the synoptics is the possible significance of patterns of their agreement. It is a commonplace that as one approaches and enters the passion narrative, the agreements or parallels become more numerous. This is, of course, true, although there are perplexing disharmonies also. With respect to the resurrection narratives an even more striking

---

[24] Some such view of John's purpose is set forth or implicit in the work of many contemporary scholars: Peder Borgen, Raymond E. Brown, Wayne A. Meeks, Klaus Wengst, *et al*. Of pivotal importance in this regard is the work of one of Paul Meyer's former students, J. Louis Martyn, *History and Theology in the Fourth Gospel* (rev. ed.; Nashville: Abingdon, 1979).

phenomenon may be observed. On the one hand, every Johannine resurrection narrative has a synoptic parallel. On the other, the discovery of the empty tomb aside, no synoptic resurrection narrative has a parallel in another synoptic gospel. There is an interesting general analogy between the Johannine resurrection narratives and the specious longer ending of Mark (16:9-20). That longer ending seems to gather together and summarize what is reported in the other canonical gospels. John's resurrection narratives could be viewed as a conflation and/or expansion of those found in the synoptics. Even John 21:1-14 has a non-resurrection parallel in Luke 5:1-11. Yet that episode also answers to the anticipation of a resurrection appearance in Galilee raised by Mark 14:28 and 16:7. Mark, of course, contains no such story.[25] To be sure, John 20:26-29 has no synoptic parallel, but it is probably a doublet of 20:19-23 (par. Luke 24:36-43). John 21:15-23 also appears to lack any synoptic parallel, but it may be viewed as the Johannine continuation of 21:1-14. Moreover, it corresponds to the expectation aroused by the singling out of Peter in Mark 16:7, as well as to the clear indication of the restoration of Peter and his task in Luke 22:31-32. Thus on the basis of the resurrection narratives alone there would be some reason to contend that John is a conflation of the synoptic gospels.

Such a contention is less easy to support in the passion narratives, although the parallels between John and any one synoptic gospel are greater here. Yet why does John omit the Lord's Supper from the pre-passion tradition, change its calendar date and that of the crucifixion, and omit an actual trial before Jewish authorities? These kinds of problems multiply as one moves backward into the public ministry. Then only chapter 6 and the meeting with John the Baptist at the outset represent strong agreements between the Fourth Gospel and any one of the synoptics. Indeed, the entire Johannine Galilean ministry of Jesus (with the exception of the Cana miracles, which have either no synoptic parallel [2:1-12] or a parallel only in Q [4:46-54]) is found in chapter 6. As is common knowledge, typical acts and forms of speech from Jesus' synoptic ministry are missing from John: no cleansing of lepers, no demon exorcisms, no parables, no apocalyptic-prophetic words, and no pronouncement stories. One could go on. For the position that John knew the synoptics and, at least in part, based his narrative upon them, especially in the passion and resurrection and in certain other pivotal points, there are obvious arguments, as well as problems. Less obvious are the reasons for John's having abandoned the synoptic framework and

---

[25] Interestingly enough, at the point at which our MS of the Gospel of Peter breaks off (14:60), an appearance of Jesus by the sea (of Galilee) is clearly to be anticipated.

narratives in the public ministry, that is, before the final visit to Jerusalem. Nevertheless, the resurrection appearance narratives, particularly with the appendix (chapter 21), strongly support some knowledge of the synoptics at a late redactional stage (cf. 21:25, especially the allusion to the books that could be written).

Still problematic, however, are the narratives in which John is clearly parallel to the synoptics, whether in the passion or elsewhere. It is these narratives that Gardner-Smith studied in his famous book, where he argued that the similarities of John to the synoptics, even the verbal agreements, could be explained as the result of common oral tradition. Such agreements are in any case not very numerous or extensive. Stories are told somewhat differently. Apparently related sayings appear in different forms and contexts. While it is possible to contend that in these cases John based his account on the synoptics, it is not so easily possible to understand why John changed what he changed and did not alter other things. Not all the divergences from the synoptics represent Johannine theological interests, nor do they fall into a distinct pattern or patterns. In other words, on these terms John's redactional policy is not easy to understand.

We find here a certain similarity to the problem advocates of the Griesbach-Farmer hypothesis encounter in attempting to understand Mark as a conflation of Luke and Matthew. In that case it is simply difficult to imagine or conceive of the purpose of Mark's redaction. The problem is even more difficult with respect to the entire gospel than in the case of individual pericopes. Concerning the relation of John to any one, or all, of the synoptics, there is a similar situation, yet in one sense it is different. In a general way John has been and remains intelligible as a distinct theological interpretation of the Jesus who stands at the center of the synoptic gospels and tradition. It becomes more difficult, however, to discern how John's apparent purpose is served by many of his specific departures from the synoptics. If at this point Windisch's thesis is invoked, one may also observe that if John wrote to displace the synoptics, it is still not obvious why the evangelist adopted what he included from the synoptics, while omitting some things that might have been of use to him, and created pointless discrepancies and contradictions. Aside from the consideration that the interpretation of specific Johannine texts on the assumption that the Fourth Evangelist had one or more of the synoptics in view is more often than not problematic, it is difficult to conceive of an author's presupposing the very texts he intends to displace. More likely, he simply goes his own way to write a gospel relevant to the needs of his community.

John and the Synoptics

Perhaps the most fundamental options remain those represented by Gardner-Smith and Neirynck. Each proceeds from a reasonable and, to my mind, right-headed insight or instinct, opposed though they may be. Thus Gardner-Smith insists that the evangelical tradition was not in the beginning limited to, or entirely incorporated within, our canonical gospels, and there is therefore now no reason to think John's similarities to the synoptics must have been derived from them, particularly in view of the many and puzzling differences. Neirynck, on the other hand, refuses to multiply hypothetical sources and traditions when the points of contact and similarity suggest as the primary possibility John's use of the synoptics. Both beginning points are reasonable, but they obviously come into conflict. New Testament scholars are inclined to think that such conflicts can only be resolved exegetically, but, in this case, presuppositions and predispositions are crucially important.

The Question of Faith and History

It is obvious, as Dodd clearly discerned, that Gardner-Smith's position leaves open the possibility of isolating and assessing the Johannine tradition with a view to its historical worth, that is, as an independent witness to the historical Jesus. By the same token, on Neirynck's view (as also on Windisch's) the scope or range of this possibility is radically reduced, if not nullified. From such a perspective, John's principal interest in history as the horizon of revelation need not be denied. Nevertheless, over against such an evaluation of the Fourth Gospel as an entirely secondary gospel, the claims of the implied author to be a distinctive and authoritative witness (19:35; 21:24; cf. 1:14) ring rather hollow.

With Neirynck we can see that a curious change of fronts has taken place in the history of criticism. In antiquity and through most of the history of exegesis, John's knowledge of the synoptics was deemed compatible with the historical accuracy and value of the Fourth Gospel. In sum, John knew more or better than the other evangelists. But with the rise of higher criticism and the questioning of the tradition of apostolic authorship, John's differences from the synoptics began to count against its historical reliability as the Fourth Gospel was increasingly regarded as a secondary document, going beyond the synoptics in ways that were basically ahistorical. Reflecting on the criticism of the late nineteenth and early twentieth centuries, Windisch could characterize the view that John was independent of the synoptics as conservative. It was becoming the refuge, or at least the correlate, of a more positive evaluation of John's historical worth, as the still dominant view that John wrote last and with knowledge of the others more and more implied its secondary and "unreliable" character.

With Bultmann one encounters a positive valuation of history as the arena of revelation, a view ascribed to the evangelist without attributing to him much by way of utilization of historical knowledge or tradition. Obviously, Bultmann's evaluation of John as an historical witness or source in the usual sense is rather low, although he grants that John employed elements of a tradition independent of, and parallel to, the synoptics. The same may apparently be said of Neirynck, the implications of whose view of John as mainly dependent on, or derivative from, the synoptics would seem to be clear. Neirynck's position takes up and continues the tradition of the late nineteenth and early twentieth century as represented, for example, by B. W. Bacon in North America.

Obviously, then, a negative evaluation of John as an historical source for Jesus and his times is presently congenial with either John's independence of the synoptics or his dependence upon them. On the other hand, it is probably a correct observation that, except in very conservative circles, those who value the Fourth Gospel as a significant source for our knowledge of Jesus regard it as independent of the other canonical gospels. A moment's reflection will reveal why this is so. The most impressive and central divergence of John from the synoptics is its impressive, christologically elevated portrait of Jesus, which no critical scholar any longer takes to depict the way the historical Jesus presented himself. If those aspects of the narrative that are parallel to the synoptics are taken to be derivative from them, one will conclude that where John moves away from the synoptics, he departs from historical reality. If, on the other hand, the parallels with the synoptics are understood as derivative from substantially related but independent sources, the door opens wider to investigate possibly historical bases of the distinctive Johannine material. For example, in John 4:44, 12:25, and 13:16 we encounter words of Jesus with clear synoptic counterparts. Do such sayings represent the tip of an iceberg of Johannine tradition, or are they only a few odd variants, sayings derived from the synoptics?

In conclusion, we should observe that the question of the historical dimension of the Fourth Gospel, particularly in relation to the synoptics, has aspects that are scarcely touched by the evaluation of the Johannine narrative or sayings tradition on historical-critical grounds. In the first place, the Gospel of John alone among the canonical gospels attests its own reliability as an historical report (19:35; 21:24; cf. 1:14). Doubtless the synoptic evangelists maintained a similar attitude, but only Luke indicates explicitly the importance of historical reliability (Luke 1:1-4;

cf. Acts 1:21-23). Does John underscore the reliability of his witness vis-a-vis that of the others? The comparison of John and the synoptics suggests that question is a relevant one. In any event, the Gospel of John itself does not permit us to put aside as irrelevant the question of whether—or in what sense—it is a valid witness to things that have taken place.

In the second place, the Gospel of John repeatedly emphasizes, as no other gospel does, the importance of remembering, but also the role played by the Spirit in remembering (e.g., 2:22; 14:26). Therefore, valid remembering can take place only in light of the cross and resurrection, that is, the exaltation of Jesus. Only then is the Spirit given (7:39). Only from that perspective can Jesus be properly remembered and understood. Any full consideration of the problem of history in John must pay attention to the gospel's own perception of this problem. Presumably all the evangelists are aware that theologically significant knowledge of Jesus is post-resurrection knowledge, but only John makes this crystal clear.

While consideration of historical reliability or worth cannot govern the results of research into the relationship of John and the synoptics, our survey makes it evident that such concerns hover anxiously around the fringes of this problem, as they have since the second century. Therefore, the relation of John to the synoptics is likely to remain, or recur, as a pivotal issue in New Testament scholarship. In a long and distinguished career in which he has inspired, begotten, and guided many New Testament students and scholars-to-be, Paul Meyer has unfailingly identified such issues and taught us to treat them with the care and respect their complexity and importance deserve.

5

Conversations With A Friend About Romans

J. Christiaan Beker [1]

It is difficult for me not to experience a certain sadness in conducting this written conversation with Paul Meyer. I cannot help but recall the many face-to-face conversations in which we were regularly engaged at Princeton Seminary. Quite often we would leave behind the busyness of departmental affairs and escape to Paul's favorite restaurant, The Old Heidelberg in Trenton. Although our choice of menu was always monotonously the same, our conversations constituted one of the highlights of my teaching career at the Seminary.

These conversations went something like this: Paul—accompanied by his ever-present Nestle text—would focus on an exegetical issue. His exegetical precision would usually correct my speculative outbursts, but in such a gracious manner that I was never put down or made to feel inferior. Subsequently, broader theological issues would surface, manifesting the wide scope and remarkable depth of his learning and insight.

I will always be grateful to Paul as colleague and conversation partner. He exhibits one of the most noble traits of a Reformed scholar: the ability to serve the glory of God in his biblical interpretation, while

---

[1] J. Christiaan Beker is Richard J. Dearborn Professor of New Testament Theology at Princeton Theological Seminary, Princeton, New Jersey.

never succumbing to the temptation to play to the galleries or to be a peddler of God's word.

I have chosen to engage Meyer[2] in a conversation about his recently published commentary on Romans in the *Harper's Bible Commentary*.[3] Within the limits of this essay, I plan to discuss three levels of interpretation which mark this commentary:

A. the commentary as translation;
B. the commentary as interpretation; and
C. the commentary as compositional structure.

It is clear that these three levels are all intertwined and impinge on each other, yet each of them deserves special attention.

I

A. Given the formidable task of producing a commentary that, according to the mandate of the editors, "is designed to make the best current scholarship available to *general audiences*" so that it "speaks to *all* who seek to use the Bible with discernment,"[4] Meyer's use of language is truly remarkable. Contrary to many "updated" translations of the New Testament, and unlike most commentaries on Romans as well which simply stick to wooden equivalences of the Greek text, Meyer is able to achieve innovative translations of terms which evoke a new interest in the Apostle's language and argumentation. Meyer's commitment to the task of New Testament scholarship surfaces here; i.e., in the attempt to recover the original, the task to go back *ad fontes* in order to undo the many anachronisms which the history of interpretation has produced throughout the centuries.

Although it was not his task to address the modern reader directly (see later), his translation of Pauline concepts evidences not only a precision, but also a transparent hermeneutic for our time. He writes (preface to Rom 3:21-8:39):

> In Paul's usage, the controlling terms are "righteousness" and "justification"—first of God and then of human beings. This creates some problems of understanding for modern readers, but

---

[2] In this essay I address my friend Paul W. Meyer as Meyer in order not to confuse him with his namesake, the Apostle Paul.

[3] (Ed. James L. Mays; San Francisco: Harper and Row, 1988) 1130-1167.

[4] Ibid., xv; emphasis mine.

the first solution, as in every instance of listening to another person, is to follow his own explanatory line of thought....[5]

It would indeed be useful for many advocates of reader-response criticism to attend to this advice.

Meyer's "transparent hermeneutic" shows itself in several ways.

(1) The headings to the sub-sections of the letter have a marvelous and lucid flow. Consider, for instance, the headings in chapters 5-8 which concern the interpretation of "The Death of Jesus Christ as the Revelation of God's Righteousness" (3:21-26):[6]

> Justification Interpreted as Reconciliation (5:1-11);
> Justification Interpreted as Acquittal and Life (5:12-21);
> Justification as the Gift of a Reordered Life (6:1-7:6);
> Justification as the Gift of Hope in a Still Unredeemed World (8:18-30); and
> Justification as Vindication by the Love of God in Christ (8:31-39).

Furthermore, the main headings have sub-headings which not only enable the reader to follow the argument but also provide solutions to interpretive difficulties which continue to plague interpreters of the letter. For instance, with respect to 6:1-7:6:

> There are three stages to the argument of 6:1-7:6, so clearly distinguished as to amount to three separate answers to the question "Why not continue in sin?" The connection with 5:12-21 remains close, for the answers Paul now gives employ the polarities of sin and grace, death and life, disobedience and obedience that were set up by contrasting Adam and Christ.[7]

And so the sections are headed as follows: "Through Death to Life" (6:1-14); "Through Slavery to Freedom" (6:15-23); and "Through Acquittal to Commitment" (7:1-6).[8]

Meyer devises an interesting way to fit the difficult section 7:7-25 into the flow of the argument: the series "justification as" (5:1-7:6; 8:18-39) is interrupted and yet accommodated to the main sequence of chapters

---

[5] Ibid., 1139.
[6] Ibid., 1139-1153.
[7] Ibid., 1146-1147.
[8] Ibid., 1147-1148.

5-8 by a "backward look" (7:7-25) and a "forward look" (8:1-17), appropriately contrasting the power of sin with the power of the Spirit.[9]

In order to appreciate the clarity and depth of Meyer's reading of Romans 6-8, as reflected in his headings, it may be useful to compare it with headings of the same section by other scholars. For instance, James D. G. Dunn, in his recent commentary, groups 6:1-11:36 together and calls it "the outworking of this gospel in relation to the individual and to the election of grace."[10] This dubious interlocking of chapters 6-8 with chapters 9-11 erroneously suggests that Paul's focus in 6:1-8:39 is on the individual, and that the relation of Israel to the gospel (chapters 9-11) belongs to the same argumentative unit.

(2) Careful attention must be given to Meyer's innovative translation of the Apostle's terminology which in its literal translation threatens to become obsolete language to so many modern readers. Accordingly, key terms in Romans are given "a new house" of meaning: πίστις ("faith") is rendered throughout as "trust" or the "trustworthiness and reliability" of God; and δικαιοσύνη ("righteousness") as the "integrity" of both God and humans, as God's "consistency" and "faithfulness", thereby allowing δικαιοσύνη its broad and flexible connotations,[11] extending to the sense of "rectitude" and the "reordering" of human life. Another key term of Meyer's interpretation, which is closely associated with the theocentric thrust of his entire interpretation of Romans and is deftly balanced with his christological emphasis, is the concept of "the impartiality of God," which not only is characterized as the basis for God's action in Christ but also defines the enduring character of God's dealing with Jew and Gentile alike. Accordingly, the sections 2:1-16; 2:17-29; 3:27-31; 11:1-36; and 14:1-12 are all subsumed under the heading "impartiality": cf. "Before an Impartial God" (2:1-16; 2:17-20); "Before an Impartially Justifying God" (3:27-31); "The Impartiality of God's Faithfulness" (11:1-36); "Jewish and Non-Jewish Observance Before an Impartial Lord" (14:1-12).[12]

B. and C. Although all three levels of interpretation which I listed previously are interrelated, I will discuss Meyer's interpretation (B) together with his conception of the compositional structure of the letter (C). To be sure, Meyer's translation strategy impinges directly on his interpretation and on his perspective on the compositional structure of

---

[9] Ibid., 1149-1152.
[10] *Romans 1-8* (Word Biblical Commentary 38; Dallas: Word, 1988) viii.
[11] Meyer, "Romans," 1146.
[12] Ibid., 1137, 1138, 1140, 1158, 1165.

the letter. My procedure seems nevertheless justified because interpretation and composition are so closely conjoined.

In following the flow of the commentary, the focus of the interpretation becomes abundantly clear.[13] On 1:18-32 he says, "The whole argument of Romans may be summed up as an exposition of God's way of rectifying, setting right, that flawed relationship [human sinfulness] by his Son, Jesus;"[14] or on 3:21-8:39, "In Paul's usage, the controlling terms are 'righteousness' and 'justification'."[15] With respect to 8:31-39, Meyer interprets God's love in Christ in terms of justification, "the very heart of Paul's teaching on justification."[16] Regarding God's treatment of Abraham at 4:17, he writes, "That places justification as a life-giving act in an all-embracing context."[17] Although Meyer acknowledges that in chapters 5-8 an important shift in style, language, and themes occurs, he concludes, "Yet all this does not mean that the treatment of the unrighteous has been abandoned. Indeed in some respects it has become more focused."[18] Accordingly, Meyer outlines chapters 5-8 in terms of the series, "justification as..." (see above).

II

Until this point I have been a fascinated listener to Paul Meyer's conversation with Romans. When I now enter the conversation, I hope not to distort or to minimize his interpretation, which is on every page a treasure of riches and depth.

Although Meyer is in line with the Reformed tradition in specifying justification as the key to the letter, I do not believe this can be done, notwithstanding the admirable consistency of the argument which this key produces. In defense of Meyer, he defines God's righteousness in terms of multiple connotations:

> ...God's "faithfulness" has several levels of meaning. His trustworthiness is his power to do what he has promised (as in 4:20-21). But it involves also his constancy, the changelessness

---

[13] In a commentary of this length, a summary of the headings in the preface would have given the reader a clearer insight into this single-minded focus.

[14] Meyer, "Romans," 1137.

[15] Ibid., 1139.

[16] Ibid., 1153.

[17] Ibid., 1142.

[18] Ibid., 1143.

of his purpose. And another side of his reliability is the consistency with which he deals with different groups of people, i.e., the very impartiality that raised the question [of God's faithfulness to Israel] in the first place. In the end, these are all aspects of God's righteousness.[19]

Why, however, does Meyer simply identify the righteousness of God with the justification of the sinner? Why, for instance, is 3:21-8:39 specified in its heading as "the justification of the unrighteous"? Although Meyer follows Ernst Käsemann in emphasizing the *justificatio impii* (Rom 4:5) as the key to Romans, it is one of Käsemann's merits to have pointed to the cosmic coordinates of the term "the righteousness of God."[20]

Meyer's neglect of distinguishing justification from the righteousness of God leads to a (however qualified) anthropological interpretation of Romans, so that the issue of the restoration of human integrity through the Christ-event runs like a red thread through the commentary. Occasionally this emphasis leads to misinterpretation. On 9:11-11:36, he writes, *"from 1:16 on* [Paul] has always been careful not to obliterate the distinction between Jew and non-Jew (1:16; 2:9-10; 3:1-30; 4:11-12)."[21] But where is this human distinction visible in chapters 5-8? The anthropological pitch of the argument also leads Meyer to a hermeneutical device which has a strong Barthian flavor to it, with its emphasis on the idolatry of the *homo religiosus*. Notwithstanding his sensitivity to the Jewish question,[22] Meyer equates the Apostle's specific address to Gentiles, Jews, and Christians in Rome with a universal rubric. On 7:7-25, he says, "all serious religious devotion [is] subject to being taken captive by sin and subverted into distrust and defiance of God;"[23] on 2:1-16, "it is the inevitable reaction of all moral and religious people;"[24] on 5:1-11, "Paul has been describing that self-protective, unrepentant, and presumptuous confidence in God that is *a recurrent trait of religious people*, but that is irreconcilable with trust;"

---

[19] On Rom 9:1-11:36 (ibid., 1154).

[20] Ernst Käsemann, *Commentary on Romans* (ed. G. W. Bromiley; Grand Rapids: Eerdmans, 1980).

[21] Meyer, "Romans," 1154; emphasis mine.

[22] Cf. especially 7:7-25 (ibid., 1151).

[23] Ibid.

[24] Ibid., 1137.

and "[Jesus' death] occurred at just such a time as *conventional religion* would least expect it of God...."[25]

Moreover, in terms of Meyer's occasional hermeneutical forays into the present (cf. especially his profound translation strategy [see above]), I wonder whether his attacks on conventional religion and on the religious pride of people, i.e., his attacks on legalism and libertinism (however much they may have been the Apostle's concern) are really the issues which make people today resist the gospel. It seems to me that Meyer's stress on the all-sufficiency of God's act in Christ with its wholesome results for human life needs to be explored and critically reexamined in the light of its frequent disconfirmation by our human experience of reality. In other words, is every rejection of the gospel due to human pride and distortion? Are not there genuine secular and humane resistances to the christological and absolutist claims of Paul's gospel? Although Meyer's elucidation of God's decisive act in Christ is far removed from a confessional positivism, and although he makes the encounter between the human and the divine a dynamic reality, I still wonder why Meyer does not occasionally question the relevance of Paul's gospel for our time.

My major objection to Meyer's thematic interpretation of Romans in terms of justification by faith concerns his treatment of chapters 5-8. Although he acknowledges Paul's change in style, vocabulary, and themes in these chapters, he does not press this issue, but maintains that the justification of the unrighteous remains the subject matter, so that Paul proceeds here "without any fundamental change of subject."[26]

At this point, I would recast Meyer's structural composition of Romans in a very different way. It seems to me that Paul's theology in Romans is essentially a theology of hope—a hope which is grounded in the anticipatory nature of God's act in Christ. This theology of hope becomes more and more prominent in the dynamic movement of the argument, especially when we observe the different climate of the argument in chapters 5-8 compared to that of chapters 1-4. Here for the first time in the letter, Paul introduces "power" language, which gives the argument a new apocalyptic thrust.

Thus 5:1-11 manifests a decisive shift in the argument, which indicates a new departure of thought. To be sure, I agree with Meyer that this shift is not disconnected from the argument of 1:18-4:25.[27] Nevertheless, the "much more" (5:8-10), the straining of "our hope of

---

[25] Ibid., 1144; emphasis mine. Cf. also 1135, 1143.

[26] Ibid., 1143.

[27] Ibid.

sharing the glory of God" (5:2), and the new emphases on the Spirit (5:5) and on the category of "life" (5:10)—which introduces the primary antithesis of "life" and "death" in 5:12-8:39—are all indicative of an argumentative shift in 5:1-11.

In other words, the intramural argument of 1:18-4:25 which focuses on "Jew and Gentile before an impartially justifying God,"[28] i.e., concentrates on the unity of Jew and Gentile in the church, is now projected onto a larger cosmic canvas which, with its confessional style, depicts Christian existence in the world by means of cosmic-apocalyptic categories and the unity of the church (1:18-4:25) as the necessary prelude to God's coming apocalyptic triumph. Now Paul emphasizes the "either-or" of the lordship of Christ over against the lordship of the power structures that rule the world. Moreover, he does not solely discuss the church in its battle against the world (6:1-8:17), but also the solidarity of the church with the world for the sake of the world's redemption (8:18-30). Thus, whereas Meyer treats the subject of hope as a complementary issue, I would stress the trajectory of hope as the basic carrier of the argument in Romans.

In this context, it is surprising that Meyer makes so little of the doxology of 15:13 which—just before Paul announces his travel plans in 15:14-33—forms the climax to the letter as a whole. Here the thrust of Paul's argument throughout the letter manifests itself clearly: the emphasis on "the God of hope" and the exhortation in the same verse "to abound in hope by the power of the Holy Spirit" indicate that the trajectory of hope is crucial to Paul's theological intent in Romans.

This is confirmed by tracing this trajectory of hope throughout the letter: it moves from 5:1-11 (especially vv. 2, 8-10) to 5:19-21; subsequently it is picked up in 6:5-23, and in 8:11-12 and then elaborated in 8:18-39. It continues in 12:12 and 13:11-14 in order to reach its climax in 15:13. Although Meyer entitles the section 13:11-14 "Living for God's Coming Day," he skips the ἐγγύτερον ("salvation is *nearer* to us now" [13:11]) and concentrates instead on "our identification with the life-pattern of Jesus" which he (erroneously, in my opinion) links with the "image" of 8:29.[29] Moreover, notwithstanding Meyer's good comments on the futurity of salvation in connection with 8:18-30,[30] he does not give Paul's distinction between justification and salvation the emphasis it deserves—especially since

---

[28] Ibid., 1140.
[29] Ibid., 1164.
[30] Ibid., 1152.

the Apostle always reserves salvation for the future consummation of life in the glory of God.

It seems to me that a compositional structure such as I propose is not only in tune with Paul's own theology, but also is able to do justice to the cosmic perspectives that are inherent in that theology. Moreover, it resists an exclusively anthropocentric and individualistic reading of Romans and opens up hermeneutical avenues which deeply touch our human experience. Indeed, Paul's theology of hope in the coming glory of God does not occur in a vacuum, but is formulated against the awesome power of death in God's world, a power which produces immense suffering and sorrow. Thus a theology of hope bases its certainty on what God has commenced to do in Christ, and refuses to grant the Christ-event a finality which supposedly yields a sufficient answer to all the questions that suffering in our world raises.

I am not sure how Paul Meyer will react to this different conception of Romans. Moreover, it is probably unfair on my part to expect from him a greater elaboration on issues which the constraints of the *Harper's Bible Commentary* did not allow. Nevertheless, this "conversation" demonstrates that another get-together at The Old Heidelberg restaurant may be necessary to convince me of my errors! In the meantime, may all of us who are interested in Romans continue to learn from Paul Meyer's commentary and to admire his amazing accomplishments.

6

Paul's Midrash: Reflections on Romans 4

Lou H. Silberman[1]

How did the recipients of Paul's letter to the Romans understand his midrash on Gen 15:6? Had they ever heard the Hebrew of the verse: *wĕheʾemin bayhwh wayyaḥšĕbehā lô ṣĕdāqâ* or did they know it only in Greek: καὶ ἐπίστευσεν (δὲ) ʾΑβρ(α)άμ τῷ θεῷ, καὶ ἐλογίσθη αὐτῷ εἰς δικαιοσύνην (cf. Rom 4:3)? Would it have made any difference either way? To seek an answer or answers to these questions this essay will pretend a second naïveté that does not know—unlike the Church and generations of commentators—the Pauline corpus, but only the letter before the community to which it was addressed. It will not know what Paul had written and sent elsewhere, for it will not assume that the Romans were privy to such. Like them, it will know only that, among the many questions that had emerged from some variously reported and often quite differently understood events in Palestine centering on a wonder-working preacher who some were convinced was more than that, one question concerned the place of the nations in the the divine scheme of things. Or so the letter was, among other matters, saying.

What the Romans could gather from this urgent message was, it seems, that events were hastening to some predetermined end. In that context this question about the place of the nations other than Israel had

---

[1] Lou H. Silberman is Hillel Professor Emeritus of Jewish Literature and Thought at Vanderbilt University, Nashville, Tennessee, and Adjunct Professor of Judaic Studies at the University of Arizona, Tucson, Arizona.

come to play an important role in Paul's thought and perhaps in the thought of others. Paul had arrived at a point of view but an *ipse dixit* was not enough. His position had to be rooted in and confirmed by Sacred Writ were it to convince his hearers. It was evident to Paul and to his hearers that Israel, that is, the Jews, among whom many if not all of the recipients were counted, had a special role and destiny. What about the others who had heard the "good news" and who had, it would seem, sought to enroll themselves in one way or another in the community? What would become of them if there was little time left to consummate their desire? It was in answer to this question that Paul provided his midrash, his explication of the scriptural passage.

Having thus suggested the context and the dynamic, we turn away from the midrash to the biblical text. What possible meanings lay within it? Although the question "had they ever heard it in Hebrew?" was put earlier, an answer is not crucial. It may well be that the scriptural lessons were read in Hebrew in Rome as elsewhere and that there were some or even many who understood it; yet it was not the Hebrew text but a Greek translation that was undoubtedly the medium of understanding, as Paul's midrash suggests. The Greek varies from the Hebrew by introducing Abraham as the expressed subject of the verb, substituting θεῷ for the tetragrammaton and transforming the active verb with a direct object, "he reckoned it," into a passive form, "it was reckoned." At this point one may ask, how serious are the variances? Martin Buber makes this the linchpin of his interpretation of Paul and the basis of his crucial distinction between two types of faith. He writes: "Now it is said of Abraham that he 'continued to trust' God (the peculiar verbal form is meant to express this) and of God that He 'deemed' this 'as the proving true' of him." Buber continues: "We must try to grasp what the narrator meant by this, in order to estimate the difference between this and what Paul derived from the text which was not only translated into Greek but virtually Hellenized, and with which he had grown up to be familiar, so that it deeply influenced his understanding of the original. What is recorded of Abraham is an immovable steadfastness."[2] Paul, on the other hand,

> found in his Greek Bible at this point something which is immersed in a different atmosphere. Abraham does not believe "in" God, in

---

[2] Martin Buber, *Two Types of Faith* (London: Routledge and Kegan Paul, 1951) 44. What Buber means by a "peculiar form" of the verb, I do not know. On this see Ronald J. Williams, *Hebrew Syntax: An Outline* (Toronto: University of Toronto Press, 1967) 34, § 168; 36, § 177.

the sense of perseverence in Him, but he believes Him—which to be sure does not require to mean that he believed His words (such a weakening of the sentence is not in the mind of the translator), but it does denote an act of the soul in the moment described. More important still is the fact that instead of the divine consideration, deeming, ratification, there has come into being an attributing, a category in the judicial computation of items of guilt and innocence against each other, and in connexion with this instead of the proving true, a "righteousness", the rightness of conduct which justifies the individual before God."[3]

This, says Buber, is what the Greek text as over against the Hebrew means and it is this meaning that is the basis of Paul's midrash.

The crux of Buber's interpretation is his understanding of ἐπίστευσεν. As cited above, it is designated "an act of the soul in the moment described"; this is, for Buber, not what the Hebrew means. Was that indeed how Paul and his hearers understood it? Must one not assume that they did not hear it as an entry in a theological dictionary but as a form of a commonly used verb? A nineteenth-century scholar, concerned not with theology but with Greek language, comments on two related Greek verbs πείθεσθαι and πιστεύειν, and points out that their presumed root πιθ has the basic meaning of "to bind." He observes that πείθειν does not mean merely the "awakening of a particular belief by means of being convinced through words" but also "winning a person over." Similarly πιστὸς ἑταῖος is the friend bound to, united with me. "πίστις is really internal devotion to someone and πιστεύειν, 'trust,' is reliance on a person or thing not confronted as alien, indifferent, in which one senses an intimate connection with one's own strivings. "These verbs," he writes, "express such a belief in persons and things that matches a strong relationship in which we stand."[4] He summarizes his understanding thus: "πιστεύειν heisst einer Person oder Sache *vertrauen* oder von einer Sache überzeugt sein. Das ist in jedem Falle ein Glaube mit dem festen Bewusstsein das man sich nicht irrt."[5] Wherein this differs from Buber's understanding of the Hebrew text is not discernible to me. Thus Paul could not have been led astray by a Greek distortion of that meaning.

---

[3] Buber, *Two Types of Faith*, 46.

[4] J. H. H. Schmidt, *Synonymik der Griechischen Sprache* (Leipzig: Teubner, 1876) 1.335-6. The translation is mine.

[5] J. H. H. Schmidt, *Handbuch der Lateineischen und Griechischen Synonymik* (Leipzig: Teubner, 1889) 692-3, emphasis his.

Further, what about the Greek rendering of ṣĕdāqâ, δικαιοσύνην? Buber writes of the Hebrew text: "In view of a promise which he was able to believe only from this essential relationship, the patriarch enhanced this yet by strengthened surrender. This is now deemed as proving him true. As *zedek* is the pertinently-fitting verdict, the agreement of an assertion or action with reality, about which judgment is made, so *zedakah* is the manifestation of the conformity between what is done and meant in the personal conduct of life, the proving true (which idea is then transferred to God as confirmation of His benevolence.)"[6] Not so the meaning of the Greek, says Buber, but "there has come into being...a category in the judicial computation of items of guilt and innocence against each other... a 'righteousness', the rightness of conduct which justifies the individual before God."[7]

Does the Hebrew mean what Buber claims? Is it devoid of any juridical or judicial implications? Ben Jehudah deals with *ṣedeq* and *ṣĕdāqâ* at length in his dictionary. Of the latter he writes: "good and proper action, particularly in the phrase *mispāṭ ûṣĕdāqâ*" and again, "with the meaning, the quality of *ṣedeq*, the attribute of *ṣedeq* and *yôser* [uprightness] in a man's actions and words."[8] How this differs from the ordinary sense of δικαιοσύνη is not evident.[9] Indeed, a careful reading of Buber, here and elsewhere, suggests that all of this is an expression of his Wellhausenian negative attitude toward post-exilic Judaism.[10] His view is recognizable in the summary of his understanding of the two terms as he interpreted them in the Greek text and hence in Paul: "...both are a limitation, a deflation of that original fulness of life, a limitation common to Alexandrian and contemporary rabbinical Judaism."[11] It is ideology not philology that determines this comment. Unsatisfied, nonetheless, that the Greek text had in the first instance led Paul astray, he continues: "With its assumption... however the sentence

---

[6] Buber, *Two Types of Faith*, 45.

[7] Ibid., 46.

[8] Eliezer Ben Jehudah, "*sedeqa*" in *A Complete Dictionary of Ancient and Modern Hebrew* (New York: Thomas Yoseloff, 1959) 6.5397-8.

[9] See Pierre Chantraine, *Dictionnaire étymologique de la Langue Grecque: Histoire des Mots* (Paris: Klincksieck, 1968- 1981) 3.868-9.

[10] On this see my "The Human Deed in a Time of Despair: The Ethics of Apocalyptic" in *Essays in Old Testament Ethics (J. Philip Hyatt, In Memoriam)* (ed. James L. Crenshaw and John T. Willis; New York: KTAV, 1974) 195-196.

[11] Buber, *Two Types of Faith*, 46.

is penetrated by the principles of the Pauline faith and justification doctrine, and its import is changed."[12]

Here I summon up my second naïveté. I assume that Paul wrote his letter to convince his hearers of something they did not know or at least did not understand fully and completely before. If they heard the text as I have suggested in terms of the ordinary usage of the language, how were they to garner this new meaning from it? Is his midrash meant to convey it to them? Or is the midrash not at all about "faith" and "works" as Buber and generations of theological commentators assumed, but about something much more immediate and practical: what about the Gentiles?

It is not, of course, that simple. Paul's evident discomfort, his breathless mutterings and sweaty self-contradictions that at times border on incoherence, must have been a source of distress to his hearers. How were they to make their way through the cluttered verbiage of his ambiguities? It was only with the midrash that the matter became clear. Paul's move, a *gezera shava*[13] or verbal analogy, begins with his earlier quotation of Hab 2:4 in Rom 1:17—ὁ δὲ δίκαιος ἐκ πίστεως ζήσεται. Life—and for Paul, that means life in the coming future—is come by through trust in God. What that trust—and its concomitant being deemed righteous which is mediated or brought about through the divine act in Jesus Christ—encompasses is not yet evident. However, the echoing "trust" and "righteousness" of Gen 15:6 shows the way.

1. Abraham "our forefather" is an exemplar of that trust that brings in its wake divine acceptance.
2. The quotation from Psalm 32 applied to Abraham at Rom 4:7-8 describes him both as μακάριος, "blessed," and guiltless, that is, righteous.
3. This is followed by a rhetorical question: was this blessed righteous one, Abraham, circumcised or not when he was deemed righteous?
4. The answer is, of course, No! It was only after his being so declared that he was circumcised as "a sign or seal of the

---

[12] Ibid., 46-47.

[13] See Moses Mielziner, *Introduction to the Talmud* (3rd ed., New York: Bloch, 1925) 142-152, where he discusses the exegetical *gezera shava*, the linguistic analogy in which "the indefinite is to be explained by the definite." In the case at hand, the indefinites ṣadıq and ʾĕmūnātô (δίκαιος, πίστεως) are explained by ṣĕdāqâ and wêheʾĕmın (δικαιοσύνην, ἐπίστευσεν.)

righteousness which he had by trust when he was uncircumcised" (4:11).

Paul does not tarry with the implicit question: if Abraham was rewarded with the sign or seal of his righteousness with circumcision ought not all those who trust be so rewarded? It is the trust that counts and its reward will come through life. Having made his point, Paul turns to spelling it out in detail and on to his impassioned peroration.

This midrash is a fine example of the genre. It is not exegesis of the biblical text in our sense of the term, but a subtle reading that underscores and nuances possibilities within it. By crescendo and diminuendo, by halts and accelerations, and by other rhetorical devices, the text is fashioned and formed to the sought-after meaning. The classical scholar quoted earlier in this essay, commenting on quite another matter, casts a clear light on such. After discussing the problematic relationship between Greek and Latin synonyms, he continues:

> The difficulty is compounded by the fact that the matching German words are likewise very ambiguous, gaining quite different meaning through the height and depth of tone, and that a marking of these relationships serves no purpose because all textbooks deal with modern languages as though they were dead, as far as I have been able to satisfy myself. With the result that reference to what is really living in a word, tone according to height, duration, and stress, would appear to be Chinese to the reader."[14]

It is, I would add, a scholar's task not only to recognize the life of modern languages but to make the earnest attempt to revivify as best one can those "dead" languages that are the very soul of his or her intellectual endeavors. One must learn to listen to the text.[15]

---

[14] Schmidt, *Handbuch*, 693. The translation is mine.

[15] That is why I have consistently referred to Paul's hearers, not his readers.

7

On Trusting an Unpredictable God: A Hermeneutical Meditation on Romans 9-11

Wayne A. Meeks [1]

One of Paul Meyer's colleagues has shown us how important is the issue of finding a "coherent" Paul among the Apostle's varied responses to the "contingencies" of his situation.[2] Yet, for anyone who still hopes to find some guidance from the Bible in trying to form a Christian life today, there is a more urgent question: not whether Paul is consistent, but whether God is. This question is at the center of Romans 9-11, and Paul Meyer has clearly articulated it: if God's action in Christ was as radical as Paul (and subsequent Christian faith) claims, "what then becomes of God's faithfulness, that very reliability on which human trust, beginning with Abraham's, can alone depend?"[3]

Many modern commentators on the letter to the Romans have supposed this problem to be uniquely Paul's, a personal and individual

---

[1] Wayne A. Meeks is Woolsey Professor of Biblical Studies at Yale University, New Haven, Connecticut.

[2] J. Christiaan Beker, *Paul the Apostle: The Triumph of God in Life and Thought* (Philadelphia: Fortress, 1980) chap. 2 *et passim*.

[3] Paul W. Meyer, "Romans" in *Harper's Bible Commentary* (ed. James L. Mays; San Francisco: Harper & Row, 1988) 1154.

issue arising only in the case of the "convert."[4] Such a reading not only misconstrues the genre and rhetorical shape of this letter, it has the effect of confining Paul's climactic assertions to the safe realm of "religion," understood usually as either abstract doctrine or personal feelings. The stakes for Paul were much higher than those terms suggest, and if we confront the full audacity of his claims, he may provide us, by analogy, with hints about a way Christians might respond to the quite different cultural situation in which we find ourselves today.

How can faith continue to be faith—that is, neither replaced by skepticism nor converted into dogmatism—when the web of culture that has embodied that faith has been torn or dislodged from the social forms that anchored it?[5] The Christian's dilemma is a special case of a more general cultural upheaval. In the domain of ethics, for example, the philosopher Bernard Williams, for whom the age of Christianity is simply past, inquires how we can preserve that moral confidence that is necessary for the humane functioning of society when we must accept that certainty is beyond our grasp.[6] To put the question in those terms makes it obvious how very different our problem is from the one addressed by Paul. Nevertheless, the difference is not absolute, as we shall see as we turn to Paul's argument in Romans 9-11.

A Stumbling Block for the Reader

Recent critical discussion of Romans 9-11 has at length recognized that these chapters are not a mere "appendix" or "excursus."[7] Even

---

[4] Even as perceptive a commentary as that by Ulrich Wilckens, despite his emphasis on *heilsgeschichtlich* elements in Paul's argument and the ecumenical and interfaith sensitivities of his commentary, falls into the individualizing mode of interpretation by construing the whole letter as essentially an *apology* vis à vis a (hypothetical) "jüdischer Gesprächspartner" (*Der Brief an die Römer* [EKK VI/2; Zürich, Einsiedeln, Cologne: Benzinger; Neukirchen-Vluyn: Neukirchener, 1980] *passim*).

[5] For an acute diagnosis of this dilemma, see Nicholas Lash, "Theologies at the Service of a Common Tradition" in *Theology on the Way to Emmaus* (London: SCM, 1986) 18-33.

[6] Bernard Williams, *Ethics and the Limits of Philosophy* (Cambridge: Harvard University Press, 1985). Compare Jeffrey Stout, *The Flight from Authority: Religion, Morality, and the Quest for Autonomy* (Notre Dame and London: University of Notre Dame Press, 1981) and of course, with quite a different project in view, Alasdair MacIntyre, *After Virtue: A Study in Moral Theory* (2nd ed.; Notre Dame and London: University of Notre Dame Press, 1984). In his more recent book, *Ethics after Babel: The Languages of Morals and Their Discontents* (Boston: Beacon, 1988), Stout argues vigorously and interestingly that acknowledgment of the cultural relativity of all kinds of justification does not commit us to moral skepticism or relativism.

[7] See, e.g., Wilckens's criticism of Dodd (*Römer* 2:181 and n. 804.)

now, however, the connection with what immediately precedes is not so clear. There is, as everyone notices, a sharp break between 8:39 and 9:1. The chain of inferential particles (ἄρα νῦν, ἄρα οὖν, γάρ, κτλ) is interrupted for a moment, only to resume immediately in v. 3. Nevertheless, the asseverations of 9:1-2 are perfectly at home in the diatribal style that has dominated the discussion since chap. 6 and continues in 9-11, and the specific theme of the latter chapters, which 9:1-5 dramatically introduces, is an essential counterpoint to the theme that has just reached its crescendo in chap. 8. The latter theme, announced triumphantly at the beginning of chap. 5 and defended in chaps. 6 and 7 against misunderstandings, declares the confidence that all those who are "justified" can have in God. Chapter 8 begins with a statement of that confidence in the forensic terms appropriate to the argument of chap. 7: "Thus there is now no condemnation for those who are in Christ Jesus." There follows a discourse on the ways in which the gift of the Spirit (interchangeably called the Spirit of God and the Spirit of Christ) confirms that confidence by pointing forward to the eschatological liberty and δόξα for which not only the believers but the whole creation yearns (vv. 5-30). A reprise of the forensic language in vv. 31-34 prepares the way for the climax in a small rhetorical circle, introduced by the question of v. 35, "Who will separate us from the love of Christ?" and concluded by the answer of vv. 38-39, "[Nothing] will be able to separate us from the love of God that is in Christ Jesus our Lord." The modulation from question ("love of Christ") to answer ("love of God in Christ") is important; it hints at a point to which we shall return.

Having so carefully and forcefully declared the confidence in God that is the very substance of faith, Paul then astonishes his hearers by solemnly swearing that his own heart is full of the opposite of confidence: "great sorrow and unceasing anguish" (9:2, RSV), and, moreover, he "would have vowed"[8] to be banned from the very love from which he has just told us nothing in heaven or earth could separate us (v. 3).[9] By waiting to name the objects of his anxiety until v. 3b, Paul

---

[8] Most commentators take the imperfect ηὐχόμην as conative or else as the expression of a wish, or some combination of both. Richard B. Hays has recently argued for a habitual sense, "I used to pray" (*Echoes of Scripture in the Letters of Paul* [New Haven and London: Yale University Press, 1989] 62), but that seems to me not to fit the context as well.

[9] John Chrysostom captures the astonishing turn with a rhetorical question that paraphrases Paul: τί λέγεις, ὦ Παῦλε; Ἀπὸ τοῦ χριστοῦ τοῦ ποθουμένου, οὗ μήτε βασιλεία σε, μήτε γέενα ἐχώριζε, μήτε τὰ ὁρώμενα, μήτε τὰ νοούμενα, μήτε ἄλλα τοσαῦτα, ἀπὸ τούτου νῦν εὔχῃ ἀνάθεμα εἶναι; (*Hom. in epist. ad Rom.* 16, *PG* 60:549A).

heightens the power of his reversal. Once he has named them, however, he emphasizes the objects with his solemn, polysyndetic list, which at the same time shifts attention from his personal connection ("my brothers, my kinsfolk by flesh") to the objective and universally significant gifts that belong to "Israelites" (vv. 4-5a). This shift is essential, because the disruptive issue is not merely an accident of Paul's personal history; it goes to the heart of what is to be believed about God. The formulaic blessing that rounds off this sentence implicitly acknowledges this point,[10] but it is hardly enough to allay the unease that Paul has induced in his readers. That the stumbling block Paul has placed in our path is deliberate is confirmed by the more elaborate liturgical piece that concludes the whole of this portion of Romans: it is precisely the inscrutability of God's judgments, the unsearchableness of his ways, the unknowability of his mind that are celebrated (11:33-36). These are hardly qualities that reinforce confidence.

The function of chaps. 9-11 is thus not to continue but to disrupt the smooth assurances of confidence that have capped the whole argument of chaps. 1-8. The reader is not to be allowed to think that confidence depends on knowing just how God will act in the future (that confidence is the same as certainty, as Bernard Williams would put it[11]). Paul has already hinted at that false step in 8:24: "Hope made visible is not hope." Now the paradigmatic challenge to a confidence that would depend on our knowing has to be faced: the trick that God has played on Israel. For if Christians are to accept Paul's assurance that "nothing will be able to separate us from the love of God," they must face the fact that the Jews have rested upon exactly the same assurance, and the radicality of Paul's claims throughout the letter so far has undermined that assurance. Does the collapsing of the διαστολή between Jew and Gentile (chaps. 1-3) not mean the canceling of Israel's election? Has the word of God "fallen away" (9:6)? "Is there injustice with God?"

---

[10] All the more reason to punctuate v. 5 with a full stop after κατὰ σάρκα, as most recent commentators agree. Cf. the discussion in Wilckens, 189; Käsemann, 259-60; Hans Lietzmann, *An die Römer* (HNT 8; Tübingen: J. C. B. Mohr [Paul Siebeck], 1933) 89-90; C. H. Dodd, *The Epistle of Paul to the Romans* (MNTC; London: Hodder and Stoughton, 1932) 152-53. Otto Michel, *Der Brief an die Römer* (KEK 4, 10th ed.; Göttingen: Vandenhoeck & Ruprecht, 1955) 197-99, offers a cautious argument for construing ὁ ὤν with χριστός while admitting to ultimate uncertainty; C. K. Barrett, *The Epistle to the Romans* (HNTC; New York and San Francisco: Harper, 1957) 178-79, leaves the question open. However, C. E. B. Cranfield (*A Critical and Exegetical Commentary on the Epistle to the Romans* [ICC 27, 6th ed.; Edinburgh: T. & T. Clark, 1975-79] 2:464-70) thinks the case for a christological referent "overwhelming."

[11] *Ethics and the Limits*, chap. 9.

(9:14). "Has God rejected his people?" (11:1). If God has abandoned that "chosen people" and taken another—as later Christian interpreters, beginning with Matthew, would claim, then how can we really be sure that God will not eventually do the same with this "new Israel"—as later interpreters, but never Paul, would call the church? These are all objections—and misunderstandings—that must be answered. Hence there is a tight internal logic in Paul's taking up at just this point the question of the continuing relationship between "Israel after the flesh" and the God who, like Abraham, "did not spare his own son, but gave him up for us all" (8:32).

Moreover, the logical dilemma is not only an intellectual one. It is not only the ideas that his readers hold about God that Paul wants to straighten out, but also the forms of communal life that embody those beliefs. For that reason the themes of Romans 1-11 continue to echo in the admonitions that follow in 12:1-15:13.[12] In one respect, however, circumstances make the task of social embodiment impossible to complete. There is, from Paul's perspective, a fundamental anomaly in the existence of the household-based groups that Paul and other Christian travelers have established. They are anomalous because they are the ἐκκλησία τοῦ θεοῦ and the "Israel of God" (Gal 6:16), yet they exist in complete isolation from the organized Jewish communities in the same cities.[13] This is an anomaly that Paul himself was unable to resolve, and no subsequent interpreters who have left any trace in the history of Christian exegesis have even sensed the problem.[14] Within this letter, Paul attempts only to point toward an eschatological

---

[12] See Wayne A. Meeks, "Judgment and the Brother: Romans 14:1-15:13" in *Tradition and Interpretation in the New Testament: Essays in Honor of E. Earle Ellis* (ed. Gerald F. Hawthorne; Grand Rapids: Eerdmans, Tübingen: J. C. B. Mohr [Paul Siebeck], 1987) 290-300.

[13] See Wayne A. Meeks, "Breaking Away: Three New Testament Pictures of Christianity's Separation from the Jewish Communities" in *"To See Ourselves as Others See Us": Christians, Jews, "Others" in Late Antiquity* (ed. Jacob Neusner and Ernest S. Frerichs; Chico: Scholars, 1985) 93-115, esp. 105-108.

[14] There have doubtless been Christians through the ages who did sense the anomaly, but they are mostly voiceless in the record. Ironically, the "Judaizers" at Antioch whom John Chrysostom railed against in his homilies *Adversus Iudaeos* in 386-387 C.E., seem in practice if not in theory to have intuited that something was lacking in a Christianity separated from Israel, but the leaders of the churches were still too insecure to see anything positive in such practice. See Wayne A. Meeks and Robert L. Wilken, *Jews and Christians in Antioch in the First Four Centuries of the Common Era* (SBLSBS 13; Missoula: Scholars, 1978) and Robert L. Wilken, *John Chrysostom and the Jews: Rhetoric and Reality in the Late 4th Century* (The Transformation of the Classical Heritage 4; Berkeley, Los Angeles, and London: University of California Press, 1983).

resolution and, within the household ἐκκλησία alone, a fitting communal ethos (Rom 14:1-15:13).

A Strategy of Paradox and Misreading

The tricks Paul plays on the Christians listening to his letter force them to think about the trick God has played on Israel. Two determinative features of his rhetorical strategy are his use of paradox and his peculiar interpretation of scripture.

Paradox

Paradoxical statements are not uncommon in Paul's letters, but they are especially thick in Romans 9-11. Consider the following examples. First, there is Paul's impossible vow in 9:3, directly contradicting what he has said immediately before, as we have already observed. Second, the transitional verses 9:30-31, drawing out the lesson of the scriptural catena cited in vv. 25-29, are formulated as a paradoxical antithesis. The Gentiles, not striving, have succeeded, where Israel, striving, has failed. The point, in different language, is repeated in 10:20-21 and 11:7. Third, immediately after, in 9:32-33, comes what Paul Meyer calls "one of the most remarkable of Paul's OT quotations because of what it attributes to God: placing in the midst of his people a base of security that is at the same time an obstacle over which they will stumble."[15] Finally, there is the summation of Israel's present status in chap. 11, which brings to a climax the almost unbearable tension that Paul has generated in chaps. 9 and 10 and leads to his remarkable statement, in 11:11-32, of the double reversal of status of Jews and Gentiles before God. Israel has indeed "stumbled," but they have not "fallen" (11:11). Most of them have suffered a "hardening" that puts them into the same category as the rejected Ishmael and Esau and even the prototypical enemy, Pharaoh (9:6-23). Indeed, this majority who have rejected Jesus as Messiah— because of their zeal for God's Torah—are classed not with that prophet whose zeal for the law was the Deuteronomist's paradigm, but precisely with Elijah's opponents, the followers of Ba'al (11:2-5). Nevertheless, their gifts and calling from God are ἀμεταμέλητα (11:26). Israel is simultaneously "enemies" (κατὰ τὸ εὐαγγέλιον) and "beloved" (κατὰ τὴν ἐκλογήν, 11:28).

We could, of course, call Paul's argument "dialectical" rather than paradoxical, but we must avoid two popular misunderstandings hidden

---

[15] Meyer, "Romans," 1157.

under that term. One attributes to Paul a logical process in which two partial insights are placed over against each other only to be transcended by a more comprehensive truth. We may eventually decide that we need to make some such move in order to appropriate Paul's thought for ourselves, but it is important to see that Paul himself does not do this.[16] His paradoxes rather set up work for the reader to do. The other way of conceiving Paul as a dialectician is simpler and more pernicious—and more common. The dialectic is seen to operate between succeeding stages of the history of salvation. The history of Israel is encompassed entirely under *Unheilsgeschichte*, which continues to have importance for Christians only as the symbol of that condemnatory function of the law that, in pietist and evangelical schemes, must precede and prepare for the reception of the gospel, the *Heilsgeschehen* which supplants all that went before.[17] Against such a reading, Paul's paradoxes bespeak the inscrutability of God's actions in present and future as well as in the past. The expectations upon which Christians, both Jew and Gentile, place their hope are set about with the mystery of yet undisclosed dimensions of God's grace, and that mystery also pervades the history of Israel. Consequently, Paul's reading of scripture is also fraught with paradox.

Misreading

In their recent books, very different in method and aim but effectively complementary, Dietrich-Alex Koch and Richard B. Hays have advanced our understanding of Paul's use of scripture well beyond previous studies of this relatively neglected topic.[18] Both give special attention to these chapters of Romans. Koch lists 66 instances of Paul's use of citations introduced by explicit introductory formulas. Of these, exactly a third, 22, occur in Romans 9-11. Including all seven of his categories of unequivocal citations, the list comes to a total of 89, of which 27 (30%) are in Romans 9-11. Reflecting on these facts, Hays argues that the whole letter ought to be read as "an *intertextual*

---

[16] Compare the remarks of Paul W. Meyer, "Romans 10:4 and the 'End' of the Law" in *The Divine Helmsman: Studies on God's Control of Human Events, Presented to Lou H. Silberman* (ed. James L. Crenshaw and Samuel Sandmel; New York: KTAV, 1980) 70.

[17] The commentary of Wilckens is still explicitly dominated by this dialectical scheme—surprising when one considers his ecumenical intention and many profound exegetical insights. Käsemann has come much closer to freeing himself from it.

[18] Dietrich-Alex Koch, *Die Schrift als Zeuge des Evangeliums: Untersuchungen zur Verwendung und Verständnis der Schrift bei Paulus* (BHT 69; Tübingen: J. C. B. Mohr [Paul Siebeck], 1986; Hays, *Echoes*.

conversation between Paul and the voice of Scripture,"[19] a judgment especially appropriate to chaps. 9-11. In what follows I depend on the detailed textual analyses of Koch and especially on the penetrating literary and interpretive insights of Hays. Accordingly it will be sufficient here to mention only a few examples of Paul's extraordinary readings of his Bible.

Hays argues that Paul's use of scripture is not rightly defined by any of the terms that have been in vogue among NT scholars, like "proof-texting," "allegory," "typology," or "midrash." Rather, much of the range of Paul's ways of using his Bible resembles the way in which modern poets "echo" their precursors.[20] A corollary is this: often when Paul refers to a passage of scripture, a reader who knows the context of that passage will discover in Paul's argument more or less subtle resonances of that context. As Hays recognizes, it is impossible to know whether any of the Roman Christians who first heard Paul's letter read to them would have caught these echoes. It is not easy to decide whether Paul really *intended* them. We can say only that in several instances the whole of Paul's rhetorical strategy gains depth and subtlety when we become aware of the unspoken contexts. A good example is in Rom 9:25, where Paul cites two verses from Hosea—initially quite against their context. Paul takes the prophet's words, addressed to Israel, to refer to *Gentiles* (very much as the author of 1 Peter does in 1 Pet 2:10). It is Christians from pagan origins who are the "non-people" who have become the people of God, the "unloved" who have become "beloved." Yet for a reader who knows the prophetic text, it is obvious that the same dialectic that Paul will make explicit in chap. 11 is the contextual sense of Hosea 1-3. The prophet declares that God, by "divorcing" Israel, has made them a "non-people," but as surely as Hosea obeys God's command to "Go again and love" an adulterous wife, God will reclaim Israel for himself. Thus while Paul's use of the text in Rom 9:25-26 is on its face a mere "proof-texting," atomistic and arbitrary, it already hints—to the knowing auditor—of that peripeteia of Paul's argument and of Israel's destiny toward which we are being carried as we listen.[21]

The same ambiguity affects the quotations from Isaiah that follow; indeed it is because Isa 10:22 begins with a clause almost identical to Hos 2:1 that Paul can link the two together by a mixed citation in Rom 9:27b. Initially, it sounds as though Paul is contrasting the promise made

---

[19] Hays, *Echoes*, 35, emphasis his.

[20] Hays, *Echoes*, chap. 1.

[21] For a similar analysis, see Hays, *Echoes*, 67.

to the Gentile "non-people" with Isaiah's threat against Israel. That, and the antithesis implied between the protasis and the apodosis, seem to justify the insertion of "only" before "a remnant," as the RSV and most other modern translations do.[22] However, Paul immediately proceeds to add to his chain of quotations Isa 1:9, which does not issue a threat but assures miraculous (and gracious) salvation. Linked with the quotation from Isa 10:22-23 by ἐγκατέλιπεν's reprise of ὑπόλειμμα, this new citation also adds something else to Paul's advancing argument. It reintroduces the word σπέρμα, which Paul has loaded with semantic freight in 9:6-9. Further, the recurrence of that word here brings a corrective to the earlier passage. There, Paul was dividing Israel: not all belong to the promise; not all deserve the name "seed." Here, he emphasizes the other side of the coin: nevertheless, God has promised to leave to Israel "seed." In light of this further development, then, we see that we would have been wrong to read "only a remnant" in v. 27— not because the negative judgment implied by the "only" is absent from the Isaiah passages as Paul reads them, but because the "only" would foreclose the other side of the prophet's word, the promise that Paul also hears there.[23]

The most brazen of Paul's "misreadings" of scripture, as all commentators recognize, often with embarrassment, is his transformation of Deut 30:12-13 in Rom 10:6-8. Here Paul explicitly cites a text that speaks unmistakably of the Torah and makes it speak instead of Christ and "the word of faith that we proclaim." His exegetical τοῦτ' ἔστιν, which has rightly reminded recent commentators of the interpretive rubrics in the Qumran *pesharim*,[24] emphasizes the deliberateness of the shifted referent. Just here, where the informed reader must make the most severe adjustment, Paul forces us to pay attention.

In order to understand what Paul is up to here, we have to notice that he has framed this exegetical *tour de force* with double brackets, which together establish 9:30-10:21 as the centerpiece of his argument in chaps. 9-11.[25] The broader *inclusio* is established by using two verses

---

[22] The case is well argued by Käsemann, *Romans*, 275.

[23] Hence I agree with the cogent arguments of Meyer, "Romans," 1156, and Hays, *Echoes*, 68.

[24] Koch, *Schrift als Zeuge*, 319-320, exaggerates the differences between Paul's interpretations and the *pesharim*, though it is obvious, as Koch says, that Paul's eschatological timetable is different from that of the Qumran texts.

[25] Cf. Hays, *Echoes*, 74-75. James D. G. Dunn, "'Righteousness from the Law' and 'Righteousness from Faith': Paul's Interpretation of Scripture in Romans 10:1-10" in *Tradition and Interpretation in the New Testament* (ed. G. F. Hawthorne; Grand Rapids:

from Isaiah 65 in Rom 10:20-21 to repeat the antithesis stated in Paul's own words in 9:30-31: Israel, running hard, have not reached the finish line; they remain disobedient and resistant. The Gentiles, not even in the race, like the tortoise in the fable have won; not seeking or inquiring, they found the prize, received the revelation. The quotation from Isa 65:2, however, adds another note, which prepares for chap. 11: God's hands are still extended to the "disobedient and contradictory people." Nested within this *inclusio* is another, created by repeating in 10:11 the quotation from Isa 28:16 introduced, in expanded and revised form, in 9:33. We have already noticed, following Meyer's observation,[26] the paradoxicality of the longer quotation. The apostle created the paradox by substituting for Isa 28:16's phrase λίθον πολυτελῆ ἐκλεκτὸν ἀκρογωνιαῖον ἔντιμον a version of the threatening phrase in Isa 8:14, λίθον προσκόμματος καὶ πέτραν σκανδάλου.[27]

What is the stone that both trips the one who runs ὡς ἐξ ἔργων and is the ground of confidence of everyone who puts trust in it? Nearly all commentators assume that it signifies Christ and point to the similar combination of texts in 1 Pet 2:6 as evidence for a Christian tradition of joining "stone" texts into christological testimonia.[28] Meyer, however, points out that there is nothing in the context to require a christological interpretation, nor any hint that the reader ought to hear the echo of yet a third "stone" text, crucial in the later christological exegesis, Ps 118(117):22. Instead, Meyer urges, the natural sense of the context "suggests that the Torah is the rock placed by God in Zion."[29] This does fit admirably with Rom 9:31 and 10:34, but creates difficulties in the context of the second citation of Isa 28:16, in Rom 10:11. Following the explicit christological content of the "confession" and "believing in the heart" of vv. 9-10, must not ἐπ' αὐτῷ be translated "on him," meaning "on Christ"? Not necessarily. While the Christian confesses, "The Lord

---

Eerdmans; Tübingen: J. C. B. Mohr [Paul Siebeck], 1987) 216-28, has not paid enough attention to the context of 10:1-10 and therefore arrives at an interpretation that is very nearly the antithesis of what I am arguing here.

[26] See above, n. 15.

[27] See the discussion in Koch, *Schrift als Zeuge*, 60, 69-71, 80.

[28] For a recent argument that Rom 9:33 presupposes such a tradition, see Koch, *Schrift als Zeuge*, 161-62, elaborating an argument already advanced by Käsemann, *Romans*, 278-279, summarizing previous discussion. Koch seems unaware of objections mounted against this hypothesis; see Meyer, "Romans 10:4," 54-65 and n. 18.

[29] Meyer, "Romans 10:4," 64; his comments in *HBC* are more ambiguous. C. K. Barrett, "Romans 9.30-10.21: Fall and Responsibility of Israel" in *Essays on Paul* (Philadelphia: Westminster, 1982) 132-53, earlier made a similar suggestion, but with the difference that he takes the same passage in 10:11 to refer to Christ, on the grounds that 10:4 means that Christ has abolished the law "in the sense that he replaces it" (144).

is Jesus," the corresponding trust in the heart is "that God raised him from the dead" (v. 9). It is ultimately *God's* action on which the Christian's faith, like the Jew's, rests; otherwise v. 12, returning to the theme of chaps. 1-3 that there is no more διαστολή between Jew and Gentile, would have no clear connection with v. 11 and would be robbed of its full weight. Therefore, at least in Rom 10:11, it would be better to understand Paul as reading Isa 28:16 to say, "Everyone who puts his trust *in God* will be vindicated." Perhaps it is a mistake to suppose that the "stone" of the text must have, in Paul's mind or in the work he sets the text to do for his readers, a single referent, as if Paul were constructing a simple allegory or, in the usual sense of the word, typology. Here Hays's comparison with the poetic trope "echo" or "metalepsis" is most helpful,[30] for it suggests a range of connections and meanings within which a text may resound. Thus we need not choose whether it is Torah, Christ, or God himself that is signified in the verse about a rock that is both obstacle and reliable foundation, as if one excluded the others.

But surely we do have to choose between Torah and Christ? That seemed to be the message of the letter to the Galatians, despite Paul's undeveloped disclaimer in Gal 3:21, but in the non-polemical context of Romans Paul's reflection on the problem is much more nuanced. We can see the difference, for example, in 9:31, where, on the usual reading of Romans, we would expect the direct object of the first verb to be not "law of righteousness," as Paul has written, but the reverse, as in the egregious mistranslation of RSV, and the object of the second to be "righteousness," not "law." Paul's surprising choice of words proclaims that the righteousness promised in the law but unattained is not the ἰδία δικαιοσύνη that stands in opposition to the righteousness of God (10:3)[31] but is God's righteousness itself, to which Torah and Prophets bear witness, even though it is manifested finally χωρὶς νόμου (3:21). Because the Torah genuinely did promise God's righteousness, and because God sent his Son "that the δικαίωμα τοῦ νόμου be fulfilled among us" (8:3-4), 10:4 can only be understood as saying that "Christ is the goal and completion of the law."[32]

We must note one more connection between 9:33 and other parts of Romans before we return to the issue of Paul's provocative exegesis of

---

[30] Above, n. 21.

[31] Dunn's tortuous exegesis in his attempt to prove the contrary shows how unnatural his construal of the text is, but it is representative of many ("Paul's Interpretation," 222-23).

[32] Meyer's argument in "Romans 10:4" ought to lay this issue to rest, but to hope so would betray too sanguine a view of NT scholarship.

Deut 30:12-13. The final clause of 9:33, following as it does Paul's bold assertions about God's δικαιοσύνη in vv. 30-31, strikingly echoes his thematic assertion in 1:16-17. As Hays says of the latter passage, "Paul is 'not ashamed' in relation to the gospel precisely because the gospel is God's eschatological vindication of those who trust in him—and consequently of God's own faithfulness."[33] And, in one of his most provocative and persuasive insights, Hays argues that Paul's introduction of Hab 2:4 into this context already foreshadows the fundamental theme of chaps. 9-11 for any reader who recalls the context of Hab 2:1-4, which is precisely the question of God's faithfulness to Israel.[34] Thus we are not allowed to perform the ellipsis that nineteen centuries of Christian reading have silently perpetrated on Rom 1:16, i.e., taking "to the Jew first" to mean only "to the Jew who has become a Christian." That misreading is disallowed because of the formidable pressure of the texts that echo here, texts that through centuries had expressed Israel's agony over God's righteousness and faithfulness—and God's agony over Israel's unfaithfulness.

Thus Paul has set his exegetical tripping stone at the center of an elaborate filigree of argument and scriptural allusion. We cannot dismiss it as an interpretive bauble decorating an argument whose weight lies elsewhere. The brazenness of his commandeering Moses' words about the Torah to be spoken by "the righteousness from faith" is transparent; no one who has read the original text can ignore it. Nor does it get Paul off the hook to observe that later rabbis sometimes play equally outrageous tricks with the words of Torah: when they do, it is not because they care nothing for the plain meaning of the texts or assume that their readers do not care. On the contrary, the overt misprisions are giant winks that say, "Pay attention!"

Is the function of Paul's misreading then a deliberate violation of everything that "is written," in order to supplant all merely scriptural authority with "the message of justification as the decisive criterion" of "a theologically reflected Christian hermeneutics"?[35] Or, by silently contradicting the plain sense of Deuteronomy in order to set it against Lev 18:5, to define two radically opposed kinds of "righteousness"?[36] If so, then everything I have said up until now is wrong.

If, however, we assume that Paul means what he says in 3:12b (the law and the prophets are witnesses to God's righteousness) and 3:31

---

[33] Hays, *Echoes*, 39.
[34] Ibid., 39-41.
[35] So Käsemann, *Romans*, 287.
[36] Koch, *Schrift als Zeuge*, 291.

(faith does not abolish but confirms the law) and chap. 7 (the law is spiritual and holy and the commandment holy, just, and good), and if 10:4 is read with rather than against those earlier statements, then Paul's parody of Deut 30:12-13 has quite a different force. Instead of abolishing the plain sense of the Torah's words, Paul requires that plain sense as the strong but unspoken counterweight to his christological confession. The resultant tension is quite specific in any reader who knows what Deuteronomy says. The plain sense that Paul suppresses, like the plain sense of Hos 2:25 and 2:1 in Rom 9:25, lodges in the mind of the competent reader as a provocation, pressing toward resolution. It is characteristic of Paul's interpretive strategy that the resolution will not come with a stroke; it is never simple.[37]

Here there are at least three steps to be taken toward resolving the tension and thus hearing the whole of what Paul is saying. First, we must remember the positive things Paul has said about the law and thus perhaps, by a kind of second hearing, revise our understanding of Paul's antitheses.[38] Second, the unresolved tension in chap. 10 prepares us for the dramatic double reversal of Jews and Gentiles in chap. 11, the climactic declaration in 11:26 that "all Israel will be saved," and the concluding doxology on the depth and inscrutability of God's wisdom. Third, Paul's heavy-handed plucking of those Deuteronomic verses may set other Deuteronomic lines ringing in our memory. For example, memory may complete the quotation of Deut 9:4 that Paul used out of context to introduce his citation of 30:12-13: "Do not say in your heart...'On account of my righteousness [plur. in the LXX] the Lord brought me in to inherit this good land...,'" and further, v. 5: "It is not because of your righteousness nor because of the holiness of your heart that you enter to inherit their land, but because of the impiety of these nations that the Lord will destroy them before your face, and in order to establish his covenant, which he swore to your fathers, Abraham and Isaac and Jacob," and more of the same.[39] Indeed, a *Leitmotiv* in Deuteronomy is that it was not because of Israel's strength, or number,

---

[37] Compare his parenetic method in 1 Corinthians: Wayne A. Meeks, "The Polyphonic Ethics of the Apostle Paul," *Annual of the Society of Christian Ethics* (1988) 17-29.

[38] For example, the antithesis in 10:5-6. Hays, *Echoes*, 76, goes so far as to say that "the righteousness from the Law" and "the righteousness from faith" here are *synonymous*. That, I think, is going too far, but it is closer to Paul's meaning than the flat contradiction that most commentators read here.

[39] Cf. Deut 8:17 and see Hays's discussion, *Echoes*, 78-79; Dunn's comments on these verses are very much to the point as well ("Paul's Interpretation", 223-25).

or military prowess, or piety, or righteousness that God chose them "to be a people peculiarly his own, beyond all the nations that are on the face of the earth," "but because the Lord loves you and keeps the oath that he swore to your fathers" (Deut 7:6,8 LXX). The theme sounds so persistently that we can readily understand how Paul could think that "the righteousness from faith" speaks Paul's own gospel through the words Moses wrote. Again, as in his use of Hosea and Habakkuk, Paul holds in reserve the very theme of the texts that he appeared initially to suppress. When the suppressed motif resurfaces, it is radically changed. The gospel spoken to Israel in Deuteronomy affirms the destruction of the ἔθνη (in Canaan) and requires for Israel's purity isolation from "the nations." Paul's gospel is that the very same divine love that chose Israel has now reached out to call a people "not only from Jews but also ἐξ ἐθνῶν (Rom 9:24), and there is to be "no separation" between them. Nevertheless, however radical this change, the gospel spoken to Israel *in the words of Torah* still stands firm.

Dare We Learn Hermeneutics from Paul?

If there are any lessons we can learn from so idiosyncratic an interpreter, it will not be by any direct imitation. Still less can we distill from Paul's multileveled strategy a method, a set of rules. We may nevertheless agree that there are three significant dimensions to Paul's use of scripture, in the sample we have in part analyzed, that will properly characterize Christian reflection even in our time. Paul's theological reflections are, first, *interpretive* in the specific sense that his rereading of the scripture and traditions of Israel is constitutive of his argument, not merely illustrative. Second, Paul's interpretation is *social*, in both context and aim. Third, it is *eschatological*. Let me briefly suggest directions in which an elaboration of these dimensions might take us.

Interpreting the Text that Interprets Us

Paul presents us with an acute instance of that dilemma which every community possessing a normative body of traditions or texts embodies: the norm must be interpreted and, by interpretation, changed. Unacknowledged, the dilemma easily produces duplicity or bad faith; acknowledged, it too often brings forth cynicism or nonchalant relativism.

In the very places where Paul most astonishingly subverts the plain sense of the ancient text, we have found that the plain sense continues to exert its more or less covert pressure, creating a dialectic with the new reading that finally brings to light a more complex and inclusive angle of vision. Paul's interpretive freedom and the return of the repressed plain meaning rest on the same foundation: confidence in the reliability of God's promises, where "confidence" (we recall) is not the same as certain knowledge. Only the recovery of that confidence might enable the postmodern interpreter, not surely to replicate the peculiar dialectic of Paul's interpretive moves, but to discover an analogous kind of dialectic. To describe what this dialectic might look like would require discussion of a number of complicated issues, such as the status of the canon.[40] At minimum, however, the dialectic would have to include the polarity between the historical meanings and functions of the texts that are reconstructed by the modern critic, on the one hand, and the premodern figural and postmodern theological readings of the same texts. My modest proposal is that historical-critical exegesis could thus play a role analogous to that of the plain sense, as Paul's contemporaries understood it, vis à vis his charismatic misreadings. That is, historical exegesis would relinquish its modernist role as umpire, no longer authorized simply to declare contemporizing interpretations "safe" or "out." Instead, it would act as a kind of *advocatus diaboli*, standing up for the past in a dialogue between Then and Now. There would be a certain poetic justice in this form of dialectic, for it was the triumph of modernist exegesis in redefining the plain sense in historical, referential terms that brought about the fateful rupture between religious and academic readings that is now so thoroughly institutionalized.[41]

A Community of Interpretation

The interpretive process we see in the letter to the Romans is a social process in two senses.[42] First, obviously, interpretation takes place

---

[40] Paul's own "canon," in the sense of those parts of the Bible he used or alluded to, is both quite selective—mainly Genesis, Deuteronomy, Isaiah, Job, the Psalms, and the Twelve (Koch, *Schrift als Zeuge*, 345-46)—and loose, in the sense that he formally cites texts that are not in our canon and in some cases not even identifiable.

[41] Hans W. Frei, *The Eclipse of Biblical Narrative: A Study in Eighteenth and Nineteenth Century Hermeneutics* (New Haven and London: Yale University Press, 1974). See, too, his further reflections in "The 'Literal Reading' of Biblical Narratives in the Christian Tradition: Does It Stretch or Will it Break?" in *The Bible and the Narrative Tradition* (ed. Frank McConnell; New York: Oxford, 1986) 36-77. My proposal is very close to that of George Lindbeck, "The Story-shaped Church: Critical Exegesis and Theological Interpretation" in *Scriptural Authority and Narrative Interpretation* (ed. Garrett Green; Philadelphia: Fortress, 1986) 161-77, although I find the canonical witness more disparate and the needed dialectic more ambiguous than he.

[42] The point I am making is different from Hays's description of Paul's interpretation as "ecclesiocentric" (*Echoes* chap. 3.), though the two are related. He means that the People

within a community and is only possible at all if there are shared elements of knowledge and practice upon which the three-way communication among texts (including traditions), interpreter, and readers can depend. Second, community is not only the context but also the goal of interpretation. Interpretive practice constitutes the community, forms and reforms it. Both sides of the dialectic are evident in several ways in Paul's dialogue with the Roman Christians.

The argument of the letter can be understood by the recipients only if they are a certain kind of group that shares a number of things with Paul. For example, they share a special group-language. They share a certain set of practices in which the specific interpretive practice required to understand the letter is embedded. Among these practices are rituals to which Paul can make specific allusion (chap. 6) and even the custom of assembling regularly in household groups (some of which are named in chap. 16), where the letter will be read aloud, within the context of familiar, customary activities.

These groups occupy a certain social space, constituted by the households within which they have been formed. Among the practical consequences of this arrangement are some that bear on Paul's principal theme in the letter and its corollary that he takes up in these chapters: the relationship between "Israel after the flesh," which is embodied in Rome in several large synagogues, and the Christian groups comprising "Jew and Greek" without διαστολή. The groups to which Paul writes consist predominantly of Gentiles, but several of the individuals he mentions by name in chap. 16 are Jewish Christians, and there must be a significant minority of them in at least some of the household groups. Thus, even though I do not share the opinion of many commentators that the letter is written primarily to deal with tensions between Gentiles and Jews in the Roman congregations,[43] it is clear that the groups in some measure embody the situation Paul presupposes in chaps. 9-11, whether or not it is for them a "problem." The larger social whole within which those Christian groups are embedded also affects the communication between Paul and his audience in complex ways. As one example, consider the communities of discourse implied by Paul's using not only the Greek language but also rhetorical conventions.

---

of God is the central character, along with God, in Paul's scriptural story. For the notion of "the hermeneutic community" with a somewhat different profile than the one I would draw, see John Howard Yoder, "The Hermeneutics of Peoplehood" in *The Priestly Kingdom: Social Ethics as Gospel* (Notre Dame: University of Notre Dame Press, 1984) 15-45.

[43] For a variety of views on this point, see, e.g., the collection of essays in *The Romans Debate* (ed. Karl P. Donfried; Minneapolis: Augsburg, 1977).

On the other hand, the functions as well as the context of the letter to the Romans are communal. The letter itself is an instrument for initiating a direct relationship and enlarging an indirect relationship between Paul and the Roman Christians. To this end, it interprets Paul's own career (1:5-17; 15:14-29) and "his gospel." However, it obviously does much more than is strictly necessary for Paul's personal self-introduction. The letter interprets God's action in Christ in such a way that a coherent practice is the appropriate response to that action. For that reason, chaps. 12-15 follow naturally and necessarily on chaps. 1-11.[44]

The obstacles in the way of a community-centered and community-forming interpretation today are formidable, but not insuperable. First, the churches must find ways to overcome the absence of even the most rudimentary knowledge of the contents of biblical texts that now prevails in all but a few fundamentalist denominations. A more difficult obstacle is the structural distance between professional interpreters and the life of the churches that has been built into our academic and ecclesiastical institutions. This distance did not first arise with the recent growth of departments of religious studies in secular universities and the consequent creation of peer communities of professionals with values distinct from those of religious groups, although that development has obviously exacerbated the division. A deeper root of the problem lies, ironically, in earlier professionalization of the Reformation emphasis on "the Word of God" into the belief that the only appropriate mode of interpretation was "theological." The concept of religion implicit in this development was cognitivist.[45] Its social matrix was a professional hierarchy whose apex was in a theological seminary. Exegetical scholars determined the correct meanings of scripture. Theologians reflected on these meanings and produced correct theological beliefs, which they taught to preachers. Preachers retailed the product to religious consumers. Whether the occupants of the hierarchy were "conservative" or "liberal" made little difference to the structure itself. Romantic reactions to idea-centered religion, whether pietist or existentialist, were potentially more interested in the life of the community, but this potential was blocked by the dominant subjectivism and individualism of those movements.

If the present distance of the biblical texts from the world of the laity is to be overcome, it will be by efforts within the congregations

---

[44] See Meeks, "Judgment and the Brother."

[45] See George Lindbeck, *The Nature of Doctrine: Religion and Theology in a Postliberal Age* (Philadelphia: Westminster, 1984).

themselves. However, some changed perspectives visible here and there in the professional hierarchy may help. On the part of biblical specialists, there are reasons to hope for some boundary-crossings between the two most innovative directions in current scholarship, the one aiming to reconstruct the social history of early Christian movements, the other a text-centered literary reading. Conversation between social historians and literary critics is by no means guaranteed to produce readings directly helpful for religious communities, but at least the results may not be simply irrelevant. On the theological side, there are calls for recognition that the proper context and aim of interpretation are not merely ideas or attitudes, but ethos and practice.[46] Thus the possibility for a creative dialogue may be emerging.

Reading Eschatologically

The phrase "but now" that introduces decisive points in Paul's arguments (like Rom 3:21) reminds us that for him what justified his novel interpretations was the conviction that God had done a new and final thing. The meaning of the past is therefore gathered and refocused on the present moment and on the community it has brought into existence (1 Cor 10:6,11; Rom 15:4).[47] Yet how can that conviction have the same force for us, living nearly two millenia after Paul died? Beker's insistence on the literalness of Paul's belief that the Parousia of Christ would come in his own time and on the inextricability of that belief from the whole of Paul's theology is a necessary warning against the ease with which we gloss over the problem, too large to handle here.[48]

Nevertheless, language about final things does a number of different kinds of work for Paul as for every apocalyptic writer. It will be enough for the moment to observe what such language is doing in Romans 9-11. The most prominent instance of what John Gager calls "end-time language"[49] in these chapters is obviously Paul's statement that Christ is the τέλος of the law (10:4). I have argued above, following Paul

---

[46] Lindbeck, "Story-shaped Church"; Nicholas Lash, "Performing the Scriptures" in *Theology on the Way to Emmaus*, 37-46; Michael G. Cartwright, "The Practice and Performance of Scripture: Grounding Christian Ethics in a Communal Hermeneutic," *The Annual of the Society of Christian Ethics* (1988) 31-53. See also Wayne A. Meeks, "A Hermeneutics of Social Embodiment," *HTR* 79 (1986) 176-86.

[47] Cf. Hays, *Echoes*, 168-73.

[48] Beker, *Paul the Apostle*.

[49] John Gager, "Functional Diversity in Paul's Use of End-Time Language," *JBL* 89 (1970) 325-37.

Meyer, that "end" in this sentence cannot merely mark the close of a period of time nor can it announce the termination of the validity of Torah. What it does is transform the way in which Torah, and therefore also the history of Israel, is to be read. That new way of reading is precisely what Paul's paradoxes in Romans 9-11 are designed to exemplify, and the course of his argument shows that the τέλος is at the same time a new beginning.

Because the End does not signify a Stop, but a new dialectic, the other prominent use of end-time language in these chapters, in 11:25-32, signals that this present time when the End has been manifested is not yet "final." It cannot be final because it has introduced a social contradiction, in Paul's understanding of God's purpose, that must yet be resolved. The contradiction is this: Christ as the End of the law has brought together Jew and Gentile into one community of the one God, abolishing the διαστολή that separated them—but in such a way that the novelty has "offended" (as the stone of stumbling) Israel-according-to-the-flesh. Thus the unity of Jew and Gentile within the church is purchased at the price of separation between the believers in Christ and empirical Israel. Paul does not allow that reversal of calling and privilege to remain the last word. The reversal itself becomes a model of God's way of acting mercifully, and thus guarantees (11:30-31) that there will be a precisely analogous reversal, in the future, of Israel's standing. He reserves God's freedom to act, yet again, in an unexpected way.

In that case, however, we are squarely up against the problem that, as Hans Frei says, "has been mentioned by commentators from Gotthold Ephraim Lessing to Frank Kermode." The problem is whether the NT narratives of Jesus are "unsurpassable," or whether their "literal sense" only "prefigures a still newer reading that displaces it in turn."[50] At this difficult point the example of Paul's dialectical reading may save us from having to choose between relativism and fanaticism. We can hardly doubt that the Christ narrative (as Paul construed it) is unsurpassable—but in the same way that God's election and promises to Israel are "irrevocable." It is within this context that perhaps we can try to understand and to make fruitful for our present situation Paul's isolated and astonishing statement in 1 Cor 15:24-28, which says quite

---

[50] Frei, "Literal Reading," 42. Frei raises the question in connection with his criticism of phenomenological hermeneutics, particularly as practiced by David Tracy, but it is clear that the "unsurpassability" (50) of the *sensus literalis* is central to his own constructive aims. He argues that hermeneutical theory cannot protect the irreplaceable Jesus story, while a less theory-laden narrative reading can. Cf. Lindbeck, "Story-shaped Church," 164.

explicitly that the time will come when the reign of Christ will be surpassed, and "God will be all in all."

Is it possible for us, as it evidently was for Paul, to hold fast to Christ as the image of God, the πνεῦμα that takes away the veil from the heart and from the reading of scripture, the goal of the Torah, the embodiment of the wisdom and the righteousness of God—and still affirm with equanimity that not Christ but God is ultimate? In the necessary and desirable pluralism of the world we have now irreversibly entered, this is a question of fundamental significance. The alternative to pluralist relativism need not be fanaticism, although evidence for that kind of religious and cultural polarization is all around us. A faithful hermeneutic of the Pauline kind, however, requires confidence in the God who, determined to have mercy on all and to bring into being the things that are not, will astonish those who are loyal to the story of God's past actions, but will not abandon them.

8

Romans 15:4—An Interpolation?

Leander E. Keck [1]

Take nothing for granted! This may well be the First Commandment of exegesis. Paul Meyer himself heeded this imperative when he argued that in Rom 9:32-33 the offending "stone" was not what exegetes assumed it was (Christ) but the law.[2] There are other NT passages where a close reading suggests that what has been taken for granted merits another look, and perhaps an alternative view. Such a passage is Rom 15:4: ὅσα γὰρ προεγράφη, εἰς τὴν ἡμετέραν διδασκαλίαν ἐγράφη, ἵνα διὰ τῆς ὑπομονῆς καὶ διὰ τῆς παρακλήσεως τῶν γραφῶν τὴν ἐλπίδα ἔχωμεν, which the RSV renders as, "For whatever was written in former days was written for our instruction, that by steadfastness and by the encouragement of the scriptures we might have hope."[3]

---

[1] Leander E. Keck is Winkley Professor of Biblical Theology at the Yale University Divinity School, New Haven, Connecticut.

[2] Paul W. Meyer, "Romans 10:4 and the 'End' of the Law" in *The Divine Helmsman: Studies on God's Control of Human Events, Presented to Lou H. Silberman* (ed. J. L. Crenshaw and S. Sandmel; New York: KTAV, 1980) 59-64.

[3] The NEB translates freely: "For all the ancient scriptures were written for our own instruction, in order that through the encouragement they give us we may maintain our hope with fortitude." The New JB reads: "And all these things which were written so long ago were written so that we, learning perseverance and the encouragement which the scriptures give, should have hope."

I

Commentators regularly refer to Rom 4:23-24; 1 Cor 9:9; 10:11 where Paul also claims that scripture was written for our benefit, and observe that in our passage Paul justifies having used, in v. 3, a christologically-interpreted quotation from Psalm 69 (LXX 68) in order to exhort "the strong" to bear with "the weak" instead of "pleasing" themselves. In other words, for Paul "the reproaches of those who reproached you [God] fell on me [Christ]" shows that Christ did not please himself, and so "the strong" are not to please themselves either. It is almost universally taken for granted that Paul wrote v. 4 in this important paragraph which brings to a head the discussion begun at 14:1. Because this assumption creates certain problems, another possibility deserves to be considered.

One begins to surmise that something is amiss here when one notes that competent commentators struggle in vain to illumine the text convincingly. Long ago, Zahn[4] saw two problems with v. 4, a major and a minor one. The latter is scarcely susceptible to a satisfactory explanation: Why did Paul, having audaciously adduced many OT quotations without justification (apart from 4:24), provide a legitimation for this one precisely here? More serious is the other observation: despite the γάρ, which clearly signals that what follows is to be regarded as warrant, there is actually no substantial connection between v. 3 and v. 4. Verse 3 uses scripture to characterize the entire life of Christ, but v. 4 concerns the Christian use of scripture "so that we might have hope." Zahn's own view of v. 4 is also unsatisfactory, however: it develops vv. 1-2 and prepares for vv. 9-10 the way v. 3 prepares for vv. 7-8.

It is instructive to note how commentators who are sensitive to the problems generated by v. 4 cope with them. Bernhard Weiss claims that "it corresponds to the free movement of the Apostle's thought that here, where he provides the purpose of such instruction through the scripture because the quoted passage speaks of suffering, he drops completely the relation to this special point for which he had adduced it, and speaks instead of the attitude of the Christian in suffering generally."[5] In other words, Paul's mind wandered as he dictated. This is possible, but hardly likely in so important a paragraph.

---

[4] Theodor Zahn, *Der Brief des Paulus an die Römer* (Leipzig: Deichert [Georg Böhme], 1910) 592-593.

[5] Bernhard Weiss, *Handbuch über den Brief des Paulus an die Römer* (KEK; Göttingen: Vandenhoeck & Ruprecht, 1886) 633- 636.

More recently, Barrett not only finds it necessary to put v. 4 in parentheses but virtually gives up trying to explain the verse in its context, saying that although Paul's real meaning may have been that "scripture exhorts us to endure in hope, and gives us good ground for doing so," one must admit that "this is not what he says."[6]

This admission is preferable to Dodd's actually substituting what we would say for what Paul wrote:

> [The words of scripture were] written in intention for contemporaries; but..., since there is a unity in the spiritual history of man, they have an application beyond their original intention whenever the like spiritual conditions and needs recur; and, further, so close is the unity of the spiritual history represented in the Bible, that there is nothing of permanent religious value in the Old Testament which has no application to Christ and, through Him, to Christians.[7]

Recently Wedderburn too has rewritten the point of v. 4, claiming that for Paul, "if the Roman Christians would heed the Old Testament scriptures they would have hope;" therefore the Apostle "points back to the Old Testament to the recurring pattern of suffering of God's faithful down the centuries."[8] Even if that were the point of the text, it would not justify the use of the quotation of Psalm 69.

Even the comments of Käsemann, who ponders this passage more carefully than most, show how difficult it is to make sense of v. 4 as a warrant for quoting the Psalm, for he must rely on rather far-reaching observations to interpret the text. One may agree that for Paul "scripture documents in advance what takes place eschatologically in correspondence of primal time and end-time," but is it pertinent to continue, "*thus* it points to their [sc. its] destiny to instruct Christ's community in the way it should conduct itself"?[9] This comment seems more appropriate for 1 Cor 10:10. Likewise, one may agree that the material justification for the underlying hermeneutic is "beyond question if Christ himself speaks in the quotation;" but does it follow that "this circumstance *makes possible* a pedagogical reading of the Old Testament"?[10]. Surely 1 Clement's pedagogical reading of the OT was

---

[6] C. K. Barrett, *Romans* (New York: Harper & Bros., 1957) 270.

[7] C. H. Dodd, *Romans* (New York: Harper & Bros., 1932) 221-222.

[8] A. J. M. Wedderburn, *The Reasons for Romans* (Edinburgh: T. & T. Clark, 1988) 86.

[9] Ernst Käsemann, *Commentary on Romans* (Grand Rapids: Eerdmans, 1980) 382.

[10] Ibid., emphasis mine.

not made possible by this hermeneutic. Käsemann thinks that the surprising mention of hope in v. 4[11] points ahead to vv. 7-13, "the eschatological uniting of the church of Jews and Gentiles." It may well be true that "to be constantly oriented to that is an integral part of the Christian hope," but is it the function of v. 4 to prepare for *this* point? Despite Käsemann's objection, Michel is right in observing that v. 4 "sounds like an inserted precept" (*eingesprengter Lehrsatz*[12])—more precisely, as Wilckens has it, a "*hermeneutischer Lehrsatz*".[13] Although Koch's monograph on Paul's use of scripture[14] sees that v. 4 significantly exceeds what the context requires, its discussion of our verse is not illuminating, largely because, like Michel and Wilckens, it claims that Paul sees in the Psalm quotation (but not in the whole Psalm) a specific reference to Jesus' passion, not to the character of the Christ-event as a whole.[15] He claims that vv. 2-3 imply that Christ is the pattern for the church's life, but in denying that the quotation is used paraenetically, he fragments the line of thought even more.

Having noted some difficulties in interpreting v. 4 *in situ*, it is appropriate to look at this *Lehrsatz* in its own right.

II

Copyists too seem to have regarded v. 4 as an important precept; that is why they made sure that the text's wording was "right" by repeatedly "correcting" their predecessors. As a result, there are more textual variants for this verse than for all five surrounding verses combined. Not a clause has come down to us free of variant readings.

Whereas the vast majority of witnesses read ὅσα γὰρ προεγράφη, B, OL, and Clement eliminate the temporal reference (heightened by the RSV's "in former days" and NEB's "ancient") by reading simply

---

[11] Ibid., 383. Cranfield is only momentarily surprised, noting that hope is appropriate to the Christian life and that Paul had spoken of it frequently in Romans—as if these considerations accounted for its appearance here (*Romans* [ICC; Edinburgh: T. & T. Clark, 1979] 2.735.

[12] Otto Michel, *Der Brief an die Römer* (KEK; Göttingen: Vandenhoeck & Ruprecht, 1978] 319-320).

[13] Ulrich Wilckens, *Römer* (EKK; Zürich: Benziger/Neukirchen: Neukirchener, 1982) 3.100.

[14] Dietrich-Alex Koch, *Die Schrift als Zeuge des Evangeliums: Untersuchungen zur Verwendung und Verständnis der Schrift bei Paulus* (BHT 69; Tübingen: J. C. B. Mohr [Paul Siebeck], 1986) 324-26.

[15] Koch does, however, reject Wilckens's view that Paul sees in the Psalm an allusion to Christ's vicarious atonement.

ἐγράφη. Perhaps the copyists/translators regarded the προ- as redundant; for the author, however, the contrast between "then" and "now" was basic. In the undisputed Pauline letters προγράφειν is used elsewhere only in Gal 3:1, where it means the public placarding of Christ as crucified; here it clearly means "written previously" (though not earlier in the same text, as in Eph 3:3). To be noted is the all-encompassing ὅσα. One may well ask whether Paul would have found such a sweeping statement necessary to warrant the citation of Psalm 69—a point made by Koch (see above). That is, despite the γάρ, the scope of the subject matter overshoots what is required, but it is appropriate to a self-contained precept which has been inserted. The unlimited scope of it is reinforced by the πάντα which BP Ψ 33 pc sy insert at the beginning of the next clause, resulting in πάντα εἰς τὴν ἡμετέραν διδασκαλίαν. (Somewhat woodenly, A Ψ 048 sy^h and the majority of Greek MSS repeat προεγράφη instead of the more likely ἐγράφη.[16])

Paul uses διδασκαλία in Rom 12:7, where it means the activity of teaching; here, however, it means "instruction," but not the thing taught, as elsewhere in the NT (especially in the Pastorals: 1 Tim 4:13, 16; 2 Tim 3:10; Tit 2:7), according to BAGD 2. Here, then, we have a second item (προγράφειν being the first) in Paul's vocabulary used in a way not found elsewhere in Paul's own letters.[17]

Somewhat unclear is the long final clause stating the purpose or goal of being instructed by scripture: ἵνα διὰ τῆς ὑπομονῆς καὶ διὰ τῆς παρακλήσεως τῶν γραφῶν τὴν ἐλπίδα ἔχωμεν. (When B vg^ms and Clement add τῆς παρακλήσεως to ἐλπίδα they restrict the hope to that of more παράκλησις.) Were one to omit the second διὰ (as do DFGP Ψ as well as many Greek minuscules, OL and Clement), the text would claim that we have hope "through the ὑπομονή and παράκλησις of the scriptures." The second διὰ, however, distinguishes the one from the other, thereby saying that only the παράκλησις is derived from scripture. This leaves διὰ τῆς ὑπομονῆς as an independent phrase referring either to attendant circumstances (so most exegetes) or to a second means of maintaining hope. Rom 8:25 similarly uses the phrase in connection with hope: "and if we hope for what we do not see, δι' ὑπομονῆς

---

[16] To my knowledge, Junji Kinoshita is alone in reversing these readings. He contends that the text originally read ὅσα ἐγράφη...προέγραφη because this supports his reconstruction of the origin of the letter we now have (see below). "Romans—Two Writings Combined: A New Interpretation of the Book of Romans," *NovT* 7 (1965) 263.

[17] Whereas διδασκαλία occurs elsewhere in the undisputed letters only at 12:7, it is a key term in the Pastorals (15 of 21 occurrences), as Dunn notes without being suspicious of what this might imply for the genuineness of v. 4 (*Romans 9-16* [Dallas: Word, 1988] 839-840).

ἀπεκδεχόμεθα;" but in 5:4 δοκιμή is the middle term between ὑπομονή and ἐλπίς. The phrase in 15:4 is therefore either Paul's own paraphrase of the idea that steadfast endurance strengthens hope or the interpolator's imitation of Paul. Either way, of course, one must ask how this disposition in which Christians are to hope justifies appealing to Ps 69:9, understood as Christ's own statement characterizing his experience.

Not to be overlooked is the fact that v. 5 goes on to speak of "the God τῆς ὑπομονῆς καὶ τῆς παρακλήσεως" as the initial phrase of the homiletic benediction.[18] In the Pauline homologoumena these benedictions sometimes take up a key word in the preceding line (e.g., in Rom 15:13 "the God of hope" takes up ἐλπιοῦσιν in the foregoing clause; in 2 Cor 13:11 "the God of love and peace" takes up the concluding word of a series of imperatives, εἰρηνεύετε. Only here, however, is the repetition so extensive. Michael suggested that it results from dittography: a copyist mistakenly inserted τῆς ὑπομονῆς καὶ διὰ τῆς παρακλήσεως into v. 4, which originally read simply ἐγράφη ἵνα διὰ τῶν γραφῶν τὴν ἐλπίδα ἔχωμεν. This error was then followed by another—the insertion of the first διὰ (resulting in διὰ τῆς ὑπομονῆς κτλ) because it was felt that ὑπομονή does not go well with τῶν γραφῶν. Those MSS which omit the second διὰ (reading καὶ ὑπομονῆς καὶ τῆς παρακλήσεως κτλ. as noted above) thus reflect "an intermediate stage when the words τῆς ὑπομονῆς κτλ. had been brought from v. 5 but διὰ had not yet been inserted."[19] Although Michael claims to have found analogous evidence elsewhere in Romans, the reconstruction is too complex to be persuasive. Nonetheless, he may have pointed in the right direction: instead of positing an accidental dittography on the part of an early copyist, one can also posit an interpolator who formulated v. 4a in such a way as to provide a transition to v. 5.

According to v. 4, "whatever was written previously was written for our instruction, so that through patient endurance and through the encouragement[20] of the scriptures we might have hope." Conceptually,

---

[18] See Robert Jewett, "The Form and Function of the Homiletic Benediction," *ATR* 51 (1969) 18-34. Gordon Wiles calls this a "prayer wish." See his formal analysis in *Paul's Intercessory Prayers* (SNTSMS 24; Cambridge: Cambridge University Press, 1974) 29-44 (exegetical discussion on pp. 79-83).

[19] J. Hugh Michael, "A Phenomenon in the Text of Romans," *JTS* 39 (1983) 150-154.

[20] The precise meaning of παράκλησις here is not obvious, partly because the word itself has a range of meanings (e.g., exhortation, encouragement, comfort, consolation), and partly because v. 5 refers to ὁ θεός...τῆς παρακλήσεως. If Paul wrote both v. 4 and v. 5, one expects the term to have the same meaning in the adjacent uses. But if v. 4 is an

no less than stylistically, this is an assertion complete in itself (apart from γάρ). Moreover, here the didactic purpose of scripture is given a clear pastoral horizon. What is not clear, however, is the relation between the human ὑπομονή and the scriptures' παράκλησις—a gap which Barrett tries to fill (see above). It is more important, however, to ask what situation is envisaged by this "hermeneutical precept." Although ὑπομονή has a range of meanings from patience to perseverence, it is frequently associated with endurance, especially of some degree of opposition or suffering. When the reader is assured in v. 4a that endurance is the means of hope, we may infer that in the shadow lurks the danger that unfavorable circumstances might diminish, if not eliminate, hope. In this light, the "encouragement of the scriptures" reminds the reader that scripture is a key resource in time of trouble. In other words, taken by itself, v. 4, as a *Lehrsatz* in its own right, would be an appropriate precept for readers in need of heartening in the midst of suffering. It is more germane to such readers than to the original readers of Romans 15.

The more clearly the nature and thrust of v. 4 come into view, the more problematic is its function in 15:1-6. On the one hand, the pastoral problem it envisages is quite different from that presented by the tensions between "the weak" and "the strong." Paul, one surmises, would scarcely have regarded "bearing with" the weak as a matter calling for ὑπομονή , especially since he characterizes it more simply as "not pleasing oneself" (v. 2). Moreover, had Paul wanted to draw a parallel between Christ's accepting the ὀνειδισμοί and Christian endurance, he could easily have written of Christ's ὑπομονή; instead, he drew a parallel between Christ's not pleasing himself and what he asks of "the strong." In other words, Zahn is right: v. 4 does not support vv. 1-

---

interpolation, then somewhat different meanings are possible—though one result of the interpolation is the assimilation of one meaning to another. Barrett uses "exhortation" for both verses, whereas Käsemann, followed by Cranfield, holds that in v. 5 (as well as in v. 4) it "obviously" means "comfort" and refers to 1 Macc 12:9 as an "excellent parallel" to this understanding. But it is at least questionable whether this is what 1 Maccabees means. The alleged parallel is found in the quoted letter from Jonathan to the Spartans (12:6-18). Jonathan, having reported receiving a letter from the Spartan king affirming that Spartans and Jews are brothers, says that such a letter is not needed: "therefore, though we have no need of such things, since we have as παράκλησις [RSV: encouragement] the holy books which are in our hands, we have undertaken to send to renew our brotherhood and friendship with you," etc. Since he goes on to mention recent victories, it appears that the RSV is correct in rendering παράκλησις as "encouragement" rather than "comfort" or "consolation" (new JB). Indeed, Jonathan A. Goldstein explicitly rejects "comfort" and translates "'source of courage' for men at war" (*1 Maccabees* [AB 41; Garden City: Doubleday, 1976] 453).

3. Nor, on the other hand, does v. 4 flow naturally into vv. 5-6, despite the reference to the God τῆς ὑπομονῆς καὶ τῆς παρακλήσεως, because these verses not only bring us back to the pastoral problem in Rome but explicitly remind the readers of Christ's example, thereby continuing the thought of vv. 1-3: τὸ αὐτὸ φρονεῖν ἐν ἀλλήλοις κατὰ Χριστὸν Ἰησοῦν, ἵνα ὁμοθυμαδὸν ἐν ἑνὶ στόματι δοξάζητε τὸν Θεὸν κτλ. In short, v. 4 does have all the marks of being an *eingesprengter Lehrsatz*, for which it is difficult to hold Paul responsible.

III

We cannot ignore the fact that elsewhere Paul says seemingly similar things about scripture. In Rom 4:23-24 he concludes his discussion of Abraham by asserting that the "it was reckoned to him" (sc. Abraham) of Gen 15:6 was written not only for his sake but also for ours as well. The argument of this chapter lays the foundation for this claim: Abraham's πίστις and Christian πίστις are structurally the same; therefore, what applies to him must apply also to everyone who has πίστις. How does this passage compare with 15:4? Even if Paul regards Genesis 15 as εἰς τὴν ἡμετέραν διδασκαλίαν ἐγράφη, the rest of v. 4a clearly has a quite different scope and thrust. The two passages would be much closer if in Romans 4 Paul were to treat Abraham as an example which Christians are urged to imitate or from which they might draw encouragement. That, however, is precisely what Paul does not say and cannot say. Moreover, in Romans 4 the view of scripture grows intimately and clearly out of the foregoing discussion, whereas in Rom 15:4 it does not. What the two passages share is the conviction that scripture pertains to the current reader, but that does not yet establish common authorship, for what early Christian would not have thought the same?

More relevant is 1 Cor 9:9. Here Paul, as a warrant for his right to church support, cites Deut 25:4: "You shall not muzzle the ox when it is treading out the grain," and comments, "Is it for oxen that God is concerned? Does he not speak entirely for our sake? It was written for our sake (δι' ἡμᾶς γὰρ ἐγράφη), because the plowman should plow in hope," etc. Paul shares a common hermeneutic with Hellenistic Jewish authors. Josephus, commenting on the same text, says, "for it is not just to exclude from the fruit your fellow laborers who toiled to produce it" (*Ant.* IV 233), likewise deflecting the original point of the text from concern for animals to concern for humans. The Letter to Aristeas makes the same move with regard to Lev 11:29, which includes the weasel and the mouse in the list of "unclean" animals:

> For you must not fall into the degrading idea that it was out of regard to mice and weasels and other such things that Moses drew up the laws with such exceeding care. All these ordinances were made for the sake of righteousness to aid the quest for virtue and the the perfecting of character (144).

The author then points out that the forbidden birds are wild and tyrannize others; usable birds, however, are tame—a sign that one is to practice righteousness and not tyrannize people (145-49). He summarizes:

> Wherefore all the rules which he has laid down with regard to what is permitted in the case of the birds and other animals he has enacted with the object of teaching us a moral lesson (150).

Philo repeatedly relies on the same interpretive strategy. For example, he says that the careful inspection of sacrificial animals to verify that they are unblemished represents

> the reformation of your conduct, for the law does not prescribe for unreasoning creatures, but for those who have mind and reason. It is anxious not that the victims should be without flaw [as clear a reversal of the text's literal meaning as Paul's statement] but that those who offer them should not suffer from any corroding passion (*de spec. Leg.* I.260).

What Paul shares with these texts is the assumption that a literal reading of such laws is misleading, and that a moral, human-oriented meaning is in fact the true one. In other words, Rom 15:4a, with its ὅσα προεγράφη reflects a common idea, and could have been written by an interpolator as well as by Paul.

In 1 Cor 10:6,11 Paul's comment about scripture justifies his use of Israel's wilderness experience to insist that baptism and eucharist do not guarantee salvation: "And these things happened as our τύποι " (v. 6); "and these things happened τυπικῶς to them but ἐγράφη δὲ πρὸς νουθεσίαν ἡμῶν (for our admonition [RSV: instruction]), upon whom the end of the ages has come" (v. 11). Given the focus on Israel's negative experiences, it is appropriate for Paul to claim that these events were written down for νουθεσίαν ἡμῶν , admonitory instructions, or warning (as the RSV renders in v. 6).[21] Interestingly, Wisd 16:6 also

---

[21] Johannes Behm, "νουθετέω, νουθεσία" in *TDNT* 4.1019-1022.

regards these events as having occurred for νουθεσία—but for the benefit of the Israelites who experienced them, not for the current reader of the text—at least not directly.[22]

Rom 15:4 is not inconsistent with these other Pauline passages, to be sure. At the same time, while they all express Paul's intent to relate the biblical text to his immediate readers, his statements should not be fused into a single "doctrine of scripture" because each has its own accent and horizon. Moreover, each statement is integral to its context—a characteristic absent from 15:4. None of them sounds like an *eingesprengter Lehrsatz*.

In certain respects, the passage closest to Rom 15:4 is found in a post-Pauline text that claims to be from Paul—2 Tim 3:16-17. Although this passage grounds the moral value of scripture in its inspired origin, here too the primary value is in its instruction, and its goal is stated in a clause (as in Rom 15:4), formulated to reflect the vocation of Timothy:

πᾶσα γραφὴ θεόπνευστος καὶ ὠφέλιμος πρὸς διδασκαλίαν, πρὸς ἐλεγμόν, πρὸς ἐπανόρθωσιν, πρὸς παιδείαν τὴν ἐν δικαιοσύνῃ, ἵνα ἄρτιος ᾖ ὁ τοῦ θεοῦ ἄνθρωπος, πρὸς πᾶν ἔργον ἀγαθὸν ἐξηρτισμένος.

Whereas 2 Tim 3:16 finds the *utility* of scripture in its διδασκαλία, Rom 15:4 sees διδασκαλία as its original *intent*. Although 2 Tim 3:15 (ἀπὸ βρέφους τὰ ἱερὰ γράμματα οἶδας) prepares for vv. 16-17, v. 16 too can stand alone as a *Lehrsatz*, made particularly pertinent to Timothy only by v. 17.

IV

It must be admitted that the data adduced do not demonstrate that Rom 15:4 is an interpolation. But neither do they disallow this possibility. What we are dealing with is a possibility suggested by the major difficulty presented by the text—the lack of continuity between v. 3 and v. 4. Omitting v. 4 improves the flow of thought, but there still remains the somewhat abrupt transition from v. 3 to vv. 5-6, and one is

---

[22] The Wisdom of Solomon is interested primarily in the transient character of the plague of serpents in Numbers 21 in order to emphasize God's gracious salvation provided by the bronze serpent. "Even when...they were perishing through the bites of the tortuous serpents, your anger did not abide to the end; only for a while were they thrown into disarray as a warning (νουθεσία), possessing as they did a symbol of your salvation to remind them of the commandment of your law" (16:6). See David Winston, *The Wisdom of Solomon* (AB 43; Garden City: Doubleday, 1979) 294.

left with the question, Why was the *Lehrsatz* inserted precisely here? Nonetheless, on the whole, depending on how seriously one takes the problematic phenomena of the text, it is probably less troublesome to trace them to the hand of an interpolator than to the drifting mind of the Apostle.

It is also simpler to regard only v. 4 as an interpolation than to see here one of the results of an editor's having spliced together two Pauline letters, as Schmithals does.[23] His solution to the problems of v. 4 and its immediate context in 15:1-13 is part of a bold, comprehensive reconstruction of the history of the whole text of Romans. He proposes that the editor of the Pauline corpus created the present letter out of three letters from Paul, two of them destined for Rome (Letter A: 1:1-4:25 + 5:12-11:36 + 15:8-13, sent when Paul's trip to Rome was delayed; and Letter B: 12:1-21 + 13:8-10 + 14:1-15:4a, 7, 5-6 + 15:11-14); one to Ephesus (16:1-20); plus fragments of correspondence originally sent to Thessalonica (5:2-11; 13:1-7, 11-14); plus marginal glosses of various origins (2:11,13,16; 5:6-7; 6:17b; 7:25b; 8:1; 10:17) as well as passages he himself wrote—our 15:4b and perhaps 5:1. Subsequently 16:24 was added. This reconstruction has not found acceptance.[24] For the purposes of this essay, it is to be noted that, on the one hand, Schmithals retains the first clause of v. 4 ("whatever was written previously was written for our instruction") because he sees it continued in v. 7 ("Therefore welcome one another as also Christ has welcomed you for the glory of God"), while on the other hand he "restores" the homiletic benediction to its allegedly "original" place after v. 7 and assigns vv. 8-13 to the previous letter altogether. At the same time, he overlooks the difficulty which is important for this essay—the transition from v. 3 to v. 4.[25] Seeing the hand of an

---

[23] Walter Schmithals, *Der Römerbrief als historisches Problem* (Götersloh: Götersloher, 1975).

[24] See, e.g., Wedderburn, *The Reasons for Romans*, 25-29.

[25] Even less convincing is Kinoshita's view ("Romans—Two Writings Combined," 263) that 15:4-13 is Paul's postscript which he added to his previously-composed "Manual of Instruction of Jewish Problems" (2:1-5, 17-29; 3:1-20; 3:27-4:25; 5:12-21; 6:1- 7:25; 9:1-11:36; 14:1-15:3), when he sent it to Ephesus, having used it previously for his teaching duties. The original letter to the Romans, a wholly Gentile church, consisted of 1:1-31; 2:6-16; 3:21-26; 5:1-11; 8:1-39; 12:1-13:14; 15:14-33. In this reconstruction our passage plays a key role. Having argued that the original text read ὅσα ἐγράφη (see above), Kinoshita claims that this means "the whole which was written here"—namely, the Manual; the reference to the "writings" (τῶν γραφῶν) also refers to this booklet. This yields the following meaning for 15:4:
 All the writings up to this point (namely, "the manual") were written previously, for the help of our (Paul and his fellow teachers') teaching the people (mainly for the

interpolator in v. 4 is also preferable to regarding all of 14:1-15:13 (or 15:6) as non-Pauline, as do John O'Neill and Winsome Munro,[26] although the former does regard v. 4 as an originally independent saying whose inclusion here was prompted by v. 3.

Increasingly it is recognized that one or more editors have left their marks on the letter to the Romans, as well as on the Pauline corpus as a whole.[27] Students must rely on internal considerations, such as those reviewed here, with but limited external evidence, in order to detect possible additions to the text. Whether such considerations are sufficient to reclassify what is proposed here for 15:4 from "possible" to "probable" will, I suspect, depend largely on one's overall assumptions about the formation and transmission of the Pauline corpus. Concretely, it is not so much the commonplace content of v. 4 as its intended function, signalled by the troublesome γάρ, that prompts one to ask seriously whether this verse might be an interpolation. In any case, that Paul wrote 15:4 should no longer be taken for granted.

Jews but not excluding the Gentiles) that by the steadfastness and the encouragement of these writings (namely, "the manual") we (Paul and his co-workers including the readers of the manual) might have hope.

[26] O'Neill regards chap. 14 as a collection of post-Pauline sayings (he finds 22 aphorisms); 15:1-13 is a similar, though earlier post-Pauline collection which had already been added to the original Romans before chap. 14 was inserted after 13:14 (*Paul's Letter to the Romans* [Harmondsworth: Penguin, 1975] 220-22; 234-36). Winsome Munro (*Authority in Paul and Peter: The Identification of a Pastoral Stratum in the Pauline Corpus and 1 Peter* [SNTSMS 45; Cambridge: Cambridge University Press, 1983]) argues that "subjectivist" teachings in much of the NT are not "isolated interpolations accrued haphazardly" but are part of a "later, redactional stratum extending across the ten-letter Pauline collection and 1 Peter," and come from the same (or similar) source as the Pastorals (p. 1). To this Trito-Pauline stratum belongs Rom 14:1-15:6. Were this bold thesis to be substantiated, it would account for the similarity between Rom 15:4 and 2 Tim 3:16-17.

[27] See the proposals, and the literature cited by William O. Walker, Jr., "Text Critical Evidence for Interpolations in the Letters of Paul," *CBQ* 50 (1988) 622-23; see also his "The Burden of Proof in Identifying Interpolations in the Pauline Letters," *NTS* 33 (1987) 610-15, as well as my contribution to the Erich Dinkler Festschrift, "The Post-Pauline Interpretation of Jesus' Death in Romans 5:6-7" in *Theologia Crucis Signum Crucis* (ed. C. Anderson and G. Klein; Tübingen: J. C. B. Mohr [Paul Siebeck] 1979) 237-48.

9

The Wisdom of God as Apocalyptic Power

E. Elizabeth Johnson [1]

Several peculiar features of 1 Cor 1:18-2:16 raise questions about its interpretation. The subject itself—wisdom and foolishness—is touched on nowhere else in Paul, although individual elements of the argument are reminiscent of passages from other letters.[2] In many respects, this is a familiar Pauline argument, although its substance is unique. Of Paul's 32 uses of σοφός and σοφία, 28 occur in 1 Corinthians, 26 of these in the first three chapters.[3] Why is it that Paul speaks at length of wisdom only here? Does this talk of wisdom originate with the Apostle or does he simply react to the Corinthians' fascination with wisdom?

Equally perplexing is the use to which Paul puts this wisdom language. He speaks of at least two kinds of wisdom—the wisdom of the world and the wisdom of God (1:20-21)—but, although presumably he knows God's wisdom, he disavows any wisdom of his own at 1:17 and

---

[1] E. Elizabeth Johnson is Associate Professor of New Testament at New Brunswick Theological Seminary, New Brunswick, New Jersey.

[2] The gospel is the power of God also at Rom 1:16 (cf. 15:19; 1 Thess 1:5), those who claim to be wise apart from God are made foolish in Rom 1:22, the wisdom of God is praised in Rom 11:33-36, and the gospel is a scandal to Jews at Rom 9:33 and Gal 5:11; the theme of weakness and strength recurs at 2 Cor 11:30-12:10 and 13:3-4, the prohibition of boasting at Rom 3:27ff; 11:18ff; 2 Cor 5:12; 11:12; Gal 6:13-14; Phil 3:13, and the work of the Spirit at 1 Cor 12:1ff and Rom 8:1ff; and the rhetorical question Paul quotes from Isa 40:13 in 1 Cor 2:16 is quoted also at Rom 11:34.

[3] Except for Rom 1:22, all of Paul's uses of μωραίνω, μωρία, and μωρός are in 1 Corinthians 1-4.

2:1-5 only to claim at 2:6 that he does speak wisdom among the τέλειοι. Does he or does he not have a wisdom teaching, and if so, of what does it consist?

Most troubling of all is the fact that, in the context of an argument which claims to counter the Corinthians' divisions, Paul himself appears to make distinctions among believers—between ψυχικοί and πνευματικοί at 2:14-15, and between τέλειοι in 2:6 and νήπιοι in 3:1-2. Does Paul, as Ulrich Wilckens suggests, suddenly speak here as a gnostic who shares his esoteric wisdom teaching only with special initiates among his churches?[4] Or does he rather, as Robin Scroggs and Hans Conzelmann maintain, merely acknowledge the existence of different spiritual abilities among believers?[5]

The distinctiveness of the argument's theme has led a number of interpreters—notably Hans Windisch and his successors[6]—to look beyond 1 Corinthians for Paul's further use of sapiential ideas, if not always wisdom language, with the result that they find in Col 1:15-20 the supposed mature expression of Paul's christology in wisdom language and read that conclusion back into 1 Corinthians 1-2. The wisdom of God in 1 Corinthians 1-2 is thus Christ, incarnate wisdom. Wilckens reverses Windisch's method in his classic *Weisheit und Torheit*, beginning with the argument in 1 Corinthians rather than a putative wisdom christology in Colossians and thus avoiding the trap of interpreting an undisputed letter by means of a letter of disputed authorship, but he nevertheless also arrives at a christological reading of Paul's argument in 1 Corinthians. Although he has since retracted some significant points,[7] the influence of *Weisheit und Torheit* is widespread among those who say that it is the Corinthians rather than the Apostle who set the sapiential agenda and that Paul's response is less a refutation of their wisdom christology (with which he is allegedly in essential agreement) than it is an apocalyptic refinement of it in terms

---

[4]*Weisheit und Torheit: Eine exegetische-religions-geschichtliche Untersuchung zu I Kor. 1 und 2* (BHT 26; Tübingen: J. C. B. Mohr, 1959) 60.

[5]Robin Scroggs, "Paul: ΣΟΦΟΣ and ΠΝΕΥΜΑΤΙΚΟΣ," *NTS* 14 (1967) 54-55; Hans Conzelmann, *1 Corinthians* (ed. G. W. MacRae; Philadelphia: Fortress, 1975) 60-61.

[6] "Die göttliche Weisheit der Juden und die paulinische Christologie" in *Neuetestamentliche Studien für Georg Heinrici* (ed. H. Windisch; Leipzig: J. C. Hinrichs, 1914) 220-234. See the discussion of Windisch's influence on succeeding studies of wisdom material in Paul in E. Elizabeth Johnson, *The Function of Apocalyptic and Wisdom Traditions in Romans 9-11* (SBLDS 109; Atlanta: Scholars, 1989) 23-49.

[7] U. Wilckens, "Zu I Kor 2,1-16" in *Theologia Crucis Signum Crucis* (ed. C. Andresen and G. Klein; Tübingen: J. C. B. Mohr, 1979) 501-537.

of cross and resurrection.[8] At the prompting of Conzelmann,[9] still others have sought evidence of Paul's reliance on wisdom traditions in contexts other than christological[10] to say that, even if it is the Corinthians rather than Paul who bring up the subject of wisdom, his position in 1 Cor 1:18-2:16 is not merely reactive; the Apostle does indeed have a wisdom teaching, although it is not the same as the Corinthians' wisdom and is not limited to christology.

The question of the relationship between 1 Cor 1:18-2:5 and 2:6-26 provokes intense debate between those who do and those who do not think Paul claims to have an esoteric wisdom teaching he reserves for a select body of the religiously mature or advanced. A common position is that the two halves of the argument are continuous, that is, that 2:6-16 represent Paul's qualification of 1:18-2:5. No, these interpreters argue, Paul does not evidence in his preaching the eloquence so prized by the Corinthians, but the wisdom he does possess—Christ crucified—is accessible to believers through the Spirit who grants faith in Christ as a gift. The Corinthians are unable to perceive this wisdom due to their factionalism and boasting.[11]

More recently, Gerd Theissen and others have emphasized the discontinuity between the two halves of the argument in 1:18-2:5 and 2:6-16, suggesting Paul's opposition of human to divine wisdom nevertheless distinguishes between common Christian wisdom ("Christ crucified," 1:23) and esoteric theological wisdom ("a secret and hidden wisdom of God," 2:7).[12] Paul's message thus contains levels of sophistication accessible variously to the church in general and to the insiders of the Pauline circle who demonstrate superior ability or receptivity. It seems, therefore, that one's answers to the first two questions raised about this passage—who sets the sapiential agenda?

---

[8] E.g., Günther Bornkamm, *Paul* (New York, Harper and Row, 1971) 162.

[9] Hans Conzelmann, "Paulus und die Weisheit," *NTS* 12 (1965) 231-244.

[10] Scroggs says Paul's wisdom teaching is "not simply about Christ himself, but about the whole eschatological drama of the final time" ("Paul," 46). Similarly, Dieter Georgi finds a wisdom "Schultradition" behind Paul's use of ἰσότης in 2 Cor 8:13ff (*Die Geschichte der Kollekte des Paulus für Jerusalem* [Hamburg: Herbert Reich, 1965] 62-67) and behind the christological hymn in Phil 2:6-11 ("Der vorpaulinische Hymnus Phil 2,6-11" in *Zeit und Geschichte: Dankesgabe an Rudolf Bultmann* [ed. E. Dinkler; Tübingen: J. C. B. Mohr (Paul Siebeck), 1964] 263-293).

[11] E.g., Gordon D. Fee, *The First Epistle to the Corinthians* (Grand Rapids: Eerdmans, 1987) 97-120; F. W. Grosheide, *Commentary on the First Epistle to the Corinthians* (Grand Rapids: Eerdmans, 1953) 62-63; Peter Lampe, "Theological Wisdom and the 'Word About the Cross'," *Int* 44 (1990) 117-131.

[12] *Psychological Aspects of Pauline Theology* (Philadelphia: Fortress, 1987) 343-393; Wilckens, *Weisheit und Torheit*; Scroggs, "Paul"; Conzelmann, *1 Corinthians*.

and what constitutes the wisdom of God?—are in some measure determined by one's answer to the third question: does Paul create (or perhaps acknowledge) degrees of difference among believers on the basis of wisdom?

Theissen's case is the most carefully nuanced, and rests on a very perceptive structural analysis of 1:18-3:23:[13]

The Preaching as Foolishness
1 Cor 1:18-25 The word of the cross as foolishness in the world

(a) is unrecognizable by the world in its wisdom (vv. 18- 22);

(b) is scandal and foolishness to Jews and Gentiles, power and wisdom for believers (vv. 22- 25).

1:26-30 Application to the community:
The foolishness of the message of the cross shows itself in its social composition.

2:1-5 Application to the Apostle:
Paul did not preach the message of the cross as wisdom teaching.

The Preaching as Wisdom
1 Cor 2:6-16 The preaching as wisdom among the perfect

(a) is unrecognizable by the rulers of this world (vv. 6-8);

(b) is foolishness to psychics, wisdom for pneumatics (vv. 9-16).

3:1-4 Application to the community:
The conflict in the community shows that its members are not yet "perfect".

3:5-23 Application to the Apostle:
No one should boast of his wisdom.

Theissen thus correctly sees that Paul's debate with the Corinthians focuses not on christology, but on the nature of Christian preaching and preachers. The overall structure of chapters 1-4, as Nils Dahl points out,[14] emphasizes that the theme of wisdom and foolishness is surrounded by Paul's overriding concern for his apostolic relationship to the church and the Corinthians' perceptions of themselves and their

---

[13] Theissen, *Psychological Aspects*, 345.

[14] "Paul and the Church at Corinth" in *Studies in Paul* (Minneapolis: Augsburg, 1977) 40-61. Cf. also Robert W. Funk, "Word and Word in 1 Corinthians 2:6-16" in *Language, Hermeneutic, and Word of God* (New York: Harper and Row, 1966) 275-305.

teachers. Paul's transition to the wisdom discussion in 1:17 speaks specifically of preaching—"Christ did not send me to baptize but to preach the gospel"—and the passage is rife with the vocabulary of proclamation.[15] What is at stake here for Paul is not the nature of Christ, but the nature of Christian preaching. On the basis of his structural analysis, Theissen concludes that, although it is the Corinthians who have initiated the debate about wisdom,[16] Paul is happy to respond, since for him the wisdom of God is both present (although not accessible) in elementary preaching about Christ crucified and also contained in a separate esoteric reflection on the meaning of the cross in which the Corinthians were—and are—not yet capable of engaging.

> The higher wisdom of Paul consists not in new contents but rather in a higher stage of consciousness in which the same contents are reflected upon. In the "initial preaching," Christians are seized by the symbol of the cross. But it is only through the "doctrine of perfection" that they grasp what seizes them. Both the immature and the perfect are affected by the same revelation, but only the perfect penetrate what happens to them and in them. In brief, perfect wisdom consists in making conscious a previously unconscious content.[17]

Despite Theissen's language about higher consciousness, this is not materially different from Scroggs's claim that "Paul must have had an esoteric wisdom teaching entirely separate from his kerygma...consistent with his theology as a whole,"[18] or Conzelmann's assertion that "wisdom would then be theology as a clarification of the proclamation" suitable for "a higher class of believer."[19]

The parallels between the two halves of the argument as Theissen arranges them, though, are so striking that one is hard-pressed to understand why he perceives such discontinuity between them, even

---

[15] λόγος/λέγειν—1:18; 2:1, 4; κήρυγμα/κηρύσσειν—1:21, 23; 2:4; λαλεῖν—2:6, 7, 13; 3:1; εὐαγγελίξεσθαι—1:17.

[16] οὐκ ἐν σοφίᾳ λόγου in 1:17 must be seen as a qualification that responds to criticism of his preaching.

[17] Theissen, *Psychological Aspects*, 352.

[18] Scroggs, "Paul," 35.

[19] Conzelmann, *1 Corinthians*, 57, 60. Cf. also Jean Héring, *The First Epistle of Saint Paul to the Corinthians* (London: Epworth, 1962) 15: "...a superior stage of Christian teaching, a kind of Christian theosophy....reserved for a Christian elite.... It is no longer pure and simple teaching of the Cross which is meant, but a more profound mystery."

though he prefers to speak of a dialectical relationship. Two prior decisions appear to control Theissen's reading: first, the decision that in 2:1-5 Paul disclaims any wisdom content at all to his "initial preaching"; and second, that Paul draws a distinction among the Corinthians between τέλειοι in 2:6 and νήπιοι in 3:1-4, and that this distinction is functionally equivalent to the distinction between ψυχικοί and πνευματικοί in 2:14-15.

Yet Theissen's own structural outline, it seems, rather places the unbelieving Jews and Gentiles of 1:22-23 parallel to the psychics of 2:14, and the elect of 1:24 parallel to the pneumatics of 2:15.[20] If that is so, then Paul does not here assign to the Spirit a specialized function among advanced Christians which is somehow absent among immature Christians. More appropriate synonyms for pneumatic and psychic seem to be 'believer' and 'unbeliever' rather than 'mature' and 'immature.' The fact that he can so easily move from the pneumatic/psychic distinction made by the Corinthians into his own more common πνεῦμα/σάρξ vocabulary at 3:1ff confirms the suspicion that he is redefining "spiritual" as a divine rather than a human trait. This is likely in any event since elsewhere (e.g., 1 Corinthians 12 and Romans 8) Paul consistently defines Christian existence itself as constituted by the Spirit. Rather than set up alternative divisions against the Corinthians' party-line divisions,[21] Paul describes how believers discern wisdom: it is a gift from God's Spirit; spiritual matters are known by spiritual means. Unbelievers rely instead on their ability to know human wisdom's persuasion and logic and therefore do not recognize the wisdom of God. 1 Corinthians 2:14-15 in its own context does not divide the Christian community into grades of religious perfection unless one has read ahead to 3:1-4 first.

To dispense with the inappropriate influence of 3:1-4, with its mature/immature contrast, on the reading of 2:14-15 does not eliminate the force of that paragraph itself. At 3:1-4 Paul seems to draw lines between childish and adult believers, between those babes in Christ who

---

[20] Cf. Funk, "Word and Word," 296-297.

[21] Scroggs concedes the difficulty of his interpretation and attempts to blunt it by saying, "Paul cannot be charged with setting up a new division in the church at the same time as he is trying to destroy the ones that exist.... Paul nowhere denies that valid *distinctions* in maturity, spiritual gifts, intellectual levels, or productivity exist. What he attacks is rather *divisions* based upon a prideful evaluation of such distinctions" ("Paul," 38, n. 4; emphasis his). The fact remains, however, that for Paul to acknowledge internal distinctions is functionally to allow divisions to exist. In effect, Wilckens, Scroggs, Conzelmann, *et al.* conclude that Paul substitutes allegedly authentic parties in the church, based on the granting or withholding of apostolic wisdom teaching, for inauthentic ones based on gnostic—or non-apostolic—teaching.

are able to consume only milk and those adult Christians who can tolerate the solid food of advanced instruction. But here again, another text beyond the passage at hand seems to exert undue influence on interpreters. Hebrews 5:11-6:3 make use of the familiar philosophic image of milk and food to describe elementary and advanced teaching for νήπιοι and τέλειοι.[22] But in Hebrews the image stands in the service of an exhortation to grow into Christian maturity, whereas Paul makes no such exhortation in 1 Cor 3:1-4. The image is one he obviously knows, and he uses it much as Hebrews does in 1 Cor 14:20, where he urges the Corinthians to be mature in thinking but children with respect to evil.[23] At 3:1-4, however, he contrasts νήπιοι not with τέλειοι, but with πνευματικοί, and describes the νήπιοι as σάρκινοι, caricaturing the Corinthians as non-Christians in the face of their claim to be spiritually advanced Christians. "Flesh" and "spirit" consistently describe the realms of unbelievers and believers in Paul's letters (e.g., Rom 8:1-17),[24] and there is no reason—beyond the existence of a technical gnostic vocabulary that post-dates Paul—to assume he uses the terms differently here.[25]

1 Corinthians 3:1-4 should then be seen as bitterly ironic. The aorist tense of ἠδυνήθην (3:1) and the imperfect of ἐδύνασθε (3:2) have encouraged interpreters to suppose that the paragraph is descriptive rather than ironic—as though Paul somehow could foresee, when he first preached in Corinth, that the community would subsequently choose up sides to see who could be most religious, and that he was therefore unable from the start to address them as spiritual people. If we instead allow the definition of πνευματικός to be established by 2:14-15 and then read the same meaning at 3:1, Paul says the Corinthians were not believers—not that they were immature believers—when he preached to them initially, and indeed they are still behaving as unbelievers. On one level, of course, he knows better: he addresses even these fractious and boastful Corinthians as the church of God (1:2), elect saints (1:2), and

---

[22] For example, Philo's observation that "for babes milk is food, but for grown men [τελείοις] wheaten bread" (*Agric.* 9). The standard Jewish and pagan texts are listed in the commentaries, e.g., Conzelmann, *1 Corinthians*, 71.

[23] Cf. also 1 Cor 13:11; 1 Pet 2:2.

[24] Cf. Herman Ridderbos, *Paul: An Outline of His Theology* (Grand Rapids: Eerdmans, 1975) 66-67.

[25] Cf. here Birger Pearson's discussion of the source of the Corinthians' anthropology (*The Pneumatikos-Psychikos Terminology in 1 Corinthians: A Study in the Theology of the Corinthian Opponents of Paul and its Relation to Gnosticism* [SBLDS 12; Missoula: Scholars, 1973] 17-24). Pearson argues that the Corinthians operate with a common Jewish rather than a gnostic vision of human nature and religious experience.

brothers and sisters (1:10, 11, 26, etc.). There is nevertheless sufficient truth to his charge that the Corinthians comport themselves in a non-Christian manner that Paul's remarks are scarcely off-hand. He is ironic—even sarcastic—but he is deadly serious. One ought therefore to read 3:1-4 as saying, in effect, "I should not have preached to you as if you could handle the gospel, since apparently you cannot. I preached wisdom to you, but it was divine wisdom, not human. You have acted as though it were mine or Apollos's to dispense, as if this wisdom were merely human rhetoric in competition with other expressions of human endeavor."[26]

So the content of Paul's wisdom is not an advanced theological system distinct from simple preaching about Christ, but the gospel itself, something Paul himself says explicitly in 2:1-5. He contrasts the ὑπεροχὴν λόγου ἢ σοφίας (2:1) and σοφίᾳ ἀνθρώπων (2:5) with the μυστήριον τοῦ θεοῦ (2:1) and δυνάμει θεοῦ (2:5), acknowledging that his preaching among the Corinthians was not marked by the superiority of human rhetoric or wisdom, since such preaching would have been foolishness with respect to God (1:18-25).[27] His preaching, he says, was instead marked by the fear and trembling appropriate to the prophetic announcement of the word of God,[28] because it contained the power of

---

[26] Several scholars have wondered how the Apostle could disavow rhetorical expertise in the very act of demonstrating it in this argument (see R. A. Horsley, "Wisdom of Word and Words of Wisdom in Corinth," *CBQ* 39 [1977] 224-239; T. H. Lim, "Not in Persuasive Words of Wisdom, But in the Demonstration of the Spirit and Power," *NovT* 29 [1987] 137-149 and the literature cited there). In response, it need only be noted that Paul himself concedes the difference between his homiletic and epistolary styles in 2 Cor 10:7-12, although he claims the content of his ministry is consistent. George A. Kennedy (*New Testament Interpretation Through Rhetorical Criticism* [Chapel Hill: University of North Carolina, 1984] 93) observes that 2 Corinthians 10-13 "shows Paul's consciousness, and his manipulation, of two different kinds of rhetoric, the radical (basically sacred) rhetoric of authority and the rhetoric of rational argumentation, which was perceived as more worldly." The same might be said to a lesser extent of 1 Corinthians 1-3. Lampe ("Theological Wisdom") argues that 1 Cor 1:18-2:16 is a *schema*, itself a well-known rhetorical device, and that Paul's *schema* is designed to oppose divine and human wisdom in such a way that the Corinthians see themselves in the contrast and understand the error of their confidence in rhetoric alone.

[27] Cf. σοφίᾳ σαρκικῇ, 2 Cor 1:12.

[28] Cf. Pss 2:11; 77:16; 119:120; Isa 66:5; Jer 5:22; Dan 6:26; 10:11; Acts 16:29; 2 Cor 7:15; Phil 2:12. See J. Louis Martyn's comment on 1 Cor 1:18: "Paul says forcefully that the preached word is not served up as a first step so that as a second step the Corinthians may apply to it their superior powers of discernment. Rather, in the preached word God is himself powerfully present and active" ("Epistemology at the Turn of the Ages: 2 Corinthians 5:15" in *Christian History and Interpretation: Studies Presented to John Knox* [ed. W. R. Farmer, C. F. D. Moule, and R. R. Niebuhr; Cambridge: Cambridge University Press, 1967] 287, n. 2).

God, the same power of God which in 1:24 he equates with the wisdom of God. Paul contrasts in 2:1-5 human wisdom and divine wisdom just as he has previously in 1:18-25. This is not his disavowal of all wisdom in his preaching, but rather his claim to know the difference between divine and human wisdom: the former he preaches, the latter he scorns.

Paul's analysis of the Corinthians' situation is that they have not only a mistaken notion of wisdom, but a correlate misunderstanding of power as well. Indeed the δύναμις/δυνάσθαι and ἰσχυρός/ἰσχύειν (ἀσθενής) language in these chapters is just as prominent as the vocabulary of preaching.[29] The very first contrast Paul draws at 1:18 is not between wisdom and foolishness, but between foolishness and power. This power of God is not simply the rhetorical force or persuasive strength of God's ideas or intelligence, but divine power that breaks into human experience to assert its right. God's wisdom does not simply make human wisdom look silly or insignificant in comparison with itself; the wisdom of God and the wisdom of the world are not merely competitors for human attention or popularity. The conflict between human and divine wisdom is, on the contrary, an eschatological power struggle between cosmic forces. Were he to have preached with the eloquence of worldly wisdom, Paul says, he would have voided the cross of Christ— not in itself but in its impact as proclamation—because he would have confused divine and human wisdom. This is precisely what the Corinthians have done, and he reminds them in 4:19-20 that the power of the kingdom of God will reveal the powerlessness of his eloquent opponents. God's judgment will itself be manifested in Paul's judgment when he arrives in Corinth, because spiritual people such as the Apostle judge τὰ πάντα (2:15).

The Corinthians equate wisdom with power—and so does Paul. But the power of God's wisdom, not their own, is what preachers demonstrate. Note, for example, Paul's sarcastic question about civil lawsuits at 6:5: "is there no one wise among you who is able to judge?" There ought to be those wise enough to be able to make judgments in the Christian community, since those who have the Spirit of God judge all things (2:15), but the Corinthians are apparently more impressed with the rhetorical abilities of non-Christian lawyers and judges than with the wisdom of the gospel which properly marks the saints (6:1).[30]

---

[29] δυνάσθαι, κτλ—1 Cor 1:18, 24, 26; 2:4, 5, 14; 3:1, 2; cf. 3:11; 4:19, 20; 5:4; 6:5, 14; 7:21; 10:13, 21; 12:3, 10, 21, 28, 29; 14:11, 31; 15:24, 43, 50, 56; ἀσθενής—1:25, 27; 2:3; cf. 4:10; 8:7, 9, 10, 11, 12; 9:22; 11:30; 12:22; 15:43; ἰσχυρός—1:25, 27; 2:3; cf. 4:10; 10:22.

[30] The contrast between appearance and reality which underlies both the sarcasm in 6:5 and the characterization of the community in 1:26-29 seems rooted in Paul's conviction of

The wisdom of God, Paul says, will put these humanly wise and powerful people to shame at the judgment (1:27).³¹ Divine wisdom will ultimately destroy³² its rivals (1:27). Just as the σοφία λόγου would nullify the cross of Christ, so the wisdom of God will destroy the wisdom of the world.

Paul speaks of his gospel as the wisdom of God in much the way his Jewish contemporaries speak of the Torah. In Sirach, the Wisdom of Solomon, 1 Enoch, 4 Ezra, 2 Baruch, at Qumran, and throughout early Judaism, the law of God is repeatedly identified as God's wisdom, that cosmic glue which holds the universe together and confronts both Israel and the nations with the alternatives: life or death, righteousness or sin.³³ So also, Paul's gospel is the powerful wisdom of God, saving those who believe and causing unbelievers to perish (1:18, cf. v. 25).³⁴ In 1 Enoch, 4 Ezra, and at Qumran, God's wisdom is further identified as the cosmic secrets of God's counsel. Here, too, Paul resembles his contemporaries, for just as the preaching of Christ crucified is God's wisdom, confronting the world and transforming the elect, so are the apocalyptic mysteries of God's plan for salvation components of divine wisdom, and therefore of Christian proclamation. All that eye has not seen, ear has not heard, nor human heart conceived of (1 Cor 2:9), as well as the message of Christ crucified, is Paul's preaching of the mystery of God (2:1).³⁵ His obscure reference to scripture at 2:9³⁶ points

---

the impartiality of God. See David M. Hay, "Paul's Indifference to Authority," *JBL* 88 (1969) 36-44. Further on the prominence of the theme of divine impartiality in the wisdom tradition, see Jouette M. Bassler, *Divine Impartiality: Paul and a Theological Axiom* (SBLDS 59; Chico, CA: Scholars, 1982) 7-44.

³¹ Paul consistently uses καταισχύνεσθαι and related words to talk about eschatological shame, that is, the potential failure or collapse of human expectations at the judgment of God. For example, he affirms that the gospel of God's righteousness will not collapse (Rom 1:16; 9:33; 10:11), that the apostolic mission will not fail (2 Cor 9:4; 10:8; Phil 1:20); and that Christian hope will not be disappointed (Rom 5:5).

³² καταργεῖν is another word fraught with eschatological meaning, e.g., Rom 3:3, 31; 4:14; 6:6; 1 Cor 13:8, 10; 15:24, 26; and so on.

³³See Johnson, *Romans* 9-11, 55-109.

³⁴Cf. Rom 10:6-8, where "the word of faith which we preach" is described as the near word of God's wisdom by means of Deut 30:12-14 and Bar 3:29-30 (ibid., 133-137).

³⁵ The variant μαρτύριον in 2:1 is probably, as Bruce M. Metzger suggests, "a recollection of 1.6, whereas μυστήριον [in earlier although fewer MSS] here prepares for its usage in ver. 7" (*A Textual Commentary on the Greek New Testament* [London: United Bible Societies, 1975 corrected] 545). On the use of μυστήριον in both apocalyptic and wisdom contexts see Raymond E. Brown, *The Semitic Background of the Term "Mystery" in the New Testament* (FBBS21; Philadelphia: Fortress, 1968).

³⁶ See Klaus Berger's review of the question in "Zur Diskussion über die Herkunft von I Kor. II.9," *NTS* 24 (1978) 270-283.

to the apocalyptic blessings yet awaiting believers, and he describes his apostolic office in 4:2 as stewardship of divine mysteries, even revealing one of those mysteries at 15:51 (cf. also Rom 11:25). All this, which Paul describes with the synecdoche, "the word of the cross", is the content of apostolic proclamation;[37] the whole cosmic drama of God's creative sovereignty, justification of sinners, and redemption of the world is the content of divine wisdom.

The wisdom of God, Paul says, is righteousness, sanctification, and redemption (1:30), that is, the full scope of the kerygma: God's justification of sinners, the Spirit's conforming the community to the image of Christ, and God's final judgment and victory. Just as Jews of the day understand God's wisdom (in the law and heavenly mysteries) to be the divine power of the world's creation, maintenance, and redemption, so Paul sees God's wisdom in Christian proclamation to be God's power to save (1:18). The gospel itself is master of those who announce it—they are servants and stewards (4:2)—and the apocalyptic urgency of the moment compels them to preach (9:6). The power resides in the message rather than the messengers, which is precisely what Paul accuses the Corinthians of having misunderstood.

It is frequently observed that Paul spends much of his time in 1 Corinthians correcting what he perceives to be misunderstandings of his own preaching.[38] Nowhere is this so true as in 1:18-2:16. The Corinthians have rightly seen Paul's preaching (and Apollos's, too, for that matter) as wisdom and power. But they have mistakenly considered the wisdom to belong to the preachers. Paul's response is to assert the divine source and content of the wisdom he preaches. It is granted as a gift rather than discerned, and its power is a function not of human ability to perceive it but of preemptive divine action. What God has prepared for those who love him has been hidden from before the ages, but now is revealed in Christian proclamation. To confuse the gift with the giver, to see Christian preachers as the source of the power to which they bear witness, is to exchange the wisdom of God for human wisdom and thus become a fool.[39] So Paul goes so far as to declare that those

---

[37] Robert G. Hamerton-Kelly, *Pre-Existence, Wisdom, and the Son of Man: A Study in the Idea of Pre-Existence in the New Testament* (Cambridge: University, 1973) 115.

[38] J. Christiaan Beker calls it "a breakdown of communications" (*Paul the Apostle: The Triumph of God in Life and Thought* [Philadelphia: Fortress, 1980] 165). Cf. Funk, "Word and Word," 276.

[39] Cf. the remarkably similar argument in Rom 1:18-32 that idolatry is the foolish (1:21-22) worship of the creature rather than the creator. Lampe observes, "The domestication of God [either by idolatry or the elevation of human over divine wisdom], this objectification of God when God is no longer allowed to be God, *this* is the sin of the fools. It is the sin

who confuse divine wisdom with human eloquence are no more enlightened than the doomed rulers of this age who failed to understand God's purpose in the cross (2:6-8). Paul finally makes no distinctions within the Corinthian community between those who are wise and those who are not. He indicts the entire community for its foolishness,[40] and says one is either foolish or wise by the Spirit's action. All boasting in human capacity or effort is therefore precluded (1:31; 9:15-16), whether in one's own capacity for insight or in the eloquence of one's teacher.[41] For Paul, the gospel of God's wisdom is the transforming power of the new age, and regardless of who preaches it, or who hears, it remains a divine rather than a human phenomenon. Although the wisdom of God is revealed to and made known by human beings, it can never become a human possession because it is a sovereign power—the very power of God.

---

against the First and Second Commandments" ("Theological Wisdom," 123; emphasis his).

[40] Whether or not the *entire* Corinthian community has actually engaged in partisan competition, Paul speaks in 1:10-16 as though it has. It seems likely that the members of Chloe's household, although they are the ones who have brought news of the community's divisiveness, are nevertheless themselves sympathetic to the group that claims allegiance to Paul, and thus are liable to his judgment that they misunderstand his apostolic role (cf. ἕκαστος, 1:12). That Paul is aware of the multiplicity of positions is evident from his passing references to τις, ἕτερος (3:4), and τινες (4:18), and he obviously has no problem taking sides occasionally in the letter. His diagnosis of the whole church's failure to perceive the nature of proclamation, however, applies to all sides in the dispute, even those who may not have actively participated in the argument. The failure is not only that of individuals, but of the church.

[41] This essay is written in honor of Paul W. Meyer not only because I am deeply indebted to him as my teacher, but also because he shares the Apostle's sense of what it means to be a teacher. Professor Meyer invariably directs the attention of his students and colleagues away from himself to the text of the New Testament, and from the text to the Word it proclaims.

10

Death and Victory in 1 Corinthians 15:51-57: The Transformation of a Prophetic Theme[1]

Walter Harrelson [2]

In 1 Corinthians 15 Paul makes many allusions to tradition that has been passed on to him, and he also includes a number of quotations from and allusions to texts of the Hebrew Bible. This essay is concerned with two of these quotations from the Hebrew Bible, quotations that may, however, also be part of the tradition that is being passed along in the Christian community of his time and place. The two quotations to be examined are, respectively, from Isa 25:8 and Hos 13:14. Neither is quoted by Paul in the form found in the Masoretic text or that found in the Septuagint.[3] Since I want to address the question of how Paul has

---

[1] It is a pleasure to contribute this brief study to the volume honoring Paul Meyer, my former colleague and longtime friend and teacher.

[2] Walter Harrelson is Professor of Hebrew Bible at the Divinity School, Vanderbilt University, Nashville, Tennessee.

[3] The most comprehensive study with which I am acquainted is E. Earle Ellis, *Paul's Use of the Old Testament* (Edinburgh: Oliver & Boyd, 1957). See also Robert G. Bratcher, *A Translator's Guide to Paul's First Letter to the Corinthians* (London: United Bible Societies, 1982).

arrived at the sense of these two texts, I will quote them below (in their contexts) in transliteration, and will then translate them quite literally.

1. Text and Translation

Isaiah 25:6-8:

> wĕ'āśâ yhwh ṣĕbā'ôt
> lĕkōl-hā 'ammîm
> bāhār hazzeh
> mištēh šĕmānîm
> mištēh šĕmārîm
> šĕmānîm mĕmuḥāyim
> šĕmārîm mĕzuqqāqîm
> ûbillaʿ bāhār hazzeh
> pĕnê-hallôṭ hallôṭ
> 'al-kōl-hā 'ammîm
> wĕhammassēkâ hannĕsûkâ
> 'al-kōl-haggôyim
> billaʿ hammāwet lāneṣaḥ
> ûmāḥâ 'ădōnāy yhwh
> dimʿâ mē 'al kōl-pānîm
> wĕḥerpat 'ammô yāsîr
> mē 'al kōl-hā 'āreṣ
> kî yhwh dibbēr

Then yhwh of hosts will make
  for all peoples on this mountain
a feast of rich foods,
  a feast of treasured wines,
rich foods with marrow,
  treasured, aged wines.
[God] will swallow up on this mountain
  the covering that is spread
  over all the peoples,
the veil that is spread out
  over all the nations.
[God] will swallow up death completely.
The Lord God will wipe away
  tears from all faces.
[God] will remove the reproach of the people
  from the whole earth—

Death and Victory

for the Lord has spoken!

Hosea 13:12-14:

ṣārûr 'äwon 'eprāyim
ṣĕpûnâ ḥaṭṭā'tô
ḥeblê yôlēdâ yābō'û lô
hû'–bēn lō' ḥākām
kî 'ēt lō'–ya'ămōd
bĕmišbar bānîm
miyyad šĕ'ôl 'epdēm
mimmāwet 'eq'ālēm
'ĕhî dĕbārêkā māwet
'ĕhî qāṭābkā [or qōṭābkā] šĕ'ôl
nōḥam yissātēr mē'ênāy

The iniquity of Ephraim is bound up,
    his sin is stored away.
The pangs of birth reach him,
    but he is an unwise son:
at the time of birth he will not situate himself
    at the place where children break out.
I will ransom them from the hand of Sheol;
[or: Shall I ransom them from the hand of Sheol?]
    I will redeem them from death.
    [or: Shall I redeem them from death?]
Where are your plagues, O death?
    Where is your destruction, O Sheol?
Vengeance [or: Compassion] is hidden from my eyes.

2. Analysis of Isaiah 25:6-8[4]

One recent study of Isaiah (Hayes/Irvine) claims that Isaiah 24-27 belongs to the eighth century prophet (along with all else found in Isaiah 1-35), but there is nearly universal agreement among scholars to the contrary. The chapters are best placed in the early post-exilic period,

---

[4] Detailed treatments of the passage are found in Hans Wildberger, *Jesaja* (BKAT 10/2; Neukirchen: Neukirchener, 1978) 959-69; and in John D. W. Watts, *Isaiah 1-33* (WBC 24; Waco, TX: Word, 1985) 327-333. See also John H. Hayes and Stuart A. Irvine, *Isaiah the Eighth Century Prophet: His Times and His Preaching* (Nashville: Abingdon, 1987) 307-10; and R. E. Clements, *Isaiah 1-39* (NCB; Grand Rapids: Eerdmans, 1980) 208-09.

along with Isa 4:2-6, Isaiah 12, and Isaiah 33-35. They speak of a coming consummation of the work of God on earth that will be preceded by divine judgment upon the peoples of earth, not excluding God's people and the central city of earth, Jerusalem/Zion. These poems use older materials, but the author has reshaped the borrowed material in order to offer a connected picture of cosmic judgment and renewal that is ready at hand.

In the midst of the section stands our text—three verses speaking of God's removal of a covering that overlies all peoples, a veil spread out over the nations. This "net" (Vulgate) is some confinement that needs to be removed in order that the consummation may proceed. What is this cosmic net, web, veil?

In Isaiah 4 and again in Isa 25:1-5 there appears a protective covering that lies over Zion. The imagery in Isaiah 4 is clearly taken from the pillar of cloud that led Israel by day in the wilderness, and the pillar of fire that led them by night. In Isa 25:1-5 the references are more general. God is a refuge from storm, a protector of the poor and the needy, apparently referring to those protected at the time of God's bringing some foreign city to ruin. The identity of the city is not known. The reference may, indeed, be to God's bringing to an end the empires of the world that have lorded it over others and exercised ruthlessness in their treatment of their subjects.[5] Now, however, God has become a cover and a shelter for the despised, and even the ruthless powers will sing God's praises and give the deity glory. Cities that were supposed to be a cover and a shelter for their inhabitants but instead have oppressed them will be replaced as protector by the One who will rightly shelter and cover them.

The covering referred to in our passage, however, is a negative reality, one that God must remove in order that the eschatological feast may proceed. One must think of the covering of the head in sorrow, of mourning rites that involved not only dust on the head and a tearing of one's clothing, but also the covering of the face and head in grief and lamentation.[6] But it is not just any kind of mourning that is suggested. The peoples and nations of earth are in mourning over the glory that has come to Zion, over their defeat by the God of Zion, and over the loss of their leaders and rulers (Isa 24:17-23).

In this context comes the assertion that God will swallow up death forever (*lāneṣaḥ*), will wipe away tears from all faces, and will remove the shame or reproach that has befallen the people of God. This

---

[5] So Watts, *Isaiah 1-33*, 318-322.

[6] Wildberger, *Jesaja* (966-69), and many others.

sweeping assertion, which (as Wildberger points out marvelously) seems almost to put the nations ahead of Israel in the day of consummation, clearly offers a picture of God's triumph over all the powers and forces of the creation that stand in opposition to the deity. God brings hostility to an end, brings weeping and lamentation to an end, and eliminates also the reproach felt by God's people Israel at the hands of the nations. No longer will God's people be despised because they have their distinct stance before the world as the people of the covenant. Israel will still be God's people, and Zion will still be the center of the universe. But the feast is one to which the nations are invited as well, and the covering of grief and shame that lies over the nations and over Israel will be swept away.

Death too will be swallowed up! Why this verb, used elsewhere in the Hebrew Bible to depict the devouring of wild animals or especially to picture the earth and Sheol and death opening up to swallow the rebellious (Num 16:31) or those under the power of the enemy's curse? Death will be swallowed up on this day, just as death has regularly swallowed up those who fell under its power. Does the text, therefore, speak about the general resurrection of the dead? Not directly, it would seem. It rather portrays the day of victory, the day of God's triumph, the season of blessedness that awaits the world.

But is that not the material from which a Jewish view of resurrection will develop? There are two strands that merge to provide a picture of resurrection in the Hebrew Bible, and both of them are present in our text. The first strand speaks more about a divine presence with sufferers and those injured by life, a presence that death itself cannot bring to an end. Our most striking passages laying out this view are Psalm 73, Job 19:23-29, and (in a different way) Psalm 139. In the first two texts, extreme suffering is found bearable and more; the divine presence in the midst of suffering is of such depth and enduringness that death itself cannot bring it to an end. One dies "in the Lord" and knows that this accompanying presence suffers no defeat or diminution in the presence of death. In the other text, Psalm 139, it is the pervasive presence of God in all aspects of the life of the psalmist that assures its permanence. No direct reference to a confrontation with death occurs, but it is made clear that God is equally sovereign over Sheol and earth and heaven. There is no escape from God, not for evildoers (139:19-22) and not for the psalmist.

This more personal and mystical portrayal of how the divine presence overcomes the power of death is balanced by the second strand of thought about death in the Hebrew Bible. The second view has more to do with the public triumph of God's righteousness and goodness than it does with the fate of the individual at death, although it will lead to an outlook that addresses the concerns of the individual. This second strand arises out of the more general question of God's justice, the question of theodicy, or how to support the claims of faith in the light of the triumph of injustice and evil in the public world. The answer given is adumbrated in our text: God's triumph over all enmity throughout the world is of such a sort as to carry over also into a triumph of God's purposes for all individuals as well as all peoples and nations.

This picture of the triumph of God over all forces in opposition to the divine will, marked as it is by God's wiping away every tear and setting right every reproach suffered by God's people, leads quite easily into the picture of resurrection found in Dan 12:2-3, where the many (which probably means all) are raised from death to receive their due reward: everlasting life or eternal shame and reproach.

It is noteworthy that our text has no place for any failures on God's part. Second Esdras (chapters 3-10) will later plead with God's angel that a better way than this be found; otherwise, most of the human race, clearly sinful and deserving of judgment, is doomed.[7]

Our text also has adumbrations of the first strand of thought addressing the question of life after death, for while it does not speak in the personal terms of Job 19 and Psalms 73 and 139, it speaks with definitiveness of death's end, once and for all, and of God's personal attention to those who lament and mourn, and to those who have suffered the indignity and reproach of being hated by the nations because of their faith and fidelity to God.

One other point requires some initial attention: is the translation of the Hebrew *lānesaḥ* correct as given above? Most commentators render the term as it clearly must be rendered in many of its occurrences in the Hebrew Bible: "forever." The basic meaning of the root is "to be preeminent," "to endure," "to be everlasting" (2 Sam 2:26, for example). But it is also clear that the meaning "to be victorious" is not at all foreign to the basic import of this verb, since it is associated with leadership, dominance, and therefore with victory. The point is that a translation like that found in 1 Corinthians 15, "in victory," which is a common meaning in Syriac and Aramaic as well as in post-biblical Hebrew, is not out of line with the word's overall meaning and usage. A temporal meaning fits well with the term "death," of course: death is swallowed up for all time and is no more. But does it fit as well in the

---

[7] See my essay, "Ezra Among the Wicked in 2 Esdras 3-10," in *The Divine Helmsman: Studies on God's Control of Human Events, Presented to Lou H. Silberman* (ed. James L. Crenshaw and Samuel Sandmel; New York: KTAV, 1980) 21-40.

context *in Isaiah 25* as does a meaning in which death is being contrasted with its opposite? I think not, and for that reason have translated "completely."

The context, as we noted, is one in which the signs of mourning and grief are being "swallowed up," swept away, and tears are being wiped away from all eyes. Israel's reproach is being removed, and God the sovereign is now ruling as Lord of all peoples and as host at the eschatological feast on Mount Zion. All the forces of destruction and death, in short, which have long raged around Mt. Zion, are now done to death, and the victorious divine sovereign rules from Zion. Death and all hostility to God have indeed been swallowed up in victory, have yielded to the One who is preeminent, who is victorious.[8]

The Greek translation εἰς νεῖκος, which is found in the LXX for a number of the occurrences of the Hebrew *lāneṣaḥ* (2 Sam 2:26; Amos 8:7; Job 36:7; Lam 5:20), may well render the meaning in our passage, given the overall context. It surely seems to offer a more satisfactory translation than does Isa 25:8 LXX: ἰσχύσας, "strongly," or the like. The word *lāneṣaḥ* is translated qualitatively in Lam 5:20 in the LXX: "Why do you [God] forget us entirely?" (literally, "to completeness," or "to victory," εἰς νεῖκος). And it is rendered qualitatively in Job 36:7 LXX: "[God] sets them [i.e., kings] victoriously, and they are exalted." It seems in order, therefore, for us to say that the LXX renderings of the term *lāneṣaḥ* show a great deal of sophistication. The LXX often translates, when the expression is clearly temporal, with εἰς τέλος or with εἰς τὸν αἰῶνα. But when some other nuance of meaning is called for, the LXX can do what Paul did in 1 Corinthians!

3. Analysis of Hosea 13:12-14[9]

Hosea 13:1-14 is very complex, and determination of its form and history of composition is difficult. Indeed, while it is clear that a new indictment of Ephraim (Hosea's favorite term for northern Israel) begins at 13:1, it is not at all clear where the unit ends. I believe it best to treat 13:1-14 as the basic unit, an indictment of Ephraim in which two

---

[8] Hayes/Irvine give an entirely political interpretation, assigning the passage to Isaiah of Jerusalem and assuming that the prophet is speaking of the coming end of Assyrian dominance over Israel and the other nations (*Isaiah*, 307-10).

[9] Excellent treatments of this passage appear in Francis I. Andersen and David Noel Freedman, *Hosea* (AB 24; Garden City, NY: Doubleday, 1983) 624-41; and Hans Walter Wolff, *Hosea* (Hermeneia; Philadelphia: Fortress, 1974) 219-30. See also the detailed study by Paul N. Franklyn, "Prophetic Cursing of Apostasy: Text, Form, and Tradition in Hosea 13" (Ph.D. dissertation, Vanderbilt University, 1986).

statements or observations by the prophet (vv. 1-3, 12-13) are followed in turn by speeches of God (vv. 4-11, 14), in which the deity alternates between third person and second person references to Ephraim. One can see that the closing unit of 13:1-16 (Hebrew 13:1-14:1), comprising verses 15 and 16 (Hebrew verses 15 and 14:1), again concerns Ephraim (v. 15) and Samaria (v. 16, Hebrew 14:1) but contains no address from God. The unit that closes the book is clearly *not* a continuation of this judgment against Ephraim. We therefore believe that it is best to treat verse 14 as the close of our unit. It must be noted, however, that treating verse 15 as the start of the new threat of judgment (the Hebrew reads, "When [or: Though] he is divided among brothers...") is difficult. Most scholars propose emendations.[10]

The passage bitterly assaults Ephraim for idolatry and apostasy from God, for ingratitude and for fawning over the images of foreign deities. God is presented in the first response as a wild animal, ripping and tearing at this prey that is already as good as dead because of its sin (v. 1: Ephraim...incurred guilt and died).

The second statement about Ephraim has a quite different tone. It is in the mode of an observation about a situation that is sad indeed: Ephraim is in a position to come to new birth, but stubbornly refuses to do so, is obdurate and will not cooperate in the process that would bring in new birth. Ready for a fresh start, Ephraim insists upon keeping the bound-up roll on which the catalogue of sins is recorded.[11] Forgiveness and new life are at hand, the text implies, but unwise Ephraim will not enter upon that new life.

The divine speech then appears, this time not canceling out the threats of the early part of the chapter but redirecting the divine wrath against the destructive powers, it would seem. A similar movement occurs in Hosea 11, where God's love for the child Israel is first recalled, the apostasy noted, and God's threat of destruction vividly and irrevocably laid down (11:1-7). But then we are introduced into the inner musings of a grieving deity (vv. 8-9): How can I do this? I am God, not a mortal, the Holy One in the midst of you. God resolves to be gracious. And that passage too is then followed by later promises (11:10-12, Hebrew 11:10-12:1), a return of the exiles to their homes and a promise that although Ephraim has proved to be apostate, Judah is still faithful. The analogy of our chapter with Hosea 11 does not prove anything, yet it is suggestive of the way in which Hosea relates divine judgment and

---

[10] See Wolff, *Hosea*, 222; Andersen/Freedman, *Hosea*, 640-41.

[11] This is the probable meaning of v. 12. See the account in Zech 5:1-4, and recall the way in which manuscripts were preserved in the caves near Qumran. See also Jer 32:9-15.

mercy, and of how Hosea's messages have been assembled and expanded.

Now we must address the most difficult question: how are we to translate verse 14? Scholars are divided over the question, and it is understandable that they should be. Among the major commentators and translators, very few have made the passage positive. The new translation of the Jewish Publication Society, *Tanakh*,[12] reads, "Vengeance is hidden from my eyes," making the passage a promise of forgiveness. Nevertheless, virtually all recent treatments of the passage understand it as a threat or, at the most, leave the interpretation open.[13]

4. Paul's Transformation of a Prophetic Theme

In my judgment, Isa 25:6-8 and Hos 13:12-14 have much in common and are ingeniously linked by Paul to support the recently developed doctrine of resurrection. They were not in their own day documents supporting the resurrection,[14] although today we cannot be as confident as once we were in affirming that the Hebrew Bible knows no doctrine of resurrection until the first third of the second century BCE. They were affirming a different point, but it is a point that is entirely compatible with the Christian understanding of resurrection as the apostle Paul affirms it in 1 Corinthians 15 and implies it in Rom 8:31-39.

This point is that God stands as sovereign over all the powers of the world, irrespective of their subtle capacity to undo human life, their uncanny hold upon persons who seek by all means to resist that hold. Sin and death belong together for Paul, and the hold of these dark forces can be broken only by divine intervention. Isaiah 25:6-8 and the surrounding unit in which it is placed (Isaiah 24-27) are speaking in their way of just such a situation. Earth itself mourns and languishes, and joy and gladness are stilled (24:4-13), until the sovereign God appears, removes the cloud and covering of sin and sadness, wipes away all tears, and "swallows up death entirely." In the expectation of that certain day, the prophet responsible for Isaiah 24-27 can promise a day when death will be done to death entirely, in that it will no longer have

---

[12] *Tanakh: The Holy Scriptures* (Philadelphia: The Jewish Publication Society, 1985).

[13] See Andersen/Freedman, *Hosea*, 640.

[14] See the intriguing treatment by John Calvin in *The First Epistle of Paul the Apostle to the Corinthians* (Edinburg: Oliver & Boyd, 1960) 344-46. See also the cogent analysis of C. K. Barrett, *A Commentary on the First Epistle to the Corinthians* (New York: Harper & Row, 1968) 382-83.

power to undo and erase the import and purpose of Israel's life, or the life of the peoples of the earth.

This theme is differently and less cosmically put in Hosea, two hundred years earlier. Hosea speaks rather of new life that is ready at hand for Ephraim, requiring only that Ephraim assist in the new birth, position himself in such fashion as to assist mother Israel in giving birth, as Israel's God serves as midwife, assisting the birth. Hosea also affirms much more outspokenly that God will not fail to engage death and plague in mortal combat. Let them come and do their worst against a sinful Ephraim! Ephraim is in God's care, beloved and dear beyond all measure (Hos 11:8-9). God does have to bring enemies against a faithless people, as Hosea clearly affirmed throughout chapters 4-13. But God, out of love and compassion, can and does turn against the bringers of death and destruction, calling a halt to the death-dealers, saying "Enough!" to endless vengeance, displaying that quality that is synonymous with Israel's God: mercy (see Exod 34:6-8).

Finally, what of Paul's rendering of the passages? Has he gone astray in his claiming of the tradition? Since in late Hebrew, in Aramaic, and in Syriac the verb $nṣḥ$ has come to mean "be victorious," "triumph," "succeed," and since such associations are already present with the biblical term, we may claim that "death is swallowed up in victory" is an acceptable rendering of the Hebrew in Isa 25:8. The Hebrew term does not have only a temporal connotation; in the Isaiah passage, the translation "completely," or "victoriously," works very well.

Moreover, it is evident from our argument above that Paul's quotation from Hos 13:14 does not use the passage out of context, as has been asserted frequently. The passage is not easy to interpret, and there is room for disagreement, of course. But I am convinced that the hapax legomenon $nōḥam$ in the verse is best rendered "settling of accounts" or "restoring the balance," and that therefore "vengeance" is the best way to render the term.

Conclusion

The apostle Paul, then, shows a striking capacity to interpret biblical texts in a way faithful to their context and appropriate to address his central concern with the doctrine of resurrection. What Paul affirms most centrally in 1 Corinthians 15 is that God's raising of Jesus is a sign that the promised day of consummation for Israel and the nations has burst in upon the world in mysterious ways, giving assurance to all that the sovereign God addresses the powers of sin and death and brings them under the divine sway. This process is under way, and those who die as well as those who live are caught up in that process and both live and die "in the Lord" (Rom 14:8).

11

The Covenants Of Hagar And Sarah[1]

J. Louis Martyn [2]

I

With the end of the second world war and the revelation of the mad attempt of the Nazi regime to exterminate European Jewry, a number of church bodies began to draft statements, declarations, even confessions designed to heal some of the wounds, and thus to better the relations between Jews and Christians. A declaration of guilt was issued in Stuttgart within months of the end of the war in 1945, and it has been followed by numerous others.[3] All of these declarations and confessions

---

[1] Genuine acquaintance with Paul Meyer began when we drove from New Haven to Montreal and back in the summer of 1963, in order to participate in a memorable conference of Biblical scholars. It is a joy to be able to say in print that that acquaintance ripened into a longstanding comradeship for which I am greatly thankful.

[2] J. Louis Martyn is the Edward Robinson Professor Emeritus of Biblical Theology, Union Theological Seminary, New York, New York.

[3] Because the Stuttgarter (Schuld) Erklärung (October 18-19, 1945) speaks of guilt in a general way by referring to the "unending suffering" that was brought upon "many peoples and countries," it belongs, important as it is, only marginally to the series of declarations pertinent to our present concerns; see Gerhard Besier and Gerhard Sauter, *Wie Christen ihre Schuld bekennen* (Göttingen: Vandenhoeck & Ruprecht, 1985) n.b. 51, n. 66. The books of Helga Croner, ed., *Stepping Stones to Further Jewish-Christian Relations* (New York: Stimulus Books, 1977) 77, and *More Stepping Stones to Jewish-Christian Relations* (New York: Paulist, 1985) 85, helpfully collect in English translation a great many of the

draw on scripture in one way or another, and, as is always the case, those who draft such statements reveal their own inner-canonical canon. This is true of the influential resolution issued in 1980 by the Synod of the Rheinische Landeskirche, a few parts of which will occupy our attention in the present essay, though I am quick to add that what will be said about it here can equally well be said about almost all of the documents referred to above.[4] Because the Rheinland resolution is drafted in the form of a confession, and because it is explicitly the result of a burning concern for the renovation of relations between German Protestants and Jews, one is not greatly surprised to see several quotations from Paul's letters, and notably from Romans 9-11. Great weight is laid, for example, on a statement of Paul often taken to be a reminder to Gentile Christians of their indebtedness to Judaism, and doubtless for that reason placed with considerable emphasis at the beginning of the resolution:

---

pertinent documents, the earliest being "The Ten Points of Seelisberg" (1947). One notes also "A Theological Understanding of the Relationship Between Christians and Jews," issued by the 199th General Assembly (1987) of the Presbyterian Church (U.S.A.); and "Guidelines for Christian-Jewish Relations; For Use in the Episcopal Church," 454-460 in *The Blue Book: Reports of the Committees, Commissions, Boards, and Agencies of the General Convention of the Episcopal Church, 1988*. In the present essay the 1980 resolution of the Landessynode der Evangelischen Kirche im Rheinland will claim our attention, not least because it has influenced subsequent statements, such as the one issued in 1987 by the Presbyterian Church U.S.A.

[4] The extensive and sometimes heated discussion elicited by the Rheinland resolution is a subject in itself. One can begin with the bibliography in *Gottes Augapfel* (2nd ed.; ed. Edna Brocke and Jürgen Seim; Neukirchen: Neukirchener Verlag, 1988); see also the essays in that volume, notably the study of Wolfgang Schrage, " '...den Juden ein Skandalon'? Der Anstoss des Kreuzes nach 1 Kor 1,23." As the Rheinland resolution will claim our attention in the present essay, and as the text of the resolution is not widely known outside Germany, I give here parts that are of particular pertinence:

(1) Wir bekennen betroffen die Mitverantwortung und Schuld der Christenheit in Deutschland am Holocaust....

(3) Wir bekennen uns zu Jesus Christus, dem Juden, der als Messias Israels der Retter der Welt ist und die Völker der Welt mit dem Volk Gottes verbindet....

(4) Wir glauben die bleibende Erwählung des jüdischen Volkes als Gottes Volk und erkennen, dass die Kirche durch Jesus Christus in den Bund Gottes mit seinem Volk hineingenommen ist....

(7) Wir stellen darum fest:

Durch Jahrhunderte wurde das Wort 'neu' in der Bibelauslegung gegen das jüdische Volk gerichtet: Der neue Bund wurde als Gegensatz zum alten Bund, das neue Gottesvolk als Ersetzung des alten Gottesvolkes verstanden...

The complete text, the explicating theses, and the accompanying essays are of great interest, and should be read as a whole: *Zur Erneuerung des Verhältnisses von Christen und Juden* (Mülheim [Ruhr], 1980), graciously sent to me by Eberhard Bethge. An English translation of the resolution itself is given in Croner, *More Stepping Stones*, 207-209.

"...it is not you that support the root, but the root that supports you." Rom 11:18b.[5]

In the same vein the Rheinland Synod declares as the fourth point of its confession:

(4) We believe in the permanent election of the Jewish people as the people of God, and we realize that through Jesus Christ the church is taken into the covenant of God with his people...[6]

These two quotations would seem to reveal the heart of the Rheinland Synod's inner-canonical canon: New Testament passages—dominantly ones in Romans 9-11—considered to be supportive of the view that the church has been taken into God's covenant with God's people Israel.

The limits of the Synod's inner-canonical canon are no less clear than its heart. Excluded by silence are Paul's comments about "the Jews who killed both the Lord Jesus and the prophets" in 1 Thessalonians 2, his nearly gnostic portrait of the Law's genesis in Galatians 3, the sharp polarity involved in his positing of two covenants in Galatians 4 and 2 Corinthians 3, and so on.[7] The major reasons for such practical exclusion are not far to seek. The history of the interpretation of these latter passages includes some dark and altogether regrettable chapters. One thinks, for example, of the famous statues that, flanking the south portal of the Strasbourg Cathedral, portray a proud and triumphant church, and a humbled and blindfolded synagogue. Those statues were obviously conceived by an artist who thought he was accurately

---

[5] The identity of the root is an important exegetical issue. A strong case can be made that Paul intended to refer to *God's gracious election*, enacted newly in each patriarchal generation, and climatically in Christ. Among the studies listed below in note 61, see especially the perceptive essay of N. Walter.

[6] For the German text see note 4 above.

[7] On 1 Thess 2:13-16 see Birger Pearson, "1 Thessalonians 2:13-16: A Deutero-Pauline Interpolation," *HTR* 64 (1971) 74-94; Hendrikus Boers, "The Form-Critical Study of Paul's Letters: I Thessalonians as a Case Study," *NTS* 22 (1976) 140-158; W. D. Davies, "Paul and the People of Israel," *NTS* 24 (1977) 4-39 (6-9); Tjitze Baarda, "Maar de toorn is over hen gekomen...'," 15-74 in Tjitze Baarda, Hans Jansen, S. J. Noorda, and J. S. Vos, *Paulus en de andere joden* (Delft: Meinema,1984); Karl P. Donfried, "Paul and Judaism: 1 Thess 2:13-16 as a Test Case," *Int* 38 (1984) 242-253; I. Broer, "'Antisemitismus' und 'Judenpolemik im Neuen Testament.' Ein Beitrag zum besseren Verständnis von 1 Thess 2,14-16," 734-772 in *Religion und Verantwortung als Elemente gesellschaftlicher Ordnung* (Beiheft zu den Siegener Studien, ohne Jahr). For a contrasting and thoroughly odious canon within the canon, see the New Testament "cleansed of Jewish relics" by the Institut zur Erforschung des jüdischen Einflusses: *Die Botschaft Gottes* (Weimar, 1941).

presenting Paul's theology as it emerges in 2 Corinthians 3, whereas he was in the main furthering the forms of anti-semitism that were widespread among Christians in medieval Europe.[8]

Small wonder that a group of European Christians, living after the Holocaust and admirably intent on rectifying some of the most grievous wrongs done to Jews by Christians, should concentrate their attention on certain parts of the Pauline corpus, to the practical exclusion of others. All exegetes work with an operative canon within the canon, their own context and thus their own history inevitably playing a significant role in their interpretive labors.[9]

It is equally true, however, that the suppressed parts of the canon often have a way of reasserting themselves, to the surprise of those who have ignored them. I am quick to say that the present essay is not designed with the presumptuous intention of instructing the framers of the Rheinland resolution as to the breadth of the Pauline canon.[10] Recognizing, however, that the term "covenant" plays a truly significant role in the resolution and that the resolution draws at several points on Paul's letters, one must at least ask whether it is wise to pen a covenant-oriented, largely Pauline resolution without reference to the earliest covenant passages in the Pauline corpus, those in the letter to the Galatians. Thus the modest goal of the present essay: to re-examine some of the issues that emerge in one of the excluded passages, Gal 4:21-5:1, as those issues might be pertinent to genuine conversation between Jews and Christians today.

---

[8] On the medieval roots of anti-Semitism see Heiko Obermann, *Wurzeln des Anti-Semitismus* (Berlin: Severin und Siedler, 1981); "Antisemitismus," in *TRE*. In a typically honest way the Rheinland Synod arranged for sermonic Bible studies on "problematic" texts, including 2 Corinthians 3 (E. Bethge) and Matt 23 (E. Schweizer), *Zur Erneuerung*, 56-71 and 72-78. Regarding 2 Corinthians 3 see notes 55, 57, and 59 below.

[9] In Baarda, Jansen, Noorda, and Vos, *Paulus en de andere joden*, 75-113, 107, n.20, Jansen points to the remarkable fact that there is not a word about Gal 4:21-31 in Karl Barth's comprehensive treatment of Galatians in *Die Kirchliche Dogmatic* (Zürich: Evangelischer Verlag, 1932-1967) IV/1, 712-718 (ET IV/1,637-642).

[10] Nor is it my intention to offer a comprehensive critique of the Synod's work, beyond saying that, in my opinion, a number of the resolution's aspects were well conceived and should prove helpful to Christians and Jews, as they seek faithful ways of relating to one another.

II
The Dominant Interpretation of Gal 4:21-5:1 and Its Grounds[11]

The history of interpretation reveals that the authors of the Rheinland resolution had reason to fear this passage, for the exegetes have been and are nearly unanimous in their opinion that it is anti-Judaic.[12] There have been a few dissenting voices, and the dominant reading itself has admitted minor variations; but in the main it has shown a remarkable vitality and tenacity from the second century to the twentieth.

Marcion. The earliest interpretation of the passage to which we have access is the one that, according to Tertullian, was given to it by Marcion. Having carefully noted Marcion's excision of the references Paul made to Abraham in Galatians 3, Tertullian expresses surprise that the man of Pontus should have let the final Abraham passage stand, even with a few changes; for, says Tertullian, it heads the list of texts one should have expected Marcion to remove in order to shape Galatians to his own theology. With this introduction, Tertullian continues by quoting and glossing the text of Gal 4:22-26 as it was read by Marcion and his followers (AM 5.4.8; Tertullian's glosses in brackets):

> For if Abraham had two sons, one by a bondmaid and the other by a free woman, but he that was by the bondmaid was born after the flesh, while he that was by the free woman was by promise: which things are allegorical,
> [which means, indicative of something else (*id est aliud portendentia*):]
> for these are two testaments (*duo testamenta*)
> [or two revelations, as I see they have translated it (*sive duae ostensiones, sicut invenimus interpretatum*)]
>
> the one from Mount Sinai referring to the synagogue of the Jews, which according to the Law gendereth to bondage: the other gendering above all principality, power, and domination, and every name that is named, not only in this world but also in

---

[11] Gal 5:1 belongs both to what precedes it and to what follows it.

[12] Markus Barth, *The People of God* (Sheffield: JSOT, 1983), for example, after thoroughly endorsing what we will shortly find to be the normative reading of Gal 4:21-31, repairs to Rom 9-11 for evidence that "after the writing of Galatians Paul progressed in his thinking"(45).

that which is to come: for she is our mother, the holy church, in whom we have expressed our faith:

[and consequently he adds, So then, brethren, we are not children of the bondwoman, but of the free. In all this the apostle has clearly shown that the noble dignity of Christianity has its allegorical type and figure in the son of Abraham born of a free woman, while the legal bondage of Judaism has its type in the son of the bondmaid: and consequently, that both the dispensations derive from that God with whom we have found the outline sketch of both the dispensations.][13]

Tertullian's expression of surprise, and notably his grounding the surprise in the claim that no passage in Galatians is more threatening to Marcion's theology, would seem to be instances of legal rhetoric, by which Tertullian was probably seeking (unconsciously?) to disguise two things.

The first is the fact that, with the possible exception of Gal 3:19 (read, as Marcion would certainly have read it—if he included it—to affirm that angels acting for the creator God ordained the Law), no part of the letter is more friendly to Marcion's theological program than the paired opposites of 4:21-5:1.[14] Indeed, one should think it a short step

---

[13] Ernest Evans, *Tertullian: Adversus Marcionem* (Oxford: Clarendon, 1972) 530-531. This highly interesting and somewhat opaque passage has elicited a great deal of discussion in the quest for Marcion's text of Paul's letters, and also in the study of Tertullian as a Biblical exegete. In addition to the classic treatment in Adolf von Harnack, *Marcion* (2nd ed.; Leipzig: J. C. Hinrichs, 1924) 46-47, 52*-53*, 75*-76*, cf. most recently Thomas P. O'Malley, S.J., *Tertullian and the Bible* (Nijmegen-Utrecht: Dekker & Van de Vegt, 1967); John J. Clabeaux, *A Lost Edition of the Letters of Paul: Reassessment of the Text of the Pauline Corpus Attested by Marcion* (Washington: Catholic Biblical Association of America, 1989). One sees that Tertullian has provided two parenthetical remarks in the course of quoting Marcion's text. It is important to note that they are not altogether coordinate. The first, *id est aliud portendentia*, is a true gloss in which Tertullian makes clear his understanding of allegory, using a term important to him (on *portendere* in Tertullian's vocabulary see O'Malley, 55, 165-165). The second parenthesis comprises the six words following *duo testamenta*, and it is hardly an attempt on Tertullian's part to clarify the term *testamenta* by a glossing reference to *ostensiones* (so Clabeaux, 56), explaining the clear by the less-clear. As interpreters from Harnack to O'Malley have recognized, Tertullian is telling his reader that at this juncture Marcion changed the text, reading *ostensiones* (perhaps ἐπιδείξεις in Greek) rather than *testamenta*. Tertullian does not object to this change, doubtless understanding the *duo ostensiones* to be the legal and graceful revelations authored by the same God.

[14] In his helpful discussion of Marcion's reading of Paul, Andreas Lindemann, *Paulus im ältesten Christentum* (Tübingen: J.C.B. Mohr [Paul Siebeck], 1979) 385, follows Harnack in holding that Marcion omitted Gal 3:15-25. On the basis of Irenaeus' citation R. Joseph

from them to Marcion's lost book entitled *Antitheses*.[15] With light retouching (Marcion thought of restoration), the passage doubtless seemed to Marcion truly representative of his beloved Paul. One can scarcely share Tertullian's surprise that Marcion should have retained it.

The second thing Tertullian disguises is the extent of his agreement with Marcion. He would have known, of course, that Marcion thought the revelation of the Sinai-bondwoman to have come from the Creator God, whereas that of the free woman would have come from the formerly unknown God of mercy. He concludes, therefore, with his customary polemic, insisting that both "dispensations," different as they are, derive from the one and only God. The observations he makes on the way toward that monotheistic correction seem, however, to be altogether harmonious with the views of Marcion.

If Marcion can find that, in speaking of the Sinai revelation, Paul was explicitly referring to "the synagogue of the Jews which according to the law begets to bondage," Tertullian can move easily to "Judaism," saying that "the legal bondage of Judaism has its type in the son of the bondmaid." And correspondingly, while Marcion (after bringing in Eph 1:21) is confident that Paul explicated his reference to "our mother" by adding the appositional expression "that holy church, in whom we have expressed our faith," Tertullian is himself similarly sure of Paul's intention to use the allegorical type of Abraham's free-born son to speak of "the noble dignity of Christianity." We see, then, that Gal 4:21-5:1, with its striking contrasts, is almost made to order for Marcion, and that

---

Hoffmann, *Marcion: on the Restitution of Christianity* (Chico, CA: Scholars, 1984) 201, argues that Marcion included 3:19, 22-25.

[15] There are, to be sure, three facets of this passage that must have been problematic for Marcion: (a) the fact that both of the sons—the one he thought connected with the church as well as the one he saw to be related to the synagogue—were sons of Abraham, (b) the presence of the word *allegoria*, and (c) the reference to *duo testamenta*. Regarding the first problem, we can presume that Marcion was willing to overlook the sons' common descent from Abraham, perhaps because, in light of the polar opposition between their mothers, the sons are emphatically contrasted with one another. The sharp polarity of the passage apparently solved the other two problems as well, providing assurance that in this instance the term *allegoria* (to which Marcion was not totally allergic) points to pairs of opposites, and that in the context of such opposites the apostle himself cannot have spoken of two complementary testaments, but rather of two exhibitions or revelations, set in stark contrast with one another. One will scarcely identify Marcion's reading as totally arbitrary; he perceptively sensed Paul's habit of thinking in terms of two orbs of power unfolding in opposition to one another (*pace* Andreas Lindemann, *Paulus*, 389-390). A major theological problem attending Marcion's rather wooden *antithesis* arises, however, when one compares them with Paul's thoroughly dynamic *antinomies*. See J. Louis Martyn, "Apocalyptic Antinomies in Paul's Letter to the Galatians," *NTS* 31 (1985) 410-424 and Martyn, "Paul and His Jewish-Christian Interpreters," *USQR* 42 (1988) 1-15.

the application of these contrasts to Judaism and Christianity—much to the cost of Judaism with its "legal bondage"—is a matter on which Marcion and Tertullian are in fundamental agreement.[16]

For the sake of brevity we make our way from Marcion and Tertullian to representative interpreters of the late twentieth century, pausing at only two points.

Luther. In his Galatians lectures of 1535, Luther, without mentioning Marcion and Tertullian, specifically linked Hagar, the slave woman, with "the synagogue" intent on the righteousness of the Law, while Sarah was the true church, "our free mother."[17]

Lightfoot. Writing in 1865, Joseph B. Lightfoot found in Paul's allegory an even sharper religious polarity. He seems, in fact, to be the first interpreter to explicate the polarity of the passage by mentioning the absolute nature of the Pythagorean table of opposites. Emphasizing these opposites, he spoke emphatically of "the slavery of Judaism," sure that Paul held Judaism to be an enslaving religion that had to disappear with the advent of Christianity. Thus, having identified "the Jews [as] children of Abraham after the flesh [and] the Christians [as] his children after the promise," Lightfoot added that, by denying the inheritance to the flesh-born sons of the slave woman (Gal 4:30, quoting Gen 21:10), Paul confidently sounded "the death-knell of Judaism."[18] Both in Luther and in Lightfoot one senses that the primary struggle is being waged between groups inside the church.[19] The fact remains that both were sure of Paul's intention to wage that inner-church struggle by linking fleshly birth and slavery with Judaism itself.

---

[16] Between the readings given our passage by Marcion and by Tertullian there may be one significant difference: Marcion's may be less monolithically negative as regards Judaism! See the very suggestive analysis of Hoffmann, *Marcion: On the Restitution of Christianity*, 226-238.

[17] Martin Luther, *Lectures on Galatians 1535* (ed. Jaroslav Pelikan, *Luther's Works* 26, St. Louis: Concordia, 1963) 441-442. Chronologically the path from Marcion's (and Tertullian's) exegesis of Gal 4:21-5:1 to that of Luther is a long one (for part of it see R. J. Kepple, "An Analysis of Antiochene Exegesis of Gal 4:24-26," *WTJ* 39 [1977] 239-249). Substantively it is very short. Luther refers to Jerome and Augustine; his silence about Marcion and Tertullian cannot hide the basic similarities.

[18] J. B. Lightfoot, *The Epistle of St. Paul to the Galatians* (1865; Grand Rapids: Zondervan, 1957) 180, 184. About Lightfoot's adjectival interpretation of the prepositional phrases κατὰ σάρκα and διὰ τῆς ἐπαγγελίας we will have more to say below.

[19] The same thing can be said about Marcion. See note 16 above. The history of Judaism in the church is a subject analyzed with considerable acumen by Leo Baeck; see J. Louis Martyn, "Leo Baeck," in *Jewish Perspectives on Christianity: The Views of Leo Baeck, Martin Buber, Franz Rosenzweig, Will Herberg, and Abraham A. Heschel* (ed. Fritz A. Rothschild; New York: Crossroad, 1990).

The Late Twentieth Century. Essentially the same exegetical conclusions emerge in the commentaries of Heinrich Schlier (12th edition 1962) and H. D. Betz (1979). Both find in Paul's allegory a polarity between Judaism and Christianity, and both discern a clear indication of the supersession of Judaism by Christianity in Paul's insistence that the inheritance falls not to Ishmael, but rather to Isaac (Gal 4:30; Gen 21:10). The statements of Betz are unequivocal:

> ...if God has given the inheritance to Gentile Christians (cf. 3:14,29; 4:1,7), the Jews are excluded from it, and the Christians constitute the Israel of God (6:16)....According to Galatians Judaism is excluded from salvation altogether...[20]

One sees, then, that Marcion's reading of the text sails through the patristic, medieval, and modern periods as though it had been an arrow shot from the bow of the most orthodox of exegetes. For, with minor variations, the exegetical conclusions of Schlier and Betz reflect the dominant interpretive line from the second to the twentieth centuries; they present, just as surely, the virtually normative exegesis of the present.[21]

The chief characteristics of this interpretation are as clear as is its hegemony:

1) The Pythagorean-like polarity of the passage is accented.
2) The prepositional phrases by which this polarity is largely expressed— "according to the flesh" versus "according

---

[20] H. D. Betz, *Galatians* (Hermeneia; Philadelphia: Fortress, 1979) 250-251. In Schlier's opinion, by speaking of Hagar and Ishmael, Paul refers to the synagogue, the Jews, Israel living under the Law; while with Sarah, the Jerusalem above, he intends the mother of the Christians. Schlier also cites with approval the comment of Worner (1882) on v 30: "...by its persecution of the heir, the Law-observant Israel only causes itself to lose the inheritance," clearly a supersessionist interpretation; Heinrich Schlier, *Der Brief an die Galater* (Meyer; Göttingen: Vandenhoeck & Ruprecht, 1962) 227. Let me add that, overall, no commentaries on Galatians have taught me more than the ones by Schlier and Betz.

[21] This normative interpretation has a very perceptive and formidable critic in Franz Mussner, *Der Galaterbrief* (Freiburg: Herder, 1974), but his own exegesis has not carried the day, as one can see from a great many studies of the passage, e.g. the perceptive treatment of C. K. Barrett, "The Allegory of Abraham, Sarah, and Hagar in the Argument of Galatians," *Rechtfertigung: Festschrift für Ernst Käsemann* (ed. J. Friedrich, W. Pöhlmann, and P. Stuhlmacher; Tübingen: J.C.B. Mohr [Paul Siebeck], 1976), and from the recent commentary of Udo Borse, *Der Brief an die Galater* (Regensburg: Verlag F. Pustet, 1984).

to the Spirit," etc.—are taken to be adjectival identity markers, differentiating from one another two existent peoples. There is a people "according to the flesh" and there is a people "according to the Spirit."
3) These two existent peoples are understood to be, respectively, the Jews and the Christians; the polarity of the passage is thus focused specifically on Judaism and Christianity.
4) Judaism is consequently characterized as the religion of slavery and Christianity as the religion of freedom.
5) Verse 29 is taken to be a reference to the synagogue's mid-first century persecution of the church.
6) And verse 30 is then read as an affirmation of the resulting supersession—according to God's will—of the synagogue by the church. Henceforth Christians are God's people; Jews are not.

As one rereads Paul's text with these characteristics in mind, one sees that the dominant interpretation stands on solid ground. The sharp polarity is unmistakable. That one of the poles is Judaism seems obvious from the presence of some of Judaism's major symbols—Sinai, the covenant of Sinai, Jerusalem— and from the way in which Paul speaks of persecution (cf. 1 Thess 2:13-16).[22] That the other pole is Christianity appears equally clear. The use of the verb "persecute" in v 29 calls specifically to mind Paul's use of this verb to characterize his own efforts as a Pharisee to exterminate the church (Gal 1:13,23; Phil 3:6).[23] And when one recalls that a major motif of the friction between mainstream Judaism and nascent Christianity had to do with the issue of inheritance (e.g., Mark 12:1-12 and parallels), one may be ready to see a reflection of the same motif in the reference to competition over inheritance in v 30. The dominant reading is far from arbitrary.

---

[22] In commenting on the passage in 1 Thessalonians, T. Holtz speaks correctly of Judaism "als es aktiv gegen die Christusbotschaft und ihre Zeugen vorgeht, indem es ihnen die Legitimation durch Gott abspricht," *Der Erste Brief an die Thessalonicher* (EKK; Zürich: Benziger/Neukirchener, 1986) 111.

[23] In addition to Gal 1:13 and 1:23 Paul employs the verb διώκω in 5:11 and 6:12, passages to which we will return below.

III
Exegetical Notes

Granted that there is much to be said for the dominant reading, one has still to ask whether there are important aspects of the text to which its proponents have given inadequate attention.

A. Gal 4:21-5:1 in Its Context[24]

Interpreters generally identify the preceding paragraph, 4:12-20, as one in which Paul rehearses the history of his personal relationship with the Galatians, doing so with great intensity of feeling, and closing with an emphatic expression of perplexity. More often than not, they then find a puzzle in the fact that, after such a richly affective section, Paul should return to a complex and sophisticated exegetical paragraph that would seem to have been better located within the argument from scripture in the letter's third chapter.[25] The puzzle becomes less puzzling when, with Beverly Roberts Gaventa, one pays serious attention to the powerful metaphor of 4:19, Paul's being in "labor pains" with the Galatians until Christ "be formed" among them.[26] For it is this startling metaphor that indicates the fundamental nature of Paul's perplexity. In part it is, to be sure, the perplexity of a debater who cannot be altogether confident that the arguments he has advanced thus far will bring the Galatians out of their foolishness (4:20 looks back to 3:1). Much more is involved, however, than the rhetoricians's anxious

---

[24] I am confident that in both of the exegetical sections of Galatians (3:6-4:7 and 4:21-5:1) Paul concerns himself with Abraham texts in Genesis because the Teachers have already used these texts very effectively, causing the Galatians to long for a relationship to the patriarch. We would know nothing of what Paul thought about Abraham (and Sarah and Hagar), had the Teachers not compelled him to speak on the subject, and had he not reworked the Abraham parts of Galatians in writing to the Romans. In the limits of the present essay we can attend to the Teachers only in passing. See C. K. Barrett, "The Allegory of Abraham, Sarah, and Hagar in the Argument of Galatians," (note 21 above); Bernard H. Brinsmead, *Galatians—Dialogical Response to Opponents* (Chico, CA: Scholars Press,1982) 107-114; and J. Louis Martyn, "A Law-Observant Mission to Gentiles: The Background of Galatians, "*SJT* 38 (1985) 307-324, where reasons are given for referring to the persons who came into Paul's Galatian churches as "the Teachers.".

[25] E.g. Albrecht Oepke, *Der Brief des Paulus an die Galater* (2nd ed., Berlin: Evangelische Verlagsanstalt, 1957).

[26] I have in mind a percipient study of Beverly Roberts Gaventa, which she kindly shared in typescript, "The Maternity of Paul: Exegetical Reflections on Galatians 4:19." [Editor's note: now available in *The Conversation Continues: Studies in Paul and John in Honor of J. Louis Martyn* (ed. Robert T. Fortna and Beverly R. Gaventa; Nashville: Abingdon, 1990) 189-201.]

impulse to call in heavy artillery (4:21-5:1) for fear of losing the argument. The astonishing metaphor of 4:19 points expressly to the perplexity, not of a debater, but rather of an expectant mother, who, thinking the child has been safely born (the genesis of the Galatian communities was untroubled; 4:14), discovers to her dismay that she herself is once again in labor pains, because, due to subsequent developments (the work of the Teachers; 4:15-18), the formation of the child has been interrupted and is therefore not yet complete.[27] The work of the Teachers, in short, is profoundly troubling to Paul, not simply because it threatens him with the possible loss of a debate, but fundamentally because it thrusts him again into both the birth pangs and the anxiety of labor, when he should be celebrating the steady maturation of a healthy new-born.[28]

Can one detect, then, a reason for Paul's turning from the perplexity of his labor pains to the allegorical exegesis of 4:21-5:1? The question is not difficult to answer, for one of the chief motifs in the new paragraph, as we will shortly see, is that of begetting and birthing. Paul can easily move from the one paragraph to the next, then, by means of the closely associated motifs of labor pains, the anxiety attendant to a difficult birth, and the coming into being of new-born children. When we search, then for the heart of the Hagar/Sarah allegory, we will do well to pay attention to the ligaments by which Paul has bound that paragraph to its predecessor. Perhaps the numerous references in 4:21-5:1 to the process of the begetting and bearing of children tell us that all the way from 4:12 to 5:1 there is only one major subject: the birthing and the consequent identity of the Galatian churches.

---

[27] On the vocables μορφοῦσθαι and μεταμορφοῦσθαι see J. Koenig, "The Motif of Transformation in the Pauline Epistles," (Dissertation, UnionTheological Seminary, 1970).

[28] Had Paul used the verb ὠδίνειν in a way that adhered strictly to the apocalyptic pattern evident in Dan 12:1, 2 Bar 68:2-3, etc. (cf. also Mark 13:8; Rev 12:2), he would have spoken of the great suffering of *the Galatians* (the people of God) at the hands of their enemies (the Teachers), as the *difficult but promising* beginning of their God-given deliverance. His modifications are striking: *he* suffers birth pangs, these renewed birth pangs bring him more anxiety than promise, and the deliverance of the people will be the *formation of Christ* in their congregations. The role played by the enemies of God's people in apocalyptic thought may be, however, in the back of his mind as he thinks of the Teachers; and as an apostle of Christ, Paul never understands his suffering to be a private and individual matter. See 1 Cor 4:8-13. As Gaventa points out, taking account of Rom 8:19, 22, the anguish Paul expresses in Gal 4:19 is more than a personal matter: "...it reflects the anguish of the whole created order, as it awaits the fulfillment of God's action in Jesus Christ."

B. The Literary Form of Gal 4:21-5:1

In form the paragraph is an exegetical argument, framed by two questions: "Tell me, you who desire to be under the rule of the Law, do you not hear what the Law actually says?" (v 21) and "What precisely does the scripture say?" (v 30). Paul's passion that the Galatians really listen to the voice of scripture, at his side rather than at the side of the Teachers, involves him in the interpretation of five texts in Genesis, all drawn from the Abraham cycle, and one text in Isaiah.[29] The fact that, after saying "It stands written in scripture," Paul initially summarizes material from the Abraham cycle, without giving formal quotations, does not lessen the exegetical nature of the paragraph. His vocabulary itself shows that he is dealing altogether seriously with the texts of Genesis 16 and 21, while taking side glances at Genesis 15 and 17, and developing the motif of promise from Genesis 15 and 18.

Galatians		Genesis (LXX)	
4:22	Abraham	16:1	Abram
	sons	:11	son (Ishmael)
	slave woman	:1	...slave woman
:23	from the slave woman	:2	from her
:24	covenants	15:18 and 17:2 etc.	covenant
:24	Hagar	16:1	Hagar
:28	Isaac	21:2-3	son...Isaac
:29	persecuted	:9	playing with (but strengthened in Jewish traditions to forms of violence)
:30	Cast out the slave woman and her son; for the son of the slave woman will not inherit with the son of the freewoman.	21:10	Cast out this slave woman and her son; for the son of this slave woman will not inherit with the son of mine, Isaac.

---

[29] Cf. Eduard Verhoef, *Er Staat Geschreven...De Oud-Testamentische Citaten in de Brief aan de Galaten* (Amsterdam: Meppel, Krips Repro, 1979) 89-104, 167-168, 200-211. For new and interesting ways of approaching Paul the exegete, see D. -A. Koch, *Die Schrift als Zeuge des Evangeliums* (Tübingen: J. C. B. Mohr [Paul Siebeck], 1986) and Richard B. Hays, *Echoes of Scripture in the Letters of Paul* (New Haven: Yale University Press,1989).

The noun "promise" and the verb "to promise" do not occur in the Abraham stories that Paul is interpreting (they are scarcely to be found in the OT), but he is certainly developing a key theological motif of these stories when he characterizes Isaac as the son born through the power of God's promise (see notably Gen 15:4-5; 18:10,14). To a considerable extent Paul stays close to the Genesis texts about which the Galatians are already hearing a great deal from the Teachers.

There are also many things in the stories of Genesis 15-21 to which Paul gives no attention at all; as most of these have to do with the term "covenant," we will return to them below. For the moment one example will suffice: the indelible connection in Genesis between the covenant and the command of circumcision. In constructing his exegesis Paul is totally silent about that matter; like all other exegetes, he is selective.[30]

He is also creative, for, as surely as the texts of Genesis 15-21 include motifs he must suppress, so they also fail to provide him with some of the terms and expressions that are crucial to his interpretation. He does not hesitate to provide them himself, and in every verse:

Galatians
- 4:22   two (sons); the free woman
- :23   was begotten according to the flesh...(was begotten) through the promise (γεννᾶν)[31]
- :24   allegorical matters
         two covenants (δύο διαθῆκαι)
         Sinai; bearing children into slavery (γεννᾶν)
- :25-26 [entire; note particularly the following:] is located in the same oppositional column (συστοιχεῖ); the present

---

[30] This instance of Paul's silence is only one facet of his apparently arbitrary exegesis of Genesis 16-21. If one leaves aside Paul's interpretive point of departure (see note 51 below), one can see that Shalom Ben-Chorin is fully justified in identifying Gal 4:21-5:1 as "eine völlige Umdrehung der Vätersage," *Paulus, der Völker Apostel in jüdischer Sicht* (München: Deutscher Taschenbuch Verlag, 1980) 132. Cf. Günter Klein, "Römer 4 und die Idee der Heilsgeschichte," *Rekonstruktion und Interpretation* (München: C. Kaiser, 1969) 145-169, "Eine brutalere Paganisierung vorgeblicher Heilsgeschichte lässt sich schwerlich noch vorstellen" (168). In order to see what Paul is talking about and what he is not talking about, one considers not only his silence regarding weighty factors in the Genesis texts, but also his silence regarding equally weighty factors in his own setting: (a) the people he will later call, in Rom 9:3, "my kinsmen by race," (b) the gospel mission to this people, and (c) those who pursue that mission while gladly accepting as part of God's work the Law-free mission to Gentiles.

[31] One may make, to be sure, a general comparison with Philo, *On the Cherubim*, 40-47; see M. Dibelius, *Botschaft und Geschichte* (Tübingen: J. C. B. Mohr, [Paul Siebeck], 1953) I, 30-34.

	Jerusalem; is in slavery; children; the Jerusalem above; mother
:27	Isa 54:1
:28	children of the promise
:29	the one begotten according to the flesh persecuted (cf. Jewish traditions based on Gen 21:10) the one (begotten) according to the Spirit (γεννᾶν)
:30	of the free woman
:31	children of the free woman

Among those items provided by Paul there are perhaps a dozen calling for extended comment. In the present essay we confine ourselves to two: the verb γεννᾶν, "to beget" (with male subject), "to bear a child" (with female subject), and the expression δύο διαθῆκαι, "two covenants."

C. The verb γεννᾶν (to "beget," "to bear")

The Genesis stories Paul is interpreting are focused on the significant births of Ishmael and Isaac, and in these stories the births are consistently referred to by the verb τίκτειν, the verb γεννᾶν being absent.[32] Paul's interpretation accents the motif of birth even more strongly than do the stories themselves. Yet in emphasizing that motif, Paul avoids the verb τίκτειν altogether, putting in its place γεννᾶν. We are immediately faced, then, with an emphatic substitution. Paul uses or clearly implies his verb γεννᾶν five times, and he spreads it throughout the whole of the passage, twice in v 23, once in v 24, and again twice in v 29. Why has Paul departed from his Genesis text in this way?

The first suggestion that comes to mind arises from the manner in which the verbs τίκτειν and γεννᾶν are used in the Septuagint as a whole. Whereas in Hebrew the verb *yld* is employed both of a man's begetting a child (*qal* and *hiphil*) and of a woman's bearing a child (*qal*), the Septuagint translators, virtually without exception, made a linguistic separation, rendering the male use with γεννᾶν and γενέσθαι and the female use with τίκτειν.[33] Since Paul begins his exegesis by

---

[32] The one instance of γεννᾶν, Gen 17:20, has no relevance to the births of Ishmael and Isaac.

[33] The book of Genesis itself provides good examples: "And Bethuel became the father of (*yālad*/γεννᾶν) Rebekah. These eight Milcah bore(*yālad*/τίκτειν) to Nahor..." (22:23). "Joseph had two sons(*yālad*/γενέσθαι), whom Asenath...bore (*yālad*/τίκτειν) to him" (41:50). One might cite as an exception Num 11:12, where Moses asks God, "Did I conceive all this people? Did I bring them forth (*yālad*/τίκτειν), that thou shouldst say to

speaking of Abraham's fathering two sons (his being the begetter is a thing taken for granted in Genesis 16 and 21), and, since Paul is interpreting stories from the Septuagint, one might suggest that he would naturally follow the Septuagint pattern of using γεννᾶν when the subject is a male. This suggestion could have some cogency for v 23 (possibly also for v 29), but one would scarcely wish to argue that it has any pertinence for v 24. After his introductory remark about Abraham, Paul lets the patriarch drop from sight altogether— he does not even allow Abraham to reemerge in the paragraph's conclusion— speaking centrally not of a man's begetting children, but rather of two women bearing children.[34] When he turns, then, to the two feminine characters, one should have expected him to return to the text of Genesis 16 and 21—and to Septuagintal usage in general—by employing the "feminine" verb τίκτειν. He does not do this.[35]

The need to explain Paul's avoidance of τίκτειν in favor of consistently using γεννᾶν becomes even more pressing in light of two further facts: (a) Paul does not avoid the verb τίκτειν when in v 27 he quotes from Isaiah: he allows it to stand in the first line of that text (the only occurrence of the verb in Paul's letters); (b) had Paul employed the birthing verb which he found in Genesis 16 and 21, he could have made use of that word to connect those Genesis texts with the one from Isaiah by *gezerah shawah* (analogy based on verbal congruity), a rule with which we know him to have been acquainted (e.g., Rom 4:3-9, where he uses the rule in order to interpret an Abraham text in Genesis).[36]

Paul's determination to give a weighty role to the verb γεννᾶν, omitting altogether the birthing verb he found in his Genesis texts, is

---

me, 'Carry them in your bosom, as a nurse carries a suckling child...'?" But this exception proves the rule with double force, for τίκτειν is needed here to be in harmony with the striking feminine imagery used of Moses.

[34] We have already noted that it is the Teachers who have directed the Galatians' attention to Abraham, exhorting them, as C. K. Barrett has put it, to join the right branch of the patriarch's family (note 21 above). Paul's concern is differently focused: he is interested in the significance of the two women, in the meaning of their two birthing processes, and in the resulting identity of their two sons.

[35] One might also suggest that Paul's employing γεννᾶν throughout is an instance of his observing classical usage, where γεννᾶν refers both to males begetting (thus Abraham) and to females bearing (thus Hagar and Sarah). Since, however, the same is true of the classical use of τίκτειν, Paul could have achieved linguistic homogeneity by employing throughout the verb present in his Genesis texts. Clearly his attention is focused neither on a Septuagintal pattern nor on a classical one.

[36] On *gezerah shawah* see, e.g., Saul Lieberman, *Hellenism in Jewish Palestine* (New York: Jewish Theological Seminary of America, 1962) 58-62.

unmistakable. We must inquire, then, about the source of this determination, and we can do that by asking the simple question: What associations has the verb γεννᾶν for Paul?

Two other passages show us that this verb is an element in Paul's mission-oriented vocabulary: When Paul speaks of the Christian birth of Onesimus through his apostolic ministry, he employs the verb γεννᾶν:

> I appeal to you for my child (τέκνον) Onesimus, whom I begot (γεννᾶν) in my imprisonment (Philemon 10).

Similarly, when he recalls the genesis of the Corinthian church, he uses the same verb:

> I do not write this to make you ashamed, but to admonish you as my beloved children (τέκνα). For though you have countless guides in Christ, you do not have many fathers. For I begot you (γεννᾶν) in Christ Jesus through the gospel (1 Cor 4:14-15).

The verb γεννᾶν (linked with the nouns τέκνον and τέκνα) is one of the expressions Paul uses to speak of the genesis of Christians and of Christian churches through the power of the gospel entrusted to him by God. Leaving aside the present passage (and the different case in Rom 9:11), we see that Paul employs this verb only to speak of the effects of his apostolic work.[37]

We can assume, then, that, had the genesis and development of the Galatian churches proceeded smoothly, Paul, after referring to the Galatians as his children (τέκνα), would have spoken in 4:19 not of protracted labor pains, but rather of joyous begetting, employing his missioning verb γεννᾶν. As we have seen, it is the apocalyptic woes associated with the Teachers' work that compel him to use the word ὠδίνειν instead.

But he suppresses his mission-oriented verb γεννᾶν only for one significant moment (4:19-20). When he turns to the allegorical exegesis of the birth stories in Genesis 16 and 21, he brings it to the fore, as we

---

[37] Birth was a metaphor employed very widely for conversion. See, e.g., the passages about proselytizing in *b Yebamoth* and *Cant Rabba* cited by K. H. Rengstorf in his part of the article on γεννᾶν in *TDNT* 1:666-668, and note in *Cant Rabba* the use of the verb "to form" (yāṣar), which may be compared with the use of the corresponding Greek verb in Gal 4:19. See also K. G. Kuhn, προσήλυτος in *TDNT* 6:727-744; the discussion of the birth metaphor in Beverly R. Gaventa, *From Darkness to Light* (Philadelphia, 1986); references to a radical break with the past in Abraham J. Malherbe, *Paul and the Thessalonians* (Philadelphia: Fortress, 1987) 44 and 38.

have noted. Why? Clouded as it is, the real birth of the Galatian churches remains his subject in 4:21-5:1; and, having realistically faced the matter of birthpangs attendant to an excruciatingly troubled delivery, he is now free to address the issue of the Galatians' birth in another mode, finally employing his missioning verb γεννᾶν, and placing it in italics. How, exactly, does he use it? Several points seize one's attention.

1. *Tense.* Paul begins his new exegetical section with the past tense. He is preparing the ground for his exegesis by honoring the story-line from his text: Abraham had two sons, one begotten from the slave woman, one begotten from the free woman. With the exegetical notice, however, that these things are to be interpreted allegorically, Paul shifts, not surprisingly, to the present tense, maintaining that tense in every subsequent verse. We can be virtually certain, however, that we are not dealing with the timeless present generally characteristic of allegory.[38] In v 29 Paul refers typologically and emphatically to the real present ("so also now"), and his conclusion in v 31 is far removed from a timeless affirmation. He speaks of the present identity of the Galatians, doubtless thinking of his own missioning activity among them as he refers to their being those born from the Jerusalem above (v 26), from the promise (v 28), by the Spirit (v 29), from the free woman (v 31).

Surprising is the fact that Paul also speaks in the present tense of a second birthing process: the Hagar/Sinai covenant is even now bearing children into slavery (the present participle γεννῶσα has essentially the same force as do the present participles in Gal 3:5). Erasmus represents the dominant interpretation when he credits Paul with saying, "...the first [mother, Hagar,] *gave birth* to a people subject to servitude of the law...."[39] Had Paul wished to say this, he would surely have used the finite form of the aorist tense. As the text stands, Paul seems clearly to be employing the mission-oriented verb γεννᾶν not only to speak of his own evangelistic work, but also to refer to the *concurrent* work of others.

2. *Complexity.* It is Paul's speaking of two birthing processes that gives the passage its basic complexity. Presumably the verb γεννᾶν retains throughout its reference to a missionary genesis, but in a way far more

---

[38] On the mixture of allegory and typology see the excellent discussion in E. Grässer, *Der Alte Bund im Neuen* (Tübingen: J. C. B. Mohr [Paul Siebeck], 1985) 70-71. Philo interprets Sarah and Hagar allegorically and timelessly, the former being self-taught virtue, the latter imperfect training; see *On the Posterity of Cain*, 130; *On Mating with the Preliminary Studies*, 23; *On the Change of Names*, 255.

[39] *Collected Works of Erasmus*, vol. 42 (ed. R. D. Sider; Toronto: University of Toronto Press, 1984) 119, emphasis added.

complex than the simple one displayed in 1 Corinthians and Philemon, as we see from the fact that Paul baptizes the verb into his picture of polar opposites.

3. *Polarity.* This picture of polar opposites deepens the complexity we have already noted, emphasizing the radical differences between the two births. Whereas in 1 Corinthians 4 and Philemon 10 he uses the verb γεννᾶν by itself to refer univocally to a single birthing, i.e., to *his* gospel-begetting of Christians and Christian churches, here he modifies the verb consistently with contrasting prepositional phrases designed to emphasize the polarity evident in these two utterly different kinds of begetting and child-bearing. These polarized phrases take us back to the Pythagorean-like columns of opposites:

v 23 begotten *according to the flesh*	begotten *via the promise*
v 24 bearing children *into slavery*	(cf. being mothered by freedom v 26)
v 29 a child begotten *according to flesh*	a child begotten *according to the Spirit*

We have already noticed the present-tense force of the clause "bearing children into slavery." Now we can add another weighty point. The phrase "into slavery" is clearly adverbial, modifying "bearing children." The resulting clause, therefore, does not present a static characteristic of Hagar that could as well be expressed by the sentence "Hagar was a slave." We are faced, then, with a matter in regard to which we have to depart from the normative interpretation sketched earlier. From Lightfoot to Betz, as we have remarked, there is a steady tendency to interpret all of the prepositional phrases laid out above on the basis of the last of them, the one in v 29, and thus—in a way that is incorrect even for v 29—to take them as fundamentally adjectival, rather than as adverbial. Explicating the columns of opposites, Betz speaks of

> the dualism of flesh and Spirit as it pertains to two kinds of people, those who are "according to [the] flesh"...and those who are "according to [the] Spirit"...(249).

But in our text Paul consistently causes the contrasting prepositional phrases to modify the verb γεννᾶν (in finite and in participial form). Consequently he does not at all speak statically of persons who *are* according to the flesh and persons who *are* according to the Spirit. He uses the prepositional phrases to refer to two different birthing processes, two different modes of birth.

When one has made this simple grammatical observation, one sees that the normative interpretation, with all of its apparent strengths, begins to unravel. It is true, as we have suggested earlier, that Paul's exegetical argument is directed toward the issue of the Galatians' identity; vv 28 and 31 show as much. He wishes to tell them who they are. But he comes to the matter of their identity only by speaking of the kind of birthing process that brought them into being—and of another birthing process that threatens to bring them into a different state of being.

4. *Imbalance.* The emphasis Paul places on the Hagar column, the fact that he develops it with a degree of detail not given to the Sarah column, tells us—as we have already seen from his reference to "bearing children into slavery"—that his attention is initially concentrated on the part of the horizon occupied by the odious danger of being born in the wrong way— according to the flesh—and into the wrong sphere of power—the orb of slavery.

5. *Initial result.* The conclusion now begins to draw itself. If Paul is here employing the verb γεννᾶν to speak of missionary labors, as he does in 1 Corinthians (and as the context set by Gal 4:19 demands), then he is not speaking in the first instance of the birth of individuals, but of the birth of churches. In short, he uses the verb, modified by the polarized phrases, to speak of *two different ways in which churches are being born at the present time,* and thus of two different *missions.* (a) On the negative and odious side, he first mentions the Hagar mission, emphasizing its connection with the slave woman, its origin in Mount Sinai, its capacity to bear children according to the flesh and thus into slavery, and its correspondence with the present Jerusalem. That mission is even now producing churches, but those churches are being born into slavery; and, while, as Isaiah prophesied, the churches being founded in this Sinai/present-Jerusalem mission are less numerous than are those being born in the other mission, its representatives are able nevertheless to persecute the children of that other mission.

To be sure, Paul's employment of the verb διώκειν in 4:29 has proved to be a mainstay to the dominant reading; for interpreters have frequently noted that the force of this verb in Gal 1:13, 23 and Phil 3:6 corresponds to its use in Matthew, Luke-Acts, and John to refer to Jewish persecution of the emerging church.[40] Read in its context,

---

[40].Thus, Charles H. Cosgrove, "The Law Has Given Sarah No Children," *NovT* 29 (1987) 219-235, has reasonably concluded: "In Gal 4:29 one thinks most naturally of this

however, Paul's reference in v 29 to persecution is harmonious with his announcement of renewed birth pangs in 4:19. Thus, the integrity of 4:12-5:1 strongly suggests that both in 4:19 (ὠδίνειν) and in 4:29 (διώκειν) Paul thinks of the odious missioning work of the Teachers, not of the persecution of the nascent church by Jews.

(b) On the positive and joyous side he refers to the Sarah/Jerusalem-above mission that is producing Isaac-like churches, begetting them by the power of God's promise, which is the same thing as birthing them by the power of the Spirit. These churches are being born into freedom, but—at least in Galatia—they have to be reminded of that fact by being told explicitly that they are not descended from the Sinai/present-Jerusalem mission (v 31). Indeed, they have to be instructed in their solemn responsibility to cleanse their communal identity, as it were, by expelling from their midst the representatives of that mission.

6. Birth "according to the flesh." The churches that are being born in the Hagar/Sinai mission are being begotten "according to the flesh" (vv 23 and 29). And what does Paul intend by this strange expression? On the story level he doubtless thinks it a good way to refer to the fact that Ishmael was begotten and born in the normal course of events, i.e. without benefit of God's promise. Allegorically he has more in mind. The significant antecedent use of the term "flesh" lies in Gal 3:3, where Paul employs it to refer to the rite of circumcision as the sign of the Galatians' incipient turning to Law-observance. The background for the strange linking of Law to flesh lies in Paul's knowing that the Galatians have been taught by the Teachers to fear the fleshly Evil Impulse and to adopt Law-observance (begun in circumcision) precisely as the opposite of the Impulse, indeed as the God-given antidote to that powerful monster.[41] Paul's response in Gal 3:3 (and even more clearly in 5:16) is,

---

familiar conflict between the church and the synagogue" (229, n. 39). It has also to be said, however, that nothing in the letter suggests that the Galatian churches—those begotten by the power of the Spirit—are being persecuted by Jews. See note 53 below, and cf. E. De Witt Burton, *The Epistle to the Galatians* (Edinburgh, 1921) 266, "In speaking of...persecution...the apostle probably has in mind chiefly the persistent efforts of the judaisers to induce the Galatians to take on the burden of the law." One notes also Paul's reference to the Teachers as persons who would themselves be subject to persecution, were they to relax their zealous proclamation of the Law (6:12). Their prospective prosecutors could be zealous Jews; but one would want to consider the possibility that Paul thinks the Teachers, were they to stray from some central aspect of the Law, would have first of all to fear the wrath of the "false brothers" in the Jerusalem church.

[41] The major key to Paul's use of the term "flesh" *as he writes to the Galatians* is given in Gal 5:16, where he speaks explicitly about the fleshly Evil Impulse (the ἐπιθυμία σαρκός), insisting that its opposite is not the (fleshly) Law, but rather the Spirit. See Joel Marcus, "The Evil Inclination in the Letters of Paul," *Irish Biblical Studies* 8 (1986) 8-21.

then, to inform the Galatians that the Teachers have incorrectly identified the opposites. Law-observance, begun in the fleshly act of circumcision, far from being the opposing antidote to the fleshly Evil Impulse, is its ally! The Galatians who believe they are taming the Impulse by circumcision/Law-observance are in fact renewing their slavery to it, merely exchanging their old, Gentile form of slavery for a new one (Gal 4:8-10)! In Gal 3:2-5 Paul has also spoken of the true and freeing antidote to the flesh: it is the Spirit.[42] He has, moreover, spoken of the Spirit and the flesh as opposites in order to contrast the Spirit-birth of the Galatian churches with their present temptation to repair to the flesh of circumcision/Law-observance ("Having begun in the Spirit, you are now being perfected in the flesh?").

From these insights we can return to our text with deeper understanding of the reasons for Paul's seeing in the birth of Ishmael from the (Sinaitic) slave Hagar a type of the birth of Gentile congregations by circumcision/Law-observance and *into* (a new form of) slavery. The contemporary reference of v 29 ("...so also now...") might be honored by rendering "to beget according to the flesh," with some such expression as "to beget by Law-observant circumcision." And that rendering enables us to bring Paul's picture into yet sharper focus, because we can now inquire into the history of the Hagar mission.

In our passage Paul is careful to coordinate three motifs: (a) "begetting according to the flesh" (begetting by circumcision), (b) "bearing children into slavery," and (c) "the present Jerusalem." Attentive listeners in the Galatian churches will have recalled that in his account of the meeting in the church of Jerusalem (Gal 2:1-10) Paul coordinated these same three motifs: (a) the false brothers' demand that converts from among the Gentiles be circumcised, (b) Paul's assessment of this demand as an attempt at enslavement, and (c) the locus in which that demand was lodged, the Jerusalem church. It is indeed in his comment about the false brothers' demand for the circumcision of Gentiles—a demand voiced in the Jerusalem church—that Paul first mentions freedom and enslavement as a pair of opposites. Paul's account of the Jerusalem meeting, then, probably puts us in touch with a key episode *in the history of the Hagar mission*, one very near to its inception. The false brothers, already at the time of the meeting influential members of the Jerusalem church, were certainly not parties to the two-mission agreement in the form in which it was signed, so to

---

[42] Cf. Eduard Schweizer, σάρξ, *TDNT* 7. 132: "Paul's...concern...is to show the bondage of man to the σάρξ from which only the power of God's Spirit can free him."

speak, by James, Peter, and John.[43] Nor is there any reason to think that after the meeting they abandoned either their membership and influence in the Jerusalem church, or their convictions regarding the nomistic conditions under which Gentiles were to be brought into God's church.

It seems likely, then, that after the Jerusalem meeting (perhaps even before it) the false brothers began to function as sponsors of the Law-observant mission to Gentiles, in which the Teachers and their like became active. James' decision to send Law-observant messengers to the Antioch church could indeed indicate that, after the meeting, the false brothers began to acquire more power, both in the Jerusalem church and beyond it, than they had had when the agreement was reached (note also Col 4:11; Acts 21:20). It would have been the support of the false brothers, then, that enabled the Teachers to say that their mission represented the true and unadulterated gospel of the Jerusalem church. [44]

These observations may enable us to hear with fresh ears Paul's reference to "the present Jerusalem," an expression that is on its face, to be sure, a symbol for "the political-religious institution of Judaism" (H. D. Betz). Considering the role of the false brothers in the Jerusalem church and the Teachers' claim that they are themselves sponsored by that church, "the present Jerusalem" may be Paul's way of referring to the Jerusalem *church*, in so far as it is sponsoring the Law-observant mission to the Gentiles, thus producing Gentile churches that are enslaved to the Law. [45] Other references show that Paul sometimes uses the name of a city to refer to the church in that place (on Jerusalem see 1 Cor 16:3). Indeed in Galatians every one of Paul's earlier uses of the word "Jerusalem" refers to the Jerusalem church (1:17, 18; 2:1). Thus

---

[43] Why does Paul not refer in Gal 2:7,9 to the Law-observant mission to Gentiles? He limits himself—as did James, Peter, and John—to missions they all perceived during the Jerusalem meeting to be authorized by God, and there were only two of these: the Law-observant one to Jews and the circumcision-free one to Gentiles (whether the latter was to be totally Law-free is an issue that was not squarely faced in the Jerusalem meeting; note Gal 2:11-14). See "A Law-Observant Mission in Gentiles," note 24 above.

[44] James himself, the leader of the Jerusalem church by the time Paul wrote to the Galatians, may never have given active support to this mission, but he does not seem to have curbed it, by openly opposing either the false brothers or the Teachers.

[45] One may pause to note that "to beget by circumcision" could be a way of referring to the proselytizing strain in Judaism itself, reflected, e.g., in Matt 23:15., and to a great extent focused on the figure of Abraham, as we know from Jewish sources. See B. J. Bamberger, *Proselytism in the Talmudic Period* (New York: 1939, 1968); W. G. Braude, *Jewish Proselyting in the First Two Centuries of the Common Era* (Providence: Brown University Press, 1940). But why should Paul speak to the Galatians about a matter regarding which they very probably know nothing (see again note 53 below)?

when the Galatians encountered the word "Jerusalem" in 4:25, they will have had reason to think in the first instance of the church in Jerusalem, rather than of the city itself, as the cultic center of Judaism.

It follows that the Hagar/Sinai mission is not Judaism, but rather the Law-observant mission to Gentiles.[46] In speaking about it, Paul does indeed refer, as we have noted, to some of the central images of Judaism: Sinai, the Sinai covenant, Jerusalem.[47] He makes these images march under the banner, however, of the dynamic verb "to give birth," clearly showing, as we have seen, that, in referring to Sinai and Jerusalem, he is speaking not of a religion, but rather of a mission.[48]

The same dynamism holds for his reference to the Jerusalem-above who is free and "our mother." She is no more Christianity than Hagar is Judaism. Nor does she refer in a general way to Christian missions. Paul thinks quite precisely and specifically of the Law-free mission pursued by himself and his co-workers, as that mission has reached into the cities of Galatia. It is true that he uses the expression *"our* mother," thus—in some sense—including himself among those born in this mission; but he does essentially the same thing elsewhere in the letter, emphatically associating himself with his Gentile converts (e.g., 3:14; 4:3).

It is, in fact, this close association of himself with the Galatians that is reflected in Paul's use of the plural of 4:31 (ἐσμέν) and 5:1a (ἡμᾶς). The initial conclusion stated in 4:28, however, has to do with the identity, not of Christians in general, but rather of the Galatians: "But you, brothers and sisters, are children [not of the flesh of circumcision,

---

[46] The discussion of Gal 4:21-5:1 in Grässer, *Bund*, 69-77, is, in many regards, one of the most perceptive and most mature analyses we have; from it and from an article by Ulrich Luz, "Der alte und der neue Bund bei Paulus und im Hebräerbrief, *EvTh* 27 (1967) 318-336 I have learned much. Like so many other exegetes, however, Grässer related the "present Jerusalem" to the Jews, and the "Jerusalem above" to the Christians, without providing grounds for this view that are any firmer than those given by others.

[47] To these Jewish images one can add Paul's reference to Abraham, and the fact that Ishmael—born according to v 24 into slavery—is a son of Abraham. Is Paul not using Ishmael, then, to refer to Judaism, portraying it as a religion of slavery? Hardly! After giving Abraham a brief appearance in v 22, Paul causes him, as we have noted, to drop from sight altogether. Like Isaac, Ishmael emerges in Paul's picture as the *son of his mother*.

[48] The sharp command of Gal 4:30 (Gen 21:10), "Throw out the slave woman and her son...," does not speak, then, of the supersession of the synagogue by the church, but rather of the enactment of God's judgment—the voice of scripture is the voice of God—against those who pursue the Law-observant Gentile mission. That mission not only lacks divine authorization (contrast Gal 2:7); it stands under God's active curse (Gal 1:8-9).

but rather] of the promise, in the pattern of Isaac."[49] It is a conclusion that specifically reflects the cause of Paul's concern, namely the difficulties he is having with the birth of his Galatian churches. His protracted birth pangs are not arising from the influence, properly speaking, of Judaism, but rather from the Law-observant mission to Gentiles as it is making its way into Galatia. That Paul deals *at all* with the Genesis stories of Abraham, Sarah, and Hagar is a response to the interpretation of these stories being offered in the Galatian churches by the Teachers, not a response to the interpretation of them in this or that synagogue!

It cannot be a cause for wonder, then, that, on the heels of his exasperated reference to birth-pangs in 4:19-20, Paul gives a full-blown portrait of the Law-observant mission to Gentiles. That mission is the cause of the difficulties in Galatia. Thus, acknowledging the existence of the Law-observant Gentile mission, and denying its divine authorization, he interprets scripture in such a way as to tell the Galatians about their true birth. Both their own memory (3:1-5) and scripture itself (3:6-4:7 and 4:21-5:1) tell them that they were not born in the Law-observant mission, but rather in the Law-free one. Their birth determines their identity. "But you, brothers and sisters, are children of the power of God's promise, according to the pattern of Isaac...you are, therefore, to stand firm, not taking on again the yoke of slavery" (4:28; 5:1b).

D. Δύο Διαθῆκαι (two covenants)

Immediately after indicating that the Genesis stories are to be read allegorically, Paul identifies the two women as two covenants, turning first to deal in detail with the one of Hagar (vv 24b-25). This is Paul's only use of the term "covenant" in our passage. The most striking observation to be made about it is that it corresponds neither to the use of the term in the stories Paul is interpreting nor to his own use of it earlier in Galatians (chapter 3).

Several things are clear about the term in the Abraham stories:

---

[49] Some manuscripts read in v 28, "But we..." That text is almost certainly the secondary work of a scribe who changed "you" to "we" (influenced, perhaps, by the plurals in 4:31 and 5:1a) and who thus participated in what we have found to be the dominant interpretation of the passage, by producing a general reference to Christians. See the discussion in Bruce M. Metzger, *A Textual Commentary on the Greek New Testament* (London/New York: United Bible Societies, 1971), and Cousar, *Galatians*, 103. The reason given by Borse for selecting "we" is not convincing (*Der Brief an die Galater*, 174).

a) God makes his covenant with Abraham and with his multiple descendants, but there is no thought that its being passed from generation to generation causes it to be several covenants:

> On that day the Lord made a covenant with Abraham, saying...I will establish my covenant between me and you and your descendants after you throughout their generations for an everlasting covenant, to be God to you and to your descendants after you (Gen 15:18; 17:7).

There is only one covenant.[50]

b) God provides Abraham with a simple and clear definition of the covenant:

> This is my covenant, which you shall keep, between me and you and your descendants after you: Every male among you shall be circumcised. You shall be circumcised in the flesh of your foreskins, and it shall be a sign of the covenant between me and you....So shall my covenant be in your flesh an everlasting covenant (Gen 17:10-13).

God's covenant is both the promise and the nomistic commandment (the circumcision of the flesh), the two being indissolubly connected to one another.
c) Abraham observed God's covenant without exception. He circumcised himself, his sons, and every male in his household (Gen 17:23-27; 21:4).
d) Although, responding to God's command, Abraham circumcised Ishmael, just as he circumcised every other male in his house, God established his covenant with Isaac and emphatically not with Ishmael, as the exchange concerning the birth of Isaac shows.

> [God promises Abraham a son by Sarah; Abraham laughs in disbelief, and preferring the certainty of the son he already has, he pleads with God:] "Oh that Ishmael might live in thy sight!"

---

[50] One may be reminded of the fact that the Hebrew word bĕrît has no plural. See the discussion by James Barr, "Some Semantic Notes on the Covenant," in *Beiträge zur alttestamentlichen Theologie: Festschrift für Heinrich Zimmerli* (ed. H. Donner, R. Hanhart, R. Smend; Göttingen: Vandenhoeck & Ruprecht, 1977). Regarding the plural in Rom 9:4, see Grässer, *Bund*, 18.

God said, "No, but Sarah your wife shall bear you a son, and you shall call his name Isaac. I will establish my covenant with him....As for Ishmael, I have heard you; behold I will bless him....But I will establish my covenant with Isaac....(Gen 17:18-21).

With regard to every one of these four points Paul departs dramatically from the stories in Genesis. He announces two covenants; he separates promise and nomistic commandment, defining one covenant as that of promise, the other as that of Sinai; he omits altogether the solemn definition of God's covenant as the commandment of circumcision; having spoken of two covenants, he identifies the first of them as the covenant of Hagar and her son, ignoring the absence in Genesis of a covenant with Ishmael. Paul's use of the noun διαθήκη shows him to be even further removed from the Genesis stories than does his use of the verb γεννᾶν.[51]

Moreover, in one regard the way in which Paul uses the term here departs from the way in which he employs it in Galatians 3. In that earlier case, having divorced the promise from the Law, much as he also does in our passage, he spoke of only one covenant, tying it exclusively to the promise, and thus issuing a divorce between the terms "covenant" and "Law." In a word, Galatians 3 does not at any point offer a reflection on the Sinai *covenant*, and it certainly gives no forecast of the thought of two covenants. The author of Gal 4:21-5:1, then, has departed in truly radical ways both from his Genesis texts and from his own earlier covenantal discourse. What was it that drove Paul—surely against all of his Pharisaic training (cf. Phil 3:4-6)—to speak of two covenants and to link that of Sinai with enslavement?

The major key lies in the fact that Paul defines the two covenants as the two women. We have already seen that Hagar is, in her child-bearing, not Judaism, but rather the Law-observant mission to Gentiles, and that Sarah, in her child-bearing, is not Christianity, but rather the Law-free Gentile mission. From these observations it is a short step to

---

[51] Both Paul's use of the verb γεννᾶν and the way in which he employs the term διαθήκη indicate clearly that the point of departure for his exegesis is not the text of scripture, but rather (a) his awareness of the birth of Gentile churches by the power of the liberating Spirit (4:29b looks back to 4:6), and thus (b) his present perception of the distinction between the Gentile mission that has been authorized by God (Gal 2:7,9) and a second Gentile mission that stands under God's curse (Gal 1:8-9), and belongs to the anti-God forces associated with the birth-pangs of the end-time. On Paul's interpretation of the Old Testament see notably Ernst Käsemann, "The Spirit and the Letter," *Perspectives on Paul* (Philadelphia: Fortress, 1971) 138-166.

the insight that Paul identifies the two women as two covenants, in order, by yet another route, to speak of these two missions. For that purpose the one-covenant picture of Galatians 3 will not suffice. Gal 4:21-5:1 is the passage in which Paul faces most openly and squarely and explicitly and analytically the existence of the Law-observant Gentile mission.

It is, then, the awesome fact of this odious development that drives Paul into the holy madness of affirming two covenants. He speaks of *two* covenants in order to establish the integrity of God's *one* church. By the mission to the Jews (presupposing their continued *adiaphoros* [non-salvific] observance of the Law) and by the Law-free mission to the Gentiles God is calling into existence this one church (2:1-10). But there are persons who wish to produce this unity under the banner of the Sinai covenant, urging Gentiles to enter that covenant. Given that development, Paul feels compelled to use the term "covenant" himself in a highly original way in order to say that those who carry out the Law-observant mission to Gentiles are in fact furthering nothing other than the enslaving Sinaitic covenant of Hagar, the slave woman; correspondingly they are violating God's covenant through Sarah, the free woman; indeed, in this way they are persecuting the Spirit-born churches of God.[52] Such people have made their way into Galatia; the Galatians are to identify them and their followers as Hagars and Ishmaels; and, casting them out, they are to cleanse their congregations as a sign that they know and affirm their own true identity as children of the Law-free mission.

---

[52] Compelled for the first time, so far as we know, to be a covenant theologian, does Paul mean to say, or at least to imply, that God is ultimately the author of both covenants, having used the Hagar covenant to imprison humanity until, climactically, he should provide the liberating covenant of Sarah (cf. the purposeful chronology of the Law and the promise in Gal 3:21-25)? There is tradition for the view that God can change his own covenantal promise (e.g., Deut 28:62-68), but that view has no pertinence to the two *simultaneously active* covenants of Galatians 4. Since the Hagar covenant *is* the Law-observant mission to Gentiles, Paul does not in any way suggest that it has its origin in God (*pace* Grässer, *Bund* 95, among others). As we have seen, it stands under God's curse; one is not surprised, therefore, to see that in speaking of the Hagar covenant Paul employs no expressions corresponding to the ἵνα clauses that function in Gal 3:22,24 to indicate God's use of the Law to his own purpose. In the Hagar covenant, by contrast, the Law is being put to a use contrary to God's will, a fact showing clearly that the Hagar covenant is not the Law as such. At least in passing, one also notes in the Septuagintal form of Psalm 83 (LXX 82) the reference to a covenant that is dangerous to God's people (for Paul the church of God) and that is authored by God's enemies, specifically, among others, by the Ishmaelites and the Hagarites.

IV. Conclusion

A. There are, then, firm grounds for thinking that the reading given most frequently to Gal 4:21-5:1, from the second century to our own day, is fundamentally flawed. To be sure, this paragraph is one of those Pauline passages marked by polar opposites, and thus a text for which Marcion was, so to speak, waiting in the wings. The possibility of Marcion's reading is, however, something of which Paul had no premonition. Specifically, he did not have in mind a polar opposition between Judaism and Christianity, but rather the crucial distinction between the two Gentile missions, one observant of the Law and one Law-free.[53] One may say that Judaism stands somewhere in the *background*, not least because other passages show Paul's firm conviction that the Law is *everywhere* impotent to curb the Evil Impulse and Sin (e.g., Gal 5:16-18; Rom 3:9).[54] In this paragraph, however, Paul is far from launching a comprehensive attack against Judaism.[55]

---

[53] As far as we can tell, there were no Jewish communities in the Galatian cities of Ancyra, Pessinus, and Tavium in the middle of the first century (see Steven Mitchell, *Regional Epigraphic Catalogues of Asia Minor II: The Inscriptions of North Galatia* [British Institute of Archaeology at Ankara, Monograph no. 4, B.A.R. International Series 135; Oxford, 1982] nos. 133, 141, 209b, 418, and 509-512). Thus, a polemic focused on Judaism itself would have been irrelevant to the Galatian situation, and would have been sensed as such by the Galatians. The history of the interpretation of Gal 4:21-5:1 would be basically different, had interpreters agreed to observe a hermeneutical rule attributed by oral tradition to Walter Bauer: Ask first how the text was understood by the initial (Greek speaking) readers, and only second how it was intended by its author. Cf. also the comment of W. G. Kümmel about Matthaus Flacius Illyricus, *Clavis Scripturae Sacrae* (1567); "Flacius erkennt auch ganz genau, dass zur Ermittlung des wörtlichen Sinnes eines biblischen Textes nötig ist, den Text im Sinn seiner ursprünglichen Leser zu verstehen *und darüber hinaus* das Ziel zu erkennen, das der biblische Schriftsteller im Auge hatte...." (W.G. Kümmel, *Das Neue Testament* [Freiburg: Karl Alber, 1958] 23, emphasis added).

[54] See again the article of Joel Marcus cited in note 41 above.

[55] One must take into account the fact that Galatians is the document in which Paul refers explicitly to "Judaism" (1:13-14), indicating that it was the locus of his *past* life (cf. Phil 3:7); likewise it is in Galatians that he speaks twice of "living in a Jewish manner" (2:14), insisting that *in mixed churches* that manner of life cannot be imposed on the formerly Gentile members, without implying that it is itself salvific, something that Paul holds to be untrue both for Jews and for Gentiles, the Law being impotent to make alive. None of these references—when addressed to former Gentiles—constitutes, however, what one would properly call an attack specifically focused on Judaism itself; in Galatians Paul makes clear that the gospel is carrying the world beyond all forms of religion, creating a community of former Jews and former Gentiles (3:28). The issues raised by 2 Corinthians 3 (notably vv 12-18) cannot be pursued in the present essay, beyond what is said in note 59

He knows of churches in Judea, for example, that retain traditional links with Judaism, in the sense that all of their members continue to observe the Law. For these communities he has only the warmest of fraternal feelings, so long as they do not try to impose the Law on Gentiles, as though it were salvific (Gal 1:22-24). Paul is altogether serious about the rule that "every one should remain in the state in which he was called...." "Was anyone at the time of his call already circumcised? Let him not seek to remove the marks of circumcision..." (1 Cor 7:20,18). Paul must himself have lived essentially in a Law-observant fashion during the meeting in the Jerusalem church (Gal 2:1-10; cf. 1 Cor 9:19-23). To be sure, he speaks in our passage of a causative connection between the Sinai covenant and enslavement. We have seen, however, that he does not draw that connection by focusing on the Sinai covenant as such, but rather by speaking of that covenant as it is imposed on Gentiles in the Law-observant mission.[56] Hence in Gal 4:21-5:1 it is Paul's intention to listen attentively to the Law, as he hears it testifying against the Law-observant mission to Gentiles and for the Law-free mission; it is a grave mistake to speak here of a polemic against Judaism itself.[57]

---

below. See again Käsemann, "The Spirit and the Letter"; Victor P. Furnish, *II Corinthians* (AB 32A; Garden City, NY: Doubleday, 1984); Grässer, *Bund*, 77-95.

[56] The study of Lloyd Gaston, "Israel's Enemies in Pauline Theology," *NTS* 28 (1982) 400-423, springs from an admirable motive, and includes some perceptive comments; but the argument is on the whole remarkably arbitrary, involving, for example, a tortured paraphrase of Gal 4:25 (410), and ending with a conclusion that owes far more to the Teachers than to Paul (the latter being credited with the view expressed in Eph 2:12,17!). Gaston never deals in a truly exegetical way with δύο διαθῆκαι and with εἰς δουλείαν γεννῶσα. For a helpful critique of Gaston's work see now E. Elizabeth Johnson, *The Function of Apocalyptic and Wisdom Traditions in Romans 9-11* (SBLDS 109; Atlanta: Scholars Press, 1989) 176-205. To some extent the arguments of James D. G. Dunn, "Works of the Law and the Curse of the Law," *NTS* 31 (1985) 523-542, are similar to those of Gaston (note again the use of Ephesians [2:13-16] to explicate Galatians!); to that extent Dunn's arguments are subject to similar critique; see the assessment by Heikki Räisänen, "Galatians 2:16 and Paul's Break with Judaism," *NTS* 31 (1985) 543-553.

[57] Were one to judge simply on the basis of Gal 4:21-5:1, one would say that, unlike Marcion and his descendants, Paul did not attack the synagogue in order to identify the Law-observant mission to Gentiles as a movement hostile to God's outreach into the world. That this passage has *implications* for Paul's perception of the synagogue has already been noted above. Galatians 4, along with 2 Corinthians 3 and other passages, presents Paul's OT hermeneutic with unmistakable clarity: apart from the liberating gospel of Christ the scripture is read and heard without being understood (cf. Grässer, *Bund*, 91). On Paul's hermeneutic see notably the article of Käsemann mentioned in note 51 above; also J. Louis Martyn, "Galatians," in *The Books of the Bible* (ed. Bernhard W. Anderson; New York: Scribners, 1989).

B. It follows that the framers of the Rheinland resolution, and the theologians who have so admirably drafted similar documents in other contexts, had no need to avoid this text for fear that it provides a basis for anti-Judaism and a support for the doctrine of supersession (see note 48). It does nothing of the sort. On the contrary, it develops a theology that could prove clarifying in conversations between Jews and Christians, precisely because it is a theology of missions *to Gentiles*.

C. Vis à vis our passage, however, the framers did have grounds for unease in light of the fourth point of their resolution, quoted earlier:

> We believe in the permanent election of the Jewish people as the people of God, and we realize that through Jesus Christ the church is taken into the covenant of God with his people...

The first clause of this sentence, clearly a polemic against the doctrine of supersession, can stand alongside Gal 4:21-5:1, in the sense that that passage says nothing about Christianity taking the place of Judaism. The theology expressed in the second clause, however, is another matter entirely, for it voices, within the context of what some are now calling a post-Auschwitz theology, a view for which no support at all can be found in the author of Gal 4:21-5:1.[58] *It is the Teachers*, not Paul, who anticipated part of the Rheinland confession, by holding quite sincerely that through their ministry God was bringing Gentiles into the covenant of Sinai. And just as clearly, as we have seen, it is their active determination to bring Gentiles into the nomistic covenant of Sinai that drove Paul—caught as he was in birth-pangs, and compelled by the

---

[58] Regarding a Christian "post-Auschwitz theology" see *Umkehr und Erneuerung* (ed. Bertold Klappert and Helmut Starck; Neukirchen-Vluyn: Neukirchener Verlag, 1980); *Auschwitz—Krise der Christlichen Theologie* (ed. Rolf Rendtorff and Ekkehard Stegemann; München: Ch. Kaiser, 1980); H. Jansen, *Christelijke theologie na Auschwitz* (den Haag, 1984); and "Exegese nach Auschwitz?" and "Zwei Heilswege?", both in Grässer, *Bund*. One recalls that in 1934 Karl Barth raised with Gerhard Kittel the question—symptomatic that it should have been necessary—whether the church could see in the "glorious " events of 1933 a second source of revelation alongside the Bible (J. Vos, "Antijudaismus/Antisemitismus im Theologischen Worterbuch zum Neuen Testament," *NedTh T* 38 [1984] 89-110 [99]). One hardly needs to say that the Holocaust is another matter altogether: see K. Haacker, "Der Holocaust als Datum der Theologiegeschichte," 137-145 in *Gottes Augapfel*. For Christians the Holocaust does most surely provide new hermeneutical lenses, without eclipsing the radical hermeneutic of the rectification of the ungodly! Even with these lenses, however, one cannot truly find in Paul's letters—including the one to the Romans—support for the view that the church has been taken into the covenant of an already-existent people of God. See the commentaries on Romans, the discussion of Rom 11:27 in Grässer, *Bund*, 20-25, the extraordinarily percipient essay of N. Walter, referred to in note 61 below, and the *Nachwort* of Grässer, *Bund*, 312-315.

theology of the Teachers to become for a moment a covenant theologian himself—to speak of the two incompatible covenants that were being carried out in the two incompatible Gentile missions.[59]

Genuinely theological conversation between Christians and Jews is comparatively rare. It is also essential to the faithful health and future of both. One is therefore grateful to those who took the step represented in the Rheinland resolution. One is also deeply thankful that, after centuries of persecution at Christian hands, Jews are yet willing to enter into dialogue. In such thanksgiving, some Christian theologians might choose, in fact, to follow the Teachers who came into Paul's Galatian churches rather than Paul, affirming both a single covenant and God's inclusion of the church in it. They would need, however, to know whom they are following, and they would do well to make the identity of their theological forebears clear to their readers; explaining, presumably, that centuries of Christian guilt vis à vis Jews—unquestionably a grave matter with which Christian theologians must deal—make it necessary to derive some aspects of Christian theology not from Paul, but rather from his Galatian opponents.[60]

---

[59] Again 2 Corinthians 3 comes to mind, with its picture of two covenants, markedly similar to the picture in Galatians 4, but also different. Two points may be mentioned here. (a) In 2 Corinthians 3 the two covenants are clearly sequential, whereas in Galatians 4, as we have seen, they are simultaneous. (b) Whereas in Galatians 4 Paul speaks of his Law-free mission as the (Sarah) covenant itself, in 2 Corinthians 3 his mission is in the *service* of the (new) covenant, a locution that may help us to understand how in Galatians Paul can include himself among the children of the Sarah/Law-free mission; note "*our* mother."

[60] In the case of the Rheinland Synod we can be confident that we are not dealing with theologians who consciously intend to substitute the theology of the Teachers for that of Paul. One might speculate that, when Paul's letters are read through the lenses of remorse for what the synod called "the co-responsibility and guilt of German Christendom for the Holocaust," those letters sound in some regards similar to ones the Teachers might have written. Thus far the result of such reading is in part, however, historically and theologically confusing, and one has to doubt that this confusing part has genuine power to eradicate anti-Semitism among Christians. It is crucial for Christian theologians to listen carefully to their Jewish counterparts (see, for example, the attempt mentioned in note 19 above), but such listening does not relieve them of the responsibility to do their own theological work on the basis of their own sources, as R. J. Zvi Werblowsky pointedly reminded the Rheinland Synod in a remarkable address on January 7, 1980: "Trennendes und Gemeinsames," 29-43 in *Zur Erneuerung des Verhältnisses von Christen und Juden* (see 35, "Es händelt sich nicht darum—wovor uns Gott bewahre—dass Christen je sich bei Juden ihre christliche Theologie holen sollten"). Looking at the period since the Holocaust, one can identify two developments that are threatening to the faithful integrity of both Jews and Christians: the danger of underestimating the degree to which that event can and must affect Christian theology; the danger of concentrating one's attention so tightly on that event as to reduce Christian theology to anti-anti-Judaism. As one thinks of Christian responsibility for Christian theology, one notices with concern that the Rheinland

Do we not find a better route, however—and one that will both clarify and deepen genuinely theological conversation between Jews and Christians today—by recognizing that the Paul whom we see in Gal 4:21-5:1 is *not* asking how "the church of God" (Gal 1:13) is related to the Israel elected by God.[61] As he writes this passage, Paul is concerned, in a tightly focused way, to bear witness to the power of God's promissory covenant, as, in the Law-free mission to Gentiles, it is giving birth to multitudes of liberated children.[62] Far from planting seeds of anti-Judaism, this Paul proves to be the theologian who, when he reads scripture, hears the Law itself saying with emphasis: The God who is now reaching out for the whole of the world—in Christ and apart from observance of the Law—is the God who promised Abraham and Sarah that he would one day do that.

---

resolution appears nowhere to speak of the rectification of the ungodly, and thus does not address the crucial issue of the relationship between that theological assertion and the affirmation of God's election of and complete redemption of Israel (Rom 5:12-21; 9:6-13; and 11:25-27,32). See Ernst Käsemann, *Romans* (Grand Rapids, MI: Eerdmans, 1980) 317.

[61] It is entirely conceivable that the Teachers gave to their colleagues in the Jerusalem church a report about Paul's letter to the Galatians, including a reading of Gal 4:21-5:1 as an attack not only on the Law-observant mission to Gentiles, but also on Judaism itself. If so, one can read parts of Romans as Paul's attempt to set the record straight (cf. J. Louis Martyn, "Paul and His Jewish-Christian Interpreters," *USQR* 42 [1988] 1-15). In any case, for the way in which Paul understood God's election of and faithfulness to *Israel*, one reads, in the first instance, not Galatians, but rather Romans 9-11. See especially the treatment of this passage in Käsemann, *Romans*; Ulrich Wilckens, *Der Brief an die Römer* (3 vols.; EKK/6; Zürich: Benziger, 1978-82; Neukirchen-Vluyn: Neukirchener Verlag, 1978-82); N. Walter, "Interpretation von Römer 9-11," *ZThK* 81 (1984) 172-195; J. S. Vos, "Israël en de goddelijke wijsheid volgens Rom. 9-11," 114-145 in Baarda, Jansen, Noorda, and Vos, *Paulus en de andere joden*; J. Christiaan Beker, "The Faithfulness of God and the Priority of Israel in Paul's Letter to the Romans," *HTR* 79 (1986) 10-16; Paul W. Meyer, "Romans," 1130-1167 in *Harper's Bible Commentary* (ed. James L. Mays; San Francisco: Harper and Row, 1988); E. Elizabeth Johnson, *The Function of Apocalyptic and Wisdom Traditions in Romans 9-11*.

[62] In light of some of the Pauline work of Lloyd Gaston (e.g., note 56 above) and its influence on the labors of others (e.g. John Gager, *The Origins of Anti-Semitism* (Oxford: Oxford University Press, 1985); Paul M. Van Buren, *A Theology of the Jewish-Christian Reality*, Parts 1-3 (San Francisco: Harper and Row, 1980, 1983, 1988), I must add a note regarding Paul's consistent conviction that God's salvific action *in the gospel of Christ* was directed to *the whole* of the enslaved world, "to the Jew first and also to the Greek." The thought never entered the apostle's head that the gospel mission to the Jews be abandoned, its being God's will that Jews should follow the path of the Law, while Gentiles should follow the path of the gospel. In writing Rom 9:6-11:24 Paul presupposes the faithful continuation of the (largely unsuccessful) mission to the Jews *until the parousia*; and the anxiety Paul experienced when he thought about the conversations he was shortly to have in the Jerusalem church (Rom 15:30-32) would have been quite differently focused had it been his view that that church should abandon the "gospel to the circumcision" (cf. Gal 2:7, 9).

12

Apostles As Babes and Nurses in 1 Thessalonians 2:7

Beverly Roberts Gaventa [1]

Over the course of his letters, Paul refers to his apostolic role in a variety of ways. Often he speaks of himself as a slave of Christ (Rom 1:1; Gal 1:10; Phil 1:1) or as a minister (1 Cor 3:5; 2 Cor 3:6; 11:23). Sometimes he characterizes himself as a workman, either a builder (1 Cor 3:10) or a fellow worker of God (1 Cor 3:9). When referring to his relationship with believers in churches founded by him, he calls himself their father (1 Thess 2:11; 1 Cor 4:14-16). In 1 Thess 2:7, however, Paul employs unusual, even provocative, imagery to describe his work as an apostle, imagery that deserves more thorough exploration than it has received to date.[2]

Among the many questions that arise from this verse, I want to address the following. First, what is the best text of this verse, and how should we translate it?

Second, what is the origin of this imagery, with which a man speaks of himself as a nurse and, as I shall argue, even as a child? What other sources employ this metaphor of the nurse? What can we learn about

---

[1] Beverly Roberts Gaventa is Professor of New Testament at Columbia Theological Seminary, Decatur, Georgia.

[2] It is a pleasure to be invited to contribute this essay to honor Paul W. Meyer, a genuine friend and a respected colleague.

the status and function of nurses in the ancient world, and how might that knowledge illumine Paul's words?

Third, what shall we make of Paul's use of metaphor here? Technically, of course, this is a *simile*, since he says ὡς ἐάν—"as if a nurse." But the distinction is grammatical rather than substantive, and most discussions of metaphor and its usage consider both types of figures. Beyond the place of metaphor in this verse, we also want to know what function the verse plays in this part of the letter, where Paul seeks to consolidate and enhance the relationship between himself and the Thessalonians. Related to that question is the larger matter of the connection between this section of the letter, with its imagery of nurture, and the apocalyptic concerns that dominate chapters 4 and 5.

I shall argue that Paul is here developing his own understanding of apostleship. If 1 Thessalonians is Paul's first letter to a Christian community, it is "an experiment in Christian writing,"[3] and we must keep the experimental character of this letter in the foreground as we read and interpret it. As part of Paul's experiment, he must explain what an apostle is and, to do so, he uses several images—of the apostles not only as fathers of believers (2:11), but also as babes and as nurses. These terms are not merely part of a conventional description of the philosopher but indicate something essential to Paul's understanding of what he and his co-workers do.

1. Text and Translation of 1 Thessalonians 2:7

As indicated above, 1 Thess 2:7 contains a significant text-critical problem. The RSV translates the verse: "But we were gentle among you, like a nurse taking care of her children." Nevertheless, the RSV also contains a footnote indicating that some ancient authorities read "babes" rather than "gentle."[4] The RSV translates according to one set of Greek manuscripts, in which the reading is, "We were gentle (ἤπιοι) among you, like a nurse taking care of her children." Another set of manuscripts, reflected in the footnote, reads, "We were babes (νήπιοι) among you, like a nurse taking care of her children."

---

[3] The phrase is Helmut Koester's ("1 Thessalonians—Experiment in Christian Writing," in *Continuity and Discontinuity in Church History: Essays Presented to George Hunston Williams on the Occasion of His 65th Birthday* [ed. F. Forrester Church and Timothy George; Leiden: Brill, 1979] 33-44).

[4] "Gentle" is also the translation of the NEB, the NASB, and the NAB. The NJB reads, "Instead, we lived unassumingly among you. Like a mother feeding and looking after her children...."

The external evidence is clear. Both the 26th edition of Nestle-Aland and the 3rd edition of the United Bible Society read νήπιοι, or babes. Although ἤπιοι appears in several of the major uncial manuscripts (including Sinaiticus, Alexandrinus, Ephraemi, Bezae), in all these manuscripts except Alexandrinus this reading comes from the hand of a corrector. Νήπιοι appears in P[65] and Vaticanus, and it is the original reading in Sinaiticus, Ephraemi, and Bezae. If we considered only the external evidence, there would be little doubt that 2:7 reads νήπιοι, or babes, rather than ἤπιοι. The explanation of the reading ἤπιοι would be that later scribes altered νήπιοι to ἤπιοι, producing with the omission of one letter a less difficult or awkward reading.

Many objections to this reading of 2:7 have been lodged, however, and they include at least the following.

1. The reading νήπιοι could easily have resulted from the simple scribal error of dittography. That is, the ν at the end of the preceding word, ἐγενήθημεν, was accidentally doubled with the result that ἤπιοι became νήπιοι.[5]

2. Paul elsewhere employs the word νήπιος when describing the immaturity of his converts, as in 1 Cor 3:1. ("But I, brethren, could not address you as spiritual persons, but as persons of the flesh, as babes in Christ.") He would scarcely use that same word with reference to himself and his co-workers.[6]

3. Since Paul immediately follows this word with the image of the nurse, only ἤπιοι fits the context. While Paul does occasionally use a mixed metaphor, it would be quite awkward to write, "we became babes among you, like a nurse...."[7]

---

[5] C. J. Ellicott, *A Critical and Grammatical Commentary on St. Paul's Epistle to the Thessalonians* (London: John W. Parker & Son, 1858) 21; Helmut Koester, "The Text of 1 Thessalonians," in *The Living Text: Essays in Honor of Ernest W. Saunders* (ed. Dennis E. Groh and Robert Jewett [Lanham, MD: University Press of America, 1985] 225).

[6] Koester, "Text of 1 Thessalonians," 225; Beda Rigaux, *Saint Paul. Les Épitres aux Thessaloniciens* (Paris: J. Gabalda, 1956) 418.

[7] Context appears to be the deciding issue for many scholars: E. von Dobschütz, *Die Thessalonicher-Briefe* (MeyerK; 7th ed.; Göttingen: Vandenhoeck & Ruprecht, 1974 [orig. 1909] 93); Martin Dibelius, *An die Thessalonicher I-II: an die Philipper* (HNT; 2nd ed.; Tübingen: J. C. B. Mohr, 1923) 9; C. G. Findlay, *The Epistles of Paul the Apostle to the Thessalonians* (Cambridge: Cambridge University Press, 1925) 32-33; William Neil, *The Epistle of Paul to the Thessalonians* (London: Hodder & Stoughton, 1950) 40; Bruce M. Metzger, *A Textual Commentary on the Greek New Testament* (London: United Bible Societies, 1970) 629-30; Ernest Best, *A Commentary on the First and Second Epistles to the Thessalonians* (London: Adam & Charles Black, 1972) 40; Ronald Ward, *Commentary on 1 and 2 Thessalonians* (Waco, TX: Word, 1973) 61-62; I. H. Marshall, *1 and 2 Thessalonians* (NCB; Grand Rapids: Eerdmans, 1983) 70; Koester, "Text of 1 Thessalonians," 225.

These arguments form a scholarly judgment that is sufficiently strong that Helmut Koester can refer to the preference for νήπιοι in the 26th editon of Nestle-Aland as "clearly wrong."[8] Yet the weight of the external evidence should prevent us from coming to a hasty conclusion that Paul "must" have meant something other than what the earliest and best manuscripts read. There are also good reasons, indeed better reasons, for concluding that Paul did in fact write νήπιοι. Among them I note five.

1. The scribal error posited by the consensus view could easily have been haplography rather than dittography. That is, a scribe wrote one ν where there should have been two, resulting in the omission of the ν in νήπιοι; hence, ἤπιοι.

2. While it is true that Paul elsewhere employs νήπιος for converts who are still new in their understanding, that usage is not uniform in the letters. He actually uses the word only five times outside of our passage in 1 Thessalonians. In addition to 1 Cor 3:1, which was noted earlier, νήπιος also appears in 1 Cor 13:11 ("when I was a child"). In Gal 4:1,3 it is used of the heir who has not yet inherited. Finally, in Rom 2:20 Paul employs it to refer to those who call themselves teachers of children but who are, in fact, hypocrites. While none of these instances could be said to have positive connotations, neither is the term clearly negative nor is it always associated with recent converts.

On the other hand, in 1 Cor 14:20 Paul does use the related verb νηπιάζειν in an admonition: "Brethren, do not be children (παῖς) in your thinking, but be babes (νηπιάζειν) with respect to evil" (cf. Rom 16:19; 1 Cor 14:20). Moreover, in some passages in the Septuagint (e.g., Pss 18 [19]:7; 118 [119]:130; Wis 10:21) and in other New Testament writings (Matt 11:25; 21:16), νήπιος does refer to those who are simple or guileless. This connotation of the term would offer, of course, an excellent contrast to the characteristics Paul has just insisted do not

---

Metzger apparently speaks for many when he invokes Daniel Mace's dictum that "no manuscript is so old as common sense" (*The Text of the New Testament, Its Transmission, Corruption, and Restoration* [New York: Oxford University Press, 1964] 230-33). What counts as "common sense," of course, fluctuates from one period to another and from one culture to another.

By contrast with the above, F. Zimmer argues that νήπιος fits the context better than does ἤπιος ("1 Thess. 2:3-8 erklärt," in *Theologische Studien: Festschrift B. Weiss* [ed. C. R. Gregory *et al.*; Göttingen: Vandenhoeck & Ruprecht, 1897] 264-65).

[8] "The Text of 1 Thessalonians," 224-25; see also Traugott Holtz, "Der Apostel des Christus: Die paulinische 'Apologie' 1 Thess 2,1-12," in *Als Boten des gekreuzigten Herrn: Festgabe für Bischof Dr. Werner Krusche zum 65. Geburtstag* (ed. Heino Falcke, Martin Onnasch, and Harald Schultze; Berlin: Evangelische, 1982) 170.

pertain to himself and his co-workers (error, guile, flattery, greed, glory-seeking, etc.).[9]

3. Certainly reading νήπιοι with the better manuscripts results in a mixed metaphor, but those are by no means uncommon in the letters of Paul! Galatians 4:19 employs another mixed metaphor, again a metaphor focusing on maternal imagery. Others are found in the marriage analogy in Rom 7:1-3 and the reference to the veil of Moses in 2 Corinthians 3. I suspect that these mixed metaphors often result, not from some defect in Paul's imagination,[10] but from his struggle to articulate all that needs to be said. (I shall address this issue again below in terms of the substance of Paul's comments in this passage.)

4. While the context of this verse may make νήπιοι difficult, the syntax does not. Paul often uses γίνομαι ("become") with a noun; indeed, he does so even in this section of 1 Thessalonians (1:5b; 1:6; 1:7; 2:14).[11] More importantly, the phrase stands parallel to ἀπόστολοι Χριστοῦ in v. 7a: "we might have made demands as apostles of Christ, but we became...." This parallel anticipates a noun following ἐγενήθημεν ("we became").[12]

5. Finally, the revered text-critical rule that the more difficult reading is earlier should incline us to regard νήπιοι as the earlier reading, since there can be no doubt that it is more difficult than ἤπιοι. It is easy to imagine why a scribe would find the mixed metaphor confusing and respond by altering νήπιοι to ἤπιοι. A deliberate or conscious change from ἤπιοι to νήπιοι is unthinkable.

---

[9] C. G. Findlay, who concludes that νήπιοι results from an early and widespread dittography, nevertheless points out that, if the reading were νήπιοι, Paul's intent would be to describe the apostles as "simple, guileless, unassuming" (*Epistles to the Thessalonians*, 42).

[10] See, for example, the comment by C. H. Dodd on Rom 7:1-6: "He lacks the gift for sustained illustration of ideas through concrete images (though he is capable of a brief illuminating metaphor). It is probably a defect of imagination" (*The Epistle of Paul to the Romans* [London: Hodder & Stoughton, 1932] 121). For a more sustained discussion of the topic, see Herbert M. Gale, *The Use of Analogy in the Letters of Paul* (Philadelphia: Westminster, 1964).

[11] The verb γίνομαι is also used with an adjective, as in 2:1,8,10. The point is that Paul might well use a noun here, not that he must do so. On the frequency of γίνομαι in this passage, see Paul Schubert, *Form and Function of the Pauline Thanksgivings* (Berlin: Töpelmann, 1930) 19-20.

[12] So also J. E. Frame, *A Critical and Exegetical Commentary on the Epistles of St. Paul to the Thessalonians* (ICC; Edinburgh: T. & T. Clark, 1912) 100.

Taken together, these considerations point to babes, or νήπιοι, as the preferred reading. This, of course, does not in itself make 1 Thess 2:7 clearer; indeed, the verse is now more rather than less confusing.[13]

The question of translation and punctuation now becomes urgent. Those who read νήπιοι sometimes suggest that this reading requires a full stop between the expressions "we became babes in your midst" and "as a nurse taking care of her children." This punctuation would provide a slight separation between the two metaphors and would result in the following translation: "But we became babes in your midst. As a nurse taking care of her children, thus we were desirous of you...." The difficulty with inserting a full stop is that the ἀλλά ("but") in v. 7b runs parallel to the ἀλλά in v. 4. In other words, vv. 4-7a state the characteristics of the apostles in a negative way—all the things they are not. The ἀλλά of v. 7b then introduces the positive claims made about them, which must also be taken together. I think we must translate: "But we became babes among you, as if a nurse taking care of her own children." Somehow these two statements belong together. They are amplified in v. 8, where Paul turns from metaphorical speech to more direct assertion: "We were pleased to share with you not only the gospel but also our selves."

2. Background of the Metaphor of the Nurse

Having established a workable text and translation of this verse, the urgent issue now becomes Paul's reference to himself and others as nurses. The most extended discussion of this reference to date is that of Abraham Malherbe, whose work on this text has found wide acceptance. Among Malherbe's early contributions to the study of 1 Thessalonians was an article, "Gentle as a Nurse," in which he argued that Paul employs in 1 Thess 2:1-12 a conventional topos concerning the work of the philosopher.[14] As a result of the number of disreputable figures

---

[13] A similar conclusion is reached by Leon Morris, *The First and Second Epistles to the Thessalonians* (NIC; Grand Rapids: Eerdmans, 1959) 76-78; Jean Gribomont, "Facti sumus parvuli: La charge apostolique (1 Th 2,1-12)," *Paul de Tarse: Apotre de notre temps* (ed. L. de Lorenzi; Rome: Abbaye de S. Paul, 1979) 311-38.

Charles Crawford ("The 'Tiny' Problem of 1 Thessalonians 2,7: The Case of the Curious Vocative," *CBQ* 54 [1973] 69-72) also argues for the reading νήπιοι, but for reasons not yet discussed. Crawford revises the suggestion of an eighteenth-century scholar, Daniel Whitby, that νήπιοι is a vocative ("But in your midst, babes, we were like a nurse..."). While this translation would resolve the difficulties of the mixed metaphor, it is grammatically indefensible.

[14] "'Gentle as a Nurse': The Cynic Background to 1 Thess ii," *NovT* 12 (1970) 203-17. Malherbe does not discuss the text-critical problem of 2:7 in this article. In a letter,

among the Cynics who were presenting themselves as public speakers, it had become advisable to distinguish oneself as a true philosopher by contrasting oneself to false philosophers by means of antithetical comparisons. Malherbe takes as a prominent example the comments of Dio Chrysostom, who contrasts the true philosopher to the charlatan. Significantly, Dio's remarks do not presuppose that he personally has been attacked, and therefore Malherbe concludes that Paul's use of the same self-description does not require us to think that he is engaged in a personal defense against charges.

Pertinent to our consideration of the metaphor of the nurse in 2:7 is Malherbe's identification of that metaphor as part of the topos regarding the behavior of the ideal philosopher. Just as the ideal philosopher speaks with παρρησία ("boldness") and acts without deceit or error, the true philosopher also should be prepared to be as gentle as a nurse. As evidence for this use of the metaphor of the nurse, Malherbe cites a number of texts (primarily from Dio Chrysostom, Epictetus, Plutarch, and Pseudo-Diogenes). For example, Dio Chrysostom, while describing a conversation between Diogenes and Alexander, explains that Diogenes knows that he has been harsh with Alexander and so he tells Alexander a story, just as nurses tell a story to comfort a child after a whipping (*Oration* 4.74). Elsewhere Dio refers to the custom of nurses to sweeten an unpleasant drink by smearing honey on the cup (*Oration* 33.10). More negative is Dio's contrast between proper instruction in knowledge and truth and the nurse who feeds her children with milk and wine and various foods (*Oration* 4.41).

As Malherbe points out, Epictetus's references to nurses are largely negative. Individuals ought to be content with what they have, not crying after things they want as children cry after their nurses (*Discourses*, 2.16.28). Some people are never willing to take solid food, but cling to their nurses (2.16.39; cf. 2.16.44). Here the nurse's charge symbolizes the immaturity of one who has not yet reached Epictetus's ideal. Similarly, Pseudo-Diogenes assaults those who, due to their own corruption, need radical surgery but instead opt for the gentle attentions of a nurse (*Ep.* 29).

Plutarch also employs the nurse as an example. In his essay, "How to Tell a Flatterer from a Friend," Plutarch employs the nurse to illustrate the need to speak gently in time of misfortune. When children fall down, their nurses do not rush up to them and berate them. Instead, they pick them up, wash them, and straighten their clothes—then they berate

---

however, he indicates that the Pauline usage elsewhere, the context, and the topos decide the debate in favor of ἤπιος (letter to Beverly Gaventa, 13 February 1989).

them (69C). When writing about the education of children, Plutarch urges that rebuke and praise should be used alternately and again mentions the practice of nurses, who cause babies to cry and then offer them nourishment ("The Education of Children," 3C-F).

Some of these texts admittedly use the imagery of a nurse's care to illustrate (either positively or negatively) aspects of the philosopher's relationship to his students. Whether there is enough consistency here to call this an established topos is, in my judgment, an open question. Quite apart from that question, however, it is problematic to connect this usage to that of Paul in 1 Thess 2:7.

1. In the texts Malherbe cites, Dio and others employ the nurse as an example. The relationship between the nurse and the speaker is actually quite remote. Not only is the nurse sometimes viewed negatively (that is, she is too soft and accommodating), but the speaker uses the nurse as an example to illustrate the point rather than as a metaphor to describe himself. For example, Dio does not say that he himself is like or unlike a nurse; he speaks of Diogenes, who in turn refers to a nurse's behavior. We might say that the difference here is that between telling a parable and decorating a sermon with an illustration.

2. In Dio's sustained descriptions of philosophers of varying types, the image of the nurse does not appear. For example, *Oration* 32, which Malherbe uses extensively to show the way in which Dio describes philosophers, makes no mention of the activity of a nurse. Instead, as noted above, the image of the nurse appears in a limited number of illustrations (e.g., *Oration* 4.73; 33.10). If there is a topos concerning the ideal philosopher, it is not clear that the topos includes the reference to the nurse.

3. Most puzzling is the fact that the word τροφός does not appear in the texts to which Malherbe points. Uniformly, these texts employ the term τίτθη for the individual described.[15] It is not immediately obvious what significance we should attach to this observation. One study of the nurse in Greek life concludes that these terms are not distinguished sharply from one another. The noun τροφός, however, appears as early as Homer and refers in a general way to one who nurtures; τίτθη appears in the literature only later and with reference more narrowly to the role of the wet-nurse.[16] Pseudo-Ammonius confirms this distinction and refers to

---

[15] This noun is not employed in the New Testament, LXX, or Josephus.

[16] Mary Rosaria Gorman, *The Nurse in Greek Life* (unpublished Ph.D. dissertation; Catholic University, 1917) 7-8.

the nurture of the τροφός after a child is weaned.¹⁷ While the two terms are clearly related to one another, they do not seem to be used interchangeably.

Given this range of problems, we may conclude that, while Malherbe has identified a topos which contrasts the ideal philosopher to the charlatan, it is far from clear that the behavior of the nurse has a fixed place in that topos.¹⁸ A more helpful approach to the nurse image, in my judgment, is one that asks how the nurse was perceived and what role she played in the social context. Here some general remarks will have to suffice. Early Greek literature usually portrays the nurse as a slave (e.g., Homer, *Od.* 7.9; *Il.* 389; Euripides, *Med.* 65), although by the fourth century BCE there are already references to free women taking on the role of the nurse as a result of dire poverty (Demosthenes, *Oration* 57.35,42). Within the household, the nurse not only had responsibility for the care of infants and small children, but often continued as the attendant for a young woman and remained in the affection of young men who were her former charges. In addition to caring for children, the nurse is portrayed as a general assistant in domestic affairs—supervising the work of others, acting as stewardess of the household, performing an array of household tasks. In some texts she appears to exercise a role of authority over others in the household, giving them directions and supervision. From Homer on, writers portray the nurse as a generous and kind figure, and there are few references to neglect or maltreatment.¹⁹ All of this suggests that Paul's metaphorical use of the nurse would conjure up in the minds of his audience an important and beloved figure. Whatever the social status of the Thessalonian Christians, they could

---

¹⁷ Ammonius 470 (11.5-8, p. 122 in the edition of K. Nickau). Cf. Eustathius, *Il.*, 6.399, p. 650. I learned of the discussion in Ammonius through von Dobschütz's commentary (p. 94). One recent study of Greek words for nursing and nurture does not even discuss the term τίτθη (Claude Moussy, *Recherches sur trephō et les verbs Grecs signifiant "nourir"* (Paris: Librairie C. Klincksieck, 1969).

¹⁸ For a critique of Malherbe's comparison of 1 Thess 2:1-12 with Cynic texts, see Wolfgang Stegemann, "Anlass und Hintergrund der Abfassung von 1 Th 2,1-12," in *Theologische Brosamen für Lothar Steiger* (ed. G. Freund and E. Stegemann; BDBAT 5; Heidelberg: Theologische Seminar, 1985) 399-401. Stegemann argues that the Pauline text is not comparable with the texts Malherbe cites, since (1) Paul is not presenting himself or his gospel for the first time but is reminding believers of their earlier experience; and (2) while Dio is attacking the authenticity of other philosophers, Paul is discussing his own teaching.

¹⁹ See Gorman, *The Nurse in Greek Life*, 9-33, and the abundant references cited there; also G. Herzog-Hauser, "Nutrix," *PW* 17, col. 1495.

understand this reference to an important social relationship—one proximate to kinship itself.[20]

Before leaving this discussion of the nurse, we need to consider briefly two important texts, one from the Hebrew Bible and the other from the Dead Sea Scrolls. These texts are important for our understanding of 1 Thess 2:7 because of the way in which a male figure attaches to himself the language of nursing.

The first text comes from Numbers 11 and is part of the traditions about Israel's wandering in the wilderness.[21] In this particular text, the people have grown weary of eating only manna and cry out for the meat, the fruit, and the vegetables of Egypt. Moses turns to God in anger and frustration with the people and cries out, "Did I conceive all this people? Did I bring them forth, that thou shouldst say to me, 'Carry them in your bosom,' as a nurse carries the sucking child?" (Num 11:12). Of course, we cannot simply leap from this passage to 1 Thess 2:7. The word τροφός does not appear in the LXX; we have no verbal connection between the two texts. Moreover, unlike Paul, Moses is complaining here; this is a role which God has thrust upon him and he would be happy to be relieved of it.

There are, however, some tantalizing connections between the two passages. We do have in both the striking application of the role of nurse to a male; and in both instances it is the male in question who identifies himself with the role. Moses, like Paul, nurtured the people. While Moses insists that he did not assume this role for himself, it is nevertheless the role he continues to play in relation to Israel. In the same way, Paul continues to nurture his congregations. Paul does not explicitly link himself to the role of Moses, but he does elsewhere apply to himself language found in the prophetic call passages. I suggest that what we have here is an image that may have exerted an influence on Paul's reflection about his own role.

The second example of the use of the image of the nurse comes from the community at Qumran. There, in the Hodayoth, the Teacher of Righteousness describes himself as the father of the pious:

Thou hast appointed me to the service of thy covenant,
And through thy promise I stand firm therein.
Thou hast made me to be a father to all the children of piety,

---

[20] Indeed, in some texts the word τροφός is used of a woman who is, in fact, the mother of a character (e.g., Theocritus 27.65; Sophocles, *Ajax* 849).

[21] The similarities between these two passages were noted as early as Zimmer, "1 Thess. 2:3-8," 268.

A foster-father to men of good omen.
They open their mouth as the nursling [to his mother's breasts]
And rejoice like a child in the lap of his foster-father.[22]

Again, as with the text regarding Moses, we must not overstate the similarities between this passage and 1 Thess 2:7. The imagery here is largely paternal rather than maternal. It is intriguing, however, to find another instance of maternal imagery, and again here it is the speaker who identifies himself in language that is maternal.

This discussion about the τροφός has ranged somewhat widely, and it will therefore be useful to summarize the major points before we ask specifically what place the term has in Paul's letter. I have argued that Paul's usage of τροφός does not derive from the topos of the philosopher and his gentleness. Instead, Paul draws upon a well-known figure in the ancient world, one identified not only with the nurture of infants but also with continued affection for her charges well into adulthood. Moreover, Paul's reference to himself (and others) as nurses bears an interesting resemblance to passages in Numbers and the Hodayoth where Moses and the Teacher of Righteousness, respectively, identify themselves with nursing roles.

3. The Metaphor(s) in Context

The answers offered to the first two questions I identified at the outset of this essay confront us with what appears to be a significant contradiction. By arguing that the earliest reading is νήπιοι, I concluded that Paul applies to himself and his co-workers the metaphor of babes. By arguing that the reference to the τροφός does not simply derive from the topos of the ideal philosopher, I insist that the metaphor of the nurse is something more than conventional. It is part and parcel of what Paul wishes to say here about his work. That means that we are looking at what we usually call a mixed metaphor, although in this case the mixture is odd enough that we might term it inverted.

Before addressing the inverted or mixed character of this particular metaphor, we may profitably remind ourselves what a metaphor is and does. A metaphor is "a device which speaks of one thing (tenor) in terms which are appropriate to another (vehicle), with the vehicle

---

[22] 1QH 7:19-23,25. The similarities between this passage and 1 Thess 2:7 are noted by O. Betz, "Die Geburt der Gemeinde durch den Lehrer," *NTS* 3 (1957) 322; W. Grundmann, "Die *nepioi* in der Paränese," *NTS* 5 (1959) 200; Traugott Holtz, *Der Erste Brief an die Thessalonicher* (*EKK*; Zurich: Benziger, 1986) 83 n. 342.

serving as the source of traits to be transferred to the tenor."[23] But this distinction between tenor and vehicle should not lead us to draw a very firm line between the two parts of a metaphor. Indeed, discussions of metaphor often comment on the way in which a metaphor changes or enhances meaning by juxtaposing tenor and vehicle. I. A. Richards argued that a metaphor combines "two thoughts of different things active together and supported by a single word, or phrase, whose meaning is a resultant of their interaction."[24] The two parts of a metaphor create new meaning by their interplay.[25] Philip Wheelwright termed this interplay a kind of metamorphosis, in which the imagination reaches out and combines things that are different.[26] Wayne Booth speaks of the expansive character of metaphor; that is to say, metaphor is a process in which meanings are added or multiplied rather than subtracted.[27] Metaphor does not merely decorate or illustrate; it broadens our understandings. Indeed, to the degree that language is inherently metaphorical, one might even say that metaphor creates understandings as well as amplifies them.

The difficulty in the text under consideration is that Paul uses not one metaphor but two. He compares himself with babes and then immediately with the one who cares for those babes—the nurse. That dramatic change of metaphors has given rise to the usual comments on Paul's inability to complete an analogy. When Shakespeare uses metaphors that might be called mixed, critics speak of "rapidly shifting figures" and say that his thoughts flow faster than his speech.[28] I suggest that something similar happens to Paul in 1 Thess 2:7. Having introduced the expression "apostles of Christ," he searches for ways of explaining what those apostles are. In this section he employs two

---

[23] Norman Friedman, *Form and Meaning in Fiction* (Athens, GA: University of Georgia Press, 1975) 289; cited in Alan Culpepper, *Anatomy of the Fourth Gospel* (Philadelphia: Fortress, 1983) 181.

[24] *The Philosophy of Rhetoric* (London: Oxford University Press, 1936) 93.

[25] Ibid., 93-95, 124-25.

[26] *Metaphor and Reality* (Bloomington: Indiana University Press, 1961) 70-91.

[27] *A Rhetoric of Irony* (Chicago: University of Chicago Press, 1974) 22-23.

[28] Wolfgang Clemen, *Shakespeares Bilder: Ihre Entwicklung und ihre Funktionen im dramatischen Werk* (Dissertation: University of Bonn, 1936) 144; English trans., *The Development of Shakepeare's Imagery* (Cambridge: Harvard University Press, 1951). Quoted in Rene Wellek and Austin Warren, *Theory of Literature* (3rd ed.; New York: Harcourt, Brace & World, 1956) 302 n. 37.

metaphors, babes and nurses, and in v. 12 he will use the less jarring metaphor, fathers.²⁹

According to many reconstructions, 1 Thessalonians is Paul's first letter to a community of believers, and this letter does not begin with "Paul an apostle," or even "Paul a slave of Christ Jesus." In fact, alone among the Pauline letters, 1 Thessalonians begins with the unadorned itemization of the co-workers' names. Therefore, the mention of "apostles of Christ" in v. 6 (v. 7 in the Greek text) is the first such reference in Paul's letters. Having used the term, he must explain what it means.

In vv. 4-6, leading up to the phrase "apostles of Christ," Paul describes them negatively. That is, he contrasts himself and his co-workers to the charges sometimes made against wandering philosophers. Paul and his associates are not abusive, greedy, seeking for glory. They are, instead, apostles of Christ.

In v. 7 Paul turns to a positive description of the apostles. They are babes among the Thessalonians. Notice that "among you" or "in your midst" the apostles became babes. They were innocent characters, lacking the guile and deceit of a charlatan. In 2 Corinthians 10-13 we see Paul making a similar kind of claim about his work among the Corinthians, again contrasting himself to those who act abusively and who seek only their own glorification, who pervert Paul's own apostolic understanding (2 Cor 11:13).

But "apostles of Christ" are also nurses who care for their children. The intensity of the metaphor here is striking. It is not enough to assert that the apostles are nurses. Paul adds the verb θάλπειν, to warm, to cherish, to comfort. The nurse cares for, literally, "her own children." At this point we encounter a certain lack of clarity. The word ἑαυτῆς may mean that the nurse is caring, not for someone else's children in this instance, but for her own. However, the pronoun does not require that translation, and the way in which nurses are described in the literature makes it difficult to think of a nurse with children that were, in fact, her own biological children.³⁰ As I explained earlier, however, the affection between a nurse and the children for whom she cared was axiomatic. So, whether Paul has in mind the nurse and her own children or the nurse and her charges, the reference to the children again intensifies the

---

²⁹ I have deliberately set aside discussion of the paternal imagery because it is abundantly treated in the commentaries.

³⁰ Zimmer likewise concludes that what is in view is the affection of a nurse for the children she has reared ("1 Thess. 2:3-8," 268).

metaphor, as does the reflexive pronoun ἑαυτῆς.³¹ Verse 8 extends the comparison by speaking about the sharing not only of the gospel but also of the "selves" of the apostles.

Paul does use a mixed, perhaps even an inverted metaphor here, but for good reason. He is struggling to identify two aspects of the apostolic role. The apostle is childlike, in contrast to the charlatan who constantly works to see how much benefit he can derive from his audience. Yet the apostle is also the responsible adult, in the first instance the nurse who approaches her charges with care and affection.

But the juxtaposition of these two metaphors, babes and nurses, is itself significant, and separating them as I have done diminishes the meaning of the text. For what the text suggests is that the apostles of Christ are not to be understood in an ordinary way. To understand them, just as to understand the gospel itself, one must employ categories that seem outrageous outside the context of Pauline paradox. To apply the language of children and nurses to grown men is to create a jarring image, one that challenges and expands understanding. In later letters, this same conviction comes to expression via irony; as, for example, when Paul speaks of the apostles as the "offscouring of all things" in 1 Cor 4:13. In 1 Thessalonians 2 the imagery is that of the nursery, but it is no less shocking.³²

Although I am speaking of the theological functions of this language, the metaphors have important social and parenetic functions as well, and these various functions work together. To apply metaphors of family life (babes, nurses, fathers) to the apostles and their relationship to believers is to suggest that those believers constitute a family. As Wayne Meeks's work on the social world of the Pauline churches reveals, this kind of language serves to create a new family for those who are being disenfranchised from their families of origin and invites Christians to reconceive conventional roles in startling ways.³³ The parenetic function of these metaphors goes hand in hand with their social function. By invoking the language of family, Paul implicitly exhorts believers to continue in those relationships. Indeed, throughout

---

³¹ Stegemann suggests that ὡς ἐάν may signal that Paul knows it is unlikely that a nurse would be caring for her own children ("1 Th 2,1-12," 409).

³² Of course, the use of such outrageous imagery for describing the apostles is consistent with the proclamation of a crucified Christ. See Paul Meyer's suggestive essay on the need to reclaim the historical event of the crucifixion as the central element in New Testament theology ("Faith and History Revisited," *Princeton Seminary Bulletin* N.S. 10 (1989) 75-83.

³³ *The First Urban Christians* (New Haven: Yale University Press, 1983) 86-88.

this whole first half of the letter, the philophronetic elements set the stage for the more explicitly parenetic material in chapters 4 and 5.

While this study of 1 Thess 2:7 contributes to our understanding of this particular verse and its context, it also raises a number of questions. For example, what place do these images of vulnerability (the babes) and nurture (the nurses) occupy in relation to Paul's other ways of characterizing his apostolic office? What connections are there between this imagery and the apocalyptic language that dominates 1 Thessalonians 4-5 (and appears as early as 1:10)? Where else in Paul's letters do we find this language of vulnerability and nurture, and how should it help us to refine our understanding of Paul's thought? All of these questions call for further research and reflection—as matters both of history and of faith.[34]

---

[34] I delivered an earlier form of this article as part of the Kenneth W. Clark lectures at Duke University, April 1989. I appreciate the many helpful suggestions made on that occasion. I also want to thank C. Clifton Black II, Charles B. Cousar, David J. Lull, and J. Louis Martyn for reading and commenting on earlier drafts of this essay.

13

Job and the Problem of Doubt in Paul

David M. Hay [1]

While the topic of Paul's references to the Jewish scriptures has been the subject of many previous studies, his references to the Book of Job have been scrutinized to only a limited degree. He certainly refers to other OT books more often than to Job, but his Job references appear in prominent places and he is the only NT writer who clearly refers to specific passages in Job.[2] Among the Apostolic Fathers, only 1 Clement offers definite references to the Book of Job; and these, while extensive, do not emphasize, as Paul does, the issue of doubt.[3] This may reflect the tendency of hellenized Judaism to view Job as a model of faith despite suffering.[4]

---

[1] David M. Hay is Joseph E. McCabe Professor of Religion at Coe College, Cedar Rapids, Iowa.

[2] The familiar mention of Job's steadfastness in Jas 5:11 is a very general reference to the story of Job that ignores the impatience elaborated in Job 3-31. Among others, B. Schaller ("Zum Textcharakter der Hiobzitate im paulinischen Schriftum," *ZNW* 71 [1980] 21, n.1) suggests that James refers not to the OT book but to the general Jewish tradition as reflected in the Testament of Job, where Job is a model of patience.

[3] 1 Clem. 17.3-4; 20.7; 26.3; 30.4-5; 39.3-9; 56.6-15. 2 Clem. 6.8-9 quotes the passage in Ezekiel 14 that mentions Job as a righteous man alongside Noah and Daniel.

[4] This is strongly emphasized in the *Testament of Job*, but it is also expressed in the extant fragment of Aristeas the Exegete, *T. Abra.* 15:15, and the hellenistic synagogue prayers identified by Kohler, Bousset and others (see esp. J. H. Charlesworth, *The OT Pseudepigrapha* [New York: Doubleday, 1985] 2.687-88, 693). Philo's solitary reference to

Job and the Problem of Doubt in Paul 209

In studying these and other OT quotations and allusions in the NT, scholars have emphasized text traditions and possible intermediate sources (e.g., florilegia) in use, the Christian hermeneutics in play, the relation to Jewish exegetical principles and to Jewish interpretations of the same passages, and the bearing on Christian doctrines, especially Christology. I wish, however, to focus primarily on the significance of Paul's references to Job for an understanding of the Apostle's conceptions of religious doubt.

By "doubt" I mean conscious uncertainty or awareness of unanswered questions. It is helpful to ponder Ludwig Wittgenstein's discussions of doubt, especially his view that doubting makes no sense except in relation to an assumption that some matters are not doubted. "If you tried to doubt everything you would not get as far as doubting anything. The game of doubting itself presupposes certainty."[5] I suggest that Paul considers certain forms of doubt to be compatible with Christian faith and that he sometimes refers to the book of Job to show fellow believers that their faith needs to contain room for doubt.

In the following pages I will concentrate on the direct quotations of Job in Paul and some allusions related to them and their connection with the theme of doubt. Left out of account will be several Pauline passages which may allude to Job but in which concern with doubt does not seem prominent. These passages include 1 Thess 5:8 (Job 2:9), 5:22 (Job 1:1,8); Gal 6:7 (Job 4:8), and 1 Cor 4:6 (Job 37:15).[6] The total number of Paul's quotations and allusions and their distribution across his writings suggest that the Book of Job influenced him significantly through much of his career as a Christian apostle, if not before.[7]

Job (*Mut.* 48) calls atttention to the inevitable imperfection of human nature, which may (like 1 Clem. 17:3-4, which also cites Job 14:4) imply Job's moral greatness.

[5] *On Certainty* [New York: Harper & Row, 1969] 18, § 115. Cf. 44, § 341: "...the *questions* that we raise and our *doubts* depend on the fact that some propositions are exempt from doubt, are as it were like hinges on which those turn."

[6] I also leave out of consideration Rom 8:33, although it may allude to the accusations of Satan (presumably correlated with Christian doubts) expressed in Job 1-2 and other Jewish writings. Cf. C. E. B. Cranfield, *The Epistle to the Romans* (ICC; Edinburgh: T. & T. Clark, 1975) 1.438, n.3.

[7] There is an interesting report (*b. Shabb.* 115a) that R. Gamaliel the Elder once was observed reading a targum on Job, which may have been the same targum as that known at Qumran (11QtgJob). None of the passages quoted by Paul is included in the extant fragments of the 11QtgJob, but this rabbinic story suggests that one of Paul's teachers paid special attention to Job. See further J. P. M. van der Ploeg and A. S. van der Woude, *Le targum de Job de la grotte XI de Qumran* (Leiden: Brill, 1971) 6.

1 Corinthians 1-4

One prominently located quotation of Job appears near the end of an argument about wisdom in 1 Cor 3:19, and the wording is closer to the MT than to the LXX:[8]

(18) Let no one deceive himself. If anyone among you thinks that he is wise (σοφός) in this age, let him become a fool that he may become wise (σοφός). (19) For the wisdom (σοφία) of this world is folly with God. For it is written (γέγραπται γάρ), "He catches the wise (σοφοί) in their craftiness," (20) and again, "The Lord knows that the thoughts of the wise (οἱ σοφοί) are futile." (21) So let no one boast of men. (RSV)

A general Pauline conclusion to the preceding discussion about wisdom (vv. 18-19a) is followed by two OT quotations identified as such by "it is written." Repetition of the term "wise" enhances the connections.[9] The subject in both quotations is God. Probably Paul means that the futility of the thoughts of the wise is shown in the fact that God catches them. The quotations are succeeded by a concluding rhetorical passage strongly suggesting a Stoic background, which is introduced by ὥστε—which in turn suggests that the thought of vv. 21-23 is based at least in part on the quotations in vv. 19 and 20. The Corinthians are being urged to rely entirely on the divine wisdom manifested in Christ, with the understanding that this is part of the meaning of belonging to Christ or submitting to his lordship (1:30-31; 3:23).

On the other hand, the γάρ of v. 19 implies that it introduces scripture to support what has gone before, perhaps especially the ideas of v. 18. Verse 18, in turn, seems to look over its shoulder toward the entire argument about wisdom and folly begun in 1:18 (and adumbrated in 1:5 and 1:10-17). Given this, the quotations in vv. 19-20 also must be seen

---

[8] Job 5:13. On the textual issues see now D. -A. Koch, *Die Schrift als Zeuge des Evangeliums: Untersuchungen zur Verwendung und zum Verständnis der Schrift bei Paulus.* (BHT 69; Tübingen: Mohr [Siebeck], 1986) 71-73. He thinks Paul relied on a Hebraizing revision of the LXX, following the judgment of Schaller, "Textcharakter," 21-26.

[9] In v. 20 Paul has apparently changed ἀνθρώπων in Ps 93:11 (LXX) to σοφῶν to bring out this linkage—unless the Apostle is taking over a source or florilegium in which this substitution had already been made. For that hypothesis see esp. L. Cerfaux, "Vestiges d'un florilège dans 1 Cor. I,18-III,24?" *RHE* 27 (1931) 521-534. He argues that such a collection of OT texts might have been assembled by a non-Christian Jew who, like Philo, believed that the right sort of skepticism could lead to faith.

in relation to that entire train of thought, and indeed they help frame the whole argument.[10]

Throughout the passage Paul assumes several things as certain and beyond question: for example, that Jesus is the Christ, that God has given believers "all things" in him (e.g., 1:30-31), and that the Corinthians should accept Paul's authority (4:16-21). The chief doubts in view in the context of 1 Cor 3:19 might be stated as questions: (1) can Christian faith not be combined with (or viewed as the source of) an esoteric wisdom? (2) having the mind of Christ, do Christians not know everything? (3) is it not right for the Corinthians to evaluate leaders and missionaries and choose sides in disagreements based on their perceptions of spiritual superiority? Coupled with these doubts about religious principle would be many personal doubts: the Corinthians' doubts about Paul (presumably not all of them doubted him, and those who did had various doubts), and Paul's about them, their grasp of the kerygma, and their opinions about various leaders. In quoting Job 5:13 the Apostle implies that Christians have received spiritual wisdom in Christ, but this genuine wisdom should cause them to doubt the legitimacy of judgmentalism and party spirit and make them humbly willing to wait till the eschaton for the perfect attainment of divine knowledge.[11] Believers must be willing to be "foolish" by the world's standards, and they must have sufficient doubt of their Christian understanding to make them avoid divisiveness and indifference to Paul's teachings. Otherwise they will be trapped in spiritual futility.[12]

In 1:18-3:23 Paul is not claiming that all human wisdom is worthless but that there is a conflict between that wisdom and the wisdom of God revealed in Jesus' cross. This wisdom of the cross is explained primarily in relation to a dispute between Paul and the Corinthians. One important facet of that dispute seems to be that the Corinthians are claiming that their position is well supported by scriptural exegesis. The phrase "not beyond what is written" in 4:6 seems best regarded as alluding to

---

[10] Koch (*Schrift*, 275) notes that the OT quotations in 1:19 and 3:19-20 form an *inclusio* for the main argument.

[11] There is an obvious tension between the claim of 2:15 that the spiritual person judges "all things" (which seems an aspect of the Christian possession of "all things" in 3:22) and the warning not to pass premature judgment before the parousia when the Lord comes who will then reveal what is now hidden and disclose the purposes of every heart (4:5). This is connected with Paul's ironic "Without us you have become kings" (4:8).

[12] Cf. the argument of W. A. Meeks (*The First Urban Christians* [New Haven: Yale, 1983] 178-179) that Paul uses apocalyptic language in 4:8 and elsewhere to restrain a "realized eschatology" bent on innovation in directions he did not approve. The social effect of Paul's use of Job in 3:19, then, would be to reinforce a sense of the inevitable ambiguity and inconsistency of Christians' status in the present world.

Corinthians who claimed "We need no instructions beyond what is written. As spiritual men we can interpret the Scriptures for ourselves. Why ask Paul?"[13] In the context the slogan gets its content from the preceding citations from and allusions to what is written concerning the wisdom of God in contrast to the wisdom of human beings (cf. 1:19-20; 1:31; 2:9; 3:19-20). Similar references to "what is written" appear in 9:9; 10:7; 14:21; and 15:45. Clearly the Corinthians are able to consult scriptural texts and it is probable that a fair amount of their thinking, like Paul's, is guided by study of the OT in relation to their current situation and questions, including questions about Paul's authority.[14]

Many of these quotations in 1 Cor 1-4 speak about the vanity of human wisdom. It is true that the quotation of Isa 40:13 (LXX) in 1 Cor 2:16a is followed by a forthright claim: "But we have the mind of Christ." Yet it is by no means clear that Paul intends with those words to call into question the skepticism and humility inculcated in 2:16a.[15] If much of 2:6-16 existed before and apart from 1 Corinthians, it may have once implied an absolute Christian knowledge without limits; but within 1 Corinthians as we now have it, the claim to "have the mind of Christ" is relativized by 3:19 and 4:4 as well as 13:12. Paul's appropriation of the OT passages sets them in a "new light," not least because in their original contexts they all tend to disparage the claims of "wise persons" who are regarded as foes of God and as evil-doers. In Corinth, however, the "wise" are Christians whom Paul is by no means interested in ostracizing; they need only, in his view, learn not to boast about their wisdom.[16] At the same time, Paul has so generalized the issues in 1:18-4:10 as to imply that all human wisdom—Corinthian

---

[13] N. A. Dahl, "The Church at Corinth," in his *Studies in Paul* (Minneapolis: Augsburg, 1977) 54.

[14] H. Conzelmann (*1 Corinthians* [Hermeneia; Philadelphia: Fortress, 1975] 80) speaks of 3:19-20 as providing "a two-fold Scripture proof." To speak of "proof," however, may mislead us into supposing that Paul has only to produce OT quotations to convince his readers. Of course he quotes the OT to support and clarify his argument, but some Corinthians may not have found his OT exegesis compelling.

[15] It is not difficult to imagine that v. 16b is a slogan of the opponents Paul faces—a slogan he does not want to repudiate completely but which he wants to set in the perspective of his Isaiah quotation.

[16] Of course it is true that in 1:18-31 the wise include non-Christian Jews and Greeks who reject the "folly of the cross." But the primary concern of 1:10-4:21 is to deal with Christian "insiders" who boast on the basis of their wisdom. Cf. P. Stuhlmacher, "The Hermeneutical Significance of 1 Cor 2:6-16" in *Tradition and Interpretation in the New Testament: Essays in Honor of E. Earle Ellis* (ed. G. F. Hawthorne and O. Betz; Grand Rapids: Eerdmans, 1987) 335-36.

Christian, rhetorical, philosophical—is insufficient to be the basis of religious confidence.

In the context of 1:10-4:21 the wisdom that Paul condemns opposes the cross of Christ—and also the authority of Paul. Still, Paul does not place himself above or beyond the judgment of God (4:4). Neither does he claim to be a σοφός—rather he takes his own advice (3:18) and sets himself among Christ's fools (4:10). Hence he has found for himself, and he commends to others, a door of escape from the threat implied by his Job quotation in 3:19. Despite the claims to a special divine wisdom in chapter 2, Paul is in a sense preparing the readers for the declaration of 1 Cor 13:9-12 that even the highest Christian knowledge is imperfect and impermanent.[17] The wisdom that trips one up is the wisdom that prompts church quarrels and currently brings some Corinthian believers into a fleshly, in contrast to a spiritual, condition (3:1-5).

Does Paul in 3:19 quote from Job with any appreciation of the context of his quotation? There is no strong conflict between the sense of the original statement of Eliphaz in Job 5 and the use Paul makes of it, although there is a transformation of concern. Eliphaz was telling Job not to despair but to trust in God, despite his suffering. Paul is telling the Corinthians that what matters is not human claims to wisdom, not even good claims to wisdom; what matters is obedience to God—"and you are Christ's" (3:23). Of course this does not prove that Paul was not using a florilegium. But the sense he gives the Job quotation in 3:19 is not such that one can claim he is clearly quoting without regard to the original context.

Granting the prominence of the quotation in 3:19, we may be more disposed to recognize deliberate allusions to Job elsewhere in 1 Corinthians 1-4. Three passages in Job concerning God as transcending human understanding may be echoed before 3:19. Paul's statement in 1:20 about God making foolish the wisdom of the world may allude to Job 12:17 (where God is said to make fools of counselors and judges). The description of Christ as the power and wisdom of God in 1:24 recalls the language of Job 12:13 (LXX). The reference in 2:10 to "the

---

[17] Cf. R. Bultmann, *Theology of the New Testament* (New York: Scribner's, 1951) 1.327: despite all the development of knowledge possible to Christians as they move toward maturity, their knowledge "remains only partial knowledge, which will not be succeeded by clear comprehension without riddles until the consummation 'when that which is perfect is come' (1 Cor. 13:10- 12); for now 'we walk only by faith, not by sight' (II Cor. 5:7)." A thoughtful exploration of how Paul regards our present knowledge as imperfect is offered by P. W. Gooch, *Partial Knowledge* (Notre Dame: University of Notre Dame Press, 1987) 142-161. He relates 1 Cor 13:12 to Rom 8:28 and ends by emphasizing the ambiguities of this world which tempt believers to doubt God's love (see esp. 157-161).

depths of God" (τὰ βάθη τοῦ θεοῦ) recalls Job 11:7-8: "Can you find out the deep things of God?"[18]

Two passages in 1 Corinthians deal with judgment in ways that recall Job. A slight possibility of an allusion to the thought of Job 23:10 seems to lie in 1 Cor 3:15, both passages speaking of God's testing of persons as resembling the refining of metal in a furnace.

The strongest case for an allusion is afforded by 1 Cor 4:4: "I am not aware of anything against me [οὐδὲν γὰρ ἐμαυτῷ σύνοιδα], but I am not thereby acquitted; it is the Lord who judges." This is Paul's only use of σύνοιδα. The only similar use of that verb with the reflexive pronoun in the LXX occurs at Job (27:6), where the protagonist attacks the judgment of his friends and, indicating some deep trust in divine judgment, says "I am not conscious of having done anything wrong [οὐ γὰρ σύνοιδα ἐμαυτῷ ἄτοπα πράξας]." Paul's apparent use of the LXX is the more notable here since the MT, which employs lēbāb ("My heart does not reproach me"), does not convey the sense of conscience or consciousness in contrast to unconscious reality expressed by the Greek.[19]

Given the quotation in 3:19 and the likelihood of allusions elsewhere in 1 Cor 1-4, we may conclude that Job has significantly influenced Paul's convictions about the problematic nature of human wisdom.

Romans 11

The only other widely recognized Job quotation in Paul comes at the end of the main argument in Romans, embedded in the hymn-like conclusion to chapter 11:

(33a) O the depth [βάθος] of the riches and wisdom and knowledge of God!

(33b) How unsearchable are his judgments and how inscrutable his ways!

---

[18]. The LXX has "And there are deeper things [βαθύτερα] than those in hell—what do you know?" Note that TJob 37:6, like Paul, uses τὰ βάθη. It reads like a paraphrase of Job 11:7-8 and may reflect a period when the LXX of Job was in a fluid state and TJob and the LXX of Job were interacting. Cf. R. P. Spittler, "Testament of Job," in OTP 1.834.

[19] C. Maurer speaks of the Hebrew concept of "heart" being in this LXX passage replaced by moral "conscience" in the Greek sense ("σύνοιδα, συνείδησις" in TDNT 7.909). He does not say, however, if he regards 1 Cor 4:4 as a reference to Job. G. Theissen (Psychological Aspects of Pauline Theology [Philadelphia: Fortress, 1987] 61-62, nn. 6, 8) does so regard it. He argues that, whereas Job never thinks that he might be unconsciously guilty despite his conscious sense of innocence, Paul leaves the door open to unconscious guilt—but even so the Apostle maintains a "good conscience."

(34) "For who has known the mind of the Lord, or who has been his counselor?"
(35) "Or who has given a gift to him that he might be repaid?"
(36) For from him and through him and to him are all things. To him be glory for ever. Amen. (RSV)

John Knox urges that Paul is probably thinking of the entire argument from 1:16 on, an argument "full of gaps and of unassimilable, incompatible elements." Here "perplexity is overcome in an act of worship." But Knox thinks the quotation from Job in v.35 is "less apt" than that from Isaiah in v.34.[20] Nils Dahl writes that this paragraph "further explains why Paul does not presume to give an exact description of the future; he must leave room for surprises and for riddles." However, he also says, apparently with special reference to the Job quotation in v.35, "That no man holds God in his debt, so that what he receives from God is never merited, is a fundamental idea which underlies all of Romans."[21] In his great commentary Ernst Käsemann barely touches on v. 35 and claims that the doxology in vv. 33-36, like 1 Cor 2:16c, assumes that the revelation in Romans 9-11 has overcome the mystery of God's mind and purposes ("Paul stands here in an apocalyptic-enthusiast tradition").[22]

Clearly vv. 33-36 stand out in their hymnic form as well as their content from the preceding passage.[23] Verse 33 expresses awe at God's transcendent riches and wisdom, which must be interpreted in the light of the preceding discussion, perhaps especially in relation to 11:25-32. Verses 34-35 offer questions correlated with the divine qualities mentioned in v. 33. Although there is no introductory "as it is written," the use of "for" (γάρ) probably is intended to signal references to the OT. Verse 34, quoting Isa 40:13 (LXX), implies the mystery and room for doubt involved with the revelation Paul has just presented; and, as we shall see, this verse may contain an allusion to another passage in

---

[20] *IB* 9.577-578.

[21] "The Future of Israel" in Dahl, *Studies in Paul* (Minneapolis: Augsburg, 1977) 157.

[22] *Commentary on Romans* (Grand Rapids: Eerdmans, 1980) 320.

[23] A major historical question is whether 11:33-36, with its clear echoes of Jewish and pagan traditions, may as a whole be a pre-Pauline hymn. A strong case for an affirmative answer is detailed in E. E. Johnson, *The Function of Apocalyptic and Wisdom Traditions in Romans 9-11* (SBLDS 109; Atlanta: Scholars, 1989) 164-173. Even on this hypothesis, however, the exegete must attempt to understand the meaning Paul gave the hymn, including its OT quotations. J. D. G. Dunn (*Romans* [Word Biblical Commentary 38B; Dallas: Word Books, 1988] 2.698), by contrast, presents a good case for regarding the "hymn" as Paul's own composition.

Job. The quotation of Job 41:3 in v. 35 provides a warrant for the basic doubt about human righteousness that undergirds Romans as a whole. This citation explains the divine riches mentioned in 11:33.[24] Like 1 Cor 3:21-23, v. 36 uses Stoic language that must be interpreted in relation to Paul's Christian argumentation and the interwoven OT citations.

I am inclined to see in 11:33-36 an implication of both certainty and perplexity. Paul intends that the Roman Christians regard as certain the proposition that "all Israel will eventually be saved" because God has given irrevocable promises and set all persons under impartial judgment and mercy. Yet the Apostle does not spell out exactly how or when Israel will be saved, nor does he say if he expects everyone eventually to believe in Jesus as the Christ.[25] So, even as he offers praise to God for what has been revealed, he points out that God's revelation remains mysterious and in many respects beyond present Christian comprehension.[26] Aware that he has not answered all possible questions and objections, perhaps conscious of areas where he himself is troubled, he leaves room for doubt—but not regarding his fundamental certitudes about salvation.

It seems clear that the answer expected to the question in v. 35 is "No one." If that is so, however, it is natural to assume that negative answers are also anticipated for the questions in v. 34. The general point of the entire doxology is to say that the whole work of salvation is accomplished by God, who acts without helper or counselor.[27] Even if

---

[24] So G. Bornkamm, "The Praise of God" in *Early Christian Experience* (New York: Harper & Row, 1969) 107. Cf. Koch, *Schrift*, 179, n.41.

[25] E. Boring offers a stimulating essay that concludes that Paul affirms *both* limited salvation *and* universal salvation but never draws the logical inferences belonging to each because he never affirms the two ideas together ("The Language of Universal Salvation in Paul," *JBL* 105 [1986] 269-292). It seems logically simpler to infer that this was a topic on which Paul was consciously uncertain and felt that it was one about which no human could conscientiously claim certainty. The Apostle says what he thinks can and must be said, and in Rom 11:33-36 indicates there is a line beyond which human thought as well as language cannot venture.

[26] Similarly Bornkamm, "Praise," 107, 110; D. Zeller, *Juden und Heiden in der Mission des Paulus* (2.Aufl.; FB; Stuttgart: Katholisches Bibelwerk, 1976) 267-268; W. D. Davies, *Jewish and Pauline Studies* (Philadelphia: Fortress, 1984) 149; C. E. B. Cranfield, *The Epistle to the Romans* (ICC; Edinburgh: T. & T. Clark, 1986) 2.592.

[27] A. T. Hanson (*The New Testament Interpretation of Scripture* [London: SPCK, 1980] 87-89) argues on the contrary that the three questions in 11:34-35 imply "Yes" answers because they contain positive if concealed references to Christ. His argument is built on the later targum to Job (not 11QTgJob) and some rabbinic interpretations of Job 41:3, although he recognizes that this rabbinic evidence is late and that there is no proof that the rabbis connected Job 41:3 with Isa 40:13. The interpretation which he cites from *Pesikta de Rab Kahana* 9.2 (p. 88) offers an understanding of Job 41:3 according to which

one interprets 1 Cor 2:16b to mean that the question of Isa 40:13 has a positive answer, we are not compelled to assume that Paul interprets that OT question in the same way in Romans 11.[28]

I take it that Rom 9:1-5 is more than passion—it is also a rhetorically powerful transition to a topic of high importance. As in 1 Cor 4:1-6, Paul speaks in the first person singular about an issue which he thinks should be of concern to all believers. Part of what he wants the Roman Christians to understand is the advantage of doubting their doubts. Gentile Christians are tempted to doubt that the Jews will be saved (11:17-19). They should reconsider. That all is not plain before his eyes on this matter is suggested by the fact that Paul writes 9:6-11:24. He cannot simply "solve" the matter by announcing his "revelation" about the future (11:25-27). All the tortuous argumentation of Romans 9-11 reflects not simply riddles that he wants the Roman Christians to ponder but ones with which he has struggled. The tightness of argument suggests that some believers in Rome—independently of Paul—may have already considered the same problems and pondered some of the same OT texts to which he turns. The ways of God with Jews and Gentiles still are mysterious for Paul, and he does not claim to see everything distinctly.

Paul's quotation in 11:35 approaches the sense of our Hebrew text (41:3) and differs markedly from the LXX (41:11), which some specialists regard as better fitting the context in Job.[29] Yet Paul's version also makes sense in relation to the rest of Job 40-41, which dwells on the mysterious power of Leviathan and Behemoth only to exalt the incomprehensible greatness of their Creator. At the heart of the book of Job as a whole is the question of divine justice, particularly in relation to innocent or righteous human beings. Romans 9-11 centers in the problem of God's relation to Israel. The key to the Book of Job may be Satan's question, "Does Job serve God for nothing?" (1:9). One of the main ideas that surfaces in the dialogues is that human beings do not benefit God by their righteousness, any more than they injure Him

---

humans can earn rewards from God through works of supererogation. But this conflicts with Paul's view of human works. Finally, as Johnson (*Function*, 168) stresses, Hanson's interpretation of 11:33-36 requires that readers detect "a most subtle christological reference." See further J. Neusner (trans.), *PESIQTA deRAB KAHANA: An Analytical Translation* (Brown Judaic Studies 122; Atlanta: Scholars Press, 1987) 1.139-140.

[28] On the differences between the two passages, including the absence of a christological emphasis in Rom 11:33-36, see esp. Dunn, *Romans*, 700, 703.

[29] E.g., M. Pope, *Job* (AB; Garden City: Doubleday, 1965) 282-283.

by their sin.[30] We conclude that in 11:35, as in 1 Cor 3:19, Paul's quotation is not demonstrably at odds with its original setting in Job.

It may be that there are more allusions to Job in the immediate vicinity of v. 35. While that verse seems intended as a quotation of Job 41:3, it is also close in sense to 35:7. In Rom 11:36 the thought of everything being from, through, and to God accords with Job 41:3b, "Everything under heaven is mine."

In Rom 11:33 Paul's use of ἀνεξιχνίαστοι (used only here by Paul[31]) recalls the four passages in the LXX utilizing the term: Pr Man 6 (where it refers to the mercy of God), and Job 5:9; 9:10; and 34:24. In Job 5:9 Eliphaz speaks about committing one's cause to God who does great and "unsearchable" things, exercising providence over all the creation.[32] But the thought of Rom 11:33 also seems close to Job 9:10. Reference to the Prayer of Manasseh is not impossible, but we know that Paul knows Job and that he is about to quote it in 11:35.

Finally we note that the quotation of Isa 40:13 in Rom 11:34 might be backed up by Paul's recollection of Job 15:8 (LXX): "Has God used you as His counselor [σύμβουλος]?" Even if the Apostle did not need the authority of Job to support that of Isaiah, he or someone before him might have been led to link this quotation of Isaiah and that from Job in 11:35 because of the commonality of language and thought in Job 15:8.

The more possible allusions to other parts of Job we find in the neighborhood of Rom 11:35,[33] the more plausible becomes the view that Job had a major role in shaping the Apostle's thought, not least in relation to doubt regarding human inability to deserve or fully understand God's mercy.[34]

---

[30] Job 7:20; 22:2-3.

[31] The only other NT passage employing it is Eph 3:8, which I take to be the work of a Pauline disciple.

[32] And it will be recalled that Paul quotes Job 5:13 in 1 Cor 3:19.

[33] Dunn (*Romans*, 698) remarks that links with Job are "particularly prominent" in 11:33-36. Besides those noted above, he mentions others which are definitely possible: the concept of σοφία in line with Job 28; of κοίμα in line with Job 40:8; of the ὁδός of God—Job 21:14, 26:14, 28:13,23. He concludes (p. 703) that the central section of this hymn-like passage "may well have been originally inspired by meditation on that profound work [Job]."

[34] R. P. C. Hanson in a brief, provocative article calls the Book of Job "the Epistle to the Romans of the Old Testament" and argues that Rom 11:34-35 shows Paul deliberately building on Job's sense of the impossibility of humans being judged righteous before God ("St Paul's Quotations of the Book of Job," *Theology* 53 [1950] 250-253).

Philippians 1

In Philippians Job is quoted—but perhaps not with the assumption that the readers will recognize the quotation—to answer doubts related to Paul's personal situation. Here, more than in the other quotations, Paul seems to identify himself with Job both in experience and in paradoxical faith.[35]

In Phil 1:19 Paul writes:

For I know that through your prayers and the help of the Spirit of Jesus Christ *this will turn out for my deliverance* (τοῦτό μοι ἀποβήσεται εἰς σωτηρίαν).

In contrast to the clear indication in Rom 11:34-35 and 1 Cor 3:19 that the OT is being cited, here there is no introductory formula to invite the reader to recognize an OT reference. Perhaps the "I know" (διδα) is meant to prompt the readers to think what the basis of knowing might be, but that can hardly be meant to provide a very strong clue.[36] Philippians generally lacks obvious OT allusions as well as quotations and it is possible that Paul does not assume his readers are well acquainted with the Jewish scriptures.[37] The mention of the church's prayers and the help of Jesus' spirit in 1:19 indicate that Paul is backing his confidence with more than the quotation from Job. Still, the confidence expressed here must have been stronger for Paul because he felt it had a scriptural basis; and he might have expected his Philippian friends to recognize that basis.[38]

---

[35] The quotation is from Job 13:16. It is worth noting that the speaker in the Joban passages quoted elsewhere was not Job: 1 Cor 3:19 quotes words of Eliphaz and Rom 11:35 words of God.

[36] Cf. the remarks on the verb in E. Lohmeyer, *Die Briefe an die Philipper, an die Kolosser und an Philemon* (13.Aufl.; MeyerK; Göttingen: Vandenhoeck & Ruprecht, 1964) 51, n.3.

[37] That Paul's language in the letter is considerably influenced by the OT does not decide if his readers would have recognized it to be so. Given the brevity of the letter and perhaps unresolvable problems of its integrity, it may be unwise to seek firm conclusions about the readers' ignorance or knowledge of the OT. Cf. A. v. Harnack, "Das Alte Testament in den Paulinischen Briefen und in den Paulinischen Gemeinden" in *Kleine Schriften zur Alten Kirche* (Leipzig: Zentralantiquariate der DDR, 1980) 2.826.

[38] J. H. Michael (*The Epistle of Paul to the Philippians* [MNTC; London: Hodder and Stoughton, 1928] 48) suggests that the Philippians may have already used Job's words in a letter sent to Paul.

Is it a quotation at all? Some scholars have dismissed the idea.[39] Yet the five italicized words are found in exactly the same sequence in Job 13:16 (LXX). Nowhere else does Paul use this word for "turn out" (ἀποβαίνειν), and nearly all the 22 uses of the term in the LXX appear in Job. No other LXX passage comes close to this phrasing with "deliverance" (σωτηρία).

It is remarkable that this quotation matches LXX Job so well,[40] given that those in Rom 11:35 and 1 Cor 3:19 diverge from the LXX so conspicuously. Three scattered quotations are not enough to demonstrate that Paul knows Job in more than one language or version and selects readings that best fit his own purposes, but that possibility cannot be excluded.

In 1:19 Paul is offering an explanation of his present and future rejoicing, which apparently is his response to a series of problems. He refers to his imprisonment and describes some who preach Christ from bad motives: competitiveness, partisanship, insincerity, and desires to augment the imprisoned Apostle's sufferings. He says he writes to convince the Philippians that the things that have happened to him have helped advance the gospel (1:12-13) and they will not prevent him from gaining his freedom and coming again to Philippi (vv. 25-26). That is, Paul is answering doubts—if not his own, then at least those he thinks some Philippian Christians are entertaining. These doubts must include wondering how a loving God could allow Paul to be imprisoned and the Philippian Christians themselves to be put in jeopardy (1:29-30). The assertion (v. 14) that certain individuals have grown bolder may respond to Philippian fears that Paul's sufferings would silence other witnesses. Some in Philippi may have thought Paul's imprisonment made his integrity suspect.[41]

Clearly 1:19 is directly related to Paul's expectations of deliverance. What kind of deliverance is he anticipating in this passage? Despite the buoyant phraseology of vv. 19-26, the Apostle seems deliberately unspecific. Death may be his only release from present imprisonment, but he indicates that for him even that would not be a loss. (Of course

---

[39] E.g. H. Vollmer (*Die alttestamentlichen Zitate bei Paulus* [Freiburg: Mohr [Siebeck], 1895] 23, n.2) doubts there is any reference to Job here. E. E. Ellis (*Paul's Use of the Old Testament* [Edinburgh: Oliver and Boyd, 1957] 154) lists it as an allusion, though perhaps an unintentional one. Koch (*Schrift*) ignores it. By contrast Schaller ("Textcharakter," 21) recognizes it as a clear citation. Others who recognize it as a quotation are Michael, *Philippians*, 46; Lohmeyer, *Briefe*, 50-51; E. F. Scott, "Exegesis of Philippians," *IB* 11.33; F. W. Beare, *The Epistle to the Philippians* (HNTC; NY: Harper & Row, 1959) 62.

[40] The MT does not substantially differ in sense from the LXX of 13:16.

[41] Cf. Michael, *Philippians*, 47.

some Philippians may have been having doubts about the afterlife.) He speaks firmly about his confidence that he will see the Philippians again—but many readers have felt he is not really certain of a physical reunion.[42] Above all Paul's greatest doubt—or the greatest doubt some Philippians might have about him—pertains to his loyalty to Christ under duress. Will he honor Christ in or with his body (v. 20)?

I would suggest that Phil 1:19 is meant to be a persuasive repudiation of some of these doubts and an indication that other doubts must simply be tolerated and endured. In the latter category is the uncertainty about when and how Paul's imprisonment may end. Also included is the uncertainty of the success or effects on churches of those who preach Christ from what Paul regards as bad motives.

Again one may say that Paul's use of these words of Job is not in sharp conflict with their original setting. In Job 13 there is a paradoxical declaration of trust in God. In the midst of complaining that his three friends are defending God with lies and that God himself treats him unfairly, Job asserts both his own innocence and God's holiness—his confidence in God's justice gives Job hope that things will "work out" for his own salvation or vindication (13:16).[43] Paul nowhere says that his suffering has made him question the righteousness of God, but his Philippian friends may have done so; and it is possible that he himself sometimes felt doubts that he chose not to express in his letters. Job 13:16 expressed hope in the midst of almost unlimited doubting, and Paul's use of these words suggests that he has thought much about Job's questions as well as his convictions.[44]

---

[42] Cf. 2:17. See esp. Lohmeyer, *Briefe*, 50-51, 69-70; Michael, *Philippians*, 60. Beare (*Epistle*, 62-63) says that in 1:19 Paul is thinking only of an eschatological deliverance but then in vv. 25-26 changes his mind and feels sure he will be released from prison and continue with his church work. Cf. P. Perkins, "Christology, Friendship and Status: The Rhetoric of Philippians," *SBLSP* (1987) 515: Paul's restraint in speaking about the future "suggests a real possibility that he will not be released."

[43] On the profundity of the paradox, see esp. S. Terrien, "Exegesis of Job," *IB* 3.1005-1006.

[44] Michael (*Philippians*, 52) suggests that Paul's words about facing death with courage remind us (and apparently, he thinks, were meant to remind us) of Job's willingness to face death bravely and without changing his position in 13:13-15. Recently Walter Wink has asked if there is "any room in Paul" for Job's defiant expressions of anger against God ("Review of G. Theissen's *Psychological Aspects of Pauline Theology*," *RelSRev* 15 [1989] 42). I would say that this side of Job is not reflected in Paul's letters, but that need not be ascribed to repression of unconscious hostility—unless, as Wink suggests, such hostility is unavoidable for theists.

Conclusions

The Book of Job is widely regarded as the supreme expression of biblical doubt, particularly in relation to the ancient Hebrew wisdom traditions, while Paul is widely regarded as a most dogmatic missionary theologian. Yet, as we have seen, Paul seems to cite Job deliberately in several passages to support his view that doubt is not always antithetical to faith. The revelation in Christ calls into question not simply human wisdom in general but specifically the wisdom claims of Corinthian Christians; it makes dubious general human efforts at self-justification and specific Christian tendencies to despise Jews. Faith means reliance on God instead of on self and requires the humility to recognize the limits of believers' understanding of God's ways and goals. Faced with the possibility of execution and the anxious perplexities of his Philippian "partners" in the Gospel, Paul affirms a confident hope that does not ignore the uncertainties of his situation or theirs.

Paul's interpretations of Job are not christological and do not typically clash with the sense of Job's words in their original context. This indicates that we need not think that Paul is interpreting the OT atomistically or relying on intermediate sources rather than a text (or texts) of the OT book. It also suggests that in applying Job's words to Christian situations Paul did not assume that Christians must interpret those words very differently from Jews.

We may wonder why Paul did not more directly and frequently incorporate words from Job into his arguments about the universality of sin and justification by faith. But other OT texts were available for those purposes. He did cite Job in several striking passages to show how Christians might live with their doubts as well as their convictions.[45]

---

[45] In conclusion I wish to express a strong sense of gratitude to the man honored in this volume. As my teacher and dissertation advisor Paul Meyer taught me many things—the need for precision in exegesis, the possibilities for creative pursuit of one's own questions, and the value (as Kafka might put it) of doubting one's doubts.

14

Faith and Its Moral Life: A Study of Individuation in the Thought World of the Apostle Paul

J. Paul Sampley [1]

For Paul, the matrix of the Christian life is community, the common life in Christ shared by all believers. Accordingly, all the extant letters of Paul[2] are addressed to communities of believers[3] and believers are frequently exhorted to focus upon how their actions affect others.

Held in equilibrium, however, with Paul's strong, fundamental commitment to community is an equally persistent emphasis upon the individual and the individual's rights. Paul's thought world gains expression in "delicate balances"[4] wherein he holds together in dialectical tension matters that are important to him, but that might on

---

[1] J. Paul Sampley is Professor of New Testament and Christian Origins at Boston University, Boston, Massachusetts.

[2] This study presupposes that Paul wrote Romans, 1 and 2 Corinthians, Galatians, Philippians, 1 Thessalonians, and Philemon.

[3] Even Philemon is written to a wider audience that includes named individuals and "the church in your house" (v. 2).

[4] J. Paul Sampley, "From Text to Thought World: The Route to Paul's Ways" in *Pauline Theology: Toward a New Synthesis* (ed. Jouette M. Bassler; Minneapolis: Fortress, 1990).

superficial notice seem to be alien to each other. A classic example is Paul's affirmation of both God's freedom and God's faithfulness,[5] where either one without the other would give less than a full picture of Paul's theological confession. The same is true with regard to Pauline claims about the community and the individual; what is said of the one must not overlook the implications for the other.[6]

Given that Paul's understandings of community[7] have been scrutinized more thoroughly than have his thoughts about the individual, our purpose in this essay will be to cast some light on an aspect of Paul's presumptions and claims about the individual, to wit a study of individuation in Paul's thought world, with a special focus upon faith and its associated moral life.

What All Believers Share

Solidarity with Christ is the foundation of Christian unity. Believers have died with Christ (Rom 6:3-4) and, being thus in Christ, they are given into the care of each other. Christian unity, therefore, is not gained by adherence to some degree of doctrinal purity or fullness, but is something done to believers, bestowed upon them. So unity is not purchased via uniformity of creed or deed. Other believers are characterized as ones for whom Christ died (1 Cor 8:11), as the work of God (Rom 14:20), and as ones whom Christ has welcomed (Rom 15:7).

In broad scope, believers have a common story. All believers, before faith came to them, lived under the power of sin (Rom 3:9). All believers are now free from sin and its power (Rom 6:11-12). All believers are equally dependent upon God's grace (Rom 5:2). All of them alike are persons for whom Christ has died; each is fully "in Christ" (1 Cor 15:22; 2 Cor 5:14-15). All the faithful have been granted

---

[5] Cf. my "Romans and Galatians: Comparison and Contrast," in *Understanding the Word: Essays in Honor of Bernhard W. Anderson* (ed. J. T. Butler, E. W. Conrad, and B. C. Ollenburger; *JSOTSup* 37; Sheffield: *JSOT*, 1985) 315-39.

[6] Though, to my knowledge, Paul W. Meyer has not written of the topic that I offer here in tribute to him. It has ever been Paul Meyer's genius to understand and to preserve the complexity and the nuances of Paul's argumentation and thought. Exemplary in this regard are his "Romans 10:4 and the 'End' of the Law," in *The Divine Helmsman: Studies on God's Control of Human Events, Presented to Lou H. Silberman* (ed. J. L. Crenshaw and S. Sandmel; New York: KTAV, 1980) 59-78; and his "Romans," *HBC* (ed. J. L. Mays; San Francisco: Harper & Row, 1988) 1130-67.

[7] See R. J. Banks, *Paul's Idea of Community* (Grand Rapids: Eerdmans, 1980). Cf. also my *Pauline Partnership in Christ: Christian Community and Commitment in Light of Roman Law* (Philadelphia: Fortress, 1980).

the Holy Spirit (2 Cor 1:22; 5:5); all have been given one or more gifts by that same Spirit (1 Cor 12:7); all are expected to produce the fruit of the Spirit (Gal 5:22-23). All are to avoid the vices (Rom 1:29-32 and parallels).[8] In each of these particulars, every believer shares just as fully as any other. For those who are in Christ there is neither Jew nor Greek, neither male nor female, neither slave nor free (Gal 3:28).

Within this broad net of Christian unity, however, Paul moves freely to note distinctive marks of individuals, to distinguish some individuals from others, to single out certain people, to recognize variations and differences among individuals. Personal identity and individuation are prominent in the Pauline corpus. The following study of individuation is not designed to treat all the issues on the individuation side of this "delicate balance" in Paul's thought world, but to contribute to our understanding of the complexity of Paul's claims about individuals within the context of the community of believers.

Paul's capacity to differentiate among believers has been widely noted with regard to both χαρίσματα, or spiritual gifts, and the individual's distinctive call. But beyond that, Pauline studies have taken little formal note of the range of individuation that Paul assumes or affirms. For Paul, individuation is not confined to human beings. All of nature is individuated. "Not all flesh is the same; there is one kind of flesh for people, another for animals, another for birds and still another for fish" (1 Cor 15:39). Differentiation pervades the cosmos: there are celestial bodies and terrestrial ones, with distinctive glories. "Another glory of the sun, and another glory of the moon, and another glory of the stars; yes, star differs from star in glory" (1 Cor 15:41). Differentiation characterizes the universe and all things.[9] Here, as in many other places in his letters, Paul sounds much like a stoic whose universe is replete with differentiation, from the natural world right through to human beings.

Individuation in Measure of Faith

A fundamental Pauline individuation that has not been sufficiently noted is what he once calls the "measure of faith" (Rom 12:3). A

---

[8] 1 Cor 5:9-13; 6:9-11; 2 Cor 12:20-21; and Gal 5:19-21.

[9] Individuation occurs across the Pauline corpus. Paul claims that God distinguishes between those who please God and those who do not (1 Cor 10:5), and this individuation has been true throughout history (1 Cor 10:1-13). Paul's missionary practice (1 Cor 9:19-23) and even his relations to his different churches express individuation (cf. 2 Cor 11:9-10; 1 Cor 9:15; and Phil 4:10-20).

common rhetorical device in Paul's world was to use the same term with distinctive meanings (ἀντανάκλασις).¹⁰ A classic Pauline example is linked to Abraham, who "in hope, against hope" believed God (Rom 4:18); here, "hope" (ἐλπίς) is taken in two radically different senses. So also with regard to faith (πίστις), Paul has at least two different ways in which he uses the term. The first and basic function of the term is to describe a right relationship with God, a relationship of dependent trust which affirms that God is able to do and will do what God has promised.¹¹ Abraham illustrates this proper, dependent relationship: God promised Abraham a heritage of offspring; Abraham believed God (Romans 4; Galatians 3). So, like Abraham, other people can be in right relationship with God, or they can be in an improper relationship with God. The one is faith; the other is not faith. One is either in faith or one is not.

But Paul has another, more individuated way in which he can talk about faith. In this second sense faith can be greater or lesser, weaker or stronger. Here each person has a "measure of faith which God has measured out to each" (Rom 12:3). Paul lists faith, viewed in this fashion, as one of the χαρίσματα (1 Cor 12:9), a χάρισμα given to some by the Spirit. Here Paul can write of "the faith you yourself have" (σὺ πίστιν ἔχεις; Rom 14:22) and advise the Romans individually regarding how they should know that whatever faith they have is between themselves and God and therefore not subject to judgment even by another believer. In this same sense Paul urges persons with the χάρισμα of prophecy to employ it "in proportion to faith" (κατὰ τὴν ἀναλογίαν τῆς πίστεως; Rom 12:6), with faith being understood as variable in degree.

Elsewhere the second view of faith appears when Paul discourses with the Romans about how to deal with relations between those who are "weak in respect to faith" (τὸν δὲ ἀσθενοῦντα τῇ πίστει; Rom 14:1).¹² When, in Rom 15:1, Paul turns to a discussion of "we the strong ones" (ἡμεῖς οἱ δυνατοί) it is not with reference to physical strength that he writes, but with a view to the relative strength of people's faith.¹³ So, even Abraham as the example of the faithful person "did not waver with respect to faith but grew strong with respect to faith" (Rom 4:20).

---

¹⁰ *Ad Herennium* 4.14.21.

¹¹ L. E. Keck, *Paul and His Letters* (Philadelphia: Fortress, 1979) 50-55.

¹² It is in this same context that Paul writes of "the faith that you have" (Rom 14:22).

¹³ Cf. 1 Cor 8:7-13, where a similar treatment, perhaps a Pauline rhetorical commonplace, links weak and strong with respect to conscience instead of faith.

In this second sense of faith, Paul considers that one has received a certain measure of faith that has been meted out by God, or put in a different, grace affirming way, that has been granted to the individual as a gift of the Spirit. That measure of faith may be "weak" or "strong." One's measure of faith may, as it did when Abraham gave glory to God, grow stronger (Rom 4:20). In the everyday struggles Paul had with the Corinthians, this notion of faith gave him a means of encouraging their growth: "Our hope is that as your faith increases, our field among you may be greatly enlarged..." (2 Cor 10:15 RSV).[14]

Both senses of faith are the same faith, that is, the right relationship with God, seen from two different perspectives. When considered over against sin, faith's counterpart in Paul's thought world, an individual is either in the right relation to God or not; one either has faith or sins. When faith is considered, however, within the two horizon markers of death with Christ on the inaugural extreme and the parousia of Christ on the other, then Paul envisions faith in terms of measure, in terms of degree of strength or weakness, and in terms of growth. It is the same faith. Only Paul's perspective shifts.

A conception of faith that allows for growth or improvement accords well with Paul's thought world as it gains expression in other ways. Many of his images of the church involve growth or building. The Corinthians are always short of where Paul hopes they may be in terms of their growth. In 1 Corinthians they are "babies" not ready for the "meat of things" but still dependent on "baby food" (1 Cor 3:1-2). They are not mature (2:6); they are like children with a father (4:14-15). Years later he is still praying for their "completion" (κατάρτισις; 2 Cor 13:9). Although his relations over the years were better with the Philippians, he expects to remain in the world for them, "for your advancement and joy in faith" (προκοπή, progress, furtherance; 1:25).

Paul has alternative linguistic expressions that affirm the same notion of growth or development where some people in the community of faith are more advanced than others. With the Corinthians, some of whom are so infatuated with Spirit manifestations, Paul distinguishes between the "spiritual person" (ὁ πνευματικός; 1 Cor 2:15) and the "unspiritual person" (ψυχικὸς ἄνθρωπος; 2:14). The argument in context makes it clear that the "spiritual person" is viewed by Paul as mature and solid in judgment—the same kinds of claims that he might have made of the "strong-faith person" of Romans. The appearance of the same

---

[14] A similar understanding probably lies behind Paul's earnest and continual prayer that he might be present to the Thessalonians and "complete the deficiencies of your faith" (1 Thess 3:10).

identification—the spiritual people are the ones who take care of the weaker ones and restore them—in Gal 6:1 shows that we have indeed identified a Pauline commonplace[15] about people being at different stages in their faith journey toward maturity. As strong as Paul's faith is—he always identifies with the strong-faith people—he acknowledges to the Philippians that his life, too, is marked by a pressing on toward maturity (τετελείωμαι, τέλειοι; 3:12-16). Apostles and all other believers alike have lives marked by striving, by growth. "Whatever mature people there are think this way," Paul assures the Philippians (3:15).

So Paul's understanding of faith accords with his view of the faithful life as one of growth. Whatever faith one has is a gift, is measured out by God and exists between the individual and God. But this relation to God can, even should, grow, should become stronger as time goes by. Stronger-faith people must be considerate of weaker-faith people; neither should judge or despise the other; neither is "better"—or "worse"—than the other. Each is steward before God of the faith that each one has received. Like apostles, believers can pray and work for the growth or increasing completeness of the faith of others.[16]

Individuation in Proper Self-Assessment

Directly linked with the idea of individually measured faith granted to each person is the need for each individual to know the measure of his or her own faith. One needs to have a proper self-assessment so that one knows how strong one's own faith is, in order to understand precisely where one is along the path from childhood to maturity.

Involved also is a need for each person neither to over-reach nor to under-reach. Paul expresses the immediate connection between one's measure of faith and one's self-assessment in Rom 12:3: "not to think too highly of oneself beyond what it is necessary to think." Paul cautions against an overestimation of one's progress in faith. The same note rings in Galatians: "If someone thinks himself to be something

---

[15]The term "commonplace" designates what the Latin rhetoricians called *loci communes:* set, relatively fixed pieces of tradition. Here I intend it to designate an identifiable, perduring Pauline outlook that is not simply or directly generated by the situation Paul is addressing, but is drawn from Paul's thought world and applied to the situation.

[16] Nowhere in the corpus does Paul suggest that one's faith will be judged at the eschaton; it is the works that one's faith lovingly puts into action (Gal 5:6) that alone will be judged (cf. Romans 2 and 2 Corinthians 5). At the judgment the issue is what the recipient has done with the divinely bestowed trust.

Faith and Its Moral Life 229

while being nothing, he deceives himself" (6:3). Formidable consequences await the person who misjudges: "If someone thinks he knows something, he does not yet know just as it is necessary to know" (1 Cor 8:2). The image is changed, but the point is the same in 1 Cor 10:12: "Therefore let the one supposing that he stands watch out that he not fall." Standing and falling are eschatological alternatives related to God's ultimate judgment of individuals (Rom 14:4; cf. Rom 11:20; Gal 5:1). A proper self-assessment, that is, an individuated one which does not overestimate one's progress in the life of faith, is critical to one's standing before God. Proper self-estimation is a concern for Paul also in his letter to the Philippians: "Not from selfishness, not from empty conceit, but with humility let each regard one other as surpassing himself" (2:3). It is almost as if Paul, fearful of the consequences of misestimation of an individual's place, reckoned any miscalculations to be less problematic if they occurred on the low side, in the direction of an underestimate.[17] In other matters as well, Paul shows a play-it-safe tendency in his moral counsel; perhaps this advice toward humility is another example. Paul's experience with the Corinthians, however, illustrates the hazards in this line of counsel when some of the Corinthians—possibly even the majority—become convinced of their lack of worth to the community and allow the enthusiastic but powerful minority in the church to prevail. Then Paul—for the one time in his extant correspondence—addresses the problem of low self-evaluation:

> If the foot should say, "Because I am not a hand, I do not belong to the body," that would not make it any less a part of the body. And if the ear should say, "Because I am not an eye, I do not belong to the body," that would not make it any less a part of the body. If the whole body were an eye, where would be the hearing? If the whole body were an ear, where would be the sense of smell? (1 Cor 12:15-17).

All believers, whatever their own particular qualities, are equally important to the well-being of the community. As matters played out in Corinth, individuation had become the occasion for differentiation in value, and more dangerously, for harmfully low self-estimation.

So Paul urges self-evaluation as an important individual responsibility of believers. The risks of overestimation seem great to Paul, and he warns several communities regarding it; the problem with

---

[17] Cf. Jesus' similar teaching as reflected in Luke 14:7-11.

underestimation of the value of individuals gnaws at the vitals of the Corinthian community.

Individuation Rules Out Comparison and Judgment

Likewise, comparison between individuals is inappropriate. Paul rails against his opponents in Corinth who make comparisons—which we can suppose were self-flattering—between themselves and others. "But these who measure themselves with regard to one another and compare themselves with one another do not understand" (2 Cor 10:12). In Paul's thought world, believers will be different in certain particulars. That is the way the Christian life takes shape and that is the way the Spirit enriches the life of the body of Christ. Comparison is out. Judgment is out. Encouragement and edification are in. Believers share the same point of origin and self-definition: they are those for whom Christ died, those who have died with Christ. And believers share the same destiny: they must all stand before the judgment of Christ or God. Between those two fixed points, the faithful must navigate at their own pace and with their own grace-bestowed gifts, with love, respect, consolation and encouragement for one another. Proper self-assessment gives a careful definition of one's location in the journey from infancy to maturity of faith and provides a clear point of reckoning from which one can seek not only to grow but also to engage lovingly and supportively with others as they traverse the same general course.

Individual Determination of God's Will

Believers must determine what God's will is. To be sure, God has an overall plan (Rom 16:25-27) and its shape has become clear in Christ. Every believer also must know the two framing events within which life must be lived, namely one's death with Christ and one's anticipated resurrection like his in the parousia (cf. 1 Cor 11:26). These events are the framework within which all believers live. Between the givens of death with Christ and the parousia, however, believers must discern just what it means to determine and to do God's will.

Believers do have some guidelines regarding God's will. Scripture provides instruction concerning the divine will (cf. 1 Cor 10:1-11; Rom 15:4; 1 Cor 9:10; Rom 4:23-24). Likewise, the vice lists (Rom 1:29-32 and parallels) mark out the boundaries of acceptable behavior. Here there is no individuation. No one can live the life of faith and cross into the territory delineated in Paul's vice lists.[18] Paul's letters present the vice lists as established borders, apparently not open to dispute and not in need of deliberation. People who do such things "are worthy of death" (Rom 1:32); these persons shall not inherit the kingdom of God (Gal 5:21; 1 Cor 6:9).[19] Within the boundaries formed by the vice lists, however, deliberation concerning appropriate behavior is necessary.

If the scriptures do not provide all the needed direction concerning how to live properly before God, then the renewed mind must be employed to search out, to determine and to apply God's will (Rom 12:2). God's will does not seem for Paul to have a non-particularized existence in the abstract. Within the borders defined by very specific vices, believers do not have set things that they must do in specific circumstances. Believers must, in a measure, determine God's will as they meet the everyday challenges of their individuated lives in their own specific circumstances. Paul says it directly: "Do not be conformed to this age, but be transformed by the renewal of mind so that you may determine and apply[20] what is the will of God, the good, the pleasing and the perfect" (Rom 12:2).

Matters important in Paul's thought world are often cast in maxims and gnomic sayings. Because the Pauline maxims are so frequently encapsulated in discussions of what believers are supposed to "know"— and thereby operate with reference to—it may be a fair assumption that gnomic reductions were a basic Pauline instructional device.[21] Only as one knows the broader sweeps of the Pauline thought world does one begin to see the linkages between a given gnomic saying and the rest of

---

[18] See Peder Borgen, "Catalogues of Vices, the Apostolic Decree, and the Jerusalem Meeting," in *The Social World of Formative Christianity and Judaism* (ed. J. Neusner, P. Borgen, E. S. Frerichs and R. Horsley; Philadelphia: Fortress, 1988) 126-141.

[19] The terminology "kingdom of God," rare for Paul, twice directly tied to vice lists and in Galatians pointedly noted as a tradition he had given them before, suggests not only that it was a Pauline commonplace in his moral instruction but also that he had adopted it from pre- or para-Pauline Christian tradition.

[20] C. K. Barrett (*A Commentary on the Epistle to the Romans* [New York: Harper & Row, 1957] 233), in an effort to get across the richness of δοκιμάζειν here, says that one must not only discern but also apply what one finds. Indeed, the range of meanings suggested by *BAGD* (p. 202) includes: put to the test, examine, prove by testing, accept as proved, approved.

[21] They are indeed reductions in several ways. Pithy as they are, they sometimes reduce more complicated issues to simpler propositional form, as in "all things are permissible" (1 Cor 6:12; 10:23). Maxims may also be reductionist when they do not even point to their own consequences, as in "there is no God but one" (1 Cor 8:4). Another feature of gnomic constructions is that they invite the hearer or reader into them; they require input from the individual who is invited to make application of them.

Paul's thought. Knowing as we do from Rom 12:2 that the renewed mind is to test out, discern and apply God's will, we can surmise the way in which the gnomic saying in 1 Thess 5:21 fits into Paul's thought world: "Test out/discern all things; retain the good." Nothing in the immediate context of 5:21 makes clear why it would be important to test everything. Presumably the Thessalonians had Paul's teachings in their memories from the time he was first with them, and those memories have been refreshed and no doubt even expanded by Timothy's visit. We can discern the broader reference to Paul's thought only by considering other Pauline passages such as Rom 12:2. The Christian is a discerning tester not only of what might be determined to be God's will, but also of *all* things, whether they be events, deeds, practices or whatever. This discerning testing is presumed to result in a sorting of all things so that the good might be distinguishable (τὸ καλόν in 1 Thess 5:21). Having made the discernment, the believer is supposed to hold fast those things that check out as good. Of course the maxim in 1 Thess 5:21 makes no effort to answer the question, "good with respect to what?" Nor does it need to do so. Paul has made that clear in his teaching and we see enough of it in his letters to know how it works. What is good is weighed out first as to whether it is good with respect to its impact on oneself, that is, whether an action is appropriate to the individual.[22] Then a contemplated action is evaluated with regard to its impact on others. In both of these reckonings individuation plays an important role. In the first an individual has to reckon the good with respect to one's own measure of faith, one's particular Spirit-granted gifts, and one's own relation to God. With respect to others, one must factor in the faith-strength of others, where they are on the journey of faith from childhood to maturity and what the projected action would add to or detract from the common good. So the testing and discerning that a believer is expected to do is multi-faceted and multi-directional.

The believer's fundamental task can be described in alternative but roughly equivalent ways: one is to discern and do God's will; one is to see that love is done to others. Which way Paul talks about it depends on what is his concern at the time. If he is concerned with life offered as a living sacrifice to God, Paul will talk about obedience to God's will. If he is treating how the believer, before God, relates to others, then the

---

[22] Evidence such as 1 Cor 10:24 and Phil 2:4 may be adduced to support a concern first with another and then (if ever) a concern with oneself. But those verses appear in letters written to believers who have the most basic fundamentals and whose relationships with others are at issue. Those two passages bear on a situation in which an individual might be weighing out his or her rights as over against those of others.

discussion will focus on love, the form it takes and the way it is encouraged. For the latter, the letter to Philemon may serve as an example. Philemon, known for his great love (vv. 5, 7), is not *commanded* to do "what is proper" (τὸ ἀνῆκον; v. 8). Paul could have prescribed; it was not lack of boldness that prevented him from doing so. Philemon's "good" (τὸ ἀγαθόν σου) was better arrived at voluntarily (ἑκούσιος) than by necessity (ἀνάγκη; v. 14). Philemon must relate to Onesimus as a brother in Christ (v. 16; cf. v. 20). So love is appropriate. But what would love entail in this situation? To accept Onesimus back as a slave, but without punishment or prejudice? To send him to Paul? To free him?[23] Paul does not say what Philemon ought to do. Philemon is left to determine, with the support and encouragement of the church of which he is a part (v. 2), *how* he shall do love on this occasion. The letter does not express the hope that Philemon will guess or discern the only right thing from among the many options. Rather, it mentions Philemon's love shown so clearly in the past, a need to reckon what is proper and a concern that Philemon achieve his good. Love could be shown by Philemon through more than one option. He had to decide which choice provided him the fullest expression of love in his circumstance.

The Individuation of Love

"Faith working through love" (Gal 5:6) discerns what obedience to God means in particular situations. By the functioning of the mind renewed in Christ, the believer determines what action among the many possible might most fully and directly put his or her measure of faith into operation in the situation at hand. Because faith is individuated and because the situations of life are never identical, the engagement of love in any particular instance cannot be prescriptive in a casuistic manner but must itself be individuated.

If individuated faith works itself out through love differentiated with regard to the situation at hand, then how does Paul expect an individual to discern which options may or may not be appropriate? Within the boundaries provided by the vice lists, each believer must pay attention to both conscience and doubts. Paul was indeed possessed of a "robust

---

[23] As laudable as this last option appears in our modern eyes, it is probably not to be taken very seriously as an option entertained by Paul, because other letters show that Paul is eschatologically unconcerned about slavery as a social institution (see 1 Cor 7:17-24) and even sees it as a metaphor of the believing life (see Rom 6:11-23).

conscience,"[24] but what else would one expect from a person who always identified himself as strong in faith? Conscience's warnings and an individual's doubts function for Paul as an individuated border inside the common one marked off by the vice lists. There is nothing wrong with a believer having doubts or wavering (διακρίνω; cf. Rom 14:23) with regard to the appropriateness of a particular action to one's measure of faith. A problem arises only when, having doubts, one goes ahead to do the act in question. Paul illustrates the matter in his treatment of what a believer may eat (Romans 14). "But the doubting/wavering one is condemned *if he eats* because [what the believer has done would then be] not from faith" (14:23; emphasis added).

Doubts function as a fence for Paul, marking off one's personal area of positive action. Within that border one can be expected to act with clear conscience and with conviction. In the passage where Paul shows how doubts function as border markers, Paul declares about himself: "I know and I am convinced in the Lord Jesus that nothing is common in itself" (Rom 14:14). The rhetorical doubling[25] of "knowing" and "being convinced" develops the antithesis to "doubting." For Paul, one operates out of what one knows, that is, from where one has no doubts. A good example of how this works is reflected in Philippians, where Paul, in prison, contemplates his death and considers the resulting perpetual presence with the Lord desirable. But he is convinced (τοῦτο πεποιθώς) that staying in the flesh is necessary on account of the Philippians' needs, so he knows (οἶδα) that he is remaining and staying on (μένω καὶ παραμένω) with them (1:25).[26] Conviction stakes out the territory within the boundary of doubts; conviction guides one to action that is in accord with that about which one is sure on the basis of one's measure of faith.[27]

Stronger-faith people will have a broader scope of matters about which they have clear convictions and within which they can freely act;

---

[24] Cf. K. Stendahl, "The Apostle Paul and the Introspective Conscience of the West," in *Paul Among Jews and Gentiles* (Philadelphia: Fortress, 1976) 78-96.

[25] Synonymy, *anadiplōsis;* cf. *Ad Herennium* 4.28.38.

[26] Matters about which Paul is convinced are sometimes bed-rock, foundational: nothing can separate believers from the love of God (Rom 8:38-39); believers belong to Christ (2 Cor 10:7); God who began a good work will bring it to fulfillment in the parousia (Phil 1:6).

[27] As in the Philippians passage just noted, so also elsewhere in the corpus, what one knows—whether from Israel's scriptures or from the traditions of the believers—functions as a safe, dependable base for action.

Faith and Its Moral Life

their doubts will be encountered less immediately. Weaker-faith people, on the other hand, will have a narrower range of freedom within which they may act; their fence of doubts will be encountered sooner. Some believers, therefore, will be able to eat anything, while others will be able to eat only vegetables (Rom 14:2). There is nothing wrong with either group and its behavior as long as they tend their own fences and act on their particular convictions. "Let each person be fully convinced in his own mind" (Rom 14:5)—that is the key. Then the actions of each will be appropriate to that individual.[28]

In other places Paul elaborates the individuated situation of the believer and points to some other considerations that must come into play as the believer determines what course of action is appropriate. The Corinthians wrote Paul concerning human sexuality and marriage. In his reply Paul reflects on persons who are not married. If they are beset by great passion, "let them marry" (1 Cor 7:36); it is not sin. Marriage for passion is well (καλῶς) enough, but there is a better (κρεῖσσον) way if it is appropriate and possible for the individual: "But the one who stands firmly in his heart, not having necessity, but who has authority concerning his own will and has reached a decision in his heart to keep her his virgin, he shall do well" (7:37). Two new phrases—not being driven by necessity (ἀνάγκη), and having control (ἐξουσία)—here express the same concern noted above in one's being convinced: to stand firmly in his heart and to have reached a decision in his heart. Different words express the same idea: believers' actions must be grounded in their convictions, clear from doubts.[29]

In summary, one's doubts, occurring somewhere within the outer limits marked off by the vice lists, provide the individuated fence within which one may act. What one does must proceed from that about which one is convinced or which one knows. Within the borders formed by one's doubt, love, which is one's own measure of faith in action (Gal 5:6), flourishes best (cf. Phlm 9) where conviction is present and

---

[28] Within the same passage (Rom 14:1-23), Paul marks out the alternatives for believers: to be fully convinced or to have doubts.

[29] Elsewhere Paul shows the same concern that one's actions not be forced. Paul does not command Philemon to do the appropriate thing but appeals to him so that his good might be voluntarily pursued rather than forced upon him as a necessity (μὴ ὡς κατὰ ἀνάγκην τὸ ἀγαθόν σου ᾖ ἀλλὰ κατὰ ἑκούσιον; v. 14). Likewise, in his appeal to the Corinthians concerning their participation in the collection for the Jerusalem saints, Paul consistently applies his conditions for proper behavior among believers: "Each must do just as he has determined in [his, understood] heart, not reluctantly, not from necessity" (2 Cor 9:7).

necessity and compulsion are absent. Love prefers exhortation (Phlm 9); love encourages one (μὴ ἐκ λύπης; 2 Cor 9:7) to reach out to others.

In light of these observations, we can better appreciate the dual force of Paul's claim in 2 Cor 5:14: ἡ γὰρ ἀγάπη τοῦ Χριστοῦ συνέχει ἡμᾶς. The verb συνέχω can mean to hold within bounds or control, and it can also mean to urge on or compel. For Paul both meanings are powerfully true. The love of Christ[30] holds believers within boundaries, inside the limits of appropriate action; and the love of Christ pushes believers out toward others for whom Christ died. The love of Christ rules out complacence and reluctance.

The Necessity of Continued Self-Assessment

Compelled and bounded by the love of Christ, believers should grow strong in their faith (cf. Rom 4:20). As their faith grows, believers experience a shift in the borders between their faith and their doubts. And they must adjust their actions accordingly. As faith grows for each believer, so the range of actions that might be the medium for love increases. In order to know just how strong one's faith is and, accordingly, what is appropriate to one's new measure of faith, one must constantly be self-reflective about where one stands in strength of faith.

The believer must avoid self-deception. "For if someone imagines himself to be something while being nothing, he deceives himself" (Gal 6:3). The context in Galatians suggests that a proper self-evaluation is fundamental to wholesome participation in the life of the community of believers. Only with an accurate self-evaluation will a person be able either to be gentle with those caught in trespass or to carry his or her own burdens (6:1-2).[31]

Proper self-evaluation at the Lord's Supper also affirms the connection between self-assessment and the last judgment. Only by testing oneself (δοκιμαζέτω δὲ ἄνθρωπος ἑαυτόν; 1 Cor 11:28) can one partake in such a way as to avoid judgment. Apparently some Corinthians have failed in this enterprise and are therefore already under God's wrath. Self-testing can avert judgment and its associated punishment if it leads to self-correction.[32] "But if we rendered a [correct, understood] decision

---

[30] Whether taken as an objective or a subjective genitive.

[31] See just such a careful self-assessment in Philippians, where Paul asks who has reason for confidence in the flesh and then gives a detailed catalog of his own grounds (3:2-11).

[32] With regard to the supper, Paul creatively moves from the notion of self-testing (δοκιμαζέτω δὲ ἄνθρωπος ἑαυτόν; 1 Cor 11:28) to the idea of individually discerning

about ourselves, then we should not be handed over for punishment" (11:31). Accurate self-evaluation is the *sine qua non* for proper or fitting action and therefore is critical to any hope of escaping divine judgment. Self-evaluation anticipates the eschatological judgment of God and permits the individual to make a mid-course correction.

In this context one can understand the Pauline "beatitude:" "Blessed is the one who has no occasion to judge oneself in the things which one approves" (Rom 14:22). True blessedness is a status conferred by God; such felicity occurs only when the decisions one makes provide no occasion for self-indictment and thereby, when accurately assessed, avoid God's judgment. As with one's blessedness, so also with one's being found worthy or "tried and true" (δόκιμος), only God can confer the blessing or the commendation. Human judgment cannot. "For it is not the one commending himself who is tried and true (δόκιμος),[33] but the one whom the Lord commends" (2 Cor 10:18). In some cases, such as with Paul and Timothy, believers can infer from comportment that this God-given approval is present; they cannot, however, confer it or invite it upon themselves.

Individuation of Works and God's Judgment

The works one does must be individuated and so also must be the judgment of God. Paul is very clear: God "will recompense each according to that one's works" (Rom 2:6).[34] What a person does will be the subject of judgment at the close of the age. Faith, which is God's gift, will not be what is weighed at the last judgment—for in doing so

---

(διακρίνων) how one ought to relate to the Lord's Supper (11:29), and on to the prospect of judgment by the Lord (κρινόμενοι δὲ ὑπὸ κυρίου; 11:32).

[33] One who passes the test at any given time is "approved, tried and true, genuine" (δόκιμος). The one who fails the test is ἀδόκιμος, which may be translated "disqualified" (cf. 1 Cor 9:27) in order to capture its association with athletics. Paul, again like an athlete, practices self-discipline so that he may not be found, presumably at the judgment and by God, worthless or disqualified (1 Cor 9:27; cf. 2 Cor 13:5). The practice of discipline is also rooted in the traditions of the cynic/stoic sage.

[34] One's works, when properly done with respect to the Lord (Rom 14:6), will commend one to God and may become the basis for boasting (Gal 6:4). Boasting in the neighbor's works is out of order (2 Cor 10:15; Gal 6:4). The proper boast of the believer has a circularity about it. Paul can "boast in Christ Jesus" concerning the things he does and thereby offers up to God (Rom 15:17), because the only thing Paul dares to speak of is what "Christ has achieved through me" (Rom 15:18). So the believer does works that are empowered by God; those works become the basis on which the believer will ultimately be judged. In the meantime, to boast of those works is to give glory to God concerning what God has done and is doing through the believer.

God would be weighing what was a freely bestowed grant. But faith, working itself out in love (Gal 5:6), produces what Paul generally labels "works," and those works can be judged with respect to certain particulars: (1) Are the works appropriate to the individual's measure of faith? (2) Are the works genuine expressions of love, taking into consideration their effects upon others? Paul is sure that his opponents will be found out by God even if the Corinthians are duped by them: "Their end shall be according to their works" (2 Cor 11:15).[35] Self-testing could bring one's works into accord with an appropriate life before God and align one so that the parousia would represent no hazard.

Finally, it must be observed that this complex moral reckoning present in Pauline individuation—where one must constantly keep track of the progress of one's own faith toward maturity and where, at the same time, one is to do the calculus of a contemplated action's impact upon others at various stages along their individual faith journeys—proved difficult for Paul's followers to understand and incorporate from the very start. To live the proper life before God, as Paul laid it out, was to monitor a delicate balance regarding self and others at every point in one's life. To do it well required a vigorous life of the mind and heart.

Pauline individuation with regard to faith and its moral life was at the heart of Paul's gospel and was a key to the vitality of the communities that his gospel brought into being. Despite any problems that Paul's followers had with proper differentiation, it is striking that Paul never settles for an eclipsed individuation in favor of retaining a semblance of unity. Rather, he labors intensely to emend the understanding and practice of individuation so that it maximizes the growth and richness of all who are "in Christ." For Paul, individuation is not one Christian option among others. Paul's thought world requires individuation.

---

[35] The following verses show this linkage firmly established in Paul's thought world. "For it is necessary for all of us to appear before the tribunal of Christ, so that each may receive the recompense for what he has done through the body, whether it was good or bad" (2 Cor 5:10). "The work of each will become manifest, for the day will make it clear" (1 Cor 3:13). "Do not be misled; God will not be treated with contempt, for whatever a man sows, this also shall he reap" (Gal 6:7). "Each shall receive his own pay according to his own labor" (1 Cor 3:8). "So each of us shall make an accounting concerning himself to God" (Rom 14:12). These claims, scattered across the corpus, show that Paul had a deeply held conviction that one's labors would be the subject of judgment.

15

Romans 8:1-11: Pauline Theology in Medieval Interpretation

Karlfried Froehlich [1]

Paul's epistles were written as ephemeral literature, letters directed to specific people at a specific time in a specific place. Yet the church, convinced that God's word is communicated through them as through other "canonical" writings, has consistently read them also as texts addressing all generations of Christians. Thus, over the centuries Paul's epistles have grown into much more than what their human author intended them to be. They have nourished Christian theology and piety throughout the generations and still occupy an important place in guiding the formulation of the faith of our time in the teaching, confession, and worship of all Christian churches.

Due to its role in the Reformation of the sixteenth century, Paul's letter to the Romans has taken on the mystique of a "Protestant" book, perhaps even the foremost Protestant book among the writings of the New Testament. Ever since Martin Luther's work on Romans in lectures, treatises, and sermons, the exposition of the epistle has become a major vehicle for the expression of Protestant theology, confirming basic Protestant convictions as in Melanchthon's, Bucer's, and Calvin's

---

[1] Karlfried Froehlich is Benjamin B. Warfield Professor of Ecclesiastical History at Princeton Theological Seminary, Princeton, New Jersey.

commentaries, or setting off new, creative attempts at formulating its essence as in the commentaries of John Locke, Emil Brunner, or Karl Barth.[2] It is still the challenge of a lifetime for many theologically-minded exegetes to work through the "teaching" of this profound text in order, on the one hand, to reconstruct Paul's theology and, on the other, to nourish afresh the life and witness of the contemporary church.

Paul Meyer has put his hand to this task in an exemplary fashion in his commentary on Romans in Harper's Bible Commentary.[3] Reading the Pauline text along with him, guided by the careful and disciplined analysis of a master exegete, readers find themselves face to face not only with the "historical Paul" but also with the major questions and problems of the church today. Critical interpretation of this kind, patient in listening and uncompromising in its intellectual integrity, remains the key for gaining access to the immense potential of the ancient text for bringing about new beginnings in Christian theology.

From the perspective of Romans as a "Protestant" book the medieval interpretation of Paul does not hold much interest. If modern commentators are in dialogue with the "exegetical tradition," they normally mean the last few decades of critical scholarship. At times they pay some attention to the Reformers of the sixteenth century and the patristic tradition, but the vast body of the medieval exegetical literature is passed over. That such a body does exist should surprise no one. The Pauline Epistles were well known and extensively studied in the Western church throughout the period. All major lectionaries included an "Epistle Lesson" among the readings for Sundays and feast days; three-fourths of the texts came from the Epistles of Paul, and of these nearly one-fourth derived from Romans.[4] Most of the text of Romans 8 was read every year, divided into three pericopes according to the old Roman lectionary.[5] Thus, the interpretation of Romans was a

---

[2] On the Romans commentaries of the Reformation era see T. H. L. Parker, *Commentaries on Romans, 1532-1542* (Philadelphia: Fortress, 1986). John Locke wrote *A Paraphrase and Notes on the Epistles of St. Paul to the Galatians, Corinthians, Romans, and Ephesians: To Which is Prefixed an Essay for the Understanding of St. Paul's Epistles by Consulting St. Paul Himself in 1705- 1707.*

[3] Paul W. Meyer, "Romans," in *Harper's Bible Commentary* (ed. James L. Mays; San Francisco: Harper & Row, 1988) 1130-1167.

[4] See the comparative tables of medieval Latin lectionaries in G. Godu's instructive article on "Epîtres," *Dictionnaire d'archéologie chrétienne et de liturgie*, vol. 5 (ed. F. Cabrol and H. Leclercq; Paris: Letouzey et Ané, 1922) 335-342 (cols. 245-344).

[5] The traditional Missale Romanum designated Rom 8:12-17 as the Epistle for the eighth Sunday after Pentecost, Rom 8:18-23 for the fourth Sunday after Pentecost. Rom 8:1-6 was the Wednesday Epistle in the fourth week after the *Nativitas Apostolorum* (SS. Peter and Paul, June 29) according to Alcuin's lectionary and its derivatives.

vital part of the life of the church in preaching and teaching, at the level of the local parish as well as in the schools. An important link is missing in our dialogue with the exegetical tradition if we overlook this part of our common history in studying the theology of Paul. As a tribute to a master exegete of Romans in our day, I propose to take a look at the medieval interpretation of a central text, Rom 8:1-11, in order to discover how Paul's theology fared at that time. Reading the minds of medieval exegetes is not only a fascinating historical exercise; it also opens up important perspectives on issues that continue to be debated today.

Extant medieval commentaries on Romans are numerous but hard to use; most of them are available in manuscript only.[6] For the task at hand, I have checked only printed sources, hoping that the sample is sufficiently representative. The majority is available in the standard edition of J. P. Migne's *Patrologia Latina* (217 vols.; Paris, 1844-1855 etc.), abbreviated PL. They include Romans commentaries of the following authors: Atto of Vercelli, Bruno the Carthusian, Haymo of Auxerre, Hervaeus of Bourg-Dieu, (Ps.) Hugh of St. Victor, Lanfranc of Bec, Nicholas of Lyra, Peter Abelard, Peter Lombard, Robert of Melun, Sedulius Scotus, Thomas Aquinas, William of St. Thierry. A chronological list of the quoted writings together with the page numbers in the editions where Rom 8:1-11 is interpreted, is provided in the notes.[7] Since it is relatively easy to locate the references to Rom 8:1-11

---

[6] A very useful annotated list of over fifty such commentaries is found in the appendix to Werner Affeldt's study, *Die weltliche Gewalt in der Paulusexegese: Römer 13, 1-7 in den Römerbriefkommentaren bis zum Ende des 13. Jahrhunderts* (Forschungen zur Kirchen-und Dogmengeschichte 22; Göttingen: Vandenhoeck & Ruprecht, 1969) 256-285. Affeldt was able to consult already several volumes of Friedrich Stegmüller's monumental *Repertorium Biblicum Medii Aevi* (11 vols.; Madrid: Consejo Superior de Investigaciones Científicas, Instituto Francisco Suarez, 1940-1980). His list does not include, however, the commentaries of the 14th and 15th centuries.

[7] The following list describes the sources used for this essay by author and title in chronological order. In each case, the pages containing the exegesis of Rom 8:1-11 are indicated in brackets. Further information on authors, writings, and bibliography may be found in Affeldt's Appendix (see note 6 above): Sedulius Scotus (early 9th c.), "Collectanea in Omnes Beati Pauli Epistolas," PL (= J. P. Migne, *Patrologia Latina*) 103, 9-270 [Rom 8:1-11: PL 103, 69A-73B]. Haymo of Auxerre (fl. 840/60), "Expositio in Divini Pauli Epistolas," PL 117, 361C-820C [Rom. 8:1-11: PL 117, 425D-429A]. Atto of Vercelli (mid-10th c.), "Expositio Epistolarum S. Pauli," PL 134, 125-834A [Rom 8:1-11: PL 134, 197A- 201C]. Lanfranc of Bec (mid-11th c.), "Commentarii in Omnes Pauli Epistolas," PL 150, 101B-406C [Rom 8:1-11: PL 150, 129A-132B]. Bruno the Carthusian (early 12th c.), "Expositio in Epistolas Pauli," PL 153, 11A-566C [Rom 8:1-11: PL 153, 69C- 71D]. Peter Abelard (1135/39), "Commentaria in Epistolam Pauli ad Romanos," in *Petri Abaelardi Opera Theologica* I (ed. E. M. Buytaert; Corpus Christianorum, Continuatio Mediaevalis 11; Turnhout: Brepols, 1969) pp. 41-340 [Rom 8:1-11: pp. 210:1-215:183]. "Reportatio" of Peter Abelard's Lectures: *Commentarius Cantabrigiensis in Epistolas S. Pauli e Schola Petri*

in the pages indicated, I have identified individual quotations by the name of the author only.

Medieval exegetes drew upon patristic commentaries. In the case of Romans, almost none of the Eastern Fathers was known in the West except for Origen in Rufinus' translation and John Chrysostom in an ancient Latin version. The writings of Latin authors included the works of Augustine who left several fragments on Romans but whose entire corpus was exploited as a major source of authoritative exegesis;[8] the so-called Ambrosiaster, a fourth-century commentary on the Pauline Epistles going under the name of Ambrose;[9] and Pelagius, whose Pauline commentary, written long before the "Pelagian controversy," circulated widely in two inadequately purged forms under the names of Jerome and Primasius of Hadrumetum.[10] Scholars often overlook the fact that Pelagius was indeed a major source for the medieval understanding of Paul. We will see the consequences.

Abaelardi: I. *In Epistolam ad Romanos* (ed. A. M. Landgraf; Publications in Medieval Studies 2; University of Notre Dame Press, 1937) [Rom 8:1-11: pp. 102-106]. William of St. Thierry (1138/45), "Expositio in Epistolam ad Romanos," PL 180, 547-694 [Rom 8:1-11: PL 180, 624B- 630C]. Hervaeus of Bourg-Dieu (mid-12th c.), PL 181, 591D-1692B [Rom 8:1-11: PL 181, 696D-704A]. Peter Lombard (1142-43), "Collectanea in Omnes Divi Pauli Apostoli Epistolas," PL 191, 1297 - 192, 520A [Rom 8:1-11: PL 191, 1432A-1438B]. Robert of Melun (1145/55), *Oeuvres de Robert de Melun*. II *Quaestiones de Epistolis Pauli* (ed. R. M. Martin; Spicilegium Sacrum Lovaniense 18; Louvain, 1938) [Rom 8:1-11: pp. 105-106]. (Pseudo) Hugh of St. Victor (late 12th c.), "Quaestiones in Epistolas Pauli," PL 175, 431C-634A [Rom 8:1-11: PL 175, 477D-479A; Quaestiones 185-192]. Thomas Aquinas (1270/72), *Sancti Thomae Aquinatis Super Epistolas Pauli Lectura* (ed. Raphael Cai, O. P.; vols. 1-2; Torino: Marietti, 1953) [Rom 8:1-11: vol. 1, pp. 109-114; sections 595-628]. Nicholas of Lyra (1322/31), *Postilla Super Totam Bibliam*, vol. 4 (Strassburg, 1492; reprint Frankfurt a.M.: Minerva, 1971) ad loc. (no pagination).

[8]The major sourcebook here was the magnificent *Collectaneum* of Augustinian texts interpreting the Pauline Epistles verse by verse, compiled by Florus of Lyons (mid-9th century); the list of the quotes, but not the texts, is printed in PL 119, 279A-420B [Rom 8:1-11: PL 119, 295D-297D]. For the fragments (not known in the Middle Ages), see the fine translation by Paula F. Landes: *Augustine on Romans: Propositions from the Epistle to the Romans. Unfinished Commentary on the Epistle to the Romans* (Early Christian Literature Series 6; Texts and Translations 23; Chico, CA: Scholars, 1982).

[9]*Ambrosiastri qui dicitur Commentarius in Epistolas Paulinas. I. In Epistolam ad Romanos* (ed. H. J. Vogels; Corpus Scriptorum Ecclesiasticorum Latinorum 81; Vienna: Tempsky, 1966) [Rom 8:1-11: pp. 248-268].

[10] The original text was published by A. Souter, *Pelagius' Exposition of Thirteen Epistles of St. Paul. II. Texts* (London, 1926) [Rom 8:1-11: pp. 60-63]. The versions under the name of Jerome and Primasius are printed in PL 30, 705C-707D and PL 68, 456A-459A respectively.

1. Paul's Rhetoric

In many ways the Pauline epistles were treated in a class by themselves by medieval commentators. An obvious indication is the fact that none of the medieval commentaries on Paul employs the traditional multiple senses (literal, allegorical, moral, and anagogical), or even a twofold sense of the literal and the spiritual. The explanation is quite simple. Medieval theology saw Paul on the one hand as the last of the inspired canonical writers and thus as the end of a line. On the other hand, they regarded Paul as the first "doctor evangelii," the beginning of a long line of biblical expositors. The Old Testament writers proclaimed the mysteries of the coming Christ in veiled form. When Christ had come, the apostles, especially Paul, declared openly what had been hidden before. Thus, the Pauline epistles were believed to express in their own literal understanding the full spiritual truth about the Old Testament and the new age of grace with no cover in need of being lifted. Paul's language was the norm for the very enterprise we call Christian "theology" today.

The appreciation for the clarity and theological normativity of Paul's style may account for the interest of medieval exegetes in the rhetorical analysis of his text. Some writers preface the exegesis of every verse by an explanation of its function as the next step in an argument. The practice of subdivision, *diairesis*, goes back to classical times.[11] In the commentaries on our passage, the transition between Rom 7:25 and 8:1 is often carefully noted:

> I myself, says Paul, one and the same man, serve the law of sin through the flesh, that is, by concupiscence, but the law of God through my mind, resisting concupiscence. Now someone might say: Since you serve the law of sin through the flesh, you earn damnation by this servitude, do you not? This is why Paul adds 'There is now no condemnation...' (Atto of Vercelli).

Sometimes the rhetorical analysis simply draws out the inherent logic of the argument. To Abelard the transition between vv 8 and 9 presents a beautiful example of a professional job of persuasion: Paul first drives the Romans to despair ("those in the flesh cannot please God"); then he

---

[11] On the classical origins see M. Fuhrmann, *Das systematische Lehrbuch: Ein Beitrag zur Geschichte der Wissenschaften in der Antike* (Göttingen: Vandenhoeck & Ruprecht, 1960) 126-131. On the revival of the technique among the scholastic commentators see M. D. Chenu, *Toward Understanding Saint Thomas* (Chicago: H. Regnery, 1964) 250ff.

comforts them ("you are not in the flesh"), but immediately warns them against being over-confident ("if God's spirit dwells in you") while having to stress again how important the possession of the Spirit is ("those who do not have it, are not Christ's"). In other words: in order not to cause the Romans, who had received their justification already but had lapsed into some sin, too much worry by his statement in v 8, the apostle "strokes and pets them with flattering words and yet tells them clearly what to do" (Bruno the Carthusian).

The most impressive achievement of a minute rhetorical *diairesis* is found in Thomas Aquinas' commentary. At the beginning of chapter 8, Thomas summarizes the "argument" as follows: after having shown in chapter 7 that by the grace of God we are freed from sin and the law, Paul argues in chapter 8 that we are freed from condemnation. He first establishes our liberation from guilt (vv 1-9), secondly from punishment (vv 10-11). Concerning the first point, he does two things: he proposes the theme (v 1), then he proves the proposition (v 2). His proposition comes in two parts: Paul first states the benefit which grace confers, formulating his sentence as a conclusion of earlier premises ("therefore there is now no condemnation"); secondly, he indicates the beneficiaries, noting two conditions: 1) "for those who are in Christ Jesus;" 2) "who do not walk according to the flesh." The subdivision continues, and the same format returns with every new section. Aquinas seems to enjoy Paul as a fellow professor and admires the apostle's skill in argument. In vv 5 and 6 he discovers two syllogisms, one *ex parte carnis*, the other *ex parte spiritus*. He describes the major, the minor, and the conclusion and explains how artfully Paul has interwoven them. Aquinas' wonderment at Paul's dialectical skill is only matched by his own analytical ability. He was not the only exegete concerned with establishing the logical outline. Nicholas of Lyra, for example, prefaced his interpretations with similar, though less elaborate summaries. Romans 8 for him spells out the usefulness of total adhesion to Christ: negatively in terms of the avoidance of evil (vv 1-13), positively in terms of the pursuit of the good (vv 14-34). Our text states the theme (vv 1-2) and then explains it (vv 3-11), spelling out how the law of Christ liberates us (vv 3-4) by distinguishing fleshly from spiritual living (vv 5-8) and by singling out the liberating effects of the latter, "walking according to the spirit" (vv 9-11).

In order to look more closely at the theological understanding of Paul by our medieval exegetes we will focus on some major themes which are regularly discussed in connection with Rom 8:1-11. K. H. Schelkle has drawn up a list of such themes in his treatment of the patristic evidence.[12] They include: Indicative and Imperative; the Law; Flesh and Spirit; Death and Life. We will follow his suggestion and add the interpretation of the difficult phrase in v 3: "Through Sin He Condemned Sin."

2. Indicative and Imperative

It seems that medieval exegetes had little sense for what many modern interpreters understand as the dialectic tension of the Pauline imperative growing out of the indicative. For most of them, the imperative becomes the condition for the indicative in our passage. Thus, the standard explanation of v 1b ("who do not walk according to the flesh") reads: "if someone does not walk according to the flesh." This moralistic tendency had strong support in the earlier tradition. Both Ambrosiaster and Pelagius shared it. Like the former, many medieval authors mention baptism as the turning point; but the connection with 7:25 suggested also a post-baptismal emphasis: "There is now no condemnation for those baptized Christians who, while they continue to experience carnal desires, do not consent to them" (Peter Lombard, using the Abelardian definition of sin as "consent"); or: "...for those who are baptized and no longer given to concupiscence.... Not the fighters, the losers are condemned" (Hervaeus of Bourg-Dieu). Nicholas of Lyra puts it with laconic precision: "There is now no condemnation for those who do not walk, that is, who do not work according to the flesh but rather according to the spirit through works following upon faith, since faith without works is dead as James says [cf. Jas 2:17]." The same turn to an "if" can be observed in v 4b: The justification of the law is fulfilled in us if we do not do the works of the flesh, although sometimes we may fall (Peter Lombard). Again Lyra states the point unambiguously: "We do not walk according to the flesh but according to the spirit through good works, since faith without works does not suffice for salvation because it is dead."

The appeal to human effort in the exegesis of our passage is in fact more pervasive than one might think. The reason may be partly Paul's own rhetoric, at least in Latin, where the generalizing relative pronoun ("qui," "quicumque," "quisquis") may convey the nuance of conditionality ("if someone"); partly, however, it is the influence of Pelagius' commentary. In some cases Pelagius clearly was the source.

---

[12] K. H. Schelkle, *Paulus, Lehrer der Väter: Die altkirchliche Auslegung von Römer 1-11* (Düsseldorf: Patmos, 1956) 259-281. Schelkle's book provides a fascinating summary of the patristic exegesis of Romans 1-11 section by section.

Sedulius Scotus followed the Pelagian line with almost total devotion, even though he had the Ambrosiaster among his sources also. According to Sedulius, v 1 says: "There will be no condemnation for those who serve God's law with all their minds." Verse 2 really speaks about the law of Moses which in itself was good but fulfilled a twofold function: for the guilty it spelled death; for the good life and mercy, just as was the case with the tree of life in paradise. What was impossible for "the law" (v 3a) was really impossible for fleshly people: the law was "weakened" (v 3b), not in itself but in its fleshly-minded followers. God sent his Son in the incarnation (v 3c) because without his example it would have been impossible to admonish carnal people to mortify their flesh. In the resurrection (v 11) the whole person will live on account of a good life here on earth. Every detail of the passage is scrutinized for its hortatory value, and conditional clauses such as those in vv 9bc, 10a, and 11a were gratefully acknowledged as grist for the same mill.

Another instance where the moral emphasis could easily triumph was the interpretation of the indwelling of the Spirit in vv 9b and 11a. Pelagius had stressed that the Spirit dwells in the one who shows forth the fruits of the Spirit and thought that the resurrection spoken of in v 11 was conditional: "If you are pure enough for the Spirit to dwell in you, then God will not suffer his temple to perish." While medieval exegetes did not take up this formulation, they emphasized that the Spirit's indwelling must be permanent, not transient like that of a guest. By sinning a person may lose the Spirit received in baptism (Thomas Aquinas). No one would have thought of Pelagianism here. It was well known that Augustine made the same point. The Cambridge *Reportatio* of Abelard equates "dwells" with "perseveres," and Nicholas of Lyra refers directly to Augustine's *gratia perseverantiae* in support of the moral appeal.

There was enough Augustinian precedent also for the psychologizing of "flesh" into "fleshly thinking" to prevent the full force of Paul's dialectic between indicative and imperative from being realized. "To walk according to the flesh" (vv 1, 4b) meant "living by carnal desires" (Haymo) or by "urges of concupiscence." The moral emphasis was not mitigated when exegetes tried to distinguish between "walking" and "being" according to the flesh, even though the difference could have alerted them to Paul's point. Question 189 of the Pseudo-Victorine *Quaestiones in Epistolas Pauli* draws on both Augustine and Ambrosiaster in the attempt at establishing the distinction:

> Are "walking" and "being" according to the flesh and "reeking of the things of the flesh" one and the same? Answer: No. "Walking"

means implementing the carnal desires by doing. "Being" means consenting to the desires or being disposed toward fleshly things. "Reeking of" means delighting in what the flesh judges to be the highest goods. Thus, "carnal" can refer to two kinds of people: Those who are fleshly in their lives, that is, indulging in the flesh, or in their doctrine, that is, refusing to believe that God can do anything apart from what is being observed in nature.[13]

Avoiding fleshly thoughts, deeds, and inclinations turns out to be the tenor of these exhortations. The indicative of being "in the Spirit" or "in Christ Jesus" was interpreted more as the result of such proper living than as its basis.

3. The Law

The opposition of two laws in v 2 and the reference to a third law in v 3a called for some attempt at systematizing Paul's concept of law. The medieval interpretations of v 2 often included lists of three or four kinds of law that must be distinguished in Paul. Aquinas presents the most elaborate distinction based on both chapter 7 and chapter 8: the law of Moses, the law of the "tinder" (of sin), the natural law, the new law. The last one is required for the spiritual perfection of the natural life; it is therefore identical with the "law of the spirit of life" in Rom 8:2. In other commentaries, this law is also identified with "grace and mercy which forgive, that is, which save from the habit of sinning" (Haymo of Auxerre), or with the gospel which promises eternal rather than temporal life. The Ambrosiaster is probably the source of its identification with the "law of faith" because this faith, received and confessed in baptism through the Holy Spirit (1 Cor 12:3), is life. More along ethical lines, the "law of the spirit of life" could be called "the law of the Spirit who teaches what is to be done and what is not" (Peter Lombard) or "the law of love." It is not surprising to find this latter term in Abelard, for whom the identification of Holy Spirit and Love was an important point of trinitarian theology. The Cambridge *Reportatio* puts it in simple words: "the law of the spirit of life is that highest love which has been infused into us by the Holy Spirit [cf. Rom 5:5]." Abelard's own commentary elaborates further:

> The Spirit is love. His law generates sons, not slaves. Therefore [this law] is the gospel which is totally permeated by love. Christ's

---

[13]For this last point see the Ambrosiaster on v 6a.

preaching is full of charity. The same is true of the Apostles. They received the Spirit who taught them "all doctrine," and this doctrine is charity as the flames at Pentecost signify.

Thomas Aquinas seems to echo this theme. The "spirit of life" has to do with the Holy Spirit, who not only teaches the mind but also inclines the heart to right action. In this way it is the "new law" of Jer 31:31, written on the heart, the law which leads to the life of grace or, in other words, to faith operative in love [cf. Gal 5:6]. It seems that Paul's own words here, lacking the antithesis of law and grace, encouraged the positive understanding of the law in which Pelagius had been vitally interested when he read this verse and commented: "Note that grace here is called the law."

Pelagius could make this statement because he was the only one who understood the two "laws" of v 2 as two different functions of the one law of Moses. Most medieval writers saw the difference as that of two options of the moral life for Christians. In this context the "law of sin and death" was sometimes linked to the "law in my members" (7:23). This law leads inescapably to death. It was frequently identified with the "tinder of sin" (*fomes peccati*) or concupiscence. Being "freed" from it means not to follow its suggestions. Only the law of vv 3a and 4a was regularly identified with the law of Moses in our passage. The referent of the "law of God" in v 7, however, remained somewhat ambiguous. It was generally understood to mean "God's commandment" or "precept," particularly the Decalogue, but it could also refer to its New Testament equivalent, the law of the gospel, which says: do not return evil for evil (Haymo of Auxerre). With regard to the Mosaic law, v 3b provided the warrant for speaking of its "weakness." It could not justify, only threaten. With the help of an Augustinian phrase, its function was sometimes described as "pointing out but not removing sin" (William of St. Thierry). The Mosaic law is good, even "spiritual" if it is correctly understood, i.e., "spiritually;" but it is not the "law of the spirit." Perfection is not in its power (Atto of Vercelli). Hervaeus of Bourg-Dieu considered v 3a as a reference to both natural and written law, neither of which was able to remit sin and overcome death. Elsewhere the connection of the "flesh" with the law's "weakness" appears as a kind of hermeneutical argument: fleshly understanding or carnal observance of the law stands in the way of its efficiency. Thus, the Mosaic law became the "law of the letter" or the "law of deeds." It commands but does not help (*jubet non juvat*). In this sense it is imperfect. In all this argumentation, however, one senses a reluctance of the exegetes to denigrate the old law. Even the old Pelagian excuse of the law's "infirmity," which laid the blame on the carnal concupiscence of the hearers, appears in a new, graphic form: "a doctor is only weak insofar as he cannot restore sight to the blind even though he can restore health to the sick" (Haymo of Auxerre). Basically the Mosaic law was respected in its limited, partial role before the coming of grace in Christ. By the old law the body was purified, but not the spirit (William of St. Thierry). Thus, medieval exegetes made room for the necessary perfection of the law achieved in Christ.

4. Flesh and Spirit, Death and Life

The antithesis of flesh and spirit is a constitutive element of Paul's ethics. It plays a major role in Romans 8. Verses 4b, 5, 6, 7, and 9 all use it directly and confirm Paul's value judgment: "flesh" represents the negative pole, "spirit" the positive. Moreover, our passage seems to presuppose a dichotomous anthropology. Verse 10 replaces flesh-spirit by the antithesis of body-spirit, setting up two components of the human person in opposition to each other. It would be a mistake, however, to press the anthropological dichotomy too far as a principle behind the ethical antithesis in Paul. Clearly Paul allows the tension to stand. But in our passage, v 11 demonstrates that "body" and "spirit" are not restricted to the anthropological dichotomy. The terms here refer to the whole mortal person of the Christian related to the indwelling spirit of God. Furthermore, chapter 7 posited the dilemma of flesh and spirit as the reality of two powers fighting over the control of one and the same human person in an apocalyptic horizon.

Medieval exegetes, indebted as they were to a Platonizing anthropology and its ascetic consequences, were quite aware of the problem of dichotomy and unity in their approach to the Pauline text. Different from Paul, they were not afraid to base the ethical antithesis squarely on an anthropological dichotomy. They understood "flesh" and "body" more or less as synonyms designating the lower, less positive side of the human composite. At the same time, they did not want to lose the Pauline emphasis on the unified human person as the subject of the ethical dilemma. Two factors helped their awareness. The first was a surprisingly strong exegetical tradition emphasizing the unity of the human person in our passage. The Ambrosiaster already observed that "body" in vv 10 and 11 meant the whole person, just as "soul" and "flesh" in biblical usage often designate the entire human being *quasi a parte totum*. He had made the same point in his interpretation of chapter 7 where he spoke repeatedly of the *totus homo* as the subject of Paul's description, "the one man consisting of flesh and soul." Pelagius echoed the emphasis. While his ascetic preoccupations tended to give the anthropological dichotomy greater prominence, he also found a way of using the theme of unity to promote his moralism:

> The human is made up of spirit and flesh. Therefore, when he acts carnally, the whole man is called flesh; if he acts spiritually, the whole man is called spirit. For each of the two substances loses somehow its own power and name when the one reduces the other to dependence. (on v 5)

Sedulius Scotus quoted this remark; Haymo and Atto paraphrased it. The latter used it unambiguously to mitigate a strongly antithetical statement which seemed to leave no room for any unity of flesh and spirit in the human person:

> For flesh is made from the earth, but spirit is given from heaven, and therefore both seek out their own place. Thus, if it happens that the flesh is overcome by the spirit, the whole person is called spiritual; if the spirit [is overcome] by the flesh, the whole person is called carnal.

The other factor was the lingering potential of reading v 7a ("the wisdom of the flesh is inimical to God") in a Manichean way as a reference to the "flesh" as a dualistic power independent of God. Many exegetes mention the need for an anti-Manichean interpretation. With the Ambrosiaster and Augustine they pointed out that not the flesh itself but the prudence or "wisdom" of the flesh was the enemy. This observation agreed with the tendency noted already to understand "flesh" psychologically as "carnal mind." Against the crude formulation of Pelagius, which could be read as suggesting two independent principles in the "substances" of flesh and spirit, our writers stress that prudence is an attitude, not a substance, and that "prudence of the flesh" designates a wrong attitude. Hervaeus of Bourg-Dieu engaged at this point in a long diatribe against slick diplomatic language. Prudence of the flesh is the intentional duplicity which goes by the name of urbanity; it manipulates the truth and hides behind words. Prudence of the spirit, on the other hand, opens up meaning by its very words and loves the truth as it is. Sometimes prudence itself was carefully defined as a virtue ("seeking the good and shunning evil"). Thomas Aquinas described it with Aristotle as "right reason concerning things to be done" by presupposing a final end of all human action. If this end is the enjoyment of earthly things ("flesh"), prudence becomes the cause of eternal death. The "prudence of the flesh," therefore, appears as a vice on account of its wrong goal. Many expositors explained it in this way: "It is a corruption of the mind and a vice not created by God but invented by the devil" (Atto of Vercelli).

"Wisdom of the flesh," the mental direction toward the lower, baser things of the flesh going against the natural movement of the human creature toward God, "cannot be subject to the law of God," as was generally emphasized with v 7b. "They who prefer the good of their carnality to God diminish the rule of God, inasmuch as it exists in them, and subject themselves to the rule of the flesh" (Bruno the Carthusian). This rule ends in death. "Whatever the soul seeks below God spells death for it" (William of St. Thierry). In this sense, flesh and spirit are as antithetical to each other as death and life—not as metaphysical principles but as ends and goals of human aspiration. There is no antigodly principle, no inherently evil nature. "God did not create vice but a nature which became vitiated" (William of St. Thierry). Humans can obey God's law, but fleshly wisdom cannot because by definition it does not will it (Haymo of Auxerre). Nature can, vice cannot (Lanfranc). Vice is an *aversio*, a turning away from God (Thomas Aquinas). It moves in a wrong direction.

Wrong direction, however, can be changed. The "wisdom of the flesh" can cease to exercise its influence, and then it does not exist any more. It can be turned around. The following two traditional examples are often cited. Snow cannot heat but it can melt and, ceasing to be snow, act as water that heats (Pelagius). Limping cannot be subject to the concept of right walking. But if you heal the limp you will see right walking (Augustine). "Once the vice is abolished, nature is healed" (Peter Lombard, quoting Augustine).[14]

*

The wisdom or prudence of the flesh is a way which leads to death (v 6a). This Augustinian theme was frequently sounded in the medieval interpretation of our passage. But the exact nature of this death seemed not altogether unambiguous. For Paul, basically, there was but one concept of death. It was rendered ambiguous by an extensive figurative use of the term which permeates all his writings. In v 11 he refers to Christ's bodily death and resurrection and to the resurrection of our mortal bodies from the same death. Medieval exegetes indeed saw this verse as "a most evident witness to the resurrection, such a brilliant and

---

[14] Augustine, *Sermo 155* [on Rom 8:1-11] (PL 38, 874B).

clear statement that it needs no expositor, only a reader" (Peter Lombard). The first point of reference is Christ's resurrection, but his resurrection has become the "cause" of the resurrection of our bodies also. There is a restriction implied here: Paul speaks of the resurrection of bodies for glory only; other bodies will be raised for death (Cambridge *Reportatio*). Aquinas explained that "those whose members were not temples of the Spirit will rise but will have passible bodies." This meant, as Peter Lombard suggests, that Paul assumed impassible bodies for those who would participate in the resurrection of glory, not because bodies were created for glory or would merit such an exalted state, but because of the indwelling Spirit. Abelard identified this Spirit with the Father's love, which dwells in these bodies as in temples; their sharing in the resurrection of the head, Christ, reflects the proper reverence for this indwelling Spirit.

Some authors likened these impassible bodies to angelic beings (Haymo of Auxerre; Atto of Vercelli). Much more widespread was the simple assumption that "they will no longer be mortal" (Haymo). The resurrection of glory will surpass the original glory of the human creature. Mortality itself will be gone. This interpretation had its roots in Augustine's thought. Adam before the fall was "mortal," that is, able to die, just as humans are able to fall ill (*aegrotabiles*) even though they will not necessarily be ill (*aegrotaturi*). This Augustinian comparison appeared in several commentaries. The entrance of sin brought with it the necessity of dying, death being the desert of sin (*meritum peccati*). Adam could have gone on to glory without dying. After the fall none of us can. We all will die. But our resurrection will not only abolish our death; it will also cancel mortality itself and with it the ability to sin (Atto of Vercelli).

It cannot be overlooked that in his choice of language Paul encouraged this interpretation by speaking of "mortality swallowed up by immortality" rather than "death swallowed up by life" in 1 Cor 15:53-57. For our authors, "mortal" was indeed worse than "dead;" the resurrection will transform both states. Thomas Aquinas summarized in one concise paragraph the argument which Peter Lombard or Hervaeus still had presented through lengthy quotations from Augustine:

> Our mortal bodies, not our dead bodies. For in the resurrection not only their deadness is cancelled, that is, their subjection to the necessity of dying, but even their mortality, the potential of dying which was in Adam's body before sin. After the resurrection, our bodies will be altogether immortal (Isa 26:19; Hos 6:3).

Seen in light of this expanded concept of death and resurrection, what was the meaning of the statement in v 10b that "the body is dead on account of sin?" The temptation to read "dead" figuratively for "mortal" must have been considerable. Augustine, however, had offered a more sophisticated interpretation, which appealed to the doctrine of original sin:

> Note that Paul says "dead," not "mortal;" for even before sin he was mortal, that is, able to die. But after sin he was dead, having in him the necessity of dying. Therefore, he adds appropriately: "on account of sin," namely of original sin from which this kind of mortality stems.[15]

This interpretation is often quoted, and under Augustine's influence the explanation of *propter peccatum* as a reference to the sin of Adam became standard in the Middle Ages. Nevertheless, most writers still seem to flirt with the tempting figurative equation: "Paul says 'dead' by anticipation instead of saying 'mortal and corruptible'" (Haymo of Auxerre). Only a few theologians note the much stronger Pauline dialectic:

> Note: it does not say, 'going to die', but 'dead' because the body of every human being though it seems to live yet is already dead; the reason is that there remains in it, if not removed by the resurrection, the merit of sin, that is, the necessity of dying. (Atto of Vercelli)

This, of course, is a paraphrase of Augustine. It is also good Pauline theology.

Pelagius had interpreted the figure differently. "The body is dead on account of sin," that is, it is deaf to the desires of the flesh so that the spirit may live and perform righteous deeds. Often this ascetic line was combined with the Augustinian argument, sometimes simply by juxtaposition (Bruno the Carthusian; Lombard). The most effective combination occurs in a *quaestio* inserted at this point by Abelard, Robert of Melun, and (dependent on them) Pseudo-Hugh of Saint Victor. It resolutely rejects Pelagius' interpretation of "dead" but explains the continuing presence of bodily death in moral terms. Which sin is the cause of bodily death? Answer: original sin. But if its cause, the guilt of sin, is removed in baptism, why not its punishment, bodily death? The

---

[15] Augustine, *Enarrationes in Psalmos* 85 (PL 37, 1094AB).

answer refers with a quotation from Isidore of Seville[16] to the need of humans to be educated toward the setting of the correct priorities for their moral life. If freedom from bodily death were granted in baptism, short-sighted human beings would rush to the sacrament in order to preserve the life of this body rather than care for the life of the soul. The continued existence of bodily death is therefore not a cruelty inflicted on us by an uncaring God but a merciful accommodation of God's dispensation to our human weakness.

The ascetic interest in the anthropological dichotomy which informs the differentiation between the life of the body and the life of the soul seems to lead also to a double concept of death. The Cambridge *Reportatio* confirms this impression, giving Abelard's answer in a brief form: "Someone could say: If we have God's Spirit, will we not escape the death of the body? No, but the death of the soul." This second death, the death of the soul, appears time and again as the real danger for Christians and non-Christians alike—more remote and less conspicuous than the death of the body but far more serious. The normal understanding of v 6a was that "death" here refers to the second death. Only Nicholas of Lyra dared to speak bluntly of physical death: "Those who live carnally frequently die earlier than others." But Lyra also had a simpler answer to the basic *quaestio*: Christians still die because, though Christ has sufficiently restored human nature both in body and in spirit, we must conform to his own "order;" first he had a passible body subject to physical death, then he rose to eternal life. We too will have to die the death of the body first. The disciple is not above the master.

For others, however, the concept of the second death, the death of the soul, provided the bridge between v 10 and the scope of v 11, which we have discussed already. Christ's passion delivered us from the death of the soul in this present age. This is what justification means. The resurrection will add the freedom from the death of the body for those in whom the Spirit "dwells," that is, continues to stay. "Not only does the soul live now; even the body will be transformed into the glory of immortality" (Atto of Vercelli). This formula, "not only the soul but also the body," leads us back to the merciful accommodation of God's grace to our weakness:

> Listen to the light of the apostolic wisdom! Whatever Paul says, he says lest people think they have only a small or no benefit from the grace of Christ. It is a great gift already that

---

[16] Isidore of Seville, *Sententiae* I.22.3 (PL 83, 588-589).

the spirit should live now. But do not despair of the life of your bodies either! (William of St. Thierry)

In Christ's work of redemption his main concern, our soul, has been satisfied; but the body, our main concern, is not left out of his caring either.

5. Through Sin He Condemned Sin

A final issue that vexed medieval exegetes was the difficult v 3d: "Through sin [God] condemned sin in the flesh." The context, with its reference to the incarnation, left no doubt that the phrase was a description of Christ's saving work, a topic which provoked considerable debate, particularly during the 12th century.[17] Not much of these debates seems to be reflected in the commentaries. But some new accents do appear in Abelard, Hervaeus of Bourg-Dieu, and Thomas Aquinas. For instance, while the phrase "in the flesh" remained ambiguous (in our flesh? in Christ's flesh?), Abelard insisted that Christ suffered "in his assumed humanity, not according to his divinity." It was this position that prompted Bernard and his friends to smell Nestorianism in Abelard's christology.

The difficulty centered around the two uses of *peccatum*, sin: what sin did God condemn? And through what sin? In answer to the former question, Peter Lombard offered three options: 1) God destroyed the devil himself who, as the author of sin, may be called sin; 2) God defused the tinder of sin which was the result of Adam's fall; 3) God cancelled all sins of the human race. All three options can indeed be found in the commentaries, alone or in combination. The first followed the Ambrosiaster, the second Augustine, and the third appears, e.g., in Augustine, Haymo, and William of St. Thierry. The greater problem, however, was presented by the clause, *de peccato*. It could not mean "through Christ's sin," since his sinlessness had just been established in v 3c. The reference had to be to some other "sin", or else Paul was using figurative language. Some authors tried to keep the two terms related paradoxically. Through sin (presumably the "flesh of sin," the likeness of which Christ assumed) he conquered sin, just as one says:

---

[17] On the issues, see J. Rivière, *Le dogme de la rédemption au debut du moyen-âge* (Bibliothèque Thomiste 19; Paris: Vrin, 1934). For Abelard's role in the controversy see R. E. Weingart, *The Logic of Divine Love: A Critical Analysis of the Soteriology of Peter Abailard* (Oxford: Clarendon, 1970).

through barbarians he [the king] conquers barbarians (Pelagius; Haymo of Auxerre).[18]

Generally, however, two major interpretations of the expression dominated the field. The first pointed to an alleged Old Testament usage according to which the host (*hostia*), the animal victim of a sin-offering, was itself called sin. It appears first in Pelagius, although it may go back to Origen.[19] Pelagius quoted Lev 4:29 where the Septuagint indeed supports the reading. Medieval exegetes, however, did not find the phrase as Pelagius quoted it in their Vulgate here or elsewhere, so that the sweeping statement that "it was customary in the Old Testament to call every sin-offering a sin" (Atto of Vercelli) is utterly unfounded. Thomas Aquinas, followed by Nicholas of Lyra, substituted a figurative verse from Hos 4:8 ("they eat the sins of my people") to make the same point: "sin" can mean "sacrifice for sin." Verse 3d then said that God condemned sin through Christ's sacrifice, his sinless flesh given as the host for sin. In this connection, some writers quoted 2 Cor 5:21 as an appropriate Pauline parallel. But the tenacity with which the pseudo-philological argument was used and defended remains astonishing. An Anselmian variant to this explanation was "sin" as a figure of Christ's death. Death resulted from sin and may therefore be called sin, just as the "Latin tongue" does not mean the bodily organ but the result of its action (William of St. Thierry; Hervaeus). God condemned sin *de peccato*, that is, through the death of the human flesh which Christ took upon himself.

The other interpretation took its clue from the ancient Origenistic theologoumenon of Satan's right over fallen humankind and his deception by Christ's incarnation.[20] Medieval exegetes knew it in the following form: the devil has a right to the death of all humans because of original sin. In the case of the sinless Christ, however, he exercised this right unjustly. Thus, "since he seized what was not conceded, he justly lost even what had been conceded" (Bruno Carth). According to v 3d, then, God condemned sin, that is, the devil, through the very sin the devil committed against Christ's flesh. The argument often appeared in an extended form, either stressing (with the Ambrosiaster) the appropriateness of God's action ("he condemned sin by its own sin in

---

[18] Haymo of Auxerre quotes the proverbial phrase in its fullest form: "Tale est hoc quasi quis de barbaris victoriam sumat de barbaris, et de Gothis vincat Gothos" (PL 117, 427B).

[19] Origen on Romans, ad loc. (PG = Migne, *Patrologia Graeca* 14, 890).

[20] Origen on Romans (PG 14, 864); cf. Gregory of Nyssa, *Catechetical Oration* 23 and 26; Augustine, *De Trinitate* 13.12.16.

the very place where it sinned, the flesh") or introducing "the Jews" into the picture ("through the sin against Christ committed by the Jews God condemned the sin of the devil"; Sedulius Scotus). Sometimes it was combined with the first option as in William of St. Thierry's elegant sentence: "through the sin of Satan, as is said, he condemned the sin of the penitent sinner, and through the death of his flesh he killed the death of the soul in us."

It is well known that Abelard, as did Anselm before him, rejected the theory of the "deal" with the devil and achieved its demise in the West.[21] In his commentary on Romans 8, however, Abelard still presented both interpretations of v 3d as possible options, the "host of Christ's flesh given for sin" and the "sin committed against him by the devil or the Jews." In addition, however, he proposed still another solution, which equated *peccatum* both times with death as the punishment for sin: "Through sin, that is, the punishment for sin which he underwent for us ... he condemned sin, that is, he removed from us the punishment for sin by which even the righteous were bound before." The phrase sounds Anselmian, but Bernard would have suspected a deficient concept of original sin: did Christ just remove the punishment, not the guilt of sin as well?[22]

The Cambridge *Reportatio* of Abelard's lectures contains an unusually long comment on v 3d. Indeed, here Abelard's peculiar soteriology appears in its specific contours. Christ's death is the example of that supreme love which, when it possesses us, drives out all sins, and justifies and sanctifies us for eternal life. The passage is worth quoting in full.[23] It starts with the double equation of sin = Christ's suffering = infused love.

> Through sin, that is, through that highest love which he infused in us by the passibility of the flesh in which he suffered. This love extended even to his enemies. He not only preached it but also practiced it when he said from the cross: "Father, forgive them for they know not what they do." We find the same [action] only in the passion of St. Stephen who prayed on bended knees for his enemies:

---

[21] Rivière, *Le dogme* (see note 17 above) 66-71 and 98-103.

[22] This is point 8 in Bernard's list of "errores Abaelardi," which were censured at the Synod of Sens in 1141 and condemned by the pope: see H. Denzinger and A. Schönmetzer, *Enchiridion Symbolorum* (34th ed.; Freiburg, etc.: Herder, 1967) 236 (no. 728). On the issues see H. Koester, *Urstand, Fall und Erbsünde in der Scholastik* (Handbuch der Dogmengeschichte II.3b; Freiburg, etc.: Herder, 1979) 148-153; Weingart, *The Logic of Divine Love* (see note 18 above) 42-50.

[23] "Reportatio" (Commentarius Cantabrigiensis) 103.

"Lord, do not hold this sin against them." Other saints seem to have been more cruel in their agony. Lawrence said: "It is roasted. Turn and eat!" And Vincent: "Rush in on me, devil, unleash the whole spirit of malignity! You will find me all the more ready." Thus, through this extraordinary love he extinguished sin in us. For no person, however carnal, calls to mind the Lord's so deep, so shameful suffering which he, the innocent, underwent for the guilty without all his carnality immediately departing from him. Carnality would have departed the world a long time ago if there were preachers as there should be, preachers who would give instruction by word and example, who would keep to the rigor of justice and would not sell the Lord whom they sell now for even less than the thirty pieces of silver which Judas took, when they accept money, not even silver. For this reason monks have a crucifix before their eyes in the chapter room in order that, mindful of the agony of their Lord who said: "there is no sorrow like mine" (Lamentations 1:12), they may count their own suffering for nothing, especially since they know they are burdened with them justly.

Even in such a personal interpretation we discern the careful and reverent use of the exegetical tradition. Abelard of course shared this attitude with the other exegetes of his era. It is his unusual and imaginative use of the tradition that stands out as an exception.

*

How did Paul's theology fare at the hand of medieval exegetes? It is difficult to generalize on the basis of just one text and only a handful of exegetes. But our detailed reading of the limited evidence can give us some clues toward an answer.

1. Medieval exegetes were extremely serious about Paul "the theologian"—perhaps too serious. Even the best among them, a Peter Abelard or Thomas Aquinas, never saw themselves on the same level with the Apostle but regarded themselves as pupils who admired the master teacher's every word and sentence.[24] In fact, the Latin Paul governed much of the terminology, conceptuality, and argumentation of

---

[24] Their interpretation of Romans has been the subject of extensive monographs: R. Peppermüller, *Abälards Auslegung des Römerbriefs* (Beiträge zur Geschichte der Philosophie und Theologie des Mittelalters, TU [N. F.] 10; Münster: Aschendorff, 1972); Th. Domanyi, *Der Römerbriefkommentar des Thomas von Aquin: Ein Beitrag zur Untersuchung seiner Auslegungsmethoden* (Berner und Basler Studien zur historischen und systematischen Theologie 39; Bern, etc.: Peter Lang, 1979).

Pauline Theology in Medieval Interpretation   259

their theologizing down to determining the issues that were deemed worth debating. As John was "the" theologian in the East, so was Paul in the West.

2. They were also intensely aware of text and context. Contrary to the impression created by reading late medieval *summae*, exegetes were not involved in prooftexting. They listened to the text carefully and allowed it to raise questions challenging them to find solutions which were compatible with context, parallels, and the presumed harmony of biblical teaching as a whole. It is true that the biblical *quaestiones* themselves led to the systematic theologies of the high middle ages, but the ongoing work of exegesis in schools and monasteries, tied as it was to the biblical text, acted as a safeguard against the free-wheeling subtextual speculations offered by the keen minds of an intellectually stimulating age. Abelard, one of the sharpest among them, said it with all desirable clarity: "I do not want to be a philosopher in such a way as to lord it over Paul."[25]

3. Medieval exegetes saw Paul's text as applying to their own time. While we have not found much evidence of the doctrinal battles of the day, this last quotation shows the deep involvement of the exegete in the questions of Christian ethics, life and death, faith, and personal piety. Paul's text clearly nourished the self-understanding of these Christians. They could see themselves, as William of St. Thierry formulated it in a comment on Rom 8:3c, as looking up to Christ who, "imparting the righteousness of his innocent death to the penitent sinner," has given them "faith and love into the heart, the confession of salvation into the mouth, and his body and blood into the hand" (PL 180, 626CD).

4. Medieval exegetes had a very high regard for the exegetical tradition. When Hugh of St. Victor discussed the books for the required reading of a theological student, he made it clear that the Fathers belong to the books of the New Testament.[26] "For just as after the Law come the Prophets, and after the Prophets, the Hagiographers, so after the Gospel come the Apostles, and after the Apostles the long line of doctors." We may reflect again on the crucial position of Paul in this vision of the Christian theological tradition. He is the kingpin. There are shortcomings too. It is deplorable that Western exegetes were not in touch with the Eastern tradition. It is outright dangerous that Pelagius'

---

[25] "Nolo sic esse philosophus ut recalcitrem Paulo," *Fidei Confessio ad Heloissam* (PL 178, 375C).

[26] The *Didascalicon of Hugh of St. Victor: A Medieval Guide to the Arts* (tr. Jerome Taylor; Records of Civilization 64; New York: Columbia University Press, 1961) 105.

reading of Paul enjoyed such unquestioned authority under the safe name of orthodox writers. The vulnerability of the medieval reliance on "tradition" in exegesis is obvious. But it was precisely the unmasking of the pervasive "Pelagianism" of late medieval theology by the "Augustinian" monk Martin Luther that led to the epochal Reform of the sixteenth century. Luther, of course, did not learn from Augustine only. As a good medieval exegete, he also took seriously the pressing issues of Christian life and piety in his time, the challenge of understanding Paul as a theologian, and above all the Pauline text itself. Good exegetes today will do likewise. And if they do, the biblical text will continue to display the power not only to become the mirror of an age but also to open up new horizons for the church of the future.

16

Christian Faith's Partnership with History

John D. Godsey [1]

Introduction

In his influential book, *The Meaning of Revelation*, H. Richard Niebuhr stated the basic problem in these words:

> It remains true that Christian faith cannot escape partnership with history, however many other partners it may choose. With this it has been mated and to this its loyalty belongs; the union is as indestructible as that of reason and sense experience in the natural sciences. But though this is true the question remains, how can it be true? How can revelation mean both history and God?[2]

Ever since the intensifying of historical consciousness during the so-called "Enlightenment" of the eighteenth century, the origins and history of Christianity have undergone painstaking scrutiny, and the church has had to wrestle with the question of how its faith and life are related to history. It had no other choice but to do so, since Christians claim that their faith is grounded in the life, death, and resurrection of a

---

[1] John D. Godsey is Professor Emeritus of Systematic Theology at Wesley Theological Seminary, Washington, D.C.

[2] H. Richard Niebuhr, *The Meaning of Revelation* (New York: Macmillian, 1946) 59.

real man, Jesus of Nazareth. If there were no such Jesus, all would be lost.

But what can we know of Jesus, and how important is the knowledge we gain from a historical investigation of the sources? What historiographical and hermeneutical principles are appropriate for the inquiry? How are historical and theological perspectives related to one another? How is the history of Jesus, a Jew of the first century C. E., connected with the whole sweep of Hebrew history in what Christians call the Old Testament? Or with world history in general? What does it matter that the only real source of knowledge about Jesus comes from the variety of writings gathered into the "New Testament" and that these were all written by Christians who confessed the crucified Jesus to be the risen Lord? Such questions as these point to the complexity and unavoidability of historical issues for Christians, especially scholars.

It is not surprising, then, that Paul Meyer, a Professor of New Testament, devoted his 1976 Schaffer Lectures at Yale ("The Justification of Jesus") and his 1988 presidential address at the American Theological Society ("The Issue that Wouldn't Go Away: Faith and History Revisited") to the historical/theological task of elucidating the christological claims of the church, namely, that Jesus of Nazareth is the Christ in and through whom God has wrought salvation for the world. Professor Meyer is rightly concerned lest Christian faith lose its basis in what he terms "the actual Jesus," the one whose brutal crucifixion outside the gates of Jerusalem cannot be gainsaid.

The following is my own attempt to name and explore some of the issues involved in the age-old partnership between faith and history, and I offer it as a token of my high esteem for Paul Meyer as a Christian scholar and friend.

Defining History

Look in any dictionary and you will find many definitions for the word "history." For instance, it can mean an account of what has happened, which can take the form of narrative, tale, or story; a systematic written account of past events, usually with an analysis and explanation; or the branch of knowledge that records and explains past events. In common usage, however, history is understood to involve both objective and subjective elements: a tracing of an interconnected series of events (facts) and an interpretation of the same (perspective). "Positivistic" or "scientific" historians emphasize objective factuality, identifying historical causality with natural causality and accepting as true only what accords with the modern scientific and cosmological standards of the natural sciences (*Naturwissenschaften*). "Idealistic" and "existentialistic" historians, on the other hand, place more stress on the subjective element, using historical imagination and human psychology to understand and interpret events and patterns of meaning in history in accordance with the principles of the human sciences (*Geisteswissenschaften*).

Because so much of the discussion of faith and history during the past three centuries has occurred within the German academic sphere, it seems advisable to distinguish some of the major German terms that have entered into common parlance. The customary word for history is *Geschichte*, which can mean either "history" or "story." But in theological discourse *Geschichte* is often contrasted with *Historie*, *Geschichte* referring to past events that have significance for the present and *Historie* to the objective history that can be recovered by scientific historiographical means. Used adjectively, *geschichtlich* is sometimes translated "historic," whereas *historisch* is rendered "historical." Existentialists and personalists differentiate between two approaches to history: the "*historische*," which uses a critical or scientific method in dealing with "external history," and the "*geschichtliche*," which endeavors to uncover the meaning of events for personal existence, the realm of "inner history" or historicity (*Geschichtlichkeit*).

Several other words have become important in theological dialogue. *Heilsgeschichte* ("history of salvation" or "redemptive history") refers to what many claim to be the biblical view of history: the linear movement of time from creation to consummation, within which there occur special divine redemptive acts centering in the ministry, death, and resurrection of Jesus of Nazareth. This linear view is contrasted with the Greek cyclical view of time, which takes its analogies from the recurrences of nature. A different understanding of salvation is expressed in the term *Heilsgeschehen* ("saving event" or "occurrence of salvation"), which defines salvation as that existential encounter that happens when the word of Christ preached by the church is heard and responded to by the decision of faith. Through this present encounter with God's Word the believer is moved into "eschatological existence," freed from the power of the past and open for responsible living toward God's future. *Urgeschichte* ("primal history" or "super history") is sometimes used to denote the divine history which precedes, encompasses, and determines human history but is not amenable to historical inquiry. It can refer, for example, to such "events" as God's election of grace, creation ex nihilo, and the resurrection of Jesus from the dead.

Intimately connected with theological discussions of history, and almost equally diverse in its definitions, is eschatology (literally, "discourse about the last things"). The sharpest division occurs between futuristic and presentistic versions. Because the people of Israel believed that their history had a divine purpose and was moving toward a definite goal—the Day of the Lord or the kingdom of God—they developed a future-oriented eschatology that entailed a pattern of divine promise and fulfillment within history. When persecution struck and hopes waned around 200 B.C.E. there emerged among the Israelites an apocalyptic eschatology with the belief that God would intercede to bring human history to a cataclysmic end, at which time there would be a resurrection of the dead, a final judgment, and the establishment of an everlasting kingdom for the righteous.

For the early Christians, these widespread expectations were dramatically modified under the impact of the "Christ-event." Jesus had preached the imminent coming of the reign of God, and when his life ended in crucifixion, God miraculously resurrected him from the dead. His followers expected a speedy return of their risen Lord to consummate the kingdom, but when this *"parousia"* or advent did not occur, the expectation weakened and the eschatological event was put off to an indefinite future by a developing church. A more recent version of this futuristic eschatology, with its apocalyptic framework, considers the resurrection of Jesus to be a "proleptic event" which provides the clue within history of what the God of the future intends for all peoples at the end of history, namely, the general resurrection, judgment, and the fulfillment of the kingdom.

Presentistic eschatology, on the other hand, is to be found in two main forms: "realized eschatology" proposes that the kingdom of God was fully present in the life and ministry of Jesus and continues wherever life is lived under the conditions of the kingdom, whereas "existentialist eschatology" declares the *eschaton* to be present whenever the preaching of the Word elicits the response of faith that moves one from sinful to eschatological existence. A third view, which combines both future and present elements, is called "inaugurated eschatology": the kingdom was inaugurated in the life and work of Jesus but its complete fulfillment still awaits his return at the end-time.

With these various options for understanding history and eschatology in mind, we turn now to a brief account of where they emerged and how they have been used in some of the main developments in Christian thought since the Enlightenment.

From Lessing to Troeltsch

The view of human history dominant in Western Christendom prior to the Enlightenment was set forth in *The City of God* by Augustine (354-430), who depicted history as an ongoing struggle between the powers of the "earthly city" and those of the "heavenly city" as it moved toward its transcendent end under divine providence and the ministration of the church. This interpretation, which was warranted by biblical prophecy and miracle, was called into question by the rise of science, with its inductive experimental method for obtaining truth in a mechanistically understood universe (empiricism), and the concomitant growth of confidence in the innate ability of the human mind to deduce the truth about the world, including the nature and destiny of humanity (rationalism). The spirit of the age was heralded by the German philosopher Immanuel Kant (1724-1804):

> Enlightenment is man's release from his self-incurred tutelage. Tutelage is man's inability to make use of his understanding without direction from another. Self-incurred is this tutelage when its cause lies not in lack of reason but in lack of resolution and courage to use it without direction from another. *Sapere aude!* "Have courage to use your own reason!"—that is the motto of enlightenment.[3]

The dramatist and critic Gotthold Lessing (1729-81), in his *On the Proof of the Spirit and of Power*, enunciated the Enlightenment's viewpoint: "Accidental truths of history can never become the proof of necessary truths of reason...That, then, is the ugly, broad ditch which I cannot get across."[4] In one stroke, Lessing drove a wedge between historical event and truth, questioning how something that happened in the past can have decisive significance for faith in the present, as well as how the historical gulf can be overcome so that the event can affect humans today. Theology has wrestled with these questions ever since.

Radical rationalists, as in Deism, not only undercut orthodox theology by raising doubts about the veracity of many biblical events but also effectively removed God from interaction with the world. At most, God was considered to be Author of Nature and of Nature's laws, and the

---

[3] Immanuel Kant, "What Is Enlightenment?" in *Foundations of the Metaphysics of Morals* (tr. Lewis White Beck; New York: Liberal Arts Press, 1959) 85. "Sapere aude!" means "Dare to know!" and derives from Horace's *Ars poetica*.

[4] Gotthold E. Lessing, *On the Proof of the Spirit and of Power* in *Lessing's Theological Writings* (tr. Henry Chadwick; Stanford, CA: Stanford University Press, 1957) 53, 55.

truths of Christianity were said to be universal moral truths available to any rational being. Some rationalists abandoned the "God-hypothesis" altogether. At this point, it was Kant, himself a rationalist, who in his critiques of reason argued that, whereas God cannot be known by "theoretical reason," which is bound to the world of phenomena and even then cannot penetrate to the noumenal world of the "thing in itself," the *idea* of God, along with that of soul and immortality, is a necessary postulate of "practical reason" if humans are to exercise freedom in a moral universe. Kant is a pivotal figure because he discredited metaphysics, reduced history to the role of illustration, confined God to the ethical realm of humans' innate sense of a "categorical imperative," and depicted Jesus as the supreme teacher and exemplar of moral truths. Kant's self-assessment was that he had destroyed reason in order to make way for faith, but "faith" here had no essential relation to history.

At the beginning of the nineteenth century two remarkably creative thinkers took up the challenge posed by Kant: the church theologian Friedrich D. E. Schleiermacher (1768-1834) and the idealist philosopher of religion Georg W. F. Hegel (1770-1831). Both believed a return to Protestant orthodoxy impossible, both reacted against Enlightenment rationalism and Kantian moralism, and both wanted to do more justice to history.

Schleiermacher was influenced by Romanticism—an artistic/literary movement that fostered the use of intuition and imagination—and believed that inner feelings provide better access to truth than abstract reason. Schleiermacher became convinced that religion is an innate human capacity for experiencing the presence of God and that its locus is in the realm of feeling (*Gefühl*); God is present pre-cognitively in human self-awareness or the feeling of absolute dependence. For Christians, this feeling, which has been suppressed by sinful attachments to the world, is awakened and modified by the church's witness to the redemption wrought by Jesus of Nazareth. Jesus, whose fully potent God-consciousness was, according to Schleiermacher, the veritable presence of God in him, is able to evoke faith by communicating this consciousness to others. Since there can be no direct cognition of God, theology in Schleiermacher's view has to do with doctrines of faith (*Glaubenslehren*), that is, with explications of the religious feelings of the Christian community at any particular time.

If for Schleiermacher history serves not as mere illustration but as the necessary context for the church's communication of the God-consciousness, for Hegel's philosophy of metaphysical idealism history is nothing less than the dialectical, evolutionary, revelatory movement of *Geist* (Absolute Spirit or Mind). According to Hegel, the triune God is self-revealed within the historical process because God moves out of self in order to gain self-consciousness through humanity's becoming conscious of God. Religion, for Hegel, is the human realization and expression of this relationship to *Geist*, and the history of religions discloses the upward development of the human consciousness of God from the primitive nature religions to Christianity, the latter being considered by Hegel to be the absolute religion because in the God-Man Jesus Christ the ultimate truth of the unity of God and humanity is revealed. Hegel believed that this truth, which in religion is expressed in the language of symbol, imagery, and poetry, can be communicated more adequately in the precise conceptual language of philosophy. After all, argued Hegel, the rational is the real and the real is rational, so the human mind is in immediate touch with the divine.

The work of Schleiermacher and Hegel during the first third of the century sparked within the church a lively interest in the historical investigation of the origins and development of Christianity. Some researchers used a positivistic method, striving with "disinterested objectivity" to reconstruct history as it really happened (Leopold von Ranke's *"wie es eigentlich gewesen"*); others, stressing the hermeneutical truth that historians themselves are conditioned by their own history, sought through the use of historical imagination and psychological empathy to understand and interpret the meaning of history by "re-living" the human experience involved in past events and their recording (Wilhelm Dilthey's *"nacherleben"*).

Two of the more significant inquiries undertaken by Christian historians during the remainder of the nineteenth century were these: the attempt to find the "real Jesus" and the endeavor to uncover the "essence of Christianity." The so-called "Life-of-Jesus Movement," which was dedicated to recovering the "Jesus of history" from the encrustation of centuries of church dogma, began seriously with the publication of the *Life of Jesus* in 1835-36 by David Friedrich Strauss (1808-74).[5] Strauss created an uproar among orthodox Christians by assigning all supernatural elements in the New Testament accounts of Jesus' life to the category of "myth," a literary device he believed to have been used by the early church to embellish its claims. Numerous other "lives of Jesus" followed during the century: biographies intended to humanize Jesus either by excising those elements of the gospel story that were not rationally acceptable or by trying to expose the inner

---

[5] David Friedrich Strauss, *The Life of Jesus Critically Examined* (ed. Peter C. Hodgson; Philadelphia: Fortress, 1972).

consciousness or the unifying personality that lay behind Jesus' teaching and actions.

The historical search for the "essence of Christianity" was conducted during the last third of the century under the aegis of the "liberal theology" that is identified with Albrecht Ritschl (1822-89) and his followers. The most famous undertaking was that of Adolf von Harnack (1851-1930), who in his popular book of 1900, *What Is Christianity?* (*Das Wesen des Christentums*),[6] contended that the essence is found in its origins, in the teachings of Jesus about the "fatherhood of God" and the "brotherhood of man," and that the subsequent history of Christianity represents a corruption due mainly to the early intrusion of Greek metaphysics (Hellenization). Harnack believed that a historian could separate the kernel of Christian truth from its metaphysical husk. His view was opposed by the Catholic modernist Alfred Loisy (1857-1940), who maintained that the essence is found neither in an original historical form (Harnack) nor in a dogmatic one (Rome), but "in an unbroken unity of development within the manifestation of a long succession of external forms,"[7] none of which is normative apart from the others.

Ritschl himself desired to return Christian faith to the firm historical basis of the Bible and the insights of Luther. To counter the growing materialism and naturalism of his day, he interpreted faith as a victory of the human spirit over nature. Opposed to metaphysics and to mysticism in any form, he returned to Kant's anti-metaphysical, ethical understanding of Christianity within the realm of the practical reason. The result was an historical dichotomy, if not a dualism. On the one hand, the Bible could be freely investigated according to scientific historical method, but, on the other, the content of this history is to be evaluated not in terms of disinterested science (judgments of fact) but in terms of its worth for meeting our deepest moral and religious convictions (judgments of value). Ritschl believed he was following Luther in grounding faith not in knowledge of abstract facts about the nature of God and Christ, but in knowing the nature of God and Christ "in their worth for us."[8] Against all individualistic tendencies, Ritschl's liberal theology emphasized the centrality within Christianity of the

---

[6] Adolph von Harnack, *What Is Christianity?* (tr. Thomas Bailey Saunders; New York: Harper, 1957).

[7] Hans Frei, "Niebuhr's Theological Background," in *Faith and Ethics: The Theology of H. Richard Niebuhr* (ed. Paul Ramsey; New York: Harper & Brothers, 1957) 26.

[8] Albrecht Ritschl, *The Christian Doctrine of Justification and Reconciliation* (tr. H. R. Mackintosh and A. B. Macaulay; Edinburgh: T. & T. Clark, 1902) 212.

communal idea of the "kingdom of God," which he interpreted to be an ethical realm in which God and humans strive together in opposition to the divisive "kingdom of evil."

Wilhelm Herrmann (1846-1922), a follower of Ritschl, insisted that the basis of faith (*Glaubensgrund*) cannot be the results of historical research but is the present moral power of "the inner life of Jesus" that is mediated by the church. Historical study, he admitted, is valuable for faith because it destroys false props and can produce "relative truth," but the Christian comes to faith and thus to communion with God only as "the person of Jesus reveals itself to us through the power of his inner life."[9] For Herrmann, this encounter is historical precisely in that it occurs in the history of a person and in the context of a particular historical community.

Several developments coalesced toward the end of the nineteenth century and the beginning of the twentieth to bring an end to the attempts to write "lives of Jesus" and to undermine many of the assumptions of liberal theology in general. First, biblical scholars in the History-of-Religions School (*religionsgeschichtliche Schule*) used scientific historical method to set Jesus and early Christianity within the context of the surrounding religio-philosophical world of that time, emphasizing how much Christian interpretations of Jesus had in common with the conceptuality of oriental mystery religions, Hellenistic philosophy, and Jewish apocalypticism.

Second, in 1892 Johannes Weiss (1863-1914), son-in-law of Ritschl, maintained in his book *Jesus' Proclamation of the Kingdom of God*[10] that Jesus and his preaching must be understood in the framework of apocalyptic eschatology, which meant that the kingdom Jesus anticipated was not a kingdom of ethical striving within history but a kingdom that God alone would establish and that would bring world history to an end. The devastating consequences of this view of Jesus as "apocalyptic preacher" for the increasingly psychologized, humanitarian picture of Jesus portrayed in the liberal "lives" was drawn in 1906 by Albert Schweitzer (1875-1965) in his book *The Quest of the Historical Jesus*,[11] in which he surveyed the various attempts "from Reimarus to Wrede" and demonstrated the error and futility of such efforts.

---

[9] Wilhelm Herrmann, *The Communion of the Christian with God* (2nd ed.; tr. J. Sandys Stanton; New York: G. P. Putnam's Sons, 1906) 79.

[10] Johannes Weiss, *Jesus' Proclamation of the Kingdom of God* (tr. and ed. Richard H. Hiers and David L. Holland; Philadelphia: Fortress, 1971).

[11] Albert Schweitzer, *The Quest of the Historical Jesus: A Critical Study of Its Progress from Reimarus to Wrede* (tr. W. Montgomery; New York: Macmillan, 1948).

Third, another book published in 1892, *The So-called Historical Jesus and the Historic, Biblical Christ* by the theologian Martin Kähler (1835-1912),[12] contained the thesis that all attempts to recover "the historical (*historische*) Jesus," that is, "Jesus insofar as he can be made the object of historical-critical research," would lead only to a blind alley. This is so, Kähler argued, because all New Testament writings, including the Gospels, were written from the post-resurrection perspective of believers in "the historic (*geschichtliche*) Christ," that is, "Jesus insofar as he is the object of faith, the content of preaching, and confessed by the community as Lord, Messiah, and Redeemer."[13] For Kähler, attempts to write "lives of Jesus" are not only historically impossible but theologically irrelevant, because faith lives from the present encounter with the risen Christ in the preaching of the church.

The nineteenth century ended with no clear answer to Lessing's dilemma. The historical dualism of liberal theology, which used the historical-critical method to investigate the past but found its certainty of faith in the realm of Kant's "practical reason," was firmly opposed by the historicism of the History-of-Religions School. Its theological representative, Ernst Troeltsch (1865-1923), set forth these three principles for any proper interpretation of history: criticism, analogy, and correlation. That is, historical study entails (1) a critical habit of mind that presupposes that only judgments of probabilities are possible in history and thus remains open to revisions; (2) the ability to discern analogies between past and present happenings based on the commonality of human experience; and (3) the assumption that events in history are related in a continuum of antecedents and consequences, so that no event can be dealt with in isolation.[14] Troeltsch's belief in historical relativism led him to deny the theory that Christianity is the "absolute religion" and to confine the validity of Christianity to its Western cultural context. Thus, Troeltsch's views exacerbated the problem initially posed by Lessing.

---

[12] Martin Kähler, *The So-Called Historical Jesus and the Historic Biblical Christ* (tr. and ed. Carl E. Braaten; Philadelphia: Fortress, 1964).

[13] See Carl E. Braaten's "Introduction" to *The So-called Historical Jesus and the Historic, Biblical Christ,* 20-21.

[14] Ernst Troeltsch, "Über historische und dogmatische Methode in der Theologie," in his *Gesammelte Schriften,* vol.2 (Tübingen: J.C.B. Mohr [Paul Siebeck], 1913) 731-34.

"Between the Times": Dialectical Theology

From a theological perspective, the First World War (1914-18) marks the boundary between the nineteenth and twentieth centuries, at least in Europe. This outbreak of evil shattered the prevailing cultural assumption of inevitable human progress in conquering nature and improving society, and it caused Christian thinkers to question the adequacy of liberal theology's understanding of the relationship between God and the world, especially its view of the immanence of God in humankind or in the historical process. Did this accord with the Bible?

Karl Barth (1886-1968), a Swiss Reformed pastor educated under Harnack and Herrmann, discovered "a strange new world" within the Bible and fired the first shot across the prow of liberal theology with the publication of his *Römerbrief* (a commentary on Romans) in 1919 and the completely rewritten second edition in 1922.[15] He was soon joined by others in a "dialectical theology" that aimed to do justice to God's transcendence and the miracle of revelation in the Word that comes *to* history in Jesus Christ. Those colleagues included the German Lutheran pastor Friedrich Gogarten (1887-1967), the German Lutheran New Testament scholar Rudolf Bultmann (1884-1976), and the Swiss pastor Emil Brunner (1889-1966). Also initially attracted to the group was another German Lutheran theologian, Paul Tillich (1886-1965). United mainly in what they were against, all these theologians soon assumed important university chairs and developed distinctive positions of their own.

The dialectical theology of the 1920s, which was stimulated by the crisis of culture to recover the biblical Word of God's judgment and grace, was aided in its attack on liberal theology by several other important developments: the rediscovery of eschatology, the emergence of form-criticism, the rise of existentialism, the appearance of the religious socialist movement, the renewed interest in the sixteenth-century Reformers, and the changed understanding of history introduced by the "I-Thou" personalist philosophy. Form-critical research on the Gospels, for example, further demonstrated the foolishness of the liberal attempt to write a "life of Jesus" by showing that the Gospels were creations of the early church knit together from various literary "forms" of the oral tradition and, further, that they were a combination of report

---

[15] The first edition of Barth's *Römerbrief* has never been translated: *Der Römerbrief* (ed. Hermann Schmidt; Zürich: Theologischer Verlag, 1985). The revised *Römerbrief* has been translated into English as *The Epistle to the Romans* (tr. Edwyn C. Hoskyns; London/New York: Oxford University Press, 1933).

and confession written to meet the preaching and teaching needs of the worshipping congregations.

Of special importance for the "faith and history" theme was the recovery of the insights of two nineteenth century "prophets" who had been largely overlooked in their own time. Søren Kierkegaard (1813-55), Danish "father of existentialism," combatted Hegel's idealism by asserting that the search for the objective truth of Christianity by either historical or speculative means can only lead to despair, because truth for the existing individual occurs in the realm of subjectivity and is known only in the passionate moment of decision. "An objective uncertainty held fast in an appropriation-process of the most passionate inwardness," he declared, "is the truth."[16] Furthermore, for Kierkegaard it is not the "what" but the "how" of faith that is crucial, because faith involves an existential relationship to what can only be conceived as paradox to thought, namely, the entrance of the eternal into time. Thus the multiplying of historical details about Jesus would offer no advantage to today's believer; it would have been more than enough, he wrote, if the generation contemporary with Jesus had left behind them only these words: "We have believed that in such and such a year God appeared among us in the humble figure of a servant, that he lived and taught in our community, and finally died."[17]

Toward the end of the century the Basel University church historian and skeptic, Franz Overbeck (1837-1905), attacked historicism in relation to Christianity. Convinced that the Christianity of scripture is wholly eschatological, he declared: "Historic Christianity—that is Christianity subjected to time—is an absurdity."[18] If Christianity, then not history; if history, then not Christianity! Christ, according to Overbeck, is not merely in history but is the source of history. He belongs to *Urgeschichte*, that primal history of the divine that bounds and alone gives meaning to human history in its blind course between creation and death.

Related to existentialist modes of thought were those of personalist philosophers such as Ferdinand Ebner (1882-1931) and Martin Buber (1887-1965), who distinguished between two approaches to the beings and things of this world: a disinterested, objective "I-It" relationship,

---

[16] Kierkegaard's *Concluding Unscientific Postscript* (tr. David F. Swenson; Princeton, NJ: Princeton University Press, 1944) 182.

[17] Søren Kierkegaard, *Philosophical Fragments: or a Fragment of Philosophy* (tr. David F. Swenson; Princeton, NJ: Princeton University Press, 1946) 87.

[18] Quoted by Karl Barth in "Unsettled Questions for Theology Today," in *Theology and Church* (tr. L. P. Smith; New York: Harper & Row, 1962) 61.

and an open, responsive "I-Thou" relationship. Only the latter, they maintained, is appropriate for an authentic encounter between humans or between humans and God. Following their lead, theologians were quick to claim that the revelation of God takes place in an event of encounter or in the area of "inner history" appropriate to an "I-Thou" relationship.

To sum up the general attitude of the dialectical theologians toward the relation of faith and history, we can say that they used whatever conceptual means they could find to emphasize what Kierkegaard had termed "the infinite qualitative distinction between eternity and time" and thereby to deny the results of scientific historical investigation any constitutive meaning for faith. Faith, they claimed, is grounded in God's revelatory, eschatological, trans-historical personal Word alone—and that Word is the risen Jesus Christ. To try to ground faith in history, they averred, would violate the Protestant principle of justification by faith alone.

Some Twentieth-Century Options

In many ways the period of dialectical theology was a transitory time, and since its break-up in the early '30s several major positions regarding faith and history have appeared. In what follows I will present some of the prominent options, choosing where feasible a representative figure and briefly characterizing the viewpoint.

1. Cullmann and *Heilsgeschichte*. In his book *Christ and Time* (1946) Oscar Cullmann (b.1902)[19] set forth a view echoed by many theologians, namely, that the biblical understanding of time is linear, that human history is best depicted by an upward-sloping line running from creation to consummation, and that salvation occurs in a history of special divine actions (*kairoi*) that culminate in the life, death, and resurrection of Jesus Christ. Faith is belief in Christ as the mid-point of history, the Lord whose victory over sin, death, and the devil gives meaning to every moment of time until his return at the *parousia*.

2. Bultmann and *Heilsgeschehen*. Rudolf Bultmann propounded the view that faith is not based on what can be known of Jesus and his message by use of the historical-critical method, but occurs in a "saving event" when a decision is made in response to the present preaching of the post-Easter kerygma. An *historische* approach, he contended, can demonstrate *that* Jesus existed but little more for certain. This presents

---

[19] Oscar Cullmann, *Christ and Time: The Primitive Christian Conception of Time and History* (tr. Floyd Filson; rev. ed.; Philadelphia: Westminster, 1964).

no problem, however, because hearing the word of the cross involves an eschatological encounter with God that can be interpreted existentially as an "eternal now" that produces a whole new understanding of existence. This is the realm of *Geschichte*, not *Historie*.

3. "Post-Bultmannians" and the "New Quest." A number of former students of Bultmann who agreed with his general position nevertheless became disturbed by his view that seemed to them to draw too sharp a discontinuity between the historical Jesus and the kerygmatic Christ. They had no interest in returning to the "old quest," but they came to believe it possible to pursue a new quest on different historiographical grounds. From the accounts of Jesus' words and deeds preserved in the Gospels (his peculiar authority, his faith, etc.), they believed they could discern enough of his existential self-understanding to claim the presence of an "implicit christology" and thus demonstrate a continuity between the pre-Easter Jesus and the post-Easter Christ.

4. Barth and *Urgeschichte*. "*Urgeschichte*" or "primal history" is a term Barth used early in his career, whereas later he spoke more in terms of a modified *Heilsgeschichte*. Nevertheless, it points to Barth's conviction that the biblical narrative presents two histories, the divine and the human, which coincide in the history of Jesus Christ. *Urgeschichte* is that "*unhistorische Geschichte*," God's eternal election of grace that determines and illumines all human history, a covenant of grace that is concretized in Jesus Christ, for in him the electing triune God and the elected humanity meet and unite in a once-for-all saving action. For Barth, the Bible is the "written Word" which attests to the "revealed Word of God," Jesus Christ, and provides the basis for the "proclaimed Word" of the church: one Word in three-fold form. The Bible may be investigated scientifically, but this method cannot disclose what is essential in its narrative: the concrete presence and deed of God in time. Only the "eyes of faith," awakened by the Spirit, see this truth. Since for Barth Christ is the Lord of time and the incarnation is all-embracing, there is no "ugly, broad ditch" to be crossed.

5. Pannenberg and Universal History. In reaction to theologies of the Word that tended to ghettoize revelation in a *Heilsgeschichte* or to dehistoricize it in an existential *Heilsgeschehen*, Wolfhart Pannenberg (b.1928) has proposed a theology of revelation as universal history. Eschewing all forms of historical dualism, he accepts only scientific historiography and affirms only one history. For Pannenberg, the apocalyptic view of history that pervades the New Testament, with its notion of the end-time, provides the correct framework for understanding world history. He argues that God is being self-revealed in the totality of

history, which means that only at the end will God be fully known. Nevertheless, a clue to history's end and thus to its meaning has been given "proleptically" in the fate of Jesus, in that his resurrection anticipates the universal resurrection at the end of history. Pannenberg dismisses as unscientific any historiography that rules out *a priori* the possibility of such a novel occurrence as Jesus' resurrection from the dead. Faith in God, according to Pannenberg, entails trusting in God's future, a trust grounded in Jesus' own fate.

6. Gutiérrez and Liberation History. Gustavo Gutiérrez (b.1928) of Peru is representative of a growing number of Latin American "liberation theologians" (and those of other oppressed groups around the world) who also eschew dualism and affirm one history, namely, the history of the struggle of the poor and disadvantaged to be liberated from oppression—in this case, from economic and cultural deprivation. Their zeal for justice, insists Gutiérrez, comes directly from the Bible: from the story of God's solidarity with the oppressed Hebrew people in Egypt and of Jesus' solidarity with the poor and outcasts of his time. The poor, he claims, have a hermeneutical advantage in reading the Bible, for they see things from the underside of history and thus have a better understanding of its message than those who have been dominant in Western society. Indeed, liberation theologians advocate a "hermeneutics of suspicion" when reading most Western theologians, believing that their views might be tainted with the ideology of the powerful. For Gutiérrez, praxis includes theological reflection as the "second step" following action (engaged commitment), and its task is not to produce theoretical truth but practical truth that will aid the oppressed in their struggle for freedom from inhumane treatment. Faith is trust in the God who is involved in *this* history.

Conclusion

We began with the question: "How can revelation mean both history and God?" I hope this brief survey has at least shown that the question has no easy answer and that the attempts during the past three centuries have varied according to the different construals of truth and reality, history and hermeneutics, ontology and epistemology. It is evident, I think, that a few critics have tried to use historical investigation to discredit the claims of Christianity, but by and large honest differences have surfaced among equally committed Christians.

Much of the difficulty appears to stem from the nature of the New Testament itself, for it presents a narrative that combines records of events and confessions of faith. It witnesses to the actions of *God* in history and to the unique redemptive action of God in the history of *one man*, a history that ends with crucifixion but also resurrection. The reality of the resurrection, as an incomparable event, has been the touchstone of the historical question, for on it is based the Christian claim that God has vindicated Jesus' life and death and has revealed his trans-historical significance. The problem for the historian in dealing with the New Testament witness is that no act of God, much less the act of resurrection, can be proved or disproved by historiographical means. The probability of such an event can be argued, but faith has seldom been willing to rest its case on probabilities.

Even the question of identifying Jesus is extremely complicated for the historian. Van Harvey (b.1926) underscores this in his book *The Historian and the Believer* by distinguishing between four components in the New Testament that must be related to each other: (1) "the actual Jesus" (the man who lived 2000 years ago); (2) "the historical Jesus" (what can be fairly said about the actual Jesus on the basis of inferences from our present sources); "the memory-impression of Jesus" (the perspectival image of the Christian community evident in what is selectively remembered); and "the biblical Christ" (the transformation and alteration of the memory-impression under the influence of the theological interpretation of the actual Jesus by the community).[20] Here, again, the historian can examine the sources and sort out what can be known with high probability about the actual Jesus but cannot fathom the mystery of his person as expressed in the confession of faith that he is the Word made flesh or the risen Lord.

I agree with those who insist that faith lives from the Word of God proclaimed in the present and not from a proven history, but I also confess that the risen Christ encountered in that Word is identical with the actual Jesus of history. Precisely because Jesus' very humanness is involved in the mystery of revelation, the work of the historian is not only permitted but is essential to the church—not the mere determination *that* Jesus existed, but what his life reveals. I do not think it is possible to "psychologize" Jesus, but I believe the New Testament accounts of his words and deeds disclose crucial information about his attitude, intentions, and convictions. After all, it was these that brought about his death.

One of the sanest explanations of the relationship between faith and history I know is found in an article by Günther Bornkamm (b.1905) entitled "The Significance of the Historical Jesus for Faith." He first emphasizes the negative point that "the two are not related in the sense

---

[20] Van A. Harvey, *The Historian and the Believer* (New York: Macmillan, 1966) 265-81.

that a history which has been scientifically examined could as such offer a proof for the truth of faith," but then he proceeds to state the following:

> Nevertheless, faith remains constantly directed to a specific history, although not to one that offers proofs and supports which supposedly first make faith possible. Yet everything depends for faith upon the fact that the name "Jesus Christ" which it confesses is not only a word or mere "cipher", but that faith really encounters Jesus of Nazareth, whom it confesses to be the Christ. For faith everything depends upon the identity between Jesus and the Christ, if it is not to lose itself in reliance upon a mythical figure. The center and content of faith, therefore, is that "Jesus Christ is the same yesterday, today, and for ever" (Heb 13:8).[21]

In summary, I think it safe to say that arguments over the relationship of faith and history will as little cease this side of the *eschaton* as those perennial controversies between the intellectualists and the voluntarists in the Christian tradition. The cleavages, we have found, run deep: between the *historische* approach and the *geschichtliche* approach, between revelation in history and revelation as history, between the "what" of faith (*fides quae creditur*) and the "how" of faith (*fides qua creditur*).

In the end, I am convinced that faith will always have a dialectical relationship to history because the history to which faith is related is one which involves the mystery of the union between the human and the divine. This requires one to say simultaneously, "Yes, revelation is history; but no, history per se is not revelation." It becomes revelation for me when my eyes are opened by grace through faith alone. And even then, my knowledge of revelation must be tested against the experience of countless others in the community of faith.

One final observation: I believe liberation theologians are legitimately asking today whether one can understand the Bible and come to know Christ without entering into the history of his suffering among the oppressed of the world and having one's eyes opened from that perspective from below. As Dietrich Bonhoeffer reminds us, "Acquired

---

[21] Günther Bornkamm, "The Significance of the Historical Jesus for Faith," in F. Hahn, W. Lohff, and G. Bornkamm, *What Can We Know about Jesus?* (tr. Grover Foley; Philadelphia: Fortress, 1969) 84.

knowledge cannot be divorced from the existence in which it is acquired."[22]

---

[22] Dietrich Bonhoeffer, *The Cost of Discipleship* (tr. R. H. Fuller and Irmgard Booth; rev. ed.; New York: Macmillan 1963) 55.

17

The Salvation of Jesus: A Theological Reflection on the Destiny of the Kingdom in History

Charles H. Cosgrove [1]

> To the Christian the Jew is the stubborn fellow who in a redeemed world is still waiting for the Messiah. For the Jew the Christian is a heedless fellow who in an unredeemed world affirms that somehow or other redemption has taken place.
> Martin Buber[2]

In his inaugural lecture at Princeton Seminary in 1979, Paul Meyer asked how the Christian community can withstand (and has withstood) "the withering force" of the words just cited.[3] In his own attempt to

---

[1] Charles H. Cosgrove is Associate Professor of New Testament at Northern Baptist Theological Seminary, Lombard, Illinois.

[2] As cited by Reinhold Niebuhr, "Martin Buber: 1878-1965," *Christianity and Crisis* 25 (July 12, 1965) 146. See also the letter of Buber on the same theme preserved in Franz von Hammerstein, *Das Messiasproblem bei Martin Buber* (Stuttgart: Kohlhammer, 1958).

[3] "The 'This-Worldliness' of the New Testament," *Princeton Seminary Bulletin* N.S. 2 (1979) 221.

answer Buber, Meyer directed attention to the meaning of the first proclamation of the resurrection of Jesus:

> [The] earliest missionaries were proclaiming neither a new God nor an unknown Jesus. Instead, they were declaring that the God of their fathers had made of the discredited Jesus of Nazareth the right clue and the criterion for discerning God's true intentions; the measure of the right way to talk about salvation and God's kingship and their obedience....[4]

To put it a bit differently, as God's confirmation of the crucified Jesus, the resurrection signifies the "justification of Jesus," a phrase adopted by Meyer as the title of his 1976 Shaffer Lectures at Yale Divinity School. In these lectures Meyer argued that the Jesus of history, who died as a consequence of what he said and how he lived, cannot be regarded as the mere presupposition of the kerygma (Bultmann) but must be recognized as its central content. For the resurrection as divine vindication can refer to no one else than the publicly discredited Jesus of Nazareth, and in that case the historical Jesus becomes both the "warrant" and also a "criterion" of Christian faith.

The meaning of this last statement turns on the way in which one construes the relation of Jesus' public career to his death and the way in which one construes the relation of that same death to the resurrection. It is the death of Jesus that mediates his relation to his own justification. But his death does not figure in this role as a self-contained entity carrying its meaning within itself. That meaning is determined by its relation to Jesus' life on the one hand and his vindication by God on the other. Moreover, it is the resurrection-vindication of Jesus that singles out his death as the theological key to the meaning of his words and deeds as the "right clue and the criterion for discerning God's true intentions." The Jesus who is himself a "criterion" for Christian faith is not the historical Jesus in a *general* sense but the publicly known Jesus whose execution was linked to what he said and how he lived. He is Jesus interpreted from the standpoint of his execution.

If I have understood correctly Meyer's basic approach to the question of faith and history in both his Shaffer Lectures and his Princeton address, he wishes to shed light on this question by thinking through the relation of the resurrection proclamation to the Jesus of history and discerning the particular way in which the meaning of the resurrection as "vindication" specifies that relation. What intrigues me about this

---

[4] Ibid., 227.

line of reflection is the way in which it suggests a second direction of thought, a theological movement *from* the meaning of Jesus' death in history *to* the meaning of the resurrection. What is the relation of Jesus to his own justification, and how might an analysis of this relation clarify the connection between redemption and history?

Something of this second direction of thought is evident in Meyer's assertion that the sheer historical givenness of the crucifixion of Jesus makes the idea of the resurrection itself, together with the traditional eschatological hopes for redemption associated with it, "irreversibly this-worldly."[5] What follows is an attempt to explore this insight further. It is offered as a token of esteem and gratefulness to one who has already taught us much about the significance and profundity of the very first post-Easter interpretation of Jesus, that deceptively simple declaration of the earliest preachers that the God of their fathers had vindicated Jesus of Nazareth by raising him from the dead.

I

"Jesus will help us" the Black man said. Hell,
Jesus couldn't even help his own self. He fooled
around and got himself nailed to the cross.
                                    Bumpy Johnson[6]

The question before us is how the relation of Jesus to his own justification may illumine the nature of "redemption" in an unredeemed world and thus serve as a criterion of faith's relationship to history. We can get a better idea of the nature and significance of this question by reflecting on what is certainly the most memorable phrase from the Shaffer Lectures and one that appears again in almost identical form in the later inaugural lecture. Meyer is describing the Jesus whom God justifies:

> This Jesus is the one whose teaching about the radical imperative of God's grace has no convincing claim until God shows him to be right; whose unorthodox moves to establish human community with the outcast are no different from the madness of any revolutionary until God identifies himself with this madness; whose challenges to religious tradition and convention are only as interesting or as

---

[5] Ibid., 227.
[6] As quoted by Gordon Parks, "Stokely Carmichael," *Life* (May 19, 1967) 82.

tiresome as a thousand other religious radicals until the early preachers talk of divine confirmation of his human career.[7]

It is of no small interest to note that in the Shaffer Lectures these lines serve to explicate the meaning of the resurrection, while in the inaugural they are introduced in the first instance as an interpretation of the cross. This observation points to a highly suggestive ambiguity in the description itself. About whom are these sentences speaking, about the justified Jesus or the unjustified Jesus? It ought to be clear that this ambiguity owes to the fact that the passage specifies the relationship between Jesus and his justification in narrative terms. In fact, the identity of the Jesus here described cannot be adequately grasped apart from the narrative in which that identity is embedded. This is not to suggest that the problem of faith and history can be legitimately avoided—or at least indefinitely postponed—by shifting to a realm of discourse where the category of "story" is substituted for that of history. The point is to see that the idea of "vindication," which functions in the proclamation of the resurrection to send us back to history, is a thoroughly narrative notion: it cannot be said or even thought except in a story.

What *generates* the story implicit in the proclamation of the resurrection is the idea of the resurrection as vindication. The resurrection marks the cross as *essential* to the meaning of "Jesus" and thus evokes a narrative interpretation of the subject matter of the kerygma. In so doing it singles out as the central plot of the story of Jesus those events that led to the cross. If all historical thinking is selective, this way of thinking the historical Jesus is guided in its identification of significant facts by the "disclosure" given in the resurrection. The early preachers were "declaring that the God of their fathers had made of the *discredited* Jesus the right clue and the criterion for discerning God's true intentions." The teachings and actions of the discredited Jesus are the clue—not the teachings and actions of Jesus interpreted apart from their relation to the crucifixion or construed as significant simply in spite of the crucifixion.

I say that the resurrection "generates" the story of the justified Jesus, not that it creates the public historical facts out of which this story is constructed. The Christian historian, like all historians, must reconstruct the history of Jesus without being guided by the "clue" given in the

---

[7]"The Justification of Jesus," the Shaffer Lectures at Yale Divinity School, February 10-12, 1976 (unpublished typescript in Speer Library, Princeton Theological Seminary) 58. See "The 'This-Worldliness' of the New Testament," 227.

resurrection. This is appropriate quite apart from the question whether the resurrection can be considered in any sense as an "event" in history; whatever the nature of the resurrection, it is not part of the life and death of Jesus of Nazareth. Now the task of reconstructing the Jesus of history must include an investigation of the relationship between Jesus' public life and his execution, and the results of such an investigation are of theological significance by virtue of the fact that the discredited Jesus of Nazareth is the subject of the kerygma. Nevertheless, the public Jesus about whom the historian, including the Christian historian, inquires is not unqualifiedly the "clue" of which the resurrection "speaks." For that clue includes the resurrection itself, just as the identity of the *justified* Jesus includes his justification. The question is how we are to understand this "inclusion," and our analysis thus far suggests that it can only be grasped in narrative categories.

It is well known that Rudolf Bultmann virtually identified the event of disclosure (the resurrection of which the kerygma speaks) with the object or content of that disclosure itself.[8] By contrast, the idea that the resurrection signifies the vindication of Jesus would appear to distinguish the event of disclosure from its content. Nevertheless, the idea of vindication suggests in fact a more complex relation of the two, an "inclusion" of the event of disclosure in the content of that which is disclosed by virtue of a structural connection in the story of Jesus' justification that appears highly paradoxical when translated out of narrative description into discursive speech.

The paradox I have in mind is illustrated by the threefold "until" found in Meyer's description of Jesus in the passage cited above. Clearly we have to do with the same Jesus on both sides of this temporal conjunction. But there is a decisive difference between the two. One might formulate this difference by saying that Jesus prior to the "until" is not yet who he shall be as the justified Jesus. But the qualifier "not yet" and the proleptic linking of this Jesus with his future, as if it already belonged to him ("shall be"), obscure the historical contingency that governed the life and death of Jesus of Nazareth, about whom nothing on the far side of that "until" applied. Indeed, the whole train of Meyer's argument as it is expressed in the paragraph before us leads to the conclusion, and rightly so, that the "justified Jesus" is, to use his terminology, the "warrant" and "criterion" for Christian faith. After all,

---

[8] See "The New Testament and Mythology," in *Kerygma and Myth* (ed. H. W. Bartsch; London: S.P.C.K., 1953) 41. Compare the even stronger statements to this effect by Schubert M. Ogden, "The Point of Christology," *JR* 55 (1975) 383; also Ogden, *The Point of Christology* (San Francisco: Harper & Row, 1982).

it is the vindication of Jesus by God that makes him into what the kerygma claims him to be. And yet the same narrative logic compels us just as surely to the conclusion that the justification of Jesus discloses the unjustified Jesus, about whom all the contingency and ambiguity and weakness before the "until" and none of the certainty and clarity and victory beyond it applied, to represent the true nature and authentic pattern of Christian faith and action in the world. After all, it is the crucified Jesus of Nazareth as an historically finished entity whom God marks out as the "right clue and the criterion for discerning God's true intentions."

The preceding two conclusions can be integrated only by thinking the way in which the justified Jesus includes the unjustified Jesus, and not the other way around. To say that Jesus' justification by God "makes" him into that which the kerygma claims him to be is to construe the disclosure entailed in the justification of Jesus as a constitutive act. The question is how the "act" or "event" character of Jesus' vindication is to be understood in relation to history. At this point one must carefully distinguish the "historicality" of Jesus from the history of Jesus contained in the story of his vindication. Otherwise we shall not conceive properly the way in which that story must do justice to the historical Jesus. "Historicality" refers here to the existential concreteness of Jesus "as he really *was*," where existential is taken in a socio-historical as opposed to a merely individualistic sense[9] and where concreteness is understood as entailing both contingency and particularity. By the "history of Jesus" in the story of his justification is meant the rendering of Jesus in that story as far as the "until" of divine vindication.

What is the relation of this "rendering" (the history of Jesus in the story of his vindication) to the historicality of Jesus of Nazareth? Antoine Roquentin, whose diary comprises the substance of Sartre's novel *Nausea*, poses a similar question when he considers the way in which stories distort what he takes to be the fundamentally "uneventful" character of life: "Nothing happens while you live.... But everything changes when you tell about life." For in telling (*raconter*), the end of the story is already there from the beginning "transforming

---

[9]It may be helpful to point out that Jean-Paul Sartre expanded his own existentialist anthropology beyond the individualist confines of its early expression (e.g., in *Being and Nothingness: An Essay on Phenomenological Ontology* [New York: Philosophical Library, 1956]) to include the socio-historical matrix of human existence. See especially *Critique of Dialectical Reason* (London: New Left Books, 1976).

everything."[10] Kierkegaard observed a similar distortion in the way in which we are apt to think the *familiar* story of Abraham in Genesis 22.

> We mount a winged horse, and in the same instant we are on Mount Moriah, in the same instant we see the ram. We forget that Abraham only rode an ass, which trudges along the road, that he had a journey of three days, that he needed some time to chop the firewood, to bind Isaac, and to sharpen the knife.[11]

Unlike Sartre's Roquentin, Kierkegaard's Abraham lives the moments of his life, from the reception of the divine command to the lifting of the knife, as a story in which he makes at once the infinite movement of resignation and the movement of faith. Yet both Sartre and Kierkegaard recognize that a story, by its very nature, tends to disclose meaning at the expense of concrete historicality. Further, both also seek to explore through narrative what they regard as the ultimately real in a way that discloses this disjunction and thus honors the radical temporal contingency of human existence.[12]

There is a real disjunction between the life of Jesus in its sheer historicality and the story implicit in the proclamation of the resurrection that "transforms everything." Yet the story of the justified Jesus does not obscure but incorporates this very disjunction into its own inner narrative logic; it makes the cleft between the life of Jesus of Nazareth and the narrative interpretation of that life an essential feature of its own plot. In the story of Jesus' vindication by God, it is the crucifixion that points to this cleft between the kerygmatic view of Jesus "from the end" and the life of Jesus, which not only had no *real* connection to this "end" but also suffered the destruction of its own teleology in the cross.

The resurrection is the *salvation of Jesus*. His vindication by God alters his fate by delivering his "teaching about the radical imperative of God's grace" from having "no convincing claim," by rescuing his "unorthodox moves to establish human community with the outcast" from being "no different from the madness of any revolutionary," and by

---

[10] *Nausea* (Norfolk, CT: New Directions, 1964) 39 and 40..

[11] Søren Kierkegaard, *Fear and Trembling* and *Repetition* (ed. and tr. Howard V. Hong and Edna H. Hong; Princeton: Princeton University Press, 1983) 52.

[12] A similar point about the relationship of contingency and meaning in narrative fiction is made by Roy Pascal in dissent from the radical theories about narrative fictions put forward by Roland Barthes and, to a lesser extent, Frank Kermode, both of whom build on Sartre's criticism of narrative. See Pascal, "Narrative Fictions and Reality: A Comment on Frank Kermode's *The Sense of an Ending*" *Novel* 11 (1977) 40-50.

liberating his "challenges to religious tradition and convention" from being "only as interesting or as tiresome as a thousand other religious radicals." *Now* he has a convincing claim. *Now* his madness is God's madness, and he is *no longer* as interesting or tiresome as any other religious radical but stands in a class by himself. Yet by altering his fate Jesus' vindication by God implicitly, but no less certainly, affirms the historical truth of his *having had* "no convincing claim," his *having been* "no different from" and "only as interesting or tiresome as" all the rest of those who have thrown themselves on the wheel of history and found relative success or failure in its turning. As a constitutive act, the truth that the resurrection speaks presupposes the fact that it overcomes, and in this way the resurrection accords that fact—the tragedy of Jesus' death—a certain status in its own truth. In this sense the resurrection is not simply the substitution of a right understanding of Jesus' cross-terminated life for a false judgment on the part of the disciples and the public. Something of that worldly public judgment is affirmed in the vindication of Jesus.

Hannah Arendt has remarked that "[h]uman deeds, unless they are remembered, are the most futile and perishable things on earth."[13] The kerygma, which has its warrant in God's own justification of Jesus, saves the deeds of Jesus from oblivion and in so doing belongs itself to God's constitutive act in vindicating Jesus. At the same time, the kerygma bestows upon the deeds of Jesus the order of a life remembered. Yet the story that sets this ordered remembering in motion fixes the futility of Jesus' deeds precisely *in* the memory of him. As vindication the meaning of the resurrection presupposes that Jesus' life came to nothing in the cross, which was the final disordering of his words and deeds. Hence, the Jesus whose life came to nothing by virtue of the death he died now *is* and thus *remains* to a definite point the defeated Jesus in the story of his vindication. It is essential to the meaning of his resurrection that the futility and perishability of his deeds remain fixed in the recollection of his life and death, and that this recollection preserves as well the particular form that these remembered words and deeds assumed in history. A genuine theology of the resurrection keeps vigil over the moment when every deed of Jesus was bound for destruction.

---

[13] "The Concept of History: Ancient and Modern," in Hannah Arendt, *Between Past and Future: Six Exercises in Political Thought* (New York: Viking, 1961) 84.

II

> ... Jesus' resurrection does found history. And we must view that history in realistic rather than idealistic terms. We must see it as history in an unredeemed world.
>
> Jon Sobrino[14]

Vindication is an inherently narrative idea and thus makes sense only "in time." The kind of time in which it speaks may be real or imaginary, depending on whether its linguistic referent is external or internal to the narrative in which it is found. To apply the word "vindication" to an historical person is to presuppose that its temporal aspect belongs in this case to real as opposed to imaginary time. To whatever degree the idea of the resurrection eludes historical categories, the justification of the historical Jesus that it signifies takes place in historical time, or else it is not really *his* justification.

The philosophical assumptions of modernity have made all talk about the resurrection as an "event," together with the very notion of an "act of God," problematic. The difficulty this poses for hermeneutics is the problem of how to do justice to the "eventfulness" that is essential to the New Testament understanding of the resurrection in a manner that is meaningful on post-Enlightenment assumptions. This problem is only partially resolved by construing the divine word signified by the resurrection as itself the "event" (a *Sprachereignis*) or "act of God" about which resurrection talk is really speaking. To be sure, the resurrection has this "word"-character, and it does so precisely as the vindication of Jesus. But if the notion of God's action in nature and history is "mythological" (in Bultmann's sense), the idea of a divine communication or "address" is no less so. If it seems to us otherwise, that only shows that we still tend to operate with idealist assumptions about the essentially world-transcending nature of ideas. But it is just this sort of dualism that the proclamation of God's justification of Jesus does not allow. Accordingly, if we cannot yet speak meaningfully of the "historicity" of the resurrection, we must nonetheless speak of its "historicality." For the divine word of the resurrection as vindication presupposes God's activity in history to change the fate of Jesus of Nazareth.

---

[14] *Christology at the Crossroads: A Latin American Approach* (Maryknoll, NY: Orbis Books, 1978) 253.

It is therefore significant that the early preachers proclaimed Jesus' vindication by saying that God had saved him from the power of death, not only that God disclosed something about Jesus that transformed their understanding of him. In fact, the transformation of Jesus is disclosing, not the other way around. Moreover, it is of equal significance that in elaborating on this salvation the early church came to speak of the resurrection as Jesus' exaltation to a position of inaugurated lordship over history and understood the gift of the Spirit as the ongoing presence of Jesus and his kingdom in the world. Considered together, from the standpoint of the ways in which they mutually define each other, the cross and the resurrection fix God's confirmation of Jesus as historical vindication constituted in that ongoing process (*processus iustificationis!*) by which God extends the kingdom in the world.

Historical vindication means that certain historical actions put into question or radically frustrated in history turn out to have been right by becoming true through the course of historical events. In history things that are "at stake" are really so in the moment of question, and things rejected, disconfirmed or destroyed suffer these fates in truth. The only things that can change such facts are new facts, which, to be sure, may well include the revision of old facts through reinterpretation, since history is moved and constituted by both words and deeds. Hence, historical vindication is always more than revelation, and the element of revelation that belongs to it is the new perception created by the vindicating events themselves. Thus it combines "discovery" and "reversal"[15] in a particular way. Historical vindication is revelation through eventful reversal.

The signification of the resurrection, its pointing to the historicality of the cross and the life that found its terminus there, devolves back upon the resurrection itself as a sign of its own historicality. The resurrection singles out the cross as the starting point for the interpretation of Jesus of Nazareth and in so doing begins the process of reflection that leads to an interpretation of the resurrection itself in the light of the cross. That interpretation, in which the cross stamps the resurrection with its own "this-worldliness," does not mean that the resurrection turns out to be nothing other than the proclamation of the cross.[16] Such a conclusion

---

[15] "A discovery is best when it occurs together with a reversal" (Aristotle, *Poetics*, 1452a).

[16] See, for instance, Pierre Bühler, *Kreuz und Eschatologie: Eine Auseinandersetzung mit der politischen Theologie, im Anschluss an Luthers theologia crucis* (Tübingen: J. C. B. Mohr [Paul Siebeck], 1981): "Die Auferstehungsbotschaft ist nichts anderes als die Proklamation des Kreuzes" (376).

would break the logic of the resurrection as vindication. What the interpretation of the resurrection in the light of the cross does mean is that the element of turning or change that belongs to the idea of vindication must be commensurate with the nature of the cross as the defeat of Jesus.

That defeat can be understood only by reconstructing the link between Jesus' execution and his ministry. In this space I can do no more than sketch my own assumptions about this relation, although at a later point I shall add an argument "from the resurrection" to reinforce the general tenor of what follows here. I take it to be virtually certain that Jesus regarded the powers of the kingdom as being already at work in the world and particularly in his own ministry. Whatever views he held about the end of history and the future of the kingdom at some final consummation of history, he preached the presence of the emergent kingdom in his own time.[17] I regard it as equally certain that Jesus' vision of the kingdom was basically prophetic in character. It called for the radical transformation of persons and society; hence his ministry entailed a threat to both the priestly aristocracy and ultimately the Romans as well, since it called for a reordering of a society that lay largely within their power and perceived rights.[18] For this transformation Jesus labored and for this he also died; the cross of Jesus is a sure clue to the social and political horizons of his work. Accordingly, the turning or change signified by Jesus' vindication must be regarded as historical and not only noetic; the "historic" power of the resurrection is decisive not only for so-called "inner history," but also for the "outer" course of events and the socially interlocking threads of public and private life in which "human persons grow out into the world and the world grows into them."[19] Only in this way is the vindication of Jesus adequate to the cross as the predicament of the historical Jesus.

---

[17] Space here does not permit me to defend this assertion. I will mention, however, that in my judgment a persuasive case has recently been made by Bruce J. Malina for understanding the indisputably authentic statement, "The kingdom of heaven is at hand," as implying the present emergence of the kingdom, not its imminence. See Malina, "Christ and Time: Swiss or Mediterranean?" *CBQ* 51 (1989) 1-31.

18 I find, for example, the work of Richard A. Horsley (*Jesus and the Spiral of Violence: Popular Jewish Resistance in Roman Palestine* [San Francisco: Harper & Row, 1987]) and Marcus Borg (*Jesus: A New Vision* [San Francisco: Harper & Row, 1987]) to be particularly convincing on this point. See also Borg's earlier work, *Conflict, Holiness and Politics in the Teaching of Jesus* (New York: E. Mellen, 1984).

19 Jürgen Moltmann, "Love, Death, Eternal Life: Theology of Hope—the Personal Side," in *Love: The Foundation of Hope* (ed. Frederic B. Burnham et al.; San Francisco: Harper & Row, 1988) 14.

"Human deeds, unless they are remembered, are the most futile and perishable things on earth." The early preachers did not set out to save Jesus' works from the obscurity of forgottenness. But one of the most significant effects of their preaching was the process by which Jesus' memory was kept alive in a certain way for posterity. Their preaching of Jesus along with what Justin would later call "the memoirs of the apostles" bequeathed a particular memory of Jesus to the world. This is the Jesus of our canonical gospels, the Jesus whose story is told from the vantage point of his execution by the Romans and resurrection-vindication by God. This Jesus belongs as much to the world as to the church. He is a world-historical figure of public collective memory, especially in the western world.

That Jesus belongs to the world in this sense is evident from the fact that it is not only Christians who lay claim to him. Milan Machoveč, for example, can recommend Jesus to atheists committed to world transforming Marxist praxis:

> [The Marxist] also experiences situations not infrequently in which he would rather suffer injustice than contribute to it. And so he stands on the threshold where the deepest mystery of the New Testament also appears no longer to atheists as mythology but as something radically real [*etwas radikal Aktuelles*]. An atheist who thus takes his own life and work for his beloved movement really seriously, in 'dead-earnest'... can recognize that it was one of the greatest moments of destiny in the history of humanity and human nature, as Peter discovered—although there was no external-apocalyptic miracle at Golgotha, no "Deus-ex-machina" experience, only a tormented actual dying on the cross— that Jesus is still victor.[20]

Machoveč's Jesus "reigns from the tree," to borrow the words of an early Christian interpretation of Psalm 96:1 (LXX).[21] He has won out in history over his accusers; for his life and labor, history itself has shown, did not end with his death but found their true historic beginning precisely there. Each time the world acts in accord with an authentic memory of his death as the outcome of the way he lived, the crucified Jesus enjoys a certain this-worldly vindication.

---

[20] *Jesus für Atheisten* (Berlin/Stuttgart: Kreuz, 1972) 23-24. Chapters 2-6 of this book were originally written in Czechoslovak, but the passage which I have here translated into English is from the first chapter, written originally in German.

[21] See Justin, *Dialogue with Trypho* 73.1.

The Salvation of Jesus

We ought to note two things about *this* "justified Jesus." First, he is a Jesus whose vindication is not clearly tied to the teleology of his own labors, since the distanciation that an account of historical effect must presuppose[22] looses that teleology from the process by which the memory of Jesus becomes historic. Hence, the victory of Jesus through *memoria* and the deeds it inspires (or at least justifies) turns out to be of a highly ambiguous sort. Nevertheless, this ambiguity does not mean that the divine vindication of Jesus has nothing to do with such worldly vindications. For the second thing to note about Machovec's Jesus is that although he does not appear to be in any necessary sense the resurrected Jesus—unless his "resurrection" is taken to mean nothing other than his victory in the cross—he is nonetheless the product of a way of remembering Jesus that took its decisive clue from the resurrection. He is not in that case victor through the cross alone, but he has in fact been delivered over to the memory of history by the resurrection. The question, therefore, is how we are to construe history's own vindications of Jesus within the horizon of God's vindication of Jesus in history.

This question concerns most fundamentally the relationship between the event of God's vindication of Jesus, which sets in motion and sustains certain processes in history—not least of which is the church—and the various ways in which "history" has vindicated Jesus by converting him into a world-historical figure who continues to shape history as "the only completely valid, completely convincing experience Western mankind [has] ever had with active love of goodness as the inspiring principle of all actions."[23] The words are once again from Hannah Arendt and imply her own judgment about the vindication through *memoria* of Jesus' frail deeds and the historic significance of that memory for revolution and *its* deeds. Whatever one may make of Arendt's own views on this point, the significant thing for our purposes is that this memory enters history by virtue of God's vindication of Jesus. It is itself an essential public aspect of the historicality of the resurrection. Moreover, to recognize this compels one to consider the sense in which the work of this memory in history is, at least in part, God's own ongoing work in history by which the vindication of Jesus assumes concrete shape in the world.

---

[22] See Paul Ricoeur, *Interpretation Theory: Discourse and the Surplus of Meaning* (Fort Worth, TX: Texas Christian University Press, 1976); Hans-Georg Gadamer, *Truth and Method* (New York: Seabury, 1975) esp. 235-341.

[23] Hannah Arendt, *On Revolution* (New York: Viking, 1963) 76-77.

Then there is Bonhoeffer's intriguing idea of "unconscious Christianity," in which it is not the public memory of Jesus but a form of active public struggle that constitutes the locus of God's own active presence in history, even if that presence is not recognized as such because it takes the shape of the "messianic sufferings of God."[24] Can one speak here of a vindication in history of the crucified Messiah? Only if these sufferings achieve something in history, perhaps that "something more of the meaning of our life's broken fragments," which Bonhoeffer himself wished to *see*,[25] perhaps certain historical realizations of the kingdom that a "this-worldly" redemption[26] ought to entail concretely.

"For the Jew the Christian is a heedless fellow who in an unredeemed world affirms that somehow or other redemption has taken place." One might respond to Buber's charge by disputing his understanding of what counts as redemption or by insisting that the statement "has taken place" does not do justice to the aspect of "eschatological reservation" that belongs to an authentic understanding of the gospel. Both answers have something to commend them, but to regard either or both of these answers as adequate to Buber's challenge is to miss the warrant for that challenge in the story of God's justification of Jesus itself. The nature of God's vindication of Jesus specifies the nature of redemption and thus defines the relation of redemption to history in a manner that requires one to look for redemption *in* history at least in some sense on Buber's own terms. To the public aspect of Jesus' humiliation there must correspond a public aspect of God's vindicating action to save him. To the political aspects of Jesus' defeat in history there must correspond certain political aspects of the divine reversal that grants him victory. Otherwise the resurrection is not the justification of the crucified Jesus, whose *problem* is centered in the world and its history and whose victory must include in some sense the sort of redemption that the disciples, along with the rest of the Jews who witnessed the termination of Jesus and his cause, along with Buber himself, would regard as redemption. Something of the public worldly judgment about the crucified King of

---

[24] Dietrich Bonhoeffer, *Letters and Papers from Prison* (enlarged ed.; ed. Eberhard Bethge; New York: Macmillan, 1972). Bonhoeffer takes up "unconscious Christianity" on pages 373, 380, 394, and the "messianic suffferings of God" on pages 361-362 and 369-370. "Unconscious Christianity" ought to be interpreted in the light of what Bonhoeffer has to say on the topic of "Christ, Reality and Good" in his *Ethics* (New York: Macmillan, 1955) 188-213.

[25] Ibid., 16. In "After Ten Years: A Reckoning Made at New Year 1943."

[26] Ibid., 336.

the Jews, with its informing presuppositions about what the triumph of Jesus would have meant, is ratified in God's own confirmation of Jesus.

This last conclusion provides a certain confirmation of the "prophetic-messianic" interpretation of the historical Jesus sketched earlier. At the same time it brings us to the heart of the meaning of the resurrection as the salvation of Jesus. If God's vindication of the crucified Jesus "agrees with the world" that the primary meaning of Jesus' execution is the dashing of all redemptive hopes fixed on him (Luke 24:21), it also reveals something of which this worldly verdict has no knowledge. It discloses a link between the cross and the kingdom in history. It was Jesus' *work* that was at stake in his trial and execution. In Jesus' death his "claim" about the active presence of God's kingdom in his ministry suffered apparent disconfirmation. The light of the resurrection shows this disconfirmation to have been mere appearance—the "finger of God" (Luke 11:20) really was at work in Jesus' ministry. But in lifting the veil of appearance that shrouds the truth of this claim, the resurrection also discloses something else: that the kingdom itself suffered destruction in the cross.

The resurrection reveals that the mundane tragedy for Jesus and his followers is really a great, yawning abyss in which the hope of this world disappears without a trace. Such a statement risks giving the impression that the cross itself is *not* a saving work of God but an obstacle to salvation. But what it is really meant to show is that the cross cannot be adequately grasped in its character as a saving work of God unless it is first of all seen to be the catastrophe, in reality and not simply in appearance, that the primordial meaning of the resurrection presupposes it to be. It is the resurrection taken in its primordial sense as divine vindication that draws the cross into the center of the gospel story and in so doing converts the primary meaning of Jesus' death in history into the primordial presupposition of the evangelical proclamation of that death. Accordingly, an authentic *theologia crucis* ("theology of the cross") must entail an affirmation of the tragic character of the cross as the presupposition of what it asserts about the divine wisdom and power of the cross. Otherwise it is not true to the specific history of Jesus of Nazareth, whose cross put a real end to his labor for the kingdom.

Neither the old Reformation idea that the kingdom is hidden in the world under the cross (*regnum cruce tectum*) nor the celebrated paradox of the "already but not yet" is fully adequate to describe the relation of the kingdom to the cross disclosed in God's salvation of Jesus from the power of death. In this relation the springs of all world-transforming Christian "enthusiasm" are found and at the same time radically qualified. The resurrection is the life of the kingdom against the cross and guarantees the possibility that the kingdom will take concrete shape in history without any limit in scope—except the limit of the cross. That limit is at once less confining and more brutal than most traditional ways of conceiving the possibilities for redemption in history. It is less confining because the cross interposes itself into the *midst* of Jesus' labor for the kingdom; it does not restrict Jesus' possibilities from the outset. Nor is it the last word, since the resurrection of Jesus means the salvation of his work in history. In the story of Jesus' vindication, the cross acquires a primordial location "in between" the kingdom's historical life in the ministry of Jesus and its salvation in the resurrection of Jesus. Thus there is space in the story of Jesus for the building up of the kingdom in history, a "Galilean spring"[27] before the winter of the cross.

Yet this "space," as a concrete opening in historical life, is bounded upon all sides by the threat of the cross, which signifies not only the struggle of the kingdom against the powers of sin and death but also the ever present possibility that any given manifestation of the kingdom may vanish as surely and brutally as Jesus lost the Spirit and the kingdom on the cross (Mark 15:34). Thus it turns out that the disjunction preserved in the story of Jesus' vindication is located between two stories: Jesus' venture to change the world, which belonged to a prophetic-messianic narrative framework and took shape as a project in history, and the story of his vindication by God, which presupposes the failure of Jesus' venture, the abortion of his kingdom project. This particular disjunction determines the primary meanings of the cross and resurrection for the kingdom in history. The resurrection summons faith that the life of the kingdom has entered into history, and it justifies no reduction of present possibilities for the kingdom to what human beings may regard as realistic based on their own historical experience and memories. The resurrection guarantees that the kingdom will manifest itself in personal, corporate, and historical life; the cross reveals that even should the kingdom grow and expand until it fills the whole world, that growth is not inexorable and whatever it achieves is vulnerable at any point to reversal and eclipse. The kingdom lives on both sides of the

---

[27] This expression is Adolf Jülicher's: "Ich könnte den Herrn nicht begreifen und also auch nicht lieben, wenn nicht seinem jerusalemischen Todesostern ein galiläischer Frühling voranging, sonnige Tage mit begeisterter Aussicht von hohen Bergen. An seinem Anfang muss eine Periode seliger Siegesgewissheit stehen, eine Zeit, wo er Anklang und Liebe fand, wo das Volk gerade sich zu ihm drängte und jedes Wort von seinen Lippen entzückt verschlang" (*Die Gleichnisreden Jesu* [2 vols in one; Darmstadt: Wissenschaftliche Buchgesellschaft, 1963] 1.144-145).

cross, but Christ's death in the middle of the life of the kingdom discloses the kingdom's fundamental instability in the world.

The fact that we still live in an unredeemed world ought to be interpreted with reference to this instability of the kingdom and not primarily in terms of the kingdom's "hiddenness" in history. The kingdom is not always hidden in the world, even if its presence is always subject to dispute.[28] Latin American theologians of liberation speak of *historizaciones* of the kingdom and point, for example, to the movements among the *comunidades de base* in Brazil and elsewhere as the beginnings of that spiritual labor (or Christian "praxis") by which the life of the kingdom is assuming concrete shape in their history. Are visible, if inchoate, *historizaciones* of the kingdom really emerging in Latin America? Is it legitimate to point to aspects of an historical movement or its inner dynamic as an "objectification" of kingdom life? Was the social order constructed by the Jesuits among the Guarani Indians in the area of South America now known as *Misiones* in any sense the realization of kingdom community that many European Christians took it to be? Or was it rather just another chapter in dehumanizing socialist experimentation, as Michael Novak contends?[29] Was John Chrysostom's plan to "make a heaven on earth" by freeing the slaves and feeding the poor of Constantinople not only unrealistic but also a misapplication of theological categories?[30] Did the Puritans make the same mistake when they conceived the task of their American experiment as "the planting of a new heaven and a new earth?"[31] Was the experience of *freedom* as the world-changing discovery of the "American Revolution" really a constitutive moment in the worldly life of God's ongoing labor in the world to "make and keep the life of man human,"[32] or ought one to attend instead to certain moments of

---

[28] See Jürgen Moltmann, *The Church in the Power of the Spirit: A Contribution to Messianic Ecclesiology* (New York: Harper & Row, 1977) 190: "In history... God rules in a disputed and hidden way."

[29] See Novak, *Will It Liberate? Questions About Liberation Theology* (New York/Mahwah: Paulist, 1986) 184, 186-88.

[30] *Hom. in Act.* 11.3. See Rainer Kampling, "'Have We Not Then Made a Heaven of Earth?' Rich and Poor in the Early Church," *Concilium* 187 (1986) 51-62.

[31] These words are from a sermon delivered in 1641 by Puritan parliamentary preacher Stephen Marshall, cited by Richard Shaull as a way of capturing the self-understanding of the Puritans in carrying out their English experiment. Shaull attributes the same self-understanding to the Puritans in their American venture. See Shaull, "The Death and Resurrection of the American Dream," in Gustavo Gutiérrez and Richard Shaull, *Liberation and Change* (ed. Ronald H. Stone; Atlanta: John Knox, 1977) 106.

[32] "Hacer y mantener human la vida del hombre." Paul Lehmann, "¿Que está haciendo Dios en el mundo?" *Caudernos Teológicos* 10/4 (1961) 243-68.

solidarity and breakthrough in Marxist revolutionary praxis, to which the coiner himself of the formula just cited is wont to point, as the more promising modern historical *loci* in which to look for signs of the transfiguration of politics by the living Spirit of Jesus?[33]

The foregoing hodgepodge of rhetorical questions scarcely begins to expose the complexity entailed in any effort to discern *historizaciones* of the kingdom in the world. But the point is, first, simply that the story of the vindication of Jesus requires both this task of discernment and the "works of the kingdom" that correspond to it, and, second, that this same story contains implicitly certain criteria for both this discernment and the Christian self-understanding under which these works ought to be carried out.

III

> Time present and time past
> Are both perhaps present in time future,
> And time future contained in time past.
> If all time is eternally present,
> All time is unredeemable.
> ....
> Only through time time is conquered.
>   T. S. Elliot,
>   "Burnt Norton"[34]

In the course of exploring the primordial meaning of the cross, I have stressed the public-historical horizon of Jesus' work and death in order to make a beginning toward defending the thesis that the kingdom assumes social shape in our world and is therefore deeply political in character. This no doubt risks the impression that forms of love and righteousness that do not break the surface of "public history" ought not to be counted as forms of present kingdom life, when in fact the correlation of the private and the public, which are always dialectically related, is one of the constructive tasks of the kind of discernment I have in mind. But even more central to the aims of this essay has been the attempt to delineate the ways in which the cross and the kingdom are linked in the story of the salvation of Jesus of Nazareth. I have endeavored to show that there is a primordial relation of the kingdom to the cross and

---

[33] Lehmann, *The Transfiguration of Politics* (New York: Harper & Row, 1975).

[34] *Four Quartets* (San Diego/New York/London: Harcourt, Brace, Jovanovich, 1943 and 1971) 13 and 16.

The Salvation of Jesus

resurrection that comes to light when one thinks through to the end the primordial relation of Jesus to his own vindication by God.

Yet there remain two further forms of interrelationship among these three primary realities of Christian faith (kingdom, cross, and resurrection). The second form is disclosed in the Pauline preaching of the cross as the salvation of the world. If the primordial meaning of Jesus' resurrection is the salvation of the kingdom from the power of death, this second interpretation of Jesus' death finds the birth of the kingdom already in the cross itself. Hence, the question of the relation of these two "theologies of the cross" is posed. Then there is a third fundamental meaning of the cross, its resolution in the absolute future of the resurrection. If the second meaning of the cross has always threatened to eclipse the first, this third sign of the cross (and the resurrection) has an even greater tendency to relativize the first two, if only because it is exceedingly difficult to construct an "account" of ultimate salvation in which the absolute value of the eschaton does not drain all value from that which is penultimate, whether of life or death, and thus render them less "real." Against the threat of such final monopolies of meaning and value, and as a way of insisting that the final meaning of the resurrection must be worked out in faithfulness to its first meaning, I wish to assert the first meaning of the cross and the inviolable order of values that it prescribes, beginning with the "this-worldliness" of the resurrection and the primordial relation of faith to history disclosed in God's salvation of Jesus and his kingdom.

18

What Do We Really Mean When We Say "God sent his son..."?

Eduard Schweizer [1]

Paul Meyer emphasized, in his inaugural lecture at Princeton Theological Seminary, the "this-worldliness" of the crucifixion of Jesus in the sense of a "mundane," though not a "profane," event in which "the actions and the presence of the living God and his transcendence" can be seen in faith.[2] In the resurrection God "acknowledged" "this crucified, this discredited Jesus," "not an other-worldly Jesus." It is he who is "made the right clue and the criterion for discerning God's true intentions," and "the transcendence and authority of God himself now underscore and authorize that this-worldliness."[3] Yet when Gal 4:4-5;

---

[1] Eduard Schweizer is Professor Emeritus of New Testament at the University of Zürich, Switzerland.

[2] Paul W. Meyer, "The This-Worldliness of the New Testament," *Princeton Seminary Bulletin* 2 N.S. (1979) 221. Paul Meyer's sense of responsibility to rework what he has formulated once is so distinguished that I am almost ashamed to present an essay that is still open to many new thoughts and not to be compared with his lecture with its style polished almost to perfection. However, this is my fifty-fifth contribution to a *Festschrift;* hence, Paul may, smilingly, excuse me.

[3] Ibid., 227.

God sent his son...

Rom 8:3; John 3:16-17[4]; and 1 John 4:9 declare that "God sent his son in order to (save the world)," it looks as if Paul and John spoke exactly of an "otherworldly Jesus," a divine being foreign to this world though living in it for a short time. Is this what the phrase means?[5]

I. The Old Testament, Judaism, and Hellenism

1.1 The Septuagint often speaks of God "sending" Moses (Exod 3:10, etc.) or a prophet (Isa 6:8; Jer 1:7, etc.).[6] What do the authors want to convey to the reader? In Exod 3:11 Moses answers, "Who am I that I should go...?" Isaiah cries, "I am lost, for I am a man of unclean lips!" (6:5). Jeremiah declares, "I do not know how to speak" (1:6; cf. Amos 7:14). Thus, "being sent by God" is a linguistic expression for the fact that the prophet could in no way fulfill his task by his own faculties, that whatever he says or does is a gift given to him through a specific act of God. Even when the human inability of the prophet is not mentioned, it is quite clear that he proclaims what he himself could never imagine: God's unexpected judgment or salvation (Jer 26:5-6; Isa 61:1; etc.). Thus, the prophet legitimized his message by attributing it to God's "sending him." In no way does the phrase suggest that Moses or the prophets were in heaven prior to their work on earth. It means merely that God gave them a specific mission and guided them in a special way (before and) in the completion of that mission.

The same is true when *Syb. Or.* 3:286 describes the coming rule of a Ptolemaic king, who is seen as a savior figure: "The heavenly God will send a king; he will judge every man in blood and bright fire."[7]

1.2 Stoic and Cynic philosophers call themselves "messenger," "scout," and "herald of the gods"[8] "sent" by Zeus,[9] although we cannot

---

[4] Ἔδωκεν is interchangeable with ἀπέστειλεν (v 17), also in John 14:16, 26 (referring to the paraclete). Cf. below note 15 (Wis 9:17).

[5] Cf. Eduard Schweizer, "Zum religionsgeschichtlichen Hintergrund der 'Sendungsformel' Gal 4,4f; Röm 8,3f; Joh 3,16f; 1 Joh 4,9," *ZNW* 57 (1966) 199-210; reprinted in *idem, Beiträge zur Theologie des Neuen Testaments*, (Zürich: Zwingli-Verlag, 1970) 83-95.

[6] Ἀποστέλλειν 44 + 12 x, ἐξαποστέλλειν 9 + 3 x.

[7] Πέμπειν. On the Jewish character of *Sibylline Oracles*, Book 3, see the introduction by J. J. Collins in *The Old Testament Pseudepigrapha*, vol. 1 (ed. J. H. Charlesworth; Garden City, NY: Doubleday, 1983) 355-357.

[8] ἄγγελος, κατάσκοπος, κῆρυξ (Epictetus *Diss.* 3.22.69).

[9] Epictetus *Diss.* 3.23.46; 4.8.31; and 1.24.6 using ἀποστέλλειν; 3.22.56,59 using καταπέμπειν.

be quite sure whether this is their own terminology or that of Epictetus when he refers to them.[10] In the cult of the Emperor, the title "Savior" (in the Orient even "Savior God") is certainly known in the time of the New Testament.[11] The term "to send," however, is not usual. More typically, the savior is spoken of as "given" or "created" by "providence" or "the universe,"[12] and Plutarch can write that "the mediator of all (nations) came from God."[13] In all these passages there is no hint that the philosopher or emperor dwelt in heaven before his earthly existence. They only say that it was the will of the deity that a man became philosopher or emperor, and that, therefore, God granted him what he needed for his office. Never do we find a story about the call of God, as with the prophets, let alone the image of a descent from heaven, except perhaps in Plutarch. In a more mythical way the emperor may be said to be born from a mother visited by a deity or to have descended from a divine ancestor.[14]

2.1 There is another concept of God's sending when the Septuagint speaks of God "sending" his angel, spirit, word (Logos) or wisdom (Sophia).[15] Here the "envoy" of God certainly lives with him in heaven before being sent, and again after returning to him from earth. The object of the "sending" is not a human but a transcendent being, whether imagined as a personal appearance, as in the case of an angel, or an impersonal one, as with the spirit or the word. And wisdom is

---

[10] Epictetus knew the "Galileans" (*Diss.* 4.7.6) and speaks of the one "who adopts the attitude of mind of the man who has been baptized" as a true Jew (2.9.20). He might have been familiar with some of the Jewish or Christian terms. Cf., however, 3.2 below.

[11] Plutarch *Demetrius* 10, cited in *Hellenistic Religions* (ed. F. C. Grant; New York: Liberal Arts Press, 1953) 64-65; Inscription of Halicarnassus (CAGIBM IV nr. 894).

[12] In the oft-quoted Inscription of Priene (OGIS II 458.33-36), "Providence has created Augustus by...for us and our posterity," the pivotal phrase "giving" (or even "sending") "the savior" is mere conjecture!

[13] Διαλλακτής (Alex. Fort. 6.329c: "He believed that he came from God as...a governor and mediator for all [probably nations or people, not things]").

[14] See Gerhard Delling, παρθένος, *TDNT*, vol. 5, 830; cf. NC texts in *Hellenistic Religions*, 63-69 (Demetrius Poliorcetes and Ptolemaeus V Epiphanes). Vergil *Eclogue* 4.49; Eduard Norden, *Die Geburt des Kindes* (Leipzig: Teubner, 1924) 75-76.

[15] Angel: ἀποστέλλειν (15) + ἐξαποστέλλειν (3); spirit (3 + 0); word(3 + 0x), wisdom (0 + 1x). Remarkable is Tobit 12:14-15, "God sent me..., I am (ἐγώ εἰμι) Raphael." Πέμπειν connected with "wisdom" and "spirit" occurs in Wis 9:10,17: "Send (ἐξαπόστειλον) her (wisdom) from the holy heavens, and from the throne of your glory send (πέμψον) her...You gave (ἔδωκας) wisdom and sent (ἔπεμψας) your holy spirit from the highest."

conceived now in one form, now in the other. Nevertheless, although the "envoy" is said to be sent to a particular person, it is clearly subordinate to God (like the angel), or it is not to be conceived as really separated from God, who rules the world by his spirit and speaks to all creation in his word.

This last point becomes even clearer in the Jewish texts of the first century B.C.E., which no longer dare to speak directly of the transcendent God acting in our world. Accordingly, they circumscribe the subject of God's activity: "There is one God and his *power* is revealed in all things, since his activity fills the whole world" (*Letter of Aristeas* 132; cf. 157). Obviously, the interest of Aristeas is to affirm belief in God's active (creative and preservative) presence in the world without equating God and the world in any way. Ezechiel the Tragedian describes "the divine Logos radiating from the bush."[16] He avoids making the direct statement of Exod 3:4 that *God* spoke from the bush, lest God be identified with the voice of nature. And yet, simply speaking of God's "activity" in the world or in the hearts of human beings is not enough. This specific act of God's—at a specific place and in a specific time—must become visible: it "radiates" from the bush when God's word is speaking to Moses. The most interesting document is fragment 2 of Aristobulus,[17] which deals with the anthropomorphic imagery of the Bible. Aristobulus interprets God's "hand" as the divine "power" (δύναμις), God's "building" (στάσις) as the "creation" (κατασκευή) of the world, his "descending" as his "energy" (ἐνέργεια) working on earth. This activity of God is not locally limited (τοπική), since God is everywhere. And yet, it became visible at a specific place and time because God indeed descended. Aristobulus wants to avoid the misunderstanding that would substitute a timeless divine being everywhere for an act of God. Though God does not act in a human way, with hands and feet, the imagery indicates clearly a specific act at a specific time.[18]

---

[16] *Fragmenta Pseudepigraphorum* (ed. A. M. Denis; Leiden: E. J. Brill, 1970) 211.5 (=Eusebius *Praep. Ev.* 9.29.8).

[17] Ibid., 217-221 (=Eusebius *Praep. Ev.* 8.10.1-17).

[18] Philo is much closer to Hellenistic thoughts: "For to suppose that the Deity approaches or departs, goes down or goes up..., is an impiety which may be said to transcend the bounds of the ocean or the universe itself....For we all know that when a person comes down he must leave one place and occupy another. But God fills all things.... To be everywhere and nowhere is his property.... None of the terms which express movement...are applicable to God in his aspect of pure being" (*Conf. Ling.* 134-36, 139 [LCL translation]).

This means that even in an apology elucidating the sense of primitive images which have to be relinquished, Aristobulus feels the necessity of a language that retains the conventions of God acting at specific times in specific places and in a historically contingent way. Accordingly, when explaining what the "hand of God" means, he chooses, typically, the picture of a king "sending" (ἐξαποστέλλειν) his army.

2.2 There are some parallels in the Hellenistic literature. Plutarch interprets the mythical idea of Hermes coming to the world by stating that it actually speaks of the Logos.[19] As the Logos, "Hermes" creates the world as the father of Horos, the "image" (εἰκών) of "the intellectual world" (νοητὸς κόσμος), which has been corrupted by materialization (ὕλη, σωματικόν). The Logos is the divine "nature" or "idea" (εἶδος), the "emanation" (ἀπόρροια) of God into the world.[20] Unlike the Jewish authors, he describes a "streaming" of God into Nature and wants to express the truth that the world and all that happens in it are not simply the product of a blind fate or casual happening but are meaningful and even divine.

3.1 In the time of the New Testament, the two ways of using the motif of "sending" are combined. "Sending" as both a legitimation of a human messenger as authorized by God, whether prophet or philosopher, and "sending" as an expression of God's contingent or continual influence on the world, its nature and history, are both evident, for example, in Wisdom of Solomon. In Wis 9:10, 17 we find the request that God "send" (ἐξαποστέλλειν, πέμπειν) his "wisdom" and his "spirit" "from the holy heavens and the throne of his glory," and chapters 10-11 give an account of how this happened in Israel with the fathers, beginning with Adam and Moses. Thus, it is in the biblical history that this transpires again and again, and it occurs all the more when the faithful Israelite prays to his God. Only in Wis 12:1, which concludes the enumeration of examples in chapter 11, does the idea of God's spirit living in all things appear at the margin, so to speak, and probably as a "modern" fashion of expression in a Greek-speaking world. When Wis 7:26 describes wisdom as "radiance of the invisible light," "mirror," and "image" of God's "energy" and "love," that is all Hellenistic language. And yet Wis 7:27 speaks of God's creative power, which enters afresh from generation to generation into "holy souls" to

---

[19] *Is. et Os.* 55 (373cd).
[20] Ibid., 53-59 (372-375); cf. *Quaest. Conv.* 8.2-3 (719e).

make them "friends of God and prophets," and the emphasis lies on the Spirit of God speaking to and through the prophets.

Wisdom of Solomon does not reconcile these two views of God's relation to the world. Does God speak and act in certain persons that he selects, be they prophets only or all pious people, or does he speak and act in the whole of nature? Or is it that he does the former in a more distinctive way than the latter? Clearly the author tries to say more than simply that some people, more sensitive than others (whether by nature or by divine endowment), are able to hear God's voice and to see his actions in the whole course of nature and history. He underlines the freedom of God to grant experiences to whomever he chooses. Thus God "sends" his wisdom and spirit at specific occasions, such as in answer to prayer.

3.2 A most interesting text is found in chapter 16 of Cornutus' *Theologiae Graecae Compendium*:[21]

> Hermes may well be the Logos that the gods sent to us from heaven, making man alone a rational creature (λογικός).... He is called strong (σῶκος), because he is the savior of the families.... He came into being not to do evil or damage but rather to save.... He is traditionally referred to as herald (κῆρυξ) of the gods...., because through an understandable voice he signifies the meaning of a word to the ears..., as messenger (ἄγγελος), because we recognize the will of the gods from the thoughts that are given to us (or: implanted in us) according to reason (λόγος).... They say that Hermes has been born to Zeus by Maia ("mummy"), thus suggesting again that reason (λόγος) is the creature of theory and research.... Because he is one and the same, common to all people and all gods... they rightly declare Hermes to be "the common one" (τὸ κοινόν).

The language is that of Stoic and Cynic philosophers (cf. 1.2) and speaks of an angel, a messenger or herald sent by the gods. The sending, however, is no longer the important thing, being mentioned only in a relative clause. Cornutus does not distinguish certain special persons, true philosophers specifically sent by God, from all other people. He makes an anthropological statement touching on humanity everywhere and in all times, with only minor differences. The "sending" of Hermes

---

[21] (Leipzig, 1881) 20-24 (translation mine).

has, obviously, "never happened but is always,"[22] which means nothing more than that human reason is divine, being the same power or life as that of the gods. We cannot be sure whether Cornutus believes in gods that are other than the innermost selves of human beings. His problem is the difference between human beings and the gods, and perhaps he thinks that persons who possess the nature of the gods in their reason become gods wholly only after death (and with some postmortem purifications).[23]

4. Doubtless, there has been quite some cross-fertilization between Judaism and Hellenism. Wisdom 12:1, on the one hand, and Cornutus' mythological language, on the other, prove that. The author of Wisdom equates, illogically, the event of God's revelation to a specific prophet with God's creative power in all human beings and all things. And Cornutus equates the human ability to think rationally, the logos which human beings share in common with the gods, with the mythical event of the sending of Hermes from heaven. The hermeneutical problem is to see what is implied in these statements and how important it is to the author (or his readers). It may be that some truths are presupposed as going without saying, such as the creation of the world by God and the oneness of God in the New Testament or the existence of gods and their acts in primeval time in some Hellenistic writings. It may also be that the same truths are no longer held at all, and that what one encounters in the examples from Wisdom and Cornutus are merely traditional ways of speaking that are no longer meaningful or carry very different meanings from what they once meant. In this case, such conventional ways of speaking may be abandoned by some as obsolete and misleading or retained by others as nonetheless useful in expressing one side of the truth in an especially fitting way.

II. The New Testament

5.1 In the Gospels we find the description of God as "He who sent me (Jesus)" in Mark 9:37 (par. Luke 9:48), Matt 10:40 and Luke 10:16 (Q). In each case the expression is ὁ ἀποστείλάς με. John 13:20 employs the synonymous expression ὁ πέμψάς με. All of these texts say that

---

[22] Pseudo-Sal(l)ustius, *De diis et mundo* 4.89 (p. 8.9-11 Collection des universités de France).

[23] Cf. Eduard Schweizer, "Slaves of the Elements and Worshipers of Angels: Gal 4:3,9 and Col 2:8,18,20," *JBL* 107 (1988) 458, 463. This essay supplies all the relevant texts in English translation.

whoever "receives" (or "rejects") Jesus receives (or rejects) God. The antecedent statement refers to receiving either the disciples of Jesus or a small child (an orphan).[24] The original form of the saying probably spoke of the disciples as "the little ones" of Jesus (as in Matt 10:42), which was later understood as describing small children. This shows that there was a pre-Q, pre-Markan, and pre-Johannine logion that spoke of Jesus coming to us in "the little ones" (disciples or children in need) and, probably from the beginning, also of God "who sent" Jesus and comes to us in him. In any case, the definition of Jesus as the one sent by God is rooted firmly in the tradition.

What the text emphasizes is that in our attitude toward Jesus we decide on our attitude toward God because in Jesus (and secondarily in his disciples or in some poor children) God encounters us. It does not—at least not explicitly—say more than that God speaks through the voice and acts of Jesus.

5.2 The parable in Mark 12:1-11 reports a sending of three servants and, finally, of "a beloved son" by the owner of a vineyard to his tenants. The parallelism of this story to the story of God sending his prophets and, finally, his own son is obvious and reveals something important about the use of this imagery. The figure of many servants and one son is fitting to describe both the relation of Jesus to the prophets and their respective relations to God.[25] Thus, the parable stresses the uniqueness of Jesus as the last envoy, one who is near to God like no other, without distinguishing the form, content, and goal of his mission from those of the other missions. It assumes that the son is closer than the servants to the lord of the vineyard, but its aim is certainly not any doctrinal statement about the status of the son prior to his mission. Even the infancy narratives of Matthew and Luke, which introduce the extraordinary (although in their time not unprecedented) story of his birth from a virgin and his genealogy, in order to emphasize the special status of Jesus over the prophets or John the Baptist, are totally silent about any existence of Jesus before his birth.

---

[24] The phrase (to receive a child) "in my name" in Mark 9:37 (par. Luke 9:48) recurs in Matt 10:42 (par. Mark 9:41) in the form (to receive a disciple of Jesus) "in the name of a disciple."

[25] Matthew 21:39 changes the sequence of "throwing out" and "killing" in order to adapt it to the crucifixion of Jesus outside the city, and Luke 20:11-12 avoids Mark's statement about the servants being killed by the tenants in order to stress the uniqueness of the death of Jesus.

6.1 The sending formulas in the Johannine literature (John 3:16, 17 and 1 John 4:9) and in Paul's letters (Gal 4:4-5 and Rom 8:3) all evidence the same pattern of speaking: "God" (and not the Lord, the Father, the Highest, etc.) is always the subject, "his son" is always the object,[26] and there is invariably a final clause that is always introduced by ἵνα ("in order that...") and not by εἰς with an infinitive ("in order to..."). The verb for "sending" varies. John 3:16 even speaks of "giving" in the first verse and "sending" in the next, suggesting that the two verbs are interchangeable in the formula (cf. also 14:16 with 14:26).[27] This shows that the description of the way in which God acts is still more or less variable. But the following features are strictly fixed: a) the verb is in the aorist (in one case the perfect) referring to a definite event in the past, b) the actor is God himself, and c) the one through whom God acts is related to him in a unique way. In these constructions "his son" is no longer mere imagery, and, although the wording does not say so explicitly, it is difficult to understand apart from assuming that Jesus was living in a filial relation to God before being sent by him.[28]

6.2 Much more important is the observation that the final clause in all five references points to Jesus' death. The redemption from the (curse of the) law (Gal 4:5) took place on the cross (Gal 3:13). In Rom 8:3, "for sin" is the usual phrase for a sin-offering (very often in Leviticus). The final clause in John 3:16 ("in order that whoever believes in him... should have eternal life") is a verbal repetition of the one in v 15, where Jesus' exaltation on the cross is interpreted. 1 John 4:9 is explained in v 10: "to be the expiation for our sins." This is the only place where the cross is not explicitly mentioned. Nevertheless, although 4:2 refers to the incarnation, ἱλασμός ("atonement") in 4:10 must, in view of 1:7-2:2; 3:16 and 5:6 focus on Jesus' death on the cross. There are different categories of thought: Jesus has become a curse for us, because the scripture curses everyone who hangs on a tree (Gal 3:13) and has in this way overcome the curse of the law; Jesus is a sin-offering like the

---

[26] In p63, A "his" is also attested for John 3:16,17.

[27] Compare further Wis 9:17 (see note 15).

[28] To interpret "his son" merely as the title of the king in the sense of Psalm 2:7 is scarcely possible, even for the original form of the phrase, and out of the question for Paul and John. Paul corrects the idea of an installation of the risen Christ into divine sonship (as God's king) in the formula of Rom 1:3-4 by adding "about his son" already at the beginning of v 3. John rejects the understanding of Jesus as the king of Israel in 6:15, and passages like 1:18; 3:16-18 or 8:58 show his view of the divine sonship of Jesus. The fact that in the case of Jesus there is none of the emphasis on inability to fulfill the commission by God that is so typical of the prophetic protest against God's demand (cf. 1.1 above) also distinguishes the call of a prophet from the sending of God's son.

animal that dies vicariously; Jesus on his cross is the exalted one to whom all people must look for salvation; and Jesus is the expiation or atonement for our sins. All these different statements emphasize that salvation is totally founded upon God's act in the crucifixion of Jesus, an act which took place outside of us and before our belief or obedience.

This means that all five sentences speak of the "worldly dimension" of God's decisive act in Jesus. They are not defining the status of Jesus before his incarnation, but are locating the presence of God himself exactly in the contingency of a "this-worldly" historical event, an event outside the walls of Jerusalem around 30 B.C.E.

III. Hermeneutical Observations

7.1 When we say today, for instance in a sermon, "God sent his son that he might save us," what do we mean? There may be hearers who have no difficulty at all making sense of such a statement. They may think that God sends his son from heaven to earth like the father who sends his son down the street to buy cigarettes. They may have a world-view that locates heaven above and the earth below and thus fits directly with the imagery of the Bible. In that case they will find the event of Christ's coming meaningful when it is expressed in this imagery. Accordingly, they will think of Jesus as an "otherworldly" being. The question is whether that is what the language of God's sending his son means—and what we mean when repeating it? Can and should we identify image and reality so directly?

No doubt we cannot simply rationalize ("demythologize") this imagery and divest it of its mystery. We have learned that images are not easily translatable. When Rev 4:6-8 tells us of four creatures around the throne of God, full of eyes all around and within, it creates a picture that is utterly fantastic and yet one that comes closer to the truth than simply calling God "omniscient." When Albrecht Dürer depicted the sharp two-edged sword issuing from the mouth of the one like a son of man (Rev 1:16; also 2:12 and 19:19), it looked rather ridiculous, and yet the image, though difficult to transfer to canvas, is so much truer than simply saying that Christ spoke to the prophet in his function as judge. When Isaiah says that "the strong hand seized him" (8:11), this expresses his real experience in some ways better than if he had said "God revealed himself to me" or "called me". Hence, there will always be something of the truth in the image of God sending his son that eludes our attempts at conceptual definition.

7.2 We have seen that all five of the Pauline and Johannine instances of the sending formula particularize what the "this-worldly" death of

Jesus on the cross means, and that their purpose is not to give information about the way in which Jesus was living before he was born. There are certain central beliefs that the New Testament does not mention but tacitly presupposes, such as the creation of the world by God or the oneness of God (see 4 above). Perhaps this is the case with the idea of the the son's pre-existence in heaven. The parallelism is not stringent. Jesus uses the Jewish teaching about the creation and preservation of all things by God as the starting point in his call for freedom from worry in the Sermon on the Mount (Matt 6:25-34); Paul employs it as the basis of his central proclamation of justification by grace (Rom 4:17) and of his equally central discussion of the problem of the law in the life of the congregation (1 Cor 10:26); and John adopts it as the fundamental beginning of his whole Gospel. Moreover, whatever we read in Paul, in John, or in one of the other Gospels about God would be inconceivable apart from the assumption of monotheism, even though Paul mentions this contrast of Jewish to Gentile faith explicitly only in his missionary preaching (1 Thess 1:9; cf. Rom 3:30; Gal 3:20; and 1 Cor 8:4-6).

The pre-existence of the son, however, is not presupposed in Paul and John in the same way that monotheism is. What Paul and John say about the sending of the son may suggest that the son was living with God before that mission, but in what form is unclear.[29] Although he might have been no more than a human being in a special or unique relation to God even before being called to his ministry (cf. Jer 1:5; Isa 49:1), Paul and John go further than this (see 1 Cor 8:6; 2 Cor 8:9; John 1:1-5; etc.). He might have existed as the love of God, as God's openness towards Israel or humankind or creation, which is perhaps what John 1:1-5 or 1 Cor 10:4 suggests. He might have existed in a "personal form" (whatever this may mean), which would fit statements like Phil 2:6-7 and John 8:58.

7.3 The verb "sent" refers back to an event in the past. This past is not a mythical time, but the time of the crucifixion of Jesus. Hence, it refers to an act of God within our time and space. At the same time, the verb describes a movement from one place to another.[30] Thus, God

---

[29] To this extent James D. G. Dunn, (*Christology in the Making: A New Testament Inquiry into the Origins of the Doctrine of the Incarnation* [Philadelphia: Westminster, 1980] 194-195, 258) is right, although Phil 2:6-7 and John 8:58 are certainly more explicit. Cf. the discussion in *Christology and Exegesis*, ed. Robert Jewett in *Semeia* 30 (1985) 74, 102, 108-111; also *TRE* 16:681 (2.4.3)

[30] This is exactly what Philo strictly disallows as a possibility for the deity (see note 18 above).

"transcends" the place of the crucifixion (and of the whole ministry of Jesus on earth); Jesus is not merely the substitute for God.[31] Finally, the verb describes God in the category of his acts (dynamically) and not in that of his "divine nature"[32] (substantially). This implies that God and the world are clearly to be distinguished and yet that they come together in a way that God alone initiates and completes, namely, in the reconciliation of God and the world in the death of Jesus.

8.1 What, then, shall we say with respect to the background of Hellenistic beliefs, which are in many ways modern beliefs? In the Bible, the imagery of angels or prophets sent by God usually emphasizes the mystery of God's act. Examples are the burning bush in the desert or the throne of God surrounded by seraphim, where the mere seam of God's vestment fills the whole temple. When the New Testament uses the figure of the "son," the mystery of his unique relation to God is stressed. When we repeat the term "son," we know, of course, that it cannot be understood in a physical sense. Nonetheless, we need it, because it awakens experiences that we have had with human fatherhood, and this brings us nearer to the truth of Jesus' relation to God than any attempt to define it. This way of looking at such language is totally different from the approaches of Cornutus and Philo, for whom the language of the old religious legends or texts is simply a leftover from pre-enlightenment times.[33]

8.2 Another contrast with Hellenistic ideas is that in the New Testament the nature of the son's existence prior to his mission is not interpreted in any explicit way. The sole point is that in the ministry and death of the discredited and crucified Jesus God himself was acting. This, again, is totally different from what Cornutus or Philo or Plutarch says. Cornutus also speaks of the goal of the sending of Hermes. He even calls it "saving" and means salvation in time and space. But this saving event is not "this-worldly" like the crucifixion of Jesus. It is

---

[31] Cf. Dorothee Soelle, *Stellvertretung* (Stuttgart: Kreuz-Verlag, 1965) 166-168, 175, 190.

[32] By contrast, Philo speaks in *Conf. Ling.* 138 of the "invisible and imperceptible divine being (in its neuter sense: Θεῖον)."

[33] Plutarch is a bit different, although he also "demythologizes" the myths (for instance, of Isis and Osiris). He believes in gods and demi-gods who act in the mystery religions and in oracles, but these demi-gods are human souls that, upon the physical death of the body, have not yet attained the perfection of the gods (cf. Schweizer, "Slaves of the Elements and Worshipers of Angels," 463) Hence, it is fair to ask whether he really believes in gods or only in the existence of perfectly pure souls.

something that may have happened in a mythical past, actually in an "other-worldly" sphere, hence it guarantees the "otherworldliness" of humanity's innermost self, of its reason, which is for him a timeless fact true of all people at all times.

8.3 The imagery of God sending his son from heaven to earth certainly portrays the transcendence of God. Again, by contrast with Cornutus and Plutarch, this means real transcendence. It is not an "otherworldliness" that enters humanity and becomes part of humanity, as in Cornutus, whose language leads one to doubt whether he really thinks that human beings in their final perfection are different from gods. When Cornutus speaks of Hermes being sent by the gods, he is actually talking about reason in humanity. When we repeat the New Testament phrase "God sent his son" we are talking about God and at the same time narrating a story that happened in our worldly time and space. It is the story of the living God who decided to live in our world in Jesus of Nazareth.

IV. Conclusion

9.1 Wisdom 9:10 speaks of God sending his wisdom, and in a parallel verse (17) of God sending his spirit. Philo interprets the biblical figure of God sending his angel (e.g. Exod 23:20) as a reference to the mission of the Logos, the firstborn son of God. In another context he again describes the Logos as the son of God and says that all those who become sons of the Logos become sons of God.[34] Finally, the idea of the Logos being sent by God is also found in a Hellenistic author at the beginning of the first century C.E. (cf. 3.2 above). All this comes pretty close to what Gal 4:4-6 and Rom 8:3,15-16 say about God sending his son and his spirit so that we might become God's sons or children. Hence, the background of the New Testament phrase is certainly a kind of Wisdom or Logos christology. What does this signify?

9.2 When we say "God sent his son...," we do so within the biblical framework of meaning and not in the sense of Hellenistic philosophy. Thus, it means neither a (demythologized) timeless truth (Cornutus) nor a literal description of a descent from above (Plutarch). We report a story. We say that God has acted at a specific time in our past, and in the final clause we identify this act with an event in our world, namely, the crucifixion of Jesus. In so doing we qualify this occurrence as a saving event that has changed the situation of the world. When we use the verb "send" we make clear that God is not simply identical with the event but transcends it, although he encounters us in it and does so in

---

[34] *Agric.* 51; *Conf. Ling.* 145-48.

God sent his son...

his totality. God, therefore, is not to be understood as part of the world nor the world as part of God. In using the expression "his son," we describe the relation of God to Jesus as a unique nearness. This excludes both a mere commission of a human being (a prophet) and a sending of a being that is no "partner" of God (either a subordinate being, such as an angel, or the spirit, word, and wisdom of God, which are not really distinguishable from him). What encounters us in Jesus is God's very life, indeed God's wisdom, word, love, and motion towards his creation. Whatever is truly God's revelation in the life and death of Jesus was "pre-existent" in the life of God with his creation and his people Israel. It became visible where the Bible reports the acts of God's wisdom, word, and love. But God is more than wisdom, word, and love. We cannot pray to these, but we can pray to God. Therefore, God's love encounters us definitively as a human person, and therefore as a subject who acts and reacts, speaks and listens, and in all this loves us up to his death on a cross. Again, this "personal" quality of God's motion towards his creation and his people was "pre-existent" and revealed itself in God's words and acts reported in Israel's Bible, until it became flesh in Jesus of Nazareth. When God raised him from the dead, he vindicated ("justified") the crucified and discredited Jesus.[35] He declared that he, God himself, was to be found in Jesus' whole life and death, in his ministry, and finally and definitively, in his love expressed in his death on the cross for all humankind.

9.3 Thus, we do not define God. Even a definition of a living human being (or an animal, for that matter) is not possible in the strict sense of the word, since any living being is changing every moment—let alone a definition of the living God. Hence, when we say, "God sent his son...," we tell the story of this living God, without defining him, of the God who reached out to the world in the creation and in the history of Israel, the God who finally brought the world home in Jesus Christ. We tell the story of the God whose "being is in the becoming."[36]

9.4 The trinitarian belief, and perhaps already Phil 2:6-8 or John 1:1-18 and 8:58, go one step further. When we call God "trinitarian," we also speak of God as a living God, not as an unchanging (and therefore dead) substance. God is living in his love to all his creatures and is therefore changing in his acting with them. In expressing the trinity we also tell a story and clearly avoid any definition, since one is not three and three is not one in a defining language. But, beyond the explicit

---

[35] Cf. Meyer (note 2 above) 227.
[36] Eberhard Jüngel, *Gottes Sein ist im Werden* (Tübingen: J. C. B. Mohr [Paul Siebeck, 1965]).

statements in Galatians 4, Romans 8, John 3, and 1 John 4, we say that God is even living in himself, before the creation of the world and after its consummation, as love. Love is not possible without somebody (or something) that we love and without being loved by somebody (or something). In fact, life itself is unthinkable without action and reaction, acting and experiencing. Here is the meaning of God as father and son: the living love of the father toward the son and of the son toward the father, the action of the father and the reaction of the son even before the existence of the world. This love between the father and the son radiates as the Spirit into the creation. Although it is not explicitly stated, this does seem to be already implied in the expression "God sent his son," and it remains, even in the trinitarian formula, a statement about the life of God, about his loving acts, and not a definition of his timeless being.

19

Revelation as Our Knowledge of God: An Essay in Biblical Theology

C. P. Price [1]

This essay is dedicated to Paul Meyer, in thankful recognition of his many and wise contributions to the Biblical Theologians, of which we both have been members for many years. The society fosters the encounter between biblical and systematic studies. They are, of course, interdependent. Not only are Christian theologians informed by their reading of scripture, but also what they see in scripture, what they take to be important depends, in turn, on their theological stance. One's view may be altered, even drastically, by what one finds in the Bible, but one never approaches it without an existing viewpoint.

Modern thought about revelation affords a good example of this interplay, and what follows is an effort to exhibit it.

I. Revelation in Modern Theology

Protestant theology since Schleiermacher has operated under quite a different view of revelation than its predecessors. For eighteen hundred years, Christian theologians were content to say that revelation was propositional. *Scripture was revelation.* Its words were the very words of

---

[1] C. P. Price is the William Meade Professor of Systematic Theology Emeritus, Virginia Theological Seminary, Alexandria, Virginia.

God. God revealed to the church the information and doctrine contained in the Bible. Scholastic Catholic theology was able to add to this propositional content of revelation the doctrinal results of ecumenical councils. The doctrines of the trinity and incarnation, for example, have come to be considered as revealed.

Enlightenment theologians found this propositional view of revelation untenable. In reaction against it, Schleiermacher began what has been described as "a turn to the subject." He proposed that revelation should refer to the "originality of the fact which lies at the foundation of a religious communion."[2] All persons display a "consciousness of being absolutely dependent, or which is the same thing, of being in relation to God."[3] Revelation in each religion establishes the particular quality of that feeling. A great deal of subsequent theology has understood revelation along those lines, as our personal relation to God. Revelation is the disclosure of God's self.

This move left a host of questions in its wake. Does the turn to the subject, for example, consign revelation to pure subjectivity? What is the relation between revelation so considered and the words of scripture? What is the character of the knowledge of God transmitted by revelation? Is it cognitive, and part of our ordinary knowledge? What is the relation between the knowledge of God offered by Christian revelation and the knowledge of God claimed in other religions? Can this new view of revelation be defended as itself scriptural in any sense?

These questions, and doubtless numerous others, have been articulated by many recent writers, notably Karl Barth[4], Paul Tillich[5], H. Richard Niebuhr[6], John Baillie[7], John Macquarrie[8], Wolfhart Pannenberg[9], Gerald Downing[10], and Ronald Thiemann[11]. In this essay

---

[2] F.D.E. Schleiermacher, *The Christian Faith* (ed. H. R. Mackintosh and J. S. Stewart; Edinburgh: T. and T. Clark, 1928) 50.

[3] Ibid., 12.

[4] Karl Barth, *Church Dogmatics* I/1 (tr. G. T. Thompson; New York: Scribner's, 1936).

[5] Paul Tillich, *Systematic Theology*, vol. 1 (2 vols.; Chicago: University of Chicago Press, 1951).

[6] H. Richard Niebuhr, *The Meaning of Revelation* (New York: Macmillan, 1946).

[7] John Baillie, *The Idea of Revelation in Recent Thought* (New York: Columbia University Press, 1956).

[8] John Macquarrie, *Principles of Christian Theology* (2nd ed.; New York: Scribner's, 1966).

[9] Wolfhart Pannenberg, ed., *Revelation as History* (London: Macmillan, 1968).

[10] Gerald Downing, *Has Christianity a Revelation?* (London: SCM, 1964).

[11] Ronald Thiemann, *Revelation and Theology* (Notre Dame: University of Notre Dame Press, 1985).

we shall review biblical evidence in what is hoped to be a fresh way with these questions in mind. Then we shall address them with the resultant biblical evidence in hand and conclude with an immodest proposal for an ampler approach to the doctrine of revelation.

II. A Review of Biblical Evidence with Modern Questions in Mind

Theologians approach biblical evidence with certain presuppositions and questions. In this respect our contemporaries are no different from any Christian theologians at any time in history. Our stance and our questions are different. Our results may be different. There is no reason to suppose, however, that they will be any less congruent to the evidence than earlier work, if the study is carefully done; and there is reason to hope that the study will better illuminate contemporary concerns.

When we look at the disclosure of God in the Bible, we quickly see that there are three separate but closely related major ideas that need attention: knowing, revelation, and the Spirit of God. A satisfactory modern view of the biblical understanding of revelation as providing our knowledge of God is not to be attained apart from a consideration of all three. A full-scale approach to a biblical doctrine of revelation would have to deal with other items as well: Word of God, glory, light, and others. We will have time to address these subjects only briefly. We shall find some distance in the Hebrew scripture among the three major concepts in our focus. All of them imply partial attainment in the present and eschatological fulfillment. The three converge in the New Testament, where knowledge of God and revelation are pegged to a new dispensation of the Spirit.

> When you read this, you can perceive my insight into the mystery of Christ, which was not made known to the sons of men in other generations as it has now been revealed to his holy apostles and prophets by the Spirit (Eph 3:4-5).[12]

A. Knowing God in the Old Testament

1. *Knowing and not knowing.* Although many things can be said to be known in Hebrew scripture, there is an impressive reticence about the claim to know God *tout court*. A number of people are said not to have known YHWH, as if they might have been expected to have had that

---

[12] Here and in what follows, all biblical quotations are from the RSV.

knowledge: the sons of Eli (1 Sam 2:2); the generation of Israelites who grew up in Canaan after the conquest (Jdgs 2:10). Jeremiah laments that "[my people]... proceed from evil to evil, and they do not know me, says the Lord" (Jer 9:3). Pharaoh did not know YHWH (Ex 5:1), and Samuel did not yet know the Lord (1 Sam 3:7).

We note that when the judgment is made that someone does not know the Lord, logic requires that the observer has some knowledge of the subject. Otherwise the judgment is meaningless. But especially in great matters like truth, justice, and knowing God, it is easier to conclude that one does not know something than that one does. Jeremiah himself had a relationship with YHWH of unparalleled intimacy; he was the only prophet to use God's name directly. But he never claimed to "know the Lord" in so many words.

Among the notable leaders of Israel, only Moses is depicted as having a personal relationship to YHWH. "The Lord used to speak to Moses face to face, as a man speaks to his friend" (Exod 33:11). Moses prays in the course of the same passage, presumably with some sense of being heard, that "I may know thee and find favor in thy sight" (Exod 33:13). Yet the last word on this subject reverses the relationship and speaks not of Moses' knowing YHWH, but of the Lord's knowing him. "There has not arisen a prophet since in Israel, whom the Lord knew face to face" (Deut 34:10). In these traditions there is an abiding mystery about the knowledge of God.

2. *Knowing and being known.* Somewhat similarly, we are told that the Lord knew David (2 Sam 7:20), and the suffering Servant of Second Isaiah is chosen by God "to know and believe and understand that I am He" who accomplished the "former things"—the prior acts of salvation. The phrase is perhaps not so strong as "to know me," and it is striking that the people so chosen, Israel (note the plural throughout this passage), are "blind yet have eyes... deaf yet have ears" (Isa 43:8-10). The knowledge of the Lord does not arise in ordinary empirical ways. It is imparted to certain persons by YHWH directly, without the intervention of sense-experience. It is, in fact, like love (Isa 43:4). This direct means of communicating the knowledge of God can be described as being known by God, or YHWH's knowing someone.

The awareness that the Lord "knows us" prior to, if not excluding, our knowledge of him, is given its most memorable expression in Psalm 139: "O Lord, thou has searched me out and known me..." (v 1). The psalmist is able to say, "How precious to me are thy thoughts, O God" (v 17), but he does not claim a completely reciprocal knowledge: "Such knowledge is too wonderful for me; it is high, I cannot attain it" (v 6). The body of the psalm expresses delight in the sense of God's presence in every place. The psalmist plainly has some kind of knowledge. Yet in the Old Testament, "being known" by YHWH has a different force than "knowing;" and knowing God, when it occurs, is dependent on being known.

3. *The act of knowing in interpersonal relationships.* Even when the matter of knowing God is not at stake, to claim knowledge of another person is usually—though not always—to claim extraordinary intimacy. For a man to "know" a woman often implies sexual intercourse, as is well known (Gen 4:1, 4:17, 4:25; Jdgs 19:22, 25, 21:12; 1 Sam 1:19; 1 Kgs 1:4). Although it is possible to say that one person "knows" another in a more casual sense, the usage seems to be quite rare. Jacob's question to the shepherds in Haran, "Do you know Laban... ?" (Gen 29:5), and Jehu's hasty remark about the young man whom Elisha sent to anoint him, "You know the fellow and his talk" (2 Kgs 9:11), are the only instances which come readily to light. Talk about knowing and being known by God surely carries the weight of the former. Knowing God on the human side depends on being known by God in an act of prior personal giving, even invasion. Few seem to be open to it.

4. *Knowing events as acts of God.* Although it is rare in the Hebrew canon that anyone is said to "know the Lord," it is frequently said that both Israel and the nations "shall know that I am the Lord your God." This kind of knowledge arises when something happens to vindicate the righteousness of YHWH or his concern for Israel. According to this claim, the events of history make it plain that YHWH rules the world that God created according to the righteousness God reveals. An unreflective reading of these tests—and there are many of them both early and late—might suggest that the events themselves were to lead to the conclusion that YHWH is Lord. Nevertheless, we must bear in mind that the claim is asserted by a prophet (or the disciple of a prophet writing a narrative). The writer already knows that YHWH is Lord because in a preliminary sense he already "knows the Lord." The Egyptians, as a matter of historical fact, never did come to know that YHWH was God. They knew other gods of their own. The writer of the Exodus narrative, who in some preliminary, derivative way already knew YHWH, presumably through the more intimate and perfect knowledge transmitted by Moses, could see in the destruction of Pharaoh's army the hand of a righteous God. That knowledge, the knowledge of certain fact, was imparted to Israelites who accepted that knowledge as an article of faith.

This state of affairs brings to mind William Temple's famous dictum that "revelation is... the coincidence of event and appreciation."[13] The role of the interpreter must not elude us. The understanding of history as the unfolding of divine purpose is not possible apart from some direct communication between the divine and human realms. Someone must "know YHWH" in order to say that "YHWH has done great things for us." Otherwise the only logical conclusion would be that history is self-vindicating. Moses knew the Lord. He imparted that knowledge to Israel, which then celebrated those deeds as acts of God in cultic recital (anamnesis). In this derivative and dependent sense they knew that YHWH was God. By the same token, the prophets proclaimed the word of YHWH, which reinforced and extended the message of YHWH's righteous lordship over history. This proclamation became the stuff of Israel's cultic life. Israelites knew that these events were believed to be the work of YHWH, their God, in accordance with his will revealed in Torah. But it was true oftener than not that they forgot YHWH, and did not "know him." Then their cultic observances were empty and futile. Only in the latter days, when Israel would know YHWH in their hearts and obey YHWH freely by doing God's justice, could the interpretation of history as the mighty acts of YHWH become universally intelligible. Then even the gentiles would know that YHWH is God.

In his essay, "The Concept of Revelation in Ancient Israel,"[14] Rolf Rentdorff examines all these passages carefully and concludes that "[t]hroughout it is clear that Jahweh is known in his historical acts to ancient Israel and that in them he manifests himself as he is."[15] He establishes the fact that when Hebrew texts say that YHWH "declared himself" or "appeared" or even "was known," the context is YHWH's self-revelation through his saving acts.[16] The question is left hanging: manifest, or appeared, or was known to whom? It is quite possible to take part in the cultic recitals of these saving deeds and never "know the Lord" whose deeds are proclaimed. It was to the prophets that YHWH was revealed, and, derivatively, to those who accepted the prophetic message.

5. *Knowing and obedience.* The connection between knowledge and obedience to the ethical demands of the covenant surfaces in these texts. It seems clear that "knowing God" arises in the consciousness of some obedient Israelites as a response to being known by God. It is a

---

[13] William Temple, *Nature, Man and God* (London: Macmillan, 1934) 315.
[14] In Pannenberg, *Revelation as History*, 25-53.
[15] Ibid., 47.
[16] Ibid., 30-31.

personal relationship in its deepest and truest form ("as a friend talks with a friend"). It issues in moral action. It results in faithfulness to the covenant. The fact that Israel breaks Torah means that the people do not know God (Hos 4:1-2, etc.). When Jeremiah wants to contrast Shallum with Josiah his father, he says of Josiah: "He judged the cause of the poor and needy; then it was well. Is not this to know me, says the Lord?" (Jer 22:16). One must ask, however, whether it is not just as possible to obey the covenant by rote and not "know the Lord" as to recite YHWH's mighty acts and not "know the Lord." Even the most moral person may not "be known by YHWH."

6. *Knowing God as eschatological possibility.* Despite the fact that the phrase "knowing God" is used so sparingly in the Hebrew text, it would be foolish to deny that the prophets, who were so conscious of speaking the word of YHWH, and those psalmists who record the delight of their intercourse with YHWH, had some knowledge of God, though we are finding more and more that it was partial and preliminary. As time went on knowledge of God was increasingly recognized as an eschatological possibility. That must mean that full knowledge of God was increasingly recognized as an eschatological possibility on the basis of present, partial knowledge. Otherwise it is an unintelligible statement.

In this vein, Hosea, who uses the phrase "knowledge of God" four times and "know God" at least as often, makes the point that in the present time Israel has rejected knowledge of God. He urges his people to "press on to know the Lord" in the future (Hos 6:1; cf. Hos 2:20). Jeremiah likewise recognizes the full possibilities of the covenant relationship with YHWH lie in the future. It is to be a new covenant, rather than a renewed covenant. In this new situation, the new covenant law will be written upon the hearts of the people. It would represent the concrete expression of an inward and personal relationship rather than rote obedience. "No longer shall each man teach his neighbor and each his brother, saying, 'Know the Lord,' for they shall all know me..." (Jer 31:34).

Full knowledge of God is an eschatological possibility. That truth is recognized by those whom the Lord knows, and whose response to YHWH's initiative brings them some personal knowledge of God in turn—as much as they are capable of bearing, enough to see the hand of God at work in nature and history.

B. Revelation in the Old Testament

1. *Revelation in prophetic writings.* Like knowing, revealing is both a divine and an ordinary human activity, as expressed in both Hebrew and

English. God revealed secrets to the prophets (Amos 3:7); talebearers reveal secrets to the curious (Prov 11:13). The verb (gālāh) and the object (sôd) are the same in each case. What was previously hidden to one person is disclosed by another. In the case of divine revelation, however, the receivers of the revelation are regularly the prophets. Not only is it said that God revealed his secret to the prophets, but also that "the Lord revealed himself to Samuel at Shiloh" (1 Sam 3:21). We might go on to infer that then he knew the Lord, in view of the statement about a prior time when "he did not yet know the Lord" (1 Sam 3:7). YHWH "uncovered the ear of David" (2 Sam 7:27), and revealed "deep and mysterious things to Daniel" (Dan 2:22). We do not read of revelation coming to the generality of the human race, at least during the course of history. Revelation in Israel, like knowledge of God, comes to special people.

2. *What is revealed?* In a good deal of modern theology, a sharp distinction is made between God's revealing himself and God's revealing propositions—statements or facts, doctrines or facts of history. As we found in the case of knowing, it is a subtle distinction which must not be pressed too hard. For example, when it is said that God revealed himself to Samuel (*niglāh yhwh 'el šĕmû 'ēl*), the shape of that revelation was a declaration of his judgment against the house of Eli, soon to be performed (1 Sam 3:11-14), a "secret." The revelation poured into David's uncovered ear concerned the future of the Davidic monarchy. The secret which Amos understood to be revealed to the prophets concerned God's future acts in history (Amos 3:6).

Can God (or a person, for that matter) be self-revealed without revealing some facts? At the human level, when a person is said to reveal himself or herself to another, the statement is vacuous unless there is some content to the revelation. Revelation of one self to another would seem to involve necessarily the revelation of information. At the same time we must observe that a third person may receive that information second hand, without sharing the relationship of intimacy which made the revelation possible to the initial receiver.

That is to say, the idea of revelation requires the revelation of propositional content; but the content, once received, may be transmitted to others and even acknowledged as true by them without its being recognized as proceeding from revelation. In a moment of intimacy and trust, by way of analogy, I might tell a friend that I was a homosexual. I would have revealed myself to the other; but that information could be received and accepted as true by others who did not share the relationship of trust and insight which made the self-revelation possible. Revelation requires content, knowing that content does not necessarily imply receiving the revelation. The relationship is not quite reciprocal. To receive revelation requires a relationship something like love.

The analogous situation seems to be true in the Hebrew scripture. There is no revelation of God's self apart from some words, some propositions. How else could God be self-revealed? The words themselves, on the other hand, do not necessarily carry the revelatory quality of the divine-human encounter.

3. *Universality of revelation as an eschatological possibility.* Just as knowledge of God will be a possibility for every person in "the latter days," so the late strata of Old Testament tradition understand that in the future the hidden things of God will be accessible to all persons. The revelation of "iniquity... in the day of God's wrath" or of YHWH's glory (Isa 40:15) or of God's salvation and deliverance (Isa 56:1) will be accessible to all persons. No mediation by prophet or priest is mentioned in these instances. In the days to come, God's reality will be clear to all persons everywhere. "All flesh shall see it together" (Isa 40:5).

4. *Light, glory, word.* It is not possible in this essay to give a complete account of all aspects of revelation, but at least a brief mention must be made of three: light, glory, and word. Light is an obvious and familiar symbol for revelation. It occurs in the first verse of Genesis, the first of the creative acts of God: "Let there be light." God "covers himself"—the Hebrew text means hides himself—"with light as with a garment" (Ps 104:2). This primordial light shrouds the innermost being of God in impenetrable mystery, as the symbol of the shekinah suggests, and this light which comes from the divine is the source of our knowledge of everything else. It is "the light by which we see light" (Ps 36:9), and is closely associated with salvation (Ps 27:1).

Glory, too, is something seen. It shines with divine light. Early strata of the Hebrew text represent the glory of God as shining in present circumstances as well as in God's heavenly abode (Isa 6:3; Ps 97:6). It appeared in the wilderness at critical moments before the people entered Canaan (Exod 16:7, 24:16; Deut 5:24), and thereafter usually in the temple. Later writing connects the glory of YHWH with eschatological revelation, however, as we have seen (Isa 40:5). This theme, eschatological glory, is picked up in the New Testament.

The *word* of YHWH is the vehicle of revelation to the prophets. Here we need to observe only that a word which proceeds from the depth of one person's being and enters another's whose ears and heart are opened to receive it, is truly revelatory. Words, however, can hide as well as reveal; like light and glory, even Word leaves the innermost being of God clothed in abiding mystery (cf. Isa 45:15).

C. A Note on Spirit in the Old Testament

1. *Parallels to knowledge and revelation.* It is not necessary to make a detailed examination of the teaching about the Spirit of God in the Hebrew scripture, nor does the scope of this essay permit it. There are a number of pertinent studies already in existence: Barrett[17], Eichrodt[18], Schweizer[19], and Pedersen[20]. The reader will have noticed at least two striking parallels between the development of the understanding of Spirit in the Old Testament and the material presented so far about knowing God and revelation. The first is the fact that Spirit is bestowed only upon especially selected persons—judges and kings, prophets, and the craftsmen who fashioned the tabernacle in the wilderness. The second is that by the end of the Hebrew canon, the Spirit is believed to come in fullness only as an eschatological possibility. Just as it was envisioned that knowing God and beholding the revelation of God will be made universal when the rule of God is fulfilled in the latter days, so "afterward" the Spirit of God will be poured out on "all flesh" and "[e]ven upon the men-servants and maid-servants, in those days, I will pour out my spirit" (Joel 2:19).

2. *Connections among Spirit, knowing, and revelation.* Nowhere in the Hebrew canon is it said that the Spirit of God by revelation brings knowledge; the Old Testament keeps some distance between these categories. Nevertheless there is, so to speak, a circle of not very large radius in which all three are included, and relationships among pairs of them are not hard to find, particularly in later strata of writing.

The messianic prediction of Isaiah 11, for example, unites *the Spirit of the Lord and knowledge* ("the spirit of knowledge," Isa 11:2; it is eschatological, we note). Similarly, the prophets are given the secret of the Lord God by *revelation* (Amos 3:7), and in a summary statement of prophetic inspiration it would be said that this gift had come *by the Spirit.* The Holy Spirit "spake by the prophets," according to the Nicene formulation. It is true that the eighth and seventh century prophets are notoriously silent about the operation of the Spirit. They did not want to be confused with earlier prophets, whom Hosea called *meshuggah* (mad). The earlier prophets were "men of the spirit" (Hos 9:7). The new

---

[17] C. K. Barrett, *The Holy Spirit in the Gospel Tradition* (London: SPCK, 1947).

[18] Eichrodt, *Theology of the Old Testament* (tr. J. A. Baker; Philadelphia: Westminster Press, 1961) 210-220; 315-391.

[19] Eduard Schweizer, "πνεῦμα," *TDNT* 6.331-455.

[20] Johannes Pedersen, *Israel* (London: Oxford University Press, 1926) esp. vol. I-II, 102ff; vol. III-IV, 113ff.

chapter of prophecy which opened with Amos and Hosea in the eighth century was understood to flourish under the *Word*. Yet Ezekiel reintroduced the category of the Spirit as the inspirer of his prophecies (Ezek 2:2), and subsequent prophets did not display the former reticence about the Spirit (Joel 1:18; Hag 2:6; Zech 4:6, 7:12). Word and Spirit seem to be intricately and intimately related in this literature, and Christian theology has eventually recognized their dialectical interdependence, suggesting a dialectical relationship between the non-cognitive and cognitive aspects of revelation.

These considerations lend support to an understanding of the relationship between the divine Spirit and the human spirit in its normal state. The prediction of Saul's prophesying, that he would be "turned into another man" (1 Sam 10:6), expresses the transnormal quality of inspiration by the Spirit. Prophetic insistence on inspiration by the Word expresses the other side of the dialectic, that it does not break or destroy human rationality. Being known by God is not given a cognitive description; but knowing God results in knowing things about God, nature and history.

Revelation and knowing are brought into conjunction in Daniel, which, however, does not refer to the Spirit of God in this context:

(God) gives wisdom to the wise and knowledge to those
    who have understanding;
he reveals deep and mysterious things... (Dan 2:21-22).

In the Old Testament, Spirit, revelation, and knowledge of God are found in close proximity and the trajectory of the texts we have examined suggests possible convergence.

D. New Testament Convergence of Spirit, Knowing, and Revelation.

The most significant new element introduced by the New Testament into our discussion of Spirit, knowing, and revelation is the Pentecost event. After the resurrection of Jesus, the Spirit was poured out on all members of the Christian community. Joel's prediction, Peter recognized, had come to realization in the new church (Acts 2:18). Acts and the epistles describe the life of a Spirit-filled community. Within it the knowledge of God is shared by all—although, even yet, it is only partial knowledge (1 Cor 13:12); and revelation is discerned by all, although the full revelation of glory is yet to come (Rom 8:18).

Nevertheless, a decisive step forward toward knowing God had been taken.

The foundation for this new state of affairs is indicated by the so-called "Johannine thunderbolt," a statement put on the lips of Jesus in Matthew. It is the only occasion in the synoptic tradition on which Jesus claimed to "know God," hence it is likely to have been an interpretive addition by the post-resurrection community. "...no one knows the Father but the Son and anyone to whom the Son chooses to reveal him" (Matt 11:27). From the point of view of this discourse, there is a completely reciprocal relationship between Father and Son, and the Son is able to mediate *knowledge of God*—by revelation—to those who believe in the Son.

In the Old Testament revelation was connected with the events of history. One came to know *that YHWH was God* by victories which vindicated him, usually the conquest of Israel's enemies. In the New Testament one comes to know *that Jesus is Lord* through the resurrection (Rom 1:4), and since the resurrection is the conquest of "the last enemy" of the human race, it represents God's final vindication. It is potentially the universal revelatory event. It includes all people.

Yet the resurrection is not purely and simply an historical event. It still has to be interpreted by prophetic insight, although such insight is now theoretically available to the whole Christian community. Jesus is "designated Son of God in power according to the Spirit of holiness by his resurrection" (Rom 1:4), and his risen body is a "spiritual body." There is an inescapable inward dimension to the knowledge of God in the New Testament, provided by the Spirit. Paul contrasts the present state of the Galatian Christians into whose hearts (N.B.) God had sent the Spirit of his Son with that of former times "when you did not know God" (Gal 4:8). Now the Galatians say "Abba". By the same token, the author of Colossians hopes that the congregation is "increasing in the knowledge of God" (Col 1:10) and indicates that the nature of those baptized—baptized into the death and resurrection of Christ—is "being renewed in knowledge after the image of its Creator" (Col 3:10). The author of Hebrews cites the new covenant passage from Jeremiah as a present reality (Heb 8:11). 2 Peter is bolder: "His divine power has granted to us all things that pertain to life and godliness through the knowledge of him who called us to his own glory..." (1:3). In this late epistle knowledge of Jesus is knowledge of God (1:2).

It seems reasonable to conclude that virtually every strand of New Testament tradition agrees that because of what God did through Christ, most signally by his resurrection, *all Christians can know God*. But the resurrection is not only an objective event which designates that Jesus is

Lord. It also makes possible a presence which "shines in our hearts." In language which recalls Jeremiah, Paul claims that God "had set me apart before I was born," and "was pleased to reveal his Son to me (lit. in me)" (Gal 1:16) and God has "shone in our hearts to give the light of the knowledge of the glory of God in the face of Christ" (2 Cor 4:6). As in the Old Testament, revelation in the New is inconceivable without some outward content, but it implies more than the declaration of a fact or the statement of information. It is at least as inward in us as the knowing of another person. The Spirit, in the world and in our hearts, maintains the connection between these kinds of knowing and these two loci of revelation. It is potentially for everyone.

It is also true that complete knowledge of God and full revelation are still for the future in New Testament terms. "Now I know in part. Then I shall know even as also I am known" (1 Cor 13:12). The revelation of Jesus Christ in glory so that all can see plainly remains a future possibility (2 Thess 1:7; 1 Pet 4:13, 5:1). According to the New Testament, knowledge of God in the present comes by revelation through the Spirit. All who receive the Spirit can know God. This general potential for the knowledge of God represents a decisively new situation. It has been partly realized, but the full actuality has not occurred. The content of that knowledge pertains to Gentiles as well as Jews. It is in principle universal, though in fact it has not been universally accepted. "We... who have the first fruits of the Spirit groan inwardly as we wait for our adoption as sons, the redemption of bodies" (Rom 8:23).

III. Some Comments on Modern Developments in Understanding Revelation with this Biblical Evidence in Mind

In the introduction to this paper, some questions were posed which have grown out of modern wrestling with the idea of revelation. Now we return to them.

A. Turn to the Subject

Does the turn to the subject consign revelation to pure subjectivity? If our analysis of biblical material has been persuasive, the answer to this question must be negative. There is room, even in the Old Testament, for saying that God reveals God's self, at least to Moses and to the prophets and to some of the writers of psalms. God knew them, making himself manifest in Word and light and glory. Some knew God in return although that knowledge was partial. In the New Testament, knowledge of God is a universal possibility although it is slow in actualization, and until the end of time will be incomplete.

How does one know that such knowledge is not simply a projection of one's desires and hopes? At this point the relationship between knowledge of God and knowledge *that God is the actor behind events* becomes important. The hand of God is discerned in historical events because they accomplish what human beings could not conceivably accomplish. The Exodus is the first case in point. The revelation of God to Moses at the burning bush was connected with a promise and vindicated at the Red Sea. If one observes that that was a parochial revelation pertinent only to Israel, and that Egyptians could not be expected to find God in the deliverance of Israel, one is brought up against the fact that the prophets saw the hand of God in the destruction of Israel, who did not "know God" and who did not fulfill the claims of justice. And if one continues to think that the whole prophetic development is a highly imaginary understanding of the outworking of ineluctable historical forces, one is then brought up against the fact that this whole story finds its culmination in the resurrection. If the resurrection is true, it transcends all historical possibilities and vindicates the proclamation of Christians who know God in that event. If the resurrection is true, the consciousness of Christians is the consciousness of something other than themselves.

Schleiermacher's analysis of the feeling of absolute dependence obscures at least two issues. He understands revelation as providing the originating foundation for every religion, and therefore the particular quality which that feeling has in each religion. He assumes divine causality in the process. Having said that, however, he does not use the insight. In the Christian communion, the originating fact at its foundation is the resurrection of Jesus Christ. Yet Schleiermacher's neglect of the resurrection is well known. Instead, he analyzed Jesus' own God-consciousness, which is carried over in a not very clearly specified way to the Christian community. His own assumptions should have led him to analyze the feeling of dependence of the Christian person. It might have driven him to take the resurrection more seriously.[21]

Subsequent post-liberal Protestant theology has reacted in various ways to the shortcomings of Schleiermacher's first venture in this turn, but even Karl Barth does not return to the prior identification of revelation and text. "We do the Bible a poor honor, and one unwelcome to itself, when we identify it with this something else, *this revelation*

---

[21] Schleiermacher, *The Christian Faith*, 417.

itself, the word spoken by God" (emphasis added).[22] It has been necessary to reestablish the connection between the revelation of God's self to the believing community and the events which confirm that God is the Lord of history. Here the best known and (in my view) still the most adequate statement of that relationship is William Temple's "event plus appreciation."[23] In the broad spectrum of more recent thought on the subject, Bultmann's view of the resurrection seems to reduce everything to subjectivity and Pannenberg's thesis that history is revelation omits divine intercourse with the interpreter.

I don't know of a single theologian, however, who stresses adequately the provisional character of all revelation and all knowledge of God, even Christian knowledge of God in the present time. In the effort to provide a firm epistemological foundation for Christian thought, the eschatological dynamic of revelation and its spiritual character may be too conveniently overlooked.

B. The Relation Between Revelation and the Words of Scripture

David Kelsey has shown the variety of uses of scripture in modern theology.[24] Conservative Christians continue to regard the words of scripture as being revelation. There is no content beyond them. We have already noted the thin dividing line inserted by Barth between scripture and revelation, though by the end of his discussion we find that the two are as intricately related as the persons of the Trinity. Liberal theologians allow at the most that scripture is the record of revelation.

Our analysis of the biblical evidence has yielded no real help at this point. Individual authors are not conscious of the whole collection of books. The author of Hebrews attributes some of the Old Testament passages he cites directly to God (Heb 1:5ff), some to the Holy Spirit (Heb 3:7ff), and some to the Holy Spirit through David (Heb 4:7). He probably intends no difference and he does not specify the nature of the inspiration. The famous verse, "All scripture is inspired by God" (2 Tim 3:16), brings the Old Testament within the ambit of the Spirit. Could we say less of the New? It would be consistent with what has emerged so far to insist that scripture, like events, needs an interpreter who "knows God." Faithfully interpreted, scripture has revelatory power. That is, it can potentially bring those who hear it or read it, to know God. "God

---

[22] Barth, *Church Dogmatics* I/1, 126.

[23] William Temple, *Christ's Revelation of God: Three Lectures* (London: SCM, 1956).

[24] David H. Kelsey, *The Uses of Scripture in Recent Theology* (Philadelphia: Fortress, 1975).

still speaks to us through the Bible," as the Prayer Book Catechism maintains.[25]

C. What is the Character of Knowledge Transmitted by Revelation?

If revelation were propositional, the knowledge it communicated would be cognitive. In ancient and medieval thought the propositions of revelation could not be demonstrated by reason; but they were expressed in ordinary speech and for the most part were inherently intelligible. Such as were intelligible served as the basis for a rational scheme of theology. Those that were not intelligible confirmed the mystery of the divine.

The modern situation presents a more complex picture. Theologians have tried to understand revelation as the interaction of divine being with frail, finite, rational humans. They have been unwilling to accept a theory of dictation to a passive receiver. Schleiermacher insisted that revelation had to be non-cognitive, at least at its inception, and that it operated on human beings not to insert new ideas piecemeal into a previously organized rational structure, but to alter the whole character of our apprehension of existence.[26] This process would eventually lead to cognitive formulation. "That this does not exclude doctrine but implies it, is obvious;"[27] but revelation *is not* that formulation. Barth maintains that the "revelation itself" expresses itself in scriptural words but is not identical with the scriptural words.

Tillich and Macquarrie, both in different ways dependent on Heidegger, are most explicit about the extraordinary nature of the revelatory encounter, and do most justice to the charismatic (pneumatic?) nature of it that our biblical study has brought to light. Tillich speaks of miracles received in ecstasy—which he carefully defines as reason driven beyond its normal limits,[28] not as the irrational. Macquarrie regards it as similar to (but not identical with) the human appropriation of Being in what Heidegger calls "essential" or "meditative" thinking, so different from the "calculative" thinking characteristic of superficial reflection in a technological age.[29] In both cases, revelation is understood to push human rationality beyond normal

---

[25] *The Book of Common Prayer* (Seabury, 1979) 853.
[26] Schleiermacher, *The Christian Faith*, 50.
[27] Ibid.
[28] Tillich, *Systematic Theology*, vol. 1, 11.
[29] Macquarrie, *Principles of Christian Theology*, 94.

limits and to produce a new understanding of the world. Both describe the process they envision more fully than Schleiermacher attempts to do.

In our biblical exploration we noted that the prophets received the revelation of God's self now under the auspices of Spirit, now under the auspices of Word, and suggested that there was a dialectical relation between them which could encompass both a transrational, non-cognitive aspect of revelation and a cognitive. Revelation is the communication of Light by which we see light, and it is a gift of the Holy Spirit which has both of these aspects.

Martin Buber's essay *I and Thou* has encouraged some theologians, H. R. Niebuhr being a salient example, to use the model of interpersonal relationships without significant qualifications to understand revelation.[30] Such an approach tends to miss the ecstatic and transforming power of revelatory moments.

IV. Reconstruction and Advance: An Immodest Proposal for Understanding Revelation as the Definition of Human Being

A final question was posed in that introductory list. "What is the relationship between the knowledge of God offered in Christian revelation and the knowledge of God claimed in other religions?" In this section I want to expand ideas advanced by Tillich[31] and Macquarrie[32] so that reception of revelation can be connected with the emergence of human being. Human being is being which stands in relationship to Light, and in that Light sees light.

A. Classic Revelation

Tillich speaks of "original revelation," Macquarrie of "primordial" or "classic" revelation. These terms all refer to the same phenomenon, the encounter with God of a religious leader or prophet in the midst of an ongoing history. This revelation becomes the foundation at the heart of a new religious departure, to use Schleiermacher's language. "A seer, a religious founder, a priest, a mystic—these are individuals from whom original revelation is derived by groups," Tillich writes.[33] Macquarrie puts it this way:

---

[30] Niebuhr, *The Meaning of Revelation*, 146.
[31] Tillich, *Systematic Theology*, vol. 1, 126ff.
[32] Macquarrie, *Principles of Christian Theology*, 90.
[33] Tillich, *Systematic Theology*, vol. 1, 127ff.

A community of faith, within which a theology arises, usually traces its history back to what may be called a 'classic' or a 'primordial' revelation. This classic revelation, a definitive disclosure experience of the holy granted to the founder or founders of the community, becomes as it were a paradigm for the experience of the holy in that community.[34]

Moses received revelation from God in an encounter in which God knew him face to face, and Moses (with *shining* face, according to the tradition preserved in Exod 34:30), articulated the content of that revelation for Israel. (His originating role is still acknowledged, cf. John 9:29.) Moses constitutes the primary biblical example of what Tillich and Macquarrie mean. In this paper, for reasons that will become clear, I choose to call this type of revelation *classic*.

B. Primordial Revelation

Neither Tillich nor Macquarrie deals with the following two points: (1) how revelation, bursting on the scene *in media res*, could be recognized as revelation; (2) why the communication of revelation is so uneven. Why do only a few persons "know God?"

One needs some prior knowledge of revelation in order to grasp the revelatory character of a new experience. "This is that," one must be able to say. "In order to recognize an experience as revelatory, one must possess a general concept of the form X as a reliable symptom of Y," Thiemann argues,[35] and we may agree with him so far. A revelatory experience has some qualities which are already known. Moses learned about God from the tradition he received. God was the God of Abraham, Isaac, and Jacob. That knowledge became knowledge of God at the burning bush and was decisively expanded there. Moses was led to a greater knowledge of God's involvement in history through God's promise to deliver Israel. When that deliverance occurred beyond all expectation, it confirmed the Israelite nation in its belief that Moses "knew God," or rather was first known by God. Revelation is recognized as such by its overcoming of limitations.[36] Israel knew that YHWH was the Lord in this derivative way.

---

[34] Macquarrie, *Principles of Christian Theology*, 8.

[35] Thiemann, *Revelation and Theology*, 42.

[36] Rudolf Bultmann, *Existence and Faith* (tr. Schubert Ogden; Cleveland: World, 1960) 86ff.

Genesis tells of God's encounter with Abraham, Isaac, and Jacob; behind them lies God's covenant with Noah and all his descendants, Jew and Gentile alike. God is nowhere without witnesses. Biblical material agrees with logical necessity and anthropological discovery that human beings always and everywhere have access to some encounter with the divine. I propose to call this knowledge of God, if we may dare to call it knowledge, knowledge by *primordial* revelation, and to distinguish it from classic revelation since the person of the founder of these earliest religions is not, or is no longer, known to us. Primordial reflection is the precondition of classic revelation.

I also propose to associate this idea of primordial revelation with what Heidegger calls the "disclosedness of *Dasein*,"[37] and what I would like to call the enlightening of human being. What makes human being human is that it is able to understand, care, live as an historical being, and to *forget* Being. All of these things Heidegger connects with the "potentiality-for-Being" that comes with disclosedness and which we might connect with human potential for relation with God that comes from revelation. All of these things emerge in the being which is shaped and transformed by its primordial encounter with the divine. Thereafter it has the capacity to receive revelation and to "know God." There is nothing "natural" here. It is God's work at every point.

James Barr comments negatively on a similar proposal.

> I am not saying that there is nothing there; only that (a) its status is too obscure to base anything upon; and (b) consideration of it thus becomes a speculative exercise in which we are not called to engage.[38]

One certainly must agree that the situation is obscure, but it seems to require some such speculation as this. One does not so much base anything on these results as see that reflection on human being leads to them.

Heidegger's understanding of the "forgetfulness of Being" is suggestive also.[39] We are sure at this late date that Heidegger did not have the divine or revelation in mind. But if one approaches his analysis of human being with the category of revelation in hand, one finds a new understanding of the fact that, in Old Testament terms, only a few

---

[37] Martin Heidegger, *Being and Time* (tr. John Macquarrie and Edward Robinson; New York: Harper and Row, 1962) 385.
[38] James Barr, *The Bible in the Modern World* (Harper and Row, 1973) 17, 79.
[39] Heidegger, *Being and Time*, 7, 262, 332 and *passim*.

"knew God." The general state of human being is forgetfulness of Being. The general state of Israel was forgetfulness of YHWH and consequent disobedience to Torah, the articulation of the divine will whose nucleus Moses received "in ecstasy." In this realm one cannot prove anything, but one can point out a great deal."[40]

C. Dependent Revelation

Tillich speaks of "dependent revelation"[41] and Macquarrie of "repetitive revelation"[42] to describe how classic revelation "keeps coming alive" in the life of the community which bears it. This aspect of revelation needs to be examined more sharply than either Tillich or Macquarrie has, and the role of dependent revelation specifically in the Christian community needs to be clarified.

In Israel dependent revelation took at least two forms: (1) the ongoing life of the cult; (2) the particular contribution of the prophets. We shall speak of *cultic repetition* and *prophetic criticism*. Our biblical survey showed that the prophets had some direct relationship to God, and no small part of their work was criticism of the people because they did not know God. The prophetic knowledge of the Word of God was not a revelation different from the Mosaic revelation, but rather a renewal of the Mosaic revelation under different circumstances. In general (not always) those circumstances resulted from Israel's disobedience to YHWH and the event which vindicated the prophetic pronouncement of doom was the destruction of Israel. Occasionally, as in the return from exile, there was a new act of deliverance. These new events, interpreted by the prophetic message, allowed Israel to "know that YHWH was God." The cultic recitals occurred year in and year out with "religious regularity," even when Israel did not "know the Lord." The continuation of the recital in the temple provided the occasion and the potential, nevertheless, for the continual knowledge of YHWH by some in Israel.

D. Revelation Through Jesus Christ

From a point of view outside the Christian community the revelation of God received by the Church through Jesus of Nazareth is one more instance of a classic revelation. He was the founder of a new religious

---

[40] Martin Heidegger, *Identity and Difference* (tr. Joan Stambaugh; New York: Harper and Row, 1969).

[41] Tillich, *Systematic Theology*, vol. 1, 37.

[42] Macquarrie, *Principles of Christian Theology*, 90.

community, and within that community subsequent encounters with God are dependent on him. One could speak of cultic repetition and prophetic criticism in terms somewhat similar to those used in the last paragraph.

It is impossible for a Christian theologian, however, to be satisfied with such a position, however much he or she may sympathize with the observer who stands outside the circle of faith. A Christian theologian is obliged to do justice to the new element in the New Testament. Revelation is recognized as revelation because it is a disclosure of God's power over human limits. New revelation discloses God's power in a new dimension. Otherwise it does not break the categories found adequate for the former revelation. The Mosaic revelation disclosed God's power exercised on behalf of Israel as a factor in world history. Such a revelation, however, is not universal. It excludes Israel's enemies. The Christian revelation discloses God's power exercised on behalf of humanity against "the last enemy to be destroyed." In this respect, Pannenberg is surely right. The resurrection is the event which would vindicate universally the revelation of God in Christ, where the non-cognitive side, represented by the new dispensation of the Spirit, was agape. In the resurrection of Jesus, God announced the beginning of the reconciliation of the world, and although the story is not yet finished, there are no new *revelatory* events yet to come. The resurrection is the originality of the fact which lies at the heart of the Christian community, to use Schleiermacher's words again. If it is accepted as true, as it is within the Christian community, it is precisely what humans cannot achieve for themselves; it represents a power inconceivable in a cosmos where everything is headed for death. It is hard to see any power beyond resurrection. The feeling of absolute dependence mediated through this particular revelation of the divine cannot be understood as nothing more than a very intense subjective feeling engendered by causes admitting a rational, historical, or psychological explanation.

If it is accepted as true.... This condition might be a crippling one. It is easy to see why Pannenberg, for example, wants to insist that the resurrection is an open event on the plane of history, which only the normal limitations of human finitude keep every person from accepting at face value. On the basis of our earlier analysis, however, we must press the fact that the resurrection is not yet general. The Easter event, like all other revelatory events, requires the interpretation of the Spirit-filled community. The knowledge of God communicated by revelation through the Spirit, which is articulated as God's self-giving love for the whole creation, is vindicated by the resurrection, which has as yet been known only by "chosen witnesses" (Acts 10:41). To that the church bears witness. As in prior cases, both objective and subjective sides of revelation are necessary—not in this case because the objective event is too parochial, but because the resurrection is not yet complete.

F. Dependent Revelation in the Christian Community

The eschatological character of life in the Christian community is indicated by the fact that the Spirit is accessible to every member. All have spiritual gifts. Jesus is designated Son of God through the power of the Spirit, and in the power of the Spirit all can know God.

The eschatological situation has not fully come. It is "now but not yet." Knowledge of God has entered a new stage, but there is still a partial quality to all knowledge. All can know, but we still do not know as we are known.

In this situation the cult continues. In worship the power of the resurrection of Christ and the new knowledge of God which it entails are still renewed week by week and year by year. The community still forgets and has to be recalled to faith by the more intense knowledge of God vouchsafed to some members of the community. This service is not always performed by the same persons. Although there were Christian prophets at first, they were not established as an order in the Church. After the second century one hears of them only sporadically.

Some Christians do have unusually intense experiences of God. They "know him." One thinks of the flame kindled in Justin Martyr's soul or Pascal's Night of Fire. Such moments remind Christians of the knowledge of God of which we all are capable through the revelation dependent on the originating fact of Jesus Christ.

We hold this revelation in trust for the world. It is potentially universal. But it is still unfulfilled, and until the end comes we can only welcome what new knowledge we can learn from those who know God through other revelations at the foundations of other world religions.

20

Inclusive Language and Biblical Authority

Paul S. Minear [1]

This essay ventures to analyze an issue of some importance in the history and the faith of Christian churches, an area in which exponents of inclusive language are frequently at odds with exponents of biblical authority. The former commonly regard the Bible as literature that stems from a patriarchal society, using paternal imagery to sanctify the masculine inequities of that society. Its advocates conclude that any movement toward greater equality between the sexes requires extensive changes in biblical language.

Rebellion against patriarchal and paternalist language is not, of course, limited to the struggle for sexual equality; it is found wherever the rights of minorities are denied and wherever inequalities are entrenched in economic, governmental, or ecclesiastical structures. Paternalism has become the code-word to identify the enemies of almost every reformist movement today. As A. Mitscherlich has observed, this rebellion has carried us far along on the road to a "fatherless society."[2]

---

[1] Paul S. Minear is Winkley Professor of Biblical Theology Emeritus at Yale Divinity School, New Haven, Connecticut.

[2] Cited by W. A. Visser 't Hooft in *The Fatherhood of God in an Age of Emancipation* (Philadelphia: Westminster, 1982) 1.

But while the rebellion against paternalism is universal, battles against exclusive sexist language are especially troublesome within the churches, for these battles take place almost every Sunday, and they involve words that carry the most cherished of overtones. In many parishes the language of favorite hymns and prayers has been carefully edited to eliminate masculine bias; or, if unedited versions are used, these provoke resentment among some worshipers. And since the liturgy is replete with biblical quotations, even the biblical readings are altered, to the relief of some and the shock of others. Because the Bible uses many paternal images in referring to God, the conflict often peaks at the point where biblical revelation concerning God as father and the demand for inclusive language collide. On the one hand, W. A. Visser 't Hooft is right that "we cannot eliminate fatherhood from the gospel without destroying its very meaning."[3] On the other hand, throughout its history the church has used the idea of God's fatherhood to justify all kinds of male chauvinism, a fact that would seem to justify the demand for erasing this sexual idiom from the Bible.

The National Council of Churches responded to that demand by appointing a commission whose mandate was to produce a series of lectionaries in which the alleged paternalism of the Bible would be either eliminated or minimized. Among the most complex tasks of that commission was that of editing the texts that speak of God as father and of Jesus as his son. The use of those metaphors was minimized; where they could not be eliminated, the editors succeeded in eliminating most of the masculine pronouns (he, his, him) referring to both. The goal of inclusive language seemed to dictate those changes.

During the same period another commission appointed by the same Council completed its translation of the Bible, the New Revised Standard Version, scheduled for publication in 1990. In dealing with the father/son imagery, the scholars steadily refused to follow the course adopted by the lectionary editors. As translators, they felt bound by the intent of the original authors rather than by current desires and demands. When the NRSV is published, attention will no doubt be concentrated on its treatment of sexist language, and therefore also on the contrasts between scripture and lectionary, between the work of two commissions as they fulfilled differing mandates from the same ecumenical agency.

To show some of the points of potential conflict, I cite two prayers, one from Matthew and one from John:

---

[3] Ibid., 1.

Inclusive Language and Biblical Authority

| At that time Jesus said, I thank you, Father, Lord of heaven and earth, because you have hidden these things from the wise and the intelligent and have revealed them to infants; yes, Father, for such was your gracious will. All things have been handed over to me by my Father; no one knows the Son except the Father, and no one knows the Father except the Son, and anyone to whom the Son chooses to reveal him. Matt 11:25-27 (NRSV)[4] | At that time Jesus declared, I thank you (God my Mother and) Father, Sovereign of heaven and earth, that you have hidden these things from the wise and understanding and revealed them to babes; yes, God, for such was your gracious will. All . things have been delivered to me by (God) my Father (and Mother), and no one knows the Child except God, and no one knows God except the Child, and anyone to whom the Child chooses to reveal God. Matt 11:25-27 *(Inclusive Language Lectionary)*[5] |

The major changes may readily be spotted. Because *father* is a masculine noun, either *God* is substituted or the metaphor is doubled to *father and mother*. Where the text reads *son*, the non-sexist *child* is substituted. The non-masculine *Sovereign* replaces the masculine *Lord*. The masculine pronoun *him* is replaced by the neutral *God*.

Similar changes are made in the account of Jesus' prayer in John:

| After Jesus had spoken these words, he looked up to heaven and said, Father, the hour has come; glorify your Son so that the Son may glorify you, since you have given him authority over all people, to give eternal life to all whom you have given him.... I glorified you on earth by | Having spoken these words, Jesus looked up to heaven, and said, (God my Mother and) Father, the hour has come; glorify your Child that your Child may glorify you, since you have given that Child power over all flesh, to give eternal life to all whom you have given your Child.... I glorified you |

---

[4] I have used the unpublished text of the New Revised Standard Version with the permission of Bruce M. Metzger, chairman of the Translation Committee.

[5] *An Inclusive Language Lectionary*, Cooperative Publication Society, Readings for Year A, Pentecost 7, 1983.

finishing the work that you gave me to do. So, now, Father, glorify me in your own presence.... John 17:1,2,4,5 (NRSV)	on earth, having accomplished the work which you gave me to do, and now, (God, my) Father (and Mother) glorify me in your own presence. (*Inclusive Language Lectionary*)[6]

In appraising the merits of the changes, an impartial reader may ask a series of questions:

Do the two terms *God* and *Father*, in the context of Jesus' prayer, carry equivalent meanings and nuances?
Does the joint address, *Father and Mother*, eliminate or correct the sexist element in addressing the father alone?
In this context do *child* and *son* carry the same meanings?
Is it either necessary or desirable to hide the masculine identity of Jesus who is praying, by using the neutral noun *child* or by eliminating the masculine pronoun *him*?

Given these contrasts between the lectionary and the translation, it is likely that future debates over inclusive language will further polarize the churches. Should that happen, the already heated conflict will continue to confuse rather than clarify. The NRSV translators will be accused of freezing the patriarchal prejudices of the Bible; the lectionary editors will be accused of allowing feminist prejudices to overrule the authority of scripture. Claiming innocence for itself, each side will accuse the other of guilt; claims and accusations will punctuate the struggle for power within the church, detracting attention from the claims and accusations of the gospel itself. Such recriminations aside, translators need to be as concerned with modern English usage as editors, and editors need to be as concerned with the intentions of ancient authors as translators. Both groups need to avoid the traps set by linguistic fashions, whether ancient or modern. Emotions have already been so poisoned by polemic that constructive dialogue has become difficult. One group considers as enemies those who address God as Father in prayer; refusal to use that salutation arouses the ire of the other group. In coming to church, many worshipers now carefully scrutinize the liturgy to see whether or not the language of hymns, prayers, and scripture has been satisfactorily de-sexed. For some, the choice of terminology for God has become more important than

---

[6] Ibid., Year A, Easter 7, 1983.

conversation with God. In reading the Bible it has become virtually impossible to be inclusive in language and at the same time to respect the autonomy of the biblical text.

Our goal in this essay is to explore the biblical data relevant to this debate. We limit our examination to the New Testament uses of the term Father for God and Son for Jesus (and sons for his disciples). The centrality of these two metaphors cannot be denied. The New Testament speaks of God as Father almost two hundred times. The metaphor appears in every book, excepting only 2 John, in a way that makes it intrinsic to the structure of thought and feeling. In many texts the authors consider the term God inadequate in itself without additional identification, as in the Pauline greeting, "Blessed be the God and Father of our Lord Jesus Christ, the Father of mercies..." (2 Cor 1:3). In other texts the terms son, children, brother, sister are used in ways that presuppose the idea of God as father of this elect family. References to these brothers and sisters also presuppose the idea of Jesus as brother of all believers because he is the firstborn son of their father.

These texts show that we are dealing not with two separate metaphors, father and son, but with a single way of thinking of both. As E. Lohmeyer has demonstrated, the term "Father as a designation of God is correlative to the term 'son' or 'child of God.'"[7] George H. Tavard has cited another important feature of this combined metaphor:

> The human term of the fatherhood analogy is not human fatherhood as lived by human fathers; it is the experience of human persons, women as well as men, of relating to a human father in love, gratitude and obedience. The point of comparison for the divine fatherhood is not human fatherhood; this would imply a point-by-point comparison, which proper proportionality denies radically. It is human filiation.[8]

Sallie McFague has clarified the same point:

> The images...are not meant to describe God so much as to suggest the new quality of relationship.... The models that emerge are not pictures of God, but images of a relationship.[9]

---

[7] Ernst Lohmeyer, *Our Father* (tr. John Bowden; New York: Harper & Row, 1965) 35.
[8] George H. Tavard, "Sexist Language in Theology," *TS* 36 (1975) 717.
[9] Sallie McFague, *Metaphorical Theology* (Philadelphia: Fortress, 1982) 166.

As we focus attention upon that relationship, a first question to be asked is this: Did sex play a role in the adoption and use of the Father/Son metaphor? The answer is no. "The idea of natural paternity has completely vanished from this idea of fatherhood."[10] The least ambiguous evidence for this assertion is provided by reports of the teachings of Jesus, which specify many ways in which God becomes a father to persons as they become his children. Both nouns become applicable at the moment when two divergent wills converge in one will and action. God becomes their father and persons become his sons:

- when God's love for his enemies engenders human love for enemies (Matt 5:45),
- when God's act of forgiving sins gives birth to human actions of forgiveness (Mark 11:26),
- when God's call to repentance produces human repentance, these "stones" becoming "children of Abraham" (Matt 3:7-10),
- when God's peacemaking calls peacemakers into similar action (Matt 5:9),
- when Jesus' mission as servant prompts others to become servants (Mark 8:31-38),
- when a disciple, on trial for his life, gives a faithful confession (Matt 10:20).

Jesus' prayer in Gethsemane is a decisive example. In that prayer two divergent wills become one (Mark 14:36). Equally decisive is his identification of members of his family: "Whoever does the will of God is my brother and sister and mother" (Mark 3:35).[11] The viewpoint is clear and consistent. This paternal/filial language is not gender-specific, but obedience-specific, vocation-specific, heart-specific. The willed action in which the filial relationship emerges involves persons at a level deeper than the distinction between male and female.[12] Only in becoming merciful can sons grasp the reality of a father of mercies; only such a father can bear such sons.

We may also find evidence, though perhaps more ambiguous, in Gospel texts that speak of Jesus' sonship in terms of divine epiphanies. Take the baptism stories, for example. In response to Jesus' obedience, God declares him to be "my Son, my Beloved." Neither the obedience of the Son nor the declaration by the Father entails consideration of sex.

---

[10] Lohmeyer, *Our Father*, 40.

[11] Paul S. Minear, *The God of the Gospels* (Atlanta: John Knox, 1988) 21.

[12] Lohmeyer, *Our Father*, 45; Minear, *The God of the Gospels*, 62-65.

A Lukan variant makes this clear: "Today I have begotten you" (Luke 3:22). There is a similar declaration at the transfiguration, following the prediction of Jesus' passion and the demand that the disciples share in that passion (Mark 8:31-9:1). One should include the centurion's announcement at the crucifixion (Mark 15:39). The stories of resurrection disclose the relationship between Father and Son that had been sealed in the cross (John 20:17). The metaphorical complex points to a father/son relationship that was mutually determined in the hidden origins of human desires and actions.

Should an exception be made for the birth stories that in later times encouraged different conceptions of sonship? I do not think so. Matthew's version may be ignored because the image of sonship does not appear. Not so Luke's. Here the metaphor appears as early as the annunciation (1:32-35). Of course Luke does not refer to this story in later chapters, with their more specific definitions of fatherhood and sonship. Moreover, the infancy narrative did not circulate until long after the resurrection and thus reflects the faith of that later period. It offers a retrospective view of the entire story of salvation. It echoes the song of Hannah (1 Sam 2:1-10) and early Christian hymns. Actually, the annunciation celebrates the obedient response of Mary to the miraculous promise of God. And the angel's word about Jesus was prophetic in form and predictive in substance. "He *will be* called holy, the Son of God" (2:35). Thus interpreted, the birth story ratifies our findings as to the central importance of the metaphorical complex without contradicting other Synoptic views of fatherhood and sonship. At no point does it inject sexual connotations into those views.[13]

We may draw two further inferences from the Synoptic traditions. First, because this imagery becomes relevant only in the response of repentance and faith, the paternal/filial language is intelligible only within the community of Jesus and his disciples. In his controversies with adversaries, Jesus rarely appeals to God as Father or refers to himself as son. The only major exception comes in the Markan account of his final hearing before the high priest, his final confrontation with the highest religious authority in Israel (Mark 14:62). Elsewhere the outlook of the Lord's Prayer is typical; it was meant for use only by members of this one family as they prayed for their own Father's will to be done. The Synoptics never speak of God as the Father of all human beings,

---

[13] The pattern of thinking in which God's word, by inciting obedience, gives birth to God's sons is found in the Epistles as well as the Gospels (James 1:18; 1 Peter 1:22-25). Paul found it easy to speak of his converts as his own children because they had been born in response to his revelation of God's will (1 Cor 4:14-15; 1 Thess 2:11).

and never as the Father of Jesus' adversaries, the Pharisees and Sadducees.[14] This is not so clearly true of John. However it is true that in John these adversaries uniformly rejected all claims by Jesus regarding God as his Father (2:16; 5:17-45; 6:27-65; 8:16-57; 10:15-39; 12:49, 50).

Secondly, the paternal/filial relationship is of the sort that can be realized only in the present. Children who have been forgiven by their Father cease to be his children whenever they refuse to forgive others (Matt 18:23-35). The attitude of Rabbi Judah is typical of the gospels: "If you behave as children, you are called children; if not, you are not called children."[15] Equally explicit is the author of 1 John: "Whoever loves is born of God and knows God. Whoever does not love does not know God" (4:7,8; cf. also 1 John 3:10; Heb 12:8). Preserving the priority of the Father's action, these texts disclose the necessary interconnections between his action in the heart and the visible actions of his sons.

From this evidence only one conclusion is possible: to introduce considerations of gender into the gospel traditions grossly violates the Evangelists' intentions and the imaginative structures of early Christian thinking. Moreover, the discussion of the issue at hand should be conducted only by members of the Christian community, because the language is designed to refer only to their innermost personal and communal relationships. And in their discussion of the issue they should honor the primacy of those relationships.

It is generally supposed that the paternal/filial imagery excludes the feminine half of humanity. This assumption makes it imperative to ask just whom this imagery was designed to exclude. Here we must first consider the basic purpose of metaphorical language. A metaphor arises in the effort to compare and contrast two persons or things—in this case, the divine and the human, the unknown and the known, the invisible and the visible. For example, to speak of God as Lord prompts reflection on how he is like and unlike other lords. To substitute another analogue alters the thought. The lectionary text cited above replaces Lord with Sovereign. Sovereignty, to be sure, is one feature of lordship, but it excludes other features, e.g. the lord as master of a slave, as owner of a vineyard, or as a divinity to be worshiped. The neutral sovereign reduces the range of potential meanings, overlooking the possibility that the objectionable features of lordship (e.g., the right to command his slave) may have been intended by the original author.

---

[14] Minear, *The God of the Gospels*, 98 ff.; Lohmeyer, *Our Father*, 57.

[15] Cited in Lohmeyer, *Our Father*, 43.

Or, to consider another aspect of the language, a metaphor needs only one analogue, not two or more. To introduce a second point of comparison distracts attention from the specific relationship in mind and destroys the force of the comparison and contrast. When we replace the *Father*, addressed in a prayer, with *Father and Mother*, we confuse the logic and intent of the original thought, as if we were constructing a jigsaw puzzle with pieces that belong to two separate puzzles. Whether one should do this in the words of a prayer is especially questionable. "When speaking to God, in poetry as in prayer, any sort of prevarication or ambiguity is unseemly, indeed unthinkable."[16]

It is a further misunderstanding to suppose that the selection of a particular analogue confers on it a superior status, in this case, on human fathers. Even Sallie McFague makes this mistake in her excellent book *Metaphorical Theology*:

> The human images that are chosen as metaphors for God gain in stature and take on divine qualities by being placed in an interactive relationship with the divine.[17]

This is simply not true of biblical thinking, where, for example, God is compared to an unscrupulous judge, a thief breaking into a house at night, an unjust employer, and a vintner who kills the tenants of his vineyard. To speak of him as shepherd does not denigrate the work of masons or miners. To speak of him as a consuming fire confers no blessing on arsonists. Often the metaphor stresses the repulsive aspect of an analogue in order to provoke thought (e.g. the slave δοῦλος image as adopted by apostles and prophets). The New Testament itself provides little evidence that the idea of God as Father enhanced the status of human fathers. Many texts imply no distinctions in rank between fathers and mothers (Matt 10:35,37; 15:3; 19:4,5,19,29; Mark 7:10-12; Luke 14:26). This is true of the sacrifices disciples are required to make: "Whoever loves father or mother more than me is not worthy of me" (Matt 10:37; Luke 14:26). Even alienation from both parents is declared to be a major purpose of Jesus' mission: "I have come to set a man against his father, and a daughter against her mother..." (Matt 10:35). Such texts show no preference of one sex over the other.

Even where only the male sex is under consideration, no preference is shown. Jesus commands his followers: "Call no man your father on

---

[16] Donald Davie, ed., *New Oxford Book of Christian Verse* (New York: Oxford University Press, 1981) xxix.

[17] McFague, *Metaphorical Theology*, 38.

earth..." (Matt 23:9). The unlikeness of human fathers is the necessary point of the saying: "If you (fathers) who are evil know how to give good gifts to your children, how much more will the heavenly Father..." (Luke 11:13). Even more damning is the prophecy: "A father will hand over his own child to death..." (Matt 10:21). Moreover, Jesus sees this form of cruelty to be perennial: "... so they persecuted the prophets before you" (Matt 5:12). The divine fatherhood casts no heavenly halo around earthly fathers; rather, by implication the phrase "your father in heaven" underscores the distance between this God and all the fathers on earth. "What is true of fatherhood on earth cannot be predicated of heavenly fatherhood...to speak of fatherhood in God is to negate human fatherhood as a proper image of God."[18]

We are now in a position to raise the question: whom did the father/son metaphor exclude, if not mothers and daughters? One answer has already been indicated. In the Synoptics the analogy was used by Jesus only in conversations with disciples who by accepting God's will could understand God's role as Father and their role as sons. From such an understanding, his adversaries were excluded because of their deaf ears, blind eyes, and hardened hearts. They could not fathom the thought of their God as Father of this troublemaker or the thought of these whores and traitors as his children. Previous ideas of both God and his people made this quite impossible. In all the gospels the story of Jesus' trial is told in such a way as to stress the denial on the part of the religious leaders that God could be the Father of this man or that this man could be his son. It was the use of the double metaphor that marked the distance between the judges and their victim. The verdict excluded the judges from any such filial relationship. Their revulsion over the use of such language ran far deeper than any revulsion today against the sexist taint of that same language.

Behind this self-exclusion by Jesus' enemies, the Evangelists discerned a more radical exclusion. Those who rejected Jesus' revelation of the Father, along with the revelation of this Father's family, were in fact demonstrating their filial relationship to another father. This alternative is most clearly stated in John:

If God were your Father, you would love me, for I came from God...
You are from your father the devil, and you choose to do your father's desires (8:42-44).

---

[18] Tavard, "Sexist Language in Theology," 717.

The Synoptics reflect the same outlook. Consider the temptation story in Matthew and Luke. The devil's argument—"if you are the son of God"—reveals a demonic misunderstanding of both fatherhood and sonship; but Jesus' answer discloses the true understanding of both. The later account of Peter's temptation is based on the same misunderstanding (Mark 8:31-33), with Peter accepting that misunderstanding and Jesus rejecting it. These two temptation stories provided a key to the entire drama, with its struggle between true and false ideas of the Father/Son relationship. The same key recurs in the crucifixion stories, with the dramatic repetition of Satan's "if you are the Son of God..." (Matt 27:40). From that time on, Christian faith was expressed in the confession of God as "the Father of our Lord Jesus Christ." It was by carrying his obedience so far as to die that Jesus forever defined the Father/Son relationship. After that death, this fatherhood and this sonship became as exclusive as the cross itself—and as inclusive. Here God both judged and loved the world, both judged his servants and loved his enemies. The cross clinched the command: "Love your enemies so that you may become sons... " When love of enemies is the test, how many are excluded? And how many are excluded by other commands? Such exclusiveness is more formidable than if it were a matter of sex or race or class. But by the same token, nothing is more inclusive than the definition of fatherhood and sonship enacted in the crucifixion. As the apostle Paul insisted, by excluding everyone, the cross included everyone (Rom 11:32).

Here we touch upon the deepest reason for resisting the effort to eliminate the paternal/filial language. That effort makes the same mistake with regard to the definition of fatherhood and sonship that the devil made...and Peter...and Caiaphas. It assumes that fatherhood is equivalent to superior status and arbitrary power, and that sonship is equivalent to exclusive privilege and special immunity.[19]

In recognizing the unique thrust of this language, something more important is at stake than the verbal sanctity of scripture. At stake is the authority of Jesus in both his saving word and his saving deed. And if his death is accepted as a revelation of his Father's will, then the authority of this Father is at stake. That is the precise implication of the account of the Gethsemane prayer, when the two wills, after maximum stress, converged into one. How we deal with this matter involves both history and faith. The historian has a salient contribution to make: to define the

---

[19] The terms father and son are examples of the radical linguistic revolution evoked by the prophetic teaching and vicarious death of Jesus. See Minear, *The God of the Gospels*, 64 ff.

issues on which believers must take a stand. Should they respect the gospel definitions of fatherhood and sonship, or rather, the gospel conception of the subtle relationships which those definitions presuppose? Granting the accuracy of that conception, believers must decide whether or not to exclude themselves from the realm that is ruled by those relationships.

But in making their decisions, both historians and believers are subject to other pressures that emanate from our current linguistic climate. At the outset of this essay I noted that both translators and editors should be sensitive to the connotations of these masculine metaphors in modern thought and speech. We must now look more closely at this factor. There is no denying the extent to which the revulsion of many Christians against male-dominated churches has become fused with their repudiation of the masculine language of the Bible. In their case, allergies to the texts that refer to God as Father have become as visceral as nausea, as uncontrollable as vertigo. Translators, no less than editors, must become aware of these allergies. But how can this be done without impugning the authority of the Bible, without erasing the σκάνδαλον of the Cross, without rejecting the Lord's Prayer and the people who use it? Is this an impasse that neither history nor faith can resolve?

However we answer such questions, there is work to be done that neither biblical translators nor lectionary editors can do. All these need the help of interpreters and teachers, who can spend more time in exploring the whole contested area. Such exegetes and teachers have the responsibility of penetrating the logic of metaphorical language, expounding the original sense of the texts and exploring the modern idiom for possible equivalents to biblical metaphors. In fulfilling such tasks, interpreters may move in one of two directions. One course is progressively to remove from the lexicon all metaphors that utilize masculine analogues: king, lord, father, he, his, him. This procedure has the advantage of relieving pent-up anger and resentments, but it is done at a certain cost. It fights a Sisyphean battle against the very logic and genius of metaphorical thinking which, as we have seen, thrives on using provocative and even obnoxious comparisons. It can never succeed in purging the linguistic stock of all offensive analogues. It encourages the practice of censoring the English language as it has developed through the centuries, or at least until about 1950. It seriously restricts the publication, circulation, and appreciation of all books published before the generation now living. By impoverishing the vocabulary and shrinking the library, it inhibits the imagination and constricts the freedom of speech. Within the churches, it produces analysts and critics of the liturgy rather than participants in prayers and anthems. It rejects out of hand the possibility that in speaking to the soul God might use offensive masculine terms.

What, then, is the second option that is open to teachers and interpreters of scripture? Instead of progressively diminishing the stock of acceptable images, they may expand it and in the process move toward a more flexible and catholic imagination. Instead of attacking objectionable analogues, they may cultivate the appreciation of even more objectionable ones, remembering that in the first century the whole father/son idiom was more offensive to enemies of the church than it now is to current crusaders. Teachers should point out that such offensiveness was considered essential to the success of the mission of Jesus and his apostles. As Nancy A. Hardesty has suggested, the choice ultimately is whether to limit our vocabulary to the scope of a first-grade primer or to expand it to embrace the wealth of an unabridged dictionary, on the principle that "the more ways in which we learn to understand God and to speak of God, the more deeply we will know God."[20]

Should this second course be chosen, the New Testament itself can offer great help precisely at the points where it retains the father/son imagery. The Gospel of John is a case in point. This gospel is filled with that imagery even more than the Synoptics, so if we can find help here we will be able to find help elsewhere. In John many alternative metaphorical constructions describe the relationship to God without the slightest suspicion of sexual preference. Let us look at some of the texts in which the Father/Son metaphor merges into these non-masculine alternatives.

As a first example, the familial relation is replaced by the relation of the sender to the sent. God sent the Son into the world "in order that the world might be saved through him" (3:17). Here fatherhood is defined by the act of sending, sonship by the act of being sent. This action of being sent includes many other sons: "Holy Father...as you have sent me into the world, so I have sent them into the world" (17:18). The identification of *son* with *sent* also appears in Jesus' protest to the Jews who were about to stone him: "... can you say that the one whom the Father has sanctified and sent into the world is blaspheming because I said I am God's Son?" (10:36). To say "Son of God" is to say "sent by God;" one expression is no more sexist than the other. To address God as Father is to say "I am sent by him." All who are sent belong to the

---

[20] Nancy A. Hardesty, *Inclusive Language in the Church* (Atlanta: John Knox, 1987) 14; cf. McFague, *Metaphorical Theology*, 20.

same embassy (6:57; 8:42; 13:16; 16:27; 20:17,21). This image excludes only those who are not sent, together with persons who do not welcome those who are sent. The correlation is quite exact. Father:Son::Sender:Sent.

A similar correlation is this: Father:Son::Speaker:Word spoken. To his Father Jesus said, "I have given them the words you gave to me" (17:8). To his disciples he said, "The word that you hear is not mine, but the Father's who sent me" (14:24). To his adversaries he said, "What I say, I say as the Father has commanded me" (12:49). Then he explains the reason for their exclusion: "You seek to kill me because my word finds no place in you to dwell" (8:37). The speaking of this word constitutes the moment of creation; it marks the birth of all who receive it (1:13). It has the power to shape the existence of every believer, whether for life or for death. The Father is the speaker of this Word; the world is its destination; in between are the sons who listen, obey, and relay the Word. This idiom excludes only those in whom the Word finds no place to dwell. The speaking and hearing involve no sexual connotations. Father:Son::Sender:Sent::Speaker:Word spoken.

The same relationship is also evident in the idiom of the giving and receiving of the Holy Spirit. The act of giving constitutes fatherhood, the act of receiving, sonship. The two actions occur simultaneously. At the beginning of Jesus' mission John the Baptist linked sonship to the gift of the Spirit: "The one on whom you see the Spirit descend...is the Son of God" (1:33-34). Jesus assured Nicodemus that this correlation extended to the disciples: "Only a person who is born of water and the Spirit can enter the kingdom of God" (3:5). This idiom reappears in a decisive way in the resurrection account: "Just as the Father has sent me, even so I send you....Receive the Holy Spirit" (20:21,22). Three links in the chain of thought appear in a single verse: "The one whom God has *sent* utters the *words* of God, for God does not measure out the *Spirit* grudgingly" (3:34).[21]

Let me add one other example of the shift from one idiom to another—the Johannine stress on works and working. The Father is a worker and so is the Son. Both demonstrate the paternal/filial relationship by doing the same works. "My Father is working still, and I

---

[21] This conception of the relation of sonship to the Spirit is as true of Paul as of John. Paul W. Meyer makes this clear in his commentary on Romans: "Obedience is not finally the work of the self but the result of the Spirit's leading. The Spirit produces an authentic filial relationship to God in place of slavery and verifies that gift by enabling people to address God with the intimate term 'Father'." See Meyer, "Romans," in *Harper's Bible Commentary* (ed. James L. Mays; San Francisco: Harper & Row, 1988) 1152.

am working" (5:17). The importance Jesus placed on these works is underscored in antithetical parallelism:

> If I am not doing the works of my Father, then do not believe me. But if I do them, believe the works (10:37,38).

One could hardly ask for a better indication of priorities. The works constitute a better index to the God-relationship than do verbal assertions. This is true because one definition of these works is to give life to the dead (5:21). The world also is defined by its works: "The world hates me, because I testify of it that its works are evil" (7:7). Those who do the works of the devil are sons of the devil (8:44). Some works exclude, others include. For those included, the promise is this: "Whoever believes in me will also do the works I do...and even greater things than these, because I go to the Father" (14:12). The works are visible; the hand of the ultimate worker is invisible. The basic reality is the convergence of unseen wills in the visible works. This reality is inherent in the selfhood of the believer and in the identity of the family of believers. Father:Son::Worker:Workers.

There are still other metaphorical complexes that suggest alternative ways of expressing the paternal/filial relationship:

Father: Son :: Giver of life: recipient of life
Father: Son :: Glory given: glory received
Father: Son :: Love given: love received and shared
Father: Son :: Judge: Judge
Father: Son :: Truth: Truth
Father: Son :: Light: Light
Father: Son :: the Peace of God : "my peace"
Father: Son :: God abiding in disciples: disciples abiding in God

The interactions among these images represent an amazing mixing of metaphors and a great versatility in expression. The flexibility of the Evangelist's imagination gives canonical support for readers to indulge in an equivalent flexibility. Such flexibility discourages efforts either to avoid the paternal/filial imagery or to absolutize its importance.

The correlations we have examined thus far are correlations among nouns: father, son, life, glory, truth, etc. If we extended the study to include verbs, the list would be much longer, for the number of verbs expressive of the divine-human relationship is much greater. Often the Father and the Son (or sons) are viewed as two subjects of the same verb: calling, gathering, healing, opening, blessing, going, seeing, hearing, promising, coming, giving. In function, these verbs are as metaphorical as are the nouns. Even more clearly than the nouns, they indicate the active inner character of family interdependence. The verbs accent the degree to which both Father and Son (and sons) are known through what they do; and they accent the degree to which human actions are the setting in which the presence of the divine may be discerned.[22] These verbal pictures make sense only if behind the pictures lie the personal and communal experience of a God-relationship that is creative of new selves in a new community. These conceptualizations of the God-relationship in verbs are projections of what has happened at the deepest levels of self-awareness. One may well think of various Pauline efforts to describe the miracle. "If anyone is in Christ...a new creation. Old things have passed away; the new has come" (2 Cor 5:17).[23] Nouns and verbs alike point beyond themselves to an elemental mystery that impelled apostles and prophets to redefine the simplest words of the vocabulary: birth, life, death, words, works, family. This language is rigorously exclusive—and scandalously inclusive; yet it has nothing to do with distinctions between sexes or classes. It points rather to the distinction between old things and new.

The conflict between inclusive language and biblical authority is bound to continue. It does not permit a quick resolution. But it may prove to be remarkably beneficial if it induces exegetes and teachers to fulfill their responsibilities: to bring into play the vast stock of biblical images, using each to illuminate the others, to clarify the basic virtues of metaphorical thought and speech, to listen afresh to the teachings in which Jesus disclosed his original perceptions of God as Father, to restore to the Passion story its central place in disclosing the power and wisdom of this strange God, to orient all God-talk around the experienced creation of radically new selves in a new community. Historians can indicate where the issues lie. Translators and lectionary editors can provide clear and accurate versions of the biblical texts. Sensitive interpreters can explore the rich resonances of the scriptural testimonies. In the end, however, comprehension of the meanings will

---

[22] Minear, *The God of the Gospels*, 60.

[23] My efforts to penetrate the level of self-awareness that these metaphors presuppose have reminded me time and time again of Søren Kierkegaard's analysis of the self in *Sickness Unto Death* (tr. Walter Lowrie; Princeton: Princeton University Press, 1941). In its intricate internal relationships, the self is derived from the Power that constituted it (43). Only through its relationship to this Power is the self able to recognize itself as a synthesis of the finite and the infinite (44). The various forms of despair (or "the sickness unto death") stem from various ways of rejecting these internal relationships. An older analysis of the self in its inner relation to its creator may be found in Psalm 139.

be the work of faith on the part of those who have been born anew into this unique family.

21

Pluralism and Unity in the New Testament

Oscar Cullmann [1]

I. The Problem

The New Testament is composed of 27 books. During the first century they clearly were not yet Holy Scripture, even though the epistles, and a little later the gospels, were read with fervor. For the first Christians, what we today call the "Old Testament" was the only Bible. It was especially through the *oral* preaching of witnesses that the gospel spread and converts had the daily experience, in their life and in their worship, of the presence of Christ the redeemer and Lord. But when the first generation disappeared, the eyewitnesses survived among subsequent generations through *their writings*, and thanks to these *writings*, Christians continued, and continue still today, to have the same experience as that of the first generations. To be sure, the presence of Christ, who was raised to the right hand of God, is not bound to written documents. But Christians began to feel more and more certain that these books were special *means of grace* granted to humans by God to

---

[1] Oscar Cullman is Professor Emeritus of New Testament and Early Christianity at the University of Basel, Switzerland.

This essay is translated from the French, "Pluralisme et Unite dans le Noveau Testament," by Dr. Michael J. Gorman, Assistant Director of the Council for Religion in Independent Schools, Washington, D.C.

transmit to all future generations the good news of the revelation in Christ, so that Jesus Christ might be present among them as he was present among the apostles. Thus the writings are not "dead letters," as some have said, but sources of life continuing to spring forth eternally.

When, beginning in the second century, other writings that were supposedly apostolic but were in reality of obscure and late origin (i.e., the "apocryphal" writings) began to spread and had to be set aside, our 27 books of the New Testament asserted themselves. They did so through their antiquity and their content as the word of God, as elements of the *incarnation*, as the only authentic witness from the apostolic period. When we compare these writings with the apocryphal writings, which are generally mediocre, we have to say that the Holy Spirit was truly at work in that selection. Space does not allow for a detailed discussion of the history of the formation of the Canon. In brief, little by little the 27 books came to be regarded as Holy Scripture under the name "New Testament." This New Testament was considered as the continuation of the Hebrew Bible, which the Church preserved as the "Old Testament," in contrast to certain heretics who rejected it.

The New Testament as the word of God: that brings us to our subject. Is the "word of God" compatible with a plurality of 27 books? Is the unity of the divine revelation safeguarded by so many writings that are so different from one another? And is not 27 a more or less arbitrary plurality?[2]

The diversity concerns, first of all, the authors. Among them there are apostles; only three of them, however, belong to the 12: Matthew and John (gospels) and Peter (epistle). There is also the apostle Paul, but the others are only disciples of apostles. There are different literary genres: narrative writings (the gospels, Acts), the epistles, and the Apocalypse. There are also different theologies within the writings, each of which emphasizes a particular point of view.

We will see that, especially with regard to the gospels, the plurality (four narratives of exactly the same events) was felt, even in antiquity, to be a problem. In modern times the human Jesus, as he appears especially in the synoptic gospels—preaching and healing the sick, crucified and resurrected—is considered by many readers to be completely different from the glorified Christ—seated at the right hand of God and Lord of the universe—that we meet in the epistles.

---

[2] In the Old Testament there is also a plurality, although the problem presents itself there in a slightly different manner. Here we will consider the question only with respect to the New Testament.

But from another perspective, isn't the plurality, on the contrary, a sign of richness, betokening Christian universalism? I will attempt, in fact, to show that plurality is not opposed to unity, but that it is even the *foundation* of unity. Plurality is willed by God, and its necessity is anchored in the divine revelation itself.

In order to better explicate the true bond between plurality and unity, I will begin by discussing numerical plurality and then will concentrate on the plurality of theological ideas, giving special attention to erroneous reactions to pluralism.

II. Numerical Plurality

I will take as an example the four gospels. As noted above, the plurality of the four has been considered a problem since antiquity. It did not seem natural that the same life of Jesus the Son of God was told four times, with more or less major differences, by four different authors, of whom only two (Matthew and John) belonged to the 12 apostles (Mark and Luke being only disciples of apostles). It seemed difficult to consider as a divine word a collection whose makeup appeared to be due to purely human contingencies and even to chance.

Beginning in the second century, various attempts were undertaken to substitute a single gospel, claimed to be the only authentic one, for the four. Some chose, according to their preference, to make one of our four gospels the only gospel. Thus Origen, the theologian of the third century, informs us that certain heretics recognized only Mark, others only Matthew. The great heretic of the second century, Marcion, who rejected the entire Old Testament, accepted as authentic only Luke, because the evangelist Luke was of pagan origin. Another heretical solution consisted of eliminating the four gospels and constructing a new, apocryphal gospel, erroneously linked to the authority of the *twelve* apostles, because it seemed that only together could they guarantee the faithfulness of the narrative. While the heretical character of these attempts was easily recognized, that of the second-century Syrian theologian Tatian gained acceptance in a number of churches, especially in Syria. This was a gospel "harmony," a combination of our four gospels, with one story borrowed from this gospel, another from that. In Greek this gospel harmony was called the Diatessaron, meaning "from four gospels (one)." Only later, in the fifth century, did the churches that had adopted it replace it with our four. The choice of stories was necessarily arbitrary, just as the other attempts that we have discussed rested on an arbitrary choice.

The Greek verb that means *to choose*, αἱρέομαι, is the verb from which our word *heretic* is derived. A heretic is a person who claims *to choose* arbitrarily, according to his human preferences, only certain parts of a revealed truth. But if the plurality of the gospels is part of the revelation, it cannot be the object of this kind of choice.

The plurality is, in fact, willed by God. It is the consequence of the human incarnation of Christ. The life of Jesus is so rich that it embodies a multitude of perspectives. A single disciple in his human weakness was not sufficient to embrace this richness in its totality. The gospels are testimonies of faith to the events of the life of Jesus the Son of God. Each evangelist bore his testimony according to the particular spiritual gift that he received. The Holy Spirit always acts by diversifying his gifts. The Holy Spirit unites, but he unites through diversity. Herein lies the *correct response* to the question of plurality. The apostle Paul devoted an entire chapter (1 Corinthians 12) to insisting on the unity of the Holy Spirit through diversity. Each evangelist received a special gift. The recent work of exegetes on the gospels strives precisely to define the particularities of the faith of each evangelist. Only the four testimonies *together* can prove *the* testimony to the life of Jesus Christ that is capable of eliciting faith in its readers.

What is true for the four gospels is true for the 27 books of the New Testament. Just as God revealed himself to people in a *human being*, Jesus Christ, born among a predetermined people and in a chosen land, so too God chose human beings—several human beings—to transmit the good news through their writings, always afresh to all generations. This transmission, therefore, is part of the incarnation.

III. Plurality of Theological Ideas in the New Testament

I turn now to the plurality of theological *ideas*. With respect to this, as well, the New Testament confronts us with a great diversity. Throughout the centuries, each era, and each church, has concentrated on *one* aspect of the theology of the New Testament, namely, the one that corresponded to its own charismatic identity. For each church has its own spiritual gift. We have said that the Holy Spirit inspired the authors of the New Testament by granting them different gifts. The Holy Spirit, present in the spiritual gifts of the readers, responds to the same Holy Spirit who inspired the different parts of the collection. Thus the great humanist Erasmus gave particular importance to the Sermon on the Mount, the Reformers to justification by faith as taught by the apostle Paul, the Orthodox Church to Johannine theology. And it would be interesting to study the entire history of the church from this perspective.

But then the question arises: Is there, however, a *legitimate* choice? We just said above that "to choose" in the face of the divine revelation was a sign of heresy. What is the criterion that distinguishes a legitimate choice from an illegitimate choice? The choice—that is, concentration on certain theological ideas in the New Testament—is legitimate whenever it is based on a spiritual gift and *does not entail the exclusion* of the other truths proclaimed by the New Testament but implies respect for the ideas contained in other parts of the collection.

The only "heretical" choice is one, based on preconceived ideas, that *suppresses* or *rejects* all ideas that contradict these preconceived ideas drawn from other sources. The Christian message is above our contradictions and our divisions. Thus we must guard ourselves from purely and simply discarding the theology of the Pauline epistles and a part of our gospels in order to keep only certain words and certain gospel narratives related to a very limited number of Christ's teachings. We must guard ourselves from inventing our own New Testament according to ideas that are consistent neither with the rules of historical and philological exegesis nor with a spiritual gift but originate from other sources. We must guard ourselves against working out a theology based on an arbitrarily *truncated* New Testament, a theology based on a certain number of passages that, to be sure, are found in the New Testament but are arbitrarily isolated from the rest. This isolation distorts the gospel.

To acknowledge that the different theological ideas in their diversity complete each other to form a superior synthesis is to allow other Christians and other churches, in turn, the liberty to concentrate, each through a legitimate choice according to their spiritual gifts, on other theological ideas in the New Testament. Thus diversity will not become cause for discord but, on the contrary, a reason for reciprocal respect and an encouragement to learn from one another. It is here that I see the solution to the ecumenical problem of the unity of the Christian churches: each must maintain its own spiritual gifts, yet through diversity.[3]

Even, however, in allowing for all the liberty of a legitimate choice, we must avoid one danger: the danger of division, the danger that each will interpret the New Testament *as a whole* from the ideas that correspond to their spiritual gift. In fact, we cannot be sure whether our idea is really the central idea common to *all* the authors of the New Testament. We risk creating an arbitrary perspective and destroying the harmony. Legitimate plurality must not turn into division. There has to

---

[3] See my book, *Unity Through Diversity* (Philadelphia: Fortress, 1988).

be a common unifying principle to *coordinate* all the particular spiritual gifts. There has to be a canon *within* the Canon.

How are we to find this common theological *center*? Only the New Testament itself can reveal it to us, and that leads us to our final section.

IV. The Elements of Unity in Diversity according to the New Testament

The New Testament formulates this unifying principle in the short confessions of faith that are cited in it and which are intended to summarize the essence of the Christian faith. I made a study of them in this regard several years ago. These formulas were born in the primitive community before the composition of the first writings. In citing them, the authors of the New Testament indicate to us what for *them* is the common center of their faith. These formulas agree in confessing faith in Jesus Christ, for faith in God the creator, inherited from Judaism, was presupposed as natural. Some of these formulas are very short: "Jesus Christ is Lord," "Jesus Christ is the Son of God." Others that are longer list the great christological truths. The most famous of these is the one in 1 Cor 15:3ff., which the apostle Paul explicitly says he had previously received from the community. This confession became the point of departure for the more developed creeds of the Church in the first centuries. These later creeds, in agreement with the thought of the New Testament, add a clause about faith in God the creator at the beginning. The existence of these creeds from the first centuries, still used today in worship, is important from the perspective of ecumenics. The founders of the Protestant Reformation recognized them as the essence of New Testament faith; and I am happy that a great Catholic theologian, the late Karl Rahner, at the end of his life proposed the Apostles' Creed and the Nicene-Constantinople Creed as the *common base* on which the plurality of Christian churches can and must be accepted.

If we examine the New Testament affirmations that appear to diverge from one another in light of these summaries of the Christian faith, we find connections where people have incorrectly claimed to see opposition. For example, it has been said that the doctrine of redemption through Christ's death for our sins is absent from the preaching of the earthly Jesus. However, in reality it is linked, by virtue of the role of the Suffering Servant of God of Isaiah 53 that Jesus attributed to himself in the words of institution at the Last Supper, to all of his teaching on the grace freely granted by the Father to the one who believes. Furthermore, this doctrine of redemption is linked above all to the fact, as reported in the gospels, that during his ministry on earth Jesus actually forgave sins.

But what especially unifies all of New Testament theology is the authors' conviction, shared with the Jews, that they belong to a *salvation history* that runs from the suprahistorical events of creation, through events unfolding on a straight line within secular history, toward the history of Israel and from there toward the Kingdom of God, and finally to the new creation. But whereas for the Jews the kingdom of God is only future, for the writers of the New Testament, who regard it in the light of the coming of Christ, it is *at the same time both future and present*. The central and decisive event has already taken place, and yet this event is not the conclusion; time continues until the final realization. The powers of evil and of sin are defeated, but they remain bound, so to speak, to a rope that can be stretched to the point that they can still break loose—until they are forever destroyed. In my book *Christ and Time*,[4] which I wrote during the very last phase of World War II, I used an image which, at that particular time, was appropriate: the battle that decided the final victory had taken place, but the war continued because the armistice had not yet been signed. That is exactly the situation in which the authors who wrote the books of the New Testament found themselves after the death and resurrection of Christ, and it is *our* situation. We live in an in-between time marked by the "already" of the divine victory in Christ and the "not yet" of the final conclusion. The realities of this in-between time are characterized by this duality: the existing institutions (the churches, the state, etc.) are willed by God and are to be respected for as long as this age, whose length we do not know, continues. Yet, though willed by God, they are called to give way to a future kingdom.

Here, then, is the movement of this history: from the creation of the world it becomes progressively narrower as it moves toward humanity, and toward the people of Israel. Then, becoming narrower still, it moves toward the "remnant of Israel" of which the prophets speak, and finally to the One, Jesus Christ, who is the center and norm of this entire history. From this center the movement is reversed along the "return route," this time constantly widening, from Christ to the apostles, from the apostles to the Church, from the Church to the world, and from the world to the new creation. This vision of the great stages in the second part of salvation history explains at once both the plurality of the New Testament as the result of the unfolding of time (gospels, Acts, letters,

---

[4] *The Primitive Christian Conception of Time and History* (Westminster: Philadelphia, 1950).

the Apocalypse) and the unity of the New Testament as the result of the plan of God that binds the different stages together.

Thus the New Testament, which is simultaneously a pluralism and a unity, is called to create unity also among the churches in their diversity. It is not an accident that ecumenism, some 40 years ago, received a special impulse through the common study of the Bible. But the New Testament, which connects the events to which it bears witness to those of the Old Testament, extends this unity beyond the Christian churches. Thus salvation history, despite the differences that separate us, unites us also to the people of Israel, whose history is inseparable from our own salvation history. And since the final goal of salvation history, in the New as in the Old Testament, envisions the world, we can say that within the scope of this salvation history is all of humanity. Such is the expectation expressed by the beautiful confession of the ancient hymn cited by the apostle Paul in Phil 2:10: "every knee shall bow" before the Lord. And the apostle himself speaks, in the majestic eschatological tableau of 1 Cor 15:28, of the end when "God will be all in all."

22

Calvin's Scriptural Ethical Monotheism: Interpretation, Moral Conscience, and Religious System

Wendell S. Dietrich [1]

Calvin's authorship constitutes a religious system and one that I propose to identify as a scriptural ethical monotheism.[2] This system

---

[1] Wendell S. Dietrich is Professor of Religious Studies and Professor of Judaic Studies at Brown University, Providence, Rhode Island.

[2] By authorship I intend Calvin's *Institutes*, the biblical commentaries, and the various ecclesiological treatises. This study is based principally on an extended and, I hope, independent study of the *Institutes* in the 1559 version: John Calvin, *Institutes of the Christian Religion* (ed. John T. McNeill and tr. Ford Lewis Battles; 2 vols; Philadelphia: Westminster Press, 1960). John Calvin, *Opera Selecta* (eds. Peter Barth and Wilhelm Niesel; vols. 3, 4 and 5; Chr. Kaiser, 1957). John Calvin, *L'Institution de la religion chrétienne* 4 vols; Geneva: Labor et Fides, 1955). With respect to the content of the commentaries and their place in the latter phases of Calvin's total authorship, I have been especially instructed by Gilbert Vincent, *Exigence éthique et interprétation dans l'oeuvre de Calvin* (Geneva: Labor et Fides, 1984); Harro Hoepfl, *The Christian Polity of John Calvin* (Cambridge: Cambridge University Press, 1982); T. H. L. Parker, *Calvin's New Testament Commentaries* (London: S.C.M. Press, 1971); Benjamin Charles Milner, Jr., *Calvin's Doctrine of the Church* (Leiden: E. J. Brill, 1970). Milner's book is especially valuable in calling attention to pertinent passages from Calvin's Old Testament commentaries. It also shares with my own essay an enthusiasm for Troeltsch's reading of Calvin, though Milner

claims as supreme authority and normative source the Old and New Testaments, read as a single unitary canon of sacred scripture. Calvin's method of interpreting that scripture provides one of the distinctive and defining features of his system. This essay focuses on Calvin's reading of sacred scripture in constructing his system and on his distinctive method of interpretation.

According to Calvin, the scriptural word, construed as a mode of the divine communication to humanity, is addressed to the troubled and guilty moral conscience. That is, a key feature of Calvin's system is what the recent French Calvin interpreter Gilbert Vincent[3] has termed an "ethical exigency." That means that the Christian moral life is interpreted in a distinctive way on the assumption that the human being as creature recognizes an unconditional moral obligation. God the Commander is the source of that obligation and also provides its sanction. (In Calvin's terms, God is the Governor of humankind in the context of the whole of creaturely reality.)

This construing of the Christian moral life assumes that the human person as moral and religious self is emphatically distinguished from the environing cosmos. This differentiates Calvin's view of the Christian moral life from the Thomist-Aristotelian scheme which presents the human being as a psycho-physical reality ultimately oriented by a spiritual dynamism toward fulfillment through virtuous operation and perfection of its powers, a perfection that culminates in friendship with and the vision of God.

Further, Calvin's authorship is a religious and not merely a theological system. Among Calvin's twentieth-century interpreters, Ernest Troeltsch, in volume 2 of *The Social Teaching of the Christian Churches*[4], has made this claim most compellingly. Troeltsch shows that Calvin constructs, through the selection and arrangement of items of Christian belief and the interpretation of sacred scripture, a description of reality (or view of the world) and prescriptions for a moral and social way of life. This religious system functions, at the point where the early modern period of Western civilization is emerging, to shape and energize a distinctive people of God. Calvin constitutes a "Christianity" and brings into play resources for a powerful and enduring actualization of that "Christianity" in the sphere of social life.

---

is principally occupied with a different theme: the correlation of the incarnate and scriptural Word and the Spirit.

[3] Vincent, *Exigence éthique*.

[4] Ernst Troeltsch, *The Social Teaching of the Christian Churches* (2 vols; London: George Allen and Unwin, 1931) 2, 576-660; especially in this connection, 599, 617, 618.

I shall now develop this argument in somewhat greater detail by making the following observations about Calvin's authorship. First, Calvin reads scripture as a narrative, a continuous story with forward movement[5] from the creation and fall of humanity through the "general election" of God's people of the Old Covenant (*peuple ancien*) to the identification of God with humanity in the salvific mediator (the God-human, Jesus Christ) and the establishment of the kingly rule of the risen and ascended Lord. This rule is actualized now in the Christian community under the conditions of spiritual combat and cross-bearing.[6]

Second, Calvin reaffirms in his own distinctive way the decision of the ancient church that the Old and New Testaments constitute a single and unitary canon of sacred scripture. He proposes a fresh series of strategies for working out a reading of scripture in its canonical totality "intratextually," to use the term of present-day literary theory.[7] Moreover, the books of canonical scripture in their interconnection are sharply differentiated from and assigned unique authority in contrast to any other authoritative texts of the Christian religious tradition. That is, in the language of the sixteenth century, "Scripture interprets itself."

Third, the reality of Christ in Calvin's religious system is persistently adduced, especially in the polemic of the *Institutes, in loco justificationis* (i.e., within the framework of the doctrine of justification). That means that this reality is adduced as a comfort to the tormented consciences of fallen human beings who are so alienated from God that they persistently turn in upon themselves and must constantly be converted in order that they might refer all life and its benefits to God and not to themselves.[8] In this respect, there is strong continuity between the teaching of Luther and Calvin, although Calvin gives his own characteristic formulation to self-denial and the reference of all benefits to God.[9]

---

[5] Hans W. Frei, *The Eclipse of Biblical Narrative* (London/New Haven: Yale University Press, 1974) 17-37.

[6] E. David Willis, *Calvin's Catholic Christology: The Function of the So-called Extra Calvinisticum in Calvin's Theology* (Leiden: E. J. Brill, 1966). Willis establishes the centrality for Calvin of Christ's present kingly rule at the right hand of the Father and the relation of that to his view of the moral life.

[7] George Lindbeck, "Barth and Textuality," *Theology Today* 43 (1986) 361-376.

[8] This is one theme of H. Richard Niebuhr's complex and variegated interpretation of Calvin. See Niebuhr, "John Calvin," in *Christian Ethics: Sources of the Living Tradition* (ed. Waldo Beach and H. Richard Niebuhr; New York: Ronald, 1955) 267-274.

[9] On the continuities in the teaching of Luther and Calvin, see especially B. A. Gerrish, *The Old Protestantism and the New: Essays in the Reformation Heritage* (Chicago: University of Chicago Press, 1982).

In Calvin's version of Reformation teaching, however, a special role is given to the shaping and formation of moral and social life, that is, to life-prescription on the basis of the life-description of the human being as creature, a fallen creature justified in Christ and converted to God. In the language of the sixteenth century disputes, Calvin teaches a "third use of the Law."[10]

Fourth, Calvin's system takes with special seriousness the Old Testament description of the social and political formation of God's people of the Old Covenant and also the prescriptions associated with that formation. On the other hand, Calvin employs a sophisticated strategy for classifying these prescriptions—ceremonial, political (sometimes called "judicial") and moral—and for judging which prescriptions are still valid for the present-day elect Christian community. Or, to use the language of contemporary literary theory, he has a strategy for selective recontextualization of the authoritative prescriptions initially given to God's people of the Old Covenant.

Fifth, Calvin's recontextualizing of the Biblical narrative and the Old Testament descriptions of and prescriptions for social and political life occurs at a key point, namely, the time of early modernity.[11] A disenchantment of the physical cosmos is under way and humanity the creature stands out with a certain moral and religious self-awareness over against it. In fact, Calvin, especially in his Genesis commentary, reads the creation narrative not as a theory of the origins of the cosmos but rather as a recital about humanity the creature, who is surrounded by benefits in the created world. There may well be a latent anti-natural scientific import in Calvin's denigration of secondary causes and his insistence that each action befalling humankind is a direct ordinance of the divine Providence. Indeed Calvin is reluctant to embrace the Copernican hypothesis, although his system is open to it in principle. Still, to paraphrase Vincent's daring judgment, Calvin interprets "nature" as if it had already fully undergone that desacralization, that disenchantment to which Weber points at the end of the nineteenth century.[12]

---

[10] On this point again, Troeltsch, *Social Teaching*, vol. 2, 617, 618

[11] Here I deliberately use the terminology of Max Weber and of one of Weber's most compelling present-day interpreters, Wolfgang Schluchter. See Schluchter, *The Rise of Western Rationalism: Max Weber's Developmental History* (Berkeley: University of California Press, 1981); and *idem*, "The Paradox of Rationalization: On the Relation of Ethics and Work," in Wolfgang Schluchter and Guenther Roth, *Max Weber's Vision of History: Ethics and Methods* (Berkeley: University of California Press, 1979) 11-64.

[12] Vincent, *Exigence éthique*, 239-286; *idem*, "Discours et Doctrine: Modalités de l'affirmation calvinienne de la providence," in *Ecclesiae Genevensis Custos* (ed. Wilhelm

This is linked with a further point, which David Little has so cogently argued.[13] Whatever attractions Calvin may feel to Renaissance versions of Stoic ethical thought—and they are certainly powerful attractions—Calvin nonetheless refuses to ground his ethic in a transcription of the patterns of human nature assimilated to the regularities of the physical cosmos, regularities further assumed to be sanctioned by an immanent God. Calvin's ethical maxim is not a Stoic, "Become yourself."

Even in Calvin's uses of the language of "natural law," it is the "law" prescribed to a creature whose existence is radically contingent on the will of the divine Creator and Governor. It is a "natural law" the knowledge of which must be refocused through the spectacles of scripture and the twofold knowledge of God the Creator and Redeemer available in scripture. It is a "natural law" for a creature whose future is yet open under the kingly rule of Christ.

With these general considerations in view, I proceed now to an examination of each major item in Calvin's recital of the biblical narrative, with an eye to indicating how the interpretation of each bears on the moral conscience and on the construction of socially productive scriptural ethical monotheism.

Calvin's recital of the biblical narrative of creation is constantly informed, as the Genesis commentary makes clear,[14] by the assumption that the creation of humanity also initiates humanity's election to life with God. In Eden humanity is intended to enjoy the bounty of a good creation; the "tree of life" is a sign that life is to be recognized as "blessed finitude."[15] Humanity is obligated to recognize in gratitude these benefits.

Such a reading of the Genesis narrative is likely to provoke a sharp question in the mind of a late twentieth century reader. Given the subsequent course of the disenchantment of nature in the West and the exploitative attitude toward nature in modern industrial society, can one not spot here an early instance of the drastic reduction of the significance of the non-human created world to its usefulness to humankind? Or, to put it in more classic theological categories: while Calvin refers to the creation as a theater of God's glory, is it not a

---

H. Neuser; Frankfurt: Peter Lang, 1984) 197-207; *idem*, "La rationalité herméneutique de discours theologique de Calvin," *Arch. Sc. soc. des Rel.* 63 (1987) 133-154.

[13] David Little, *Religion, Order and Law: A Study in Pre-revolutionary England* (New York: Harper and Row, 1969) 33-80; David Little, "Calvin and the Prospects for a Christian Theory of Natural Law," in *Norm and Context in Christian Ethics* (ed. Gene Outka and Paul Ramsey; New York: Charles Scribners, 1968) 199-217.

[14] See on this point Vincent, *Exigence éthique*, 191-286.

[15] Ibid., 209-215.

theater in which human beings are the sole actors? Clearly, Calvin's views do contribute, within a total complex of ideational and material factors, to the emergence of the ethos of modern organizational industrial society. But in terms of Calvin's own religious system, some careful qualifications are in order.

Perhaps the matter is best approached obliquely through Calvin's refocusing of the Christian concept of self-denial. He rejects that devaluation of this world which is the presupposition of the other-worldly asceticism characteristically institutionalized in Christian monastic life. To speak in terms of moral theory, Calvin rejects the notion of "counsels of perfection" to be carried out only by a restricted elite group, "counsels" which loosen ties to family, society, and all this-worldly activity. The divine commandments are equally obligatory for all. As Calvin interprets these commandments, he produces a version of self-denial which involves a mastery of the created world, not a flight from it.[16] He clearly does not anticipate all the ramifications of that world-mastery, but his view of the non-human created world cannot be reduced to seeing its significance only in terms of its usefulness to human beings.

According to Calvin, infidelity to God and thus disobedience to the divine command are at the root of humanity's fall. The classic Augustinian theme of sin as pride (*superbia*) is developed by Calvin in relatively brief fashion. That brevity is related to the fact that Calvin rejects the neo-Platonic Augustinian hierarchical metaphysics, which treats *superbia* as aversion from God and conversion to finite goods "below" humanity in the total hierarchy.

Moreover, although Calvin never works the matter out in an extended "thematic" presentation, the *Institutes* abounds in evidence that Calvin sees "sloth," the refusal of the creature to be energetically what he or she is called to be, as a major mode of sin. The discussion of "sloth" is usually linked to the doctrine of that "quickening" to life by the Holy Spirit which orients the believer to the risen and ascended Christ.[17] Though connected theologically to the doctrine of Christ and the Spirit, this theme of "quickening" also has an impact on Calvin's interest in instructing the moral conscience and producing new forms of ecclesiastical and societal life.

Moreover, in addition to the treatment of sin and humanity's original sin as infidelity-disobedience-pride and the further identification of sin

---

[16] Schluchter, *The Rise of Western Rationalism; idem,* "The Paradox of Rationalization."

[17] Margaret R. Miles, "Theology, Anthropology and the Human Body in Calvin's *Institutes of the Christian Religion,*" *HTR* 74 (1981) 303-323.

as sloth, Calvin's *Institutes* also suggests, though it is never stated "thematically," a doctrine of sin as suppression of the truth. Calvin's Platonizing philosophical cast of mind draws him to the notion of the suppression of the truth as a refusal to live in the light. Such suppression of the truth about reality is linked to fallen humanity's inveterate capacity for fabricating idols in violation of both the first commandment and the prohibition against graven images.

Calvin asserts the doctrine of "hereditary sin," rejecting the Pelagian notion of "imitation." However, he assigns minimal importance to the "physical" transmission of the taint and guilt of original sin in the moment of concupiscence in sexual activity. Calvin's principal intellectual initiatives are in the direction of finding political metaphors of social covenant to express the solidarity of humankind in sin, the presence of all "in" Adam and their implication in his disobedient action.

In conflict to some extent with the probe for political metaphors is Calvin's characterization of sin as "pollution" transmitted from generation to generation. But this "pollution" is not principally linked to sexuality but rather to the soteriological notion of humanity under the curse of God and the sacrifice of Christ on humanity's behalf.[18]

In reciting the biblical narrative in its forward movement, Calvin speaks of the creation of humanity, humanity's fall in Adam and the transmission of sin. Humanity's fall occurs through the ordinance of God. But Calvin is at pains to distinguish his doctrine from astrological and classic philosophical doctrines of fate. Here Calvin is most emphatically Augustinian. He will never let go of the results of the Augustinian polemic against Manichaeism. Humanity's moral responsibility precisely as a fallen sinner must always be preserved.[19]

After the creation and fall of humanity the "general election" of the people Israel is next in the forward movement of the biblical narrative. Calvin's *Commentaries on the Four Last Books of Moses, Arranged in the Form of a Harmony* and his commentaries on the Old Testament books which chronicle Israel's history under the kings[20] provide a rich elaboration of the theme of Israel's election, but the function of the doctrine in the religious system as a whole is controlled by the doctrine

---

[18] Such a notion of pollution-sacrifice cuts back behind quasi-moral penal-juridical categories and proffers a distinctive version of Old Testament pollution-sacrifice themes in interpreting the priestly work of Christ. See George H. Kehm, "Calvin on Defilement and Sacrifice," *Int* 31 (1977) 39-52.

[19] Vincent, *Exigence éthique*, 175-190.

[20] See especially Milner, *Calvin's Doctrine of the Church*.

of election and predestination in the *Institutes*. That is, the teaching about the "general election" of the people Israel is presented in connection with and as a prelude to the teaching about the "special election" of the individual believer. Hence, to understand the doctrine of Israel's general election it is necessary to grasp first the motivating drives of the doctrine of the election of the individual believer and the function of that doctrine in the system as a whole.

The doctrine of the election of the individual believer is religiously rooted in the problem of the "perseverance of the saints." For Calvin, what is at issue in that problem is the believer's certainty about and confidence in the divine benevolence and thus the related question of the believer's resolute persistence in the life of a justified sinner whose moral and societal behavior is reshaped in Christ. Moreover, the doctrine of the special election of the believer has an empirical point of departure in the observed fact that some persons respond to the gospel and some do not. Like Augustine and Luther, Calvin insists that the response of faith be attributed not to human worthiness but to divine grace. Moreover, Christ, for Calvin, is indeed the chief mirror of election. Finally, it is very important to note that Calvin never supposed that he, or his ministerial companions, could unmistakably identify a particular individual as elect or reprobate. He never invokes God's decision before all time to elect some persons to life and others to damnation in deducing theories or deciding cases in the sphere of ecclesiastical discipline or the interaction of ecclesiastical and political authority.[21]

Given this understanding of individual election, what does the doctrine of the "general election" of the people Israel look like? According to the biblical narrative, God elects Israel as a people.[22] Calvin, who constantly has in view the whole Pentateuch, further insists that God shapes the life of this elect people through ceremonial, political (sometimes called "judicial") and moral law. This emphasis gives to the whole system a communal-social dimension.

Moreover, Calvin recontextualizes the Old Testament teaching in the early modern period, a time of emerging national states. Thus, as Troeltsch shows, a number of possibilities emerge, not all of them explicitly warranted by Calvin's system as such. There is the possibility of construing the universal church as an association of churches in various nations. Indeed, as "Christian" nations they can themselves be

---

[21] Hoepfl, *The Christian Polity*, 227-240 argues this critical point about Calvin's religious system with special cogency.
[22] *Institutes* 3.21-24.

understood as "elect" peoples. Each of these nations may be seen as making and renewing a national covenant with God. Each of them can regard its own history as typologically prefigured in the history of Israel. This has ramifications for everything from the Scottish National Covenant to the Mayflower Compact or the ideology of Afrikaanerdom in the late nineteenth and twentieth centuries.[23]

The doctrine of Israel's general election portrays Israel as the object of the divine blessing. But Calvin also invokes the theme of Israel's exile and the "interruption" of Israel's election. Yet the theme of the interruption of election in exile is also linked to Israel's restoration.

Alongside this pattern of exile and restoration, Calvin develops the prophetic notion of a "remnant," the selection of a group out of the totality of the elect people. This he associates with the unfathomable and "arbitrary" selection for blessing of certain members of the elect people while others are rejected. From the outset Esau is cut off from election; Ishmael and Saul are also rejected.

At last the divine election concentrates on the singular figure of Jesus Christ; yet Calvin speaks further of the election of the Head and of the members of the body of Christ in the Head. Thus there is a communal aspect of election in the Christian dispensation. But the doctrine comes to focus on the "special election" of the Christian individual.

For Calvin, the climactic and, for all intents and purposes, terminal event of the biblical narrative is the identification of God with humanity in the salvific mediator, the God-human Jesus Christ. According to this interpretation God establishes the kingly rule of the risen and ascended Lord, a rule now actualized in the Christian community under the conditions of spiritual combat and cross-bearing.

As I have already observed, Calvin, in typical sixteenth-century Reformation style, adduces the reality of Christ *in loco justificationis* in connection with the liberating proclamation of the divine grace addressed to the tormented moral conscience. However, for Calvin it is distinctively Jesus Christ who is the mediator, true God and true human (as the Chalcedonian formula has it) and as such prophet, priest, and king.

At times in the *Institutes* Calvin seems to play with the notion that the gulf between God the Creator and humanity the creature is so vast that

---

[23] Calvin's teaching about resistance to tyranny and his projection of equality as a norm of the absolute moral law also provide resources for a twentieth-century South African theology of liberation like Allan Boesak's. See, for example, Boesak, *Farewell to Innocence: A Socio-Ethical Study of Black Theology and Black Power* (Maryknoll, NY: Orbis, 1977).

creaturely knowledge of God would have required a mediator, even apart from humanity's sin. At times, Calvin casts a furtive, favorable glance at the Scotist thesis that God would have become human, identifying himself with the human creature, even apart from sin. But when Calvin devotes himself to the presentation and ordering of the biblical narrative, he thrusts aside such "speculations" and talks of the divine "ordination" of humanity's creation and fall and the coming of the mediator in reaction to that fall.

Calvin's doctrine of Jesus Christ, the anointed one, as prophet, priest, and king attests to his preoccupation with an "intratextual" reading of the Old and New Testaments. Each of these "anointed" Old Testament figures is a type fulfilled in Christ.

To a modern, it may seem curious that a "scriptural ethical monotheism" like Calvin's is really not very fully developed on the matter of Christ as prophet. (Only nineteenth- and twentieth-century biblical criticism opens the possibility of "prophetic" ethical monotheisms in either Judaism or Christianity.) For Calvin, the prophetic figure is a teacher of true doctrine. The type is fulfilled in Christ the teacher of true doctrine who is himself the Truth.

The doctrines of Christ as priest and king are much more fully developed, though an initial inspection of the doctrine of Christ as priest may provide the most powerful counter-indication to my assertion that Calvin's religious system is an ethical monotheism. For Calvin's doctrine of Christ as priest makes at least some use of what some might call the sub-moral if not anti-moral categories of pollution-curse. Indeed, I am deeply impressed by George Kehm's contention that the Old Testament themes of pollution, curse, and sacrifice contribute a basic and irreducible element to Calvin's doctrine of Christ as priest.[24] Humans as sinners are polluted and, as such, under the curse of God; Christ the sacrificial victim bears the curse of God and cleanses humanity from the pollution of sin. These themes, Kehm contends, are rationalized in the secondary schematism of substitutionary punishment, a schematism in which one finds juridical notions of an extra-moral "physical" punishment which must be carried out in response to violations which are initially moral or at least intentional in character. I can only note further, as Kehm does, that Calvin, in line with the epistle to the Hebrews, constantly refers to the final outcome of Christ's priestly work as the "sprinkling" and cleansing of the tormented conscience. Like the book of Leviticus, Calvin seems to be able to tolerate the close

---

[24] Kehm, "Calvin on Defilement and Sacrifice."

juxtaposition of themes of pollution and sacrifice and talk about moral violations, both witting and unwitting.[25]

Calvin insists that the kingdom of the crucified and risen Lord, who rules at the right hand of God the Father, is already established. True, this kingdom is provisional in the sense that at the end of the ages Christ will deliver the kingdom over to God the Father and God will be, in the Pauline phrase, "all in all." But Christ the king really rules at present not only in the ecclesiastical community but in the "world."

Such kingly rule reaffirms the goodness of creation. That "meditation on the future life" recommended by Calvin implies no depreciation of the metaphysical status of this world. On the contrary, the "lifting up of the heart" to the risen Lord energizes moral and social activity and orients that self-discipline Weber rightly calls "inner-worldly asceticism." What is more, this interpretation of Christ's present kingly rule is linked to Calvin's interpretation of the moral instruction in the Sermon on the Mount and to his conception of how the Sermon on the Mount is related to the Ten Commandments.

The moral teaching in the Sermon on the Mount reaffirms the instruction of the Ten Commandments; and both the Sermon on the Mount and the Ten Commandments are a statement of, to use Troeltsch's problematic but useful terminology, the "relative natural law," the moral law appropriate for the whole of humanity after the fall. In this interpretation of the Sermon on the Mount, Calvin differs from Luther, who stresses a novel and radical interiorization of the law as requiring absolute purity of intention. Moreover, Calvin's doctrine of the kingdom differs from the two kingdoms doctrine of Luther with its paradoxical linking of two modes of divine rulership—the kingdom of the church where grace, love and non-coercion prevail and the this-worldly kingdom where law, justice, and coercion are normative. Furthermore, Calvin is heavily critical of the Anabaptist notion of the church as a non-violent community, separated from the surrounding social world, and forbidden to engage in the tasks of governmental action and responsibility for the whole of civilization. In fact, much of the polemic in Calvin's exposition of the Ten Commandments is directed against the non-violent wing of the Anabaptist movement, a movement with which Calvin came into most extensive contact during

---

[25] For a discussion of the themes of pollution and purity in Calvin's thought from yet another angle, see William J. Bouwsma, *John Calvin: A Sixteenth Century Portrait* (New York/Oxford: Oxford University Press, 1988). Bouwsma probes a possible connection between Calvin and psychic and social-psychic preoccupations with "purity and danger" in the social and religious turbulence and efforts at reconstruction in the sixteenth century.

his Strasbourg sojourn. It is especially the moral and societal implications of the kingly rule of Christ which permit H. Richard Niebuhr to characterize Calvin's view of "Christ and culture" as Christ transforming culture."[26]

Indeed, this central conviction about the present kingly rule of Christ shapes Calvin's expectation of a "final resurrection." There will be a transformation of the creaturely world in which the soul of each person will be newly integrated with a transformed body. But Calvin does not look forward in apocalyptic expectation to a conclusion of history that is totally against the grain of its present movement. It is therefore not inappropriate that Calvin's attention never turned to a commentary on the Revelation of John.

I propose now a close reading of the *Institutes* 2,7,9-11, which will permit a recapitulation of a number of themes already treated.[27] At some points in this exposition Calvin presents, as Hans Frei points out, a static conception of total congruence between the content of the Old Testament and the New.[28] In Calvin's terminology, there is identity of "substance" between the Old Testament and the New, though differentiation of "administration." What is present to the "Fathers" of the Old Testament, though not explicitly acknowledged by them as such, is the "grace of Christ." Thus, they really participate in the salvation mediated only by the mediator, Jesus Christ, prophet, priest and king. Further, what is conveyed to the Christian, who reads the Old Testament as Christian scripture, is the "grace of Christ." Clearly, this is a judgment about the content of the Old Testament made by a sixteenth century interpreter who proposes to read the whole canon "intratextually." "Scripture interprets itself."

This assertion of congruity of content is connected with an issue of ethical theory. Calvin wants to turn aside from Luther's sharp contrast of Old Testament law and New Testament gospel. Luther tends to characterize the whole of the Old Testament and even the Sermon on the Mount as "law" (whether as law employed politically in regulating institutional life or law convicting human beings of sin and driving them

---

[26] H. Richard Niebuhr, *Christ and Culture* (New York: Harper & Row, 1951) 206-218; especially 217-218.

[27] The titles of these chapters are in the Battles-McNeill translation: chapter 7, "The Law Was Given, Not to Restrain the Folk of the Old Covenant under Itself, but to Foster Hope of Salvation in Christ until His Coming;" chapter 9, "Christ, Although He Was Known to the Jews under the Law, Was at Length Clearly Revealed Only in the Gospel;" chapter 10, "The Similarity of Old and New Testament;" chapter 11, "The Difference Between the Two Testaments."

[28] Frei, *The Eclipse of Biblical Narrative*, 30.

to Christ). For Luther, on the other hand, the New Testament is "gospel." For Calvin both the Old and New Testaments present the grace of Christ as well as a law. This law convicts of sin but, when used politically, it also shapes social life and when used by the individual believer, shapes the moral life. In addition to this polemic against Luther, Calvin also wishes to refute the claim of the non-violent Anabaptists that the New Testament moral teaching presents an unprecedented and novel set of demands. Nevertheless, although Calvin asserts at times in this exposition a static congruity of content between the Old Testament and the New, at other times he indicates a sense of forward movement.

This idea of a forward movement is signaled by the fact that Calvin rejects the notion that all Old Testament texts refer either directly or indirectly to Christ. Some Old Testament passages are best interpreted in their original "historical" context and indeed should be exclusively so interpreted. To put it from a doctrinal point of view, the Old Testament presents a promise not yet fulfilled. Within the scheme of promise and fulfillment, Calvin focuses on the frustration of the Fathers in not yet attaining the fullness of the promise. He speaks as well of their anticipation of the promise deliberately expressed by them in "figural" rather than explicit terms. Further, Calvin asserts the insufficiency of what the Fathers have indeed thus far attained.[29]

Paired with the scheme of promise and fulfillment is one of "shadow" and "reality." The "shadow-reality" scheme provides the framework for Calvin's fundamental distinction between three types of Old Testament law: ceremonial, political (sometimes called "judicial") and moral. While the validity of the moral law of the Old Testament remains intact in the Christian dispensation, the ceremonial and political law are superseded under the kingly rule of Christ. Indeed, it is a mistake to claim that Calvin seeks to apply Old Testament political ("judicial") law directly to the reconstruction of society in his own day. On the contrary, in the exposition of the theory of civil government in the *Institutes* (4.20), Calvin recognizes the validity of a wide variety of social, political and legal systems in a plurality of circumstances, both in classical antiquity and in his own time. In fact, Calvin assigns to the "natural reason" of fallen humanity a very extensive competence in the construction and maintenance of well-ordered societies.

I propose to analyze in conclusion a concentrated statement of Calvin's system in which many of its principal elements are set out: the exposition of the Ten Commandments in the *Institutes* 2.8.13-51. For all

---

[29] Ibid., 30-32.

the major theologians of the sixteenth century Reformation, it was customary to expound the commandments as part of the catechetical instruction of a new class of educated and active lay persons. But in Calvin's case to a striking degree the exposition of the commandments provides an occasion for recapitulating elements of his system.

Like that of other Reformers, Calvin's exposition employs the notion of "two tables of the law." The first is concerned with the proper worship of God, and the second with obligations to the neighbor. In line with his basic theological position, Calvin posits a reciprocal relation between the self's proper orientation in singular devotion to God and the proper discerning and carrying out of obligations to the neighbor. Singular devotion to God includes constant conversion of the self from self-enclosure to orientation to the one God. Obligation to one's neighbor is the "eternal law" of love, which Calvin also calls a "scheme of equity." This reciprocal relation is a specific instance of the correlation between proper knowledge of God and knowledge of ourselves, which characterizes Calvin's practical non-speculative piety.

The commandments of the "second table" inscribe the moral demand which is obligatory for the whole of humanity. But this is also the "relative natural law," to use Troeltsch's terms, the law which obligates all of humanity, including Christians, under the conditions of the fall. Hence, a majority of the commandments of the "second table" are framed as prohibitions. But Calvin's uniform rule of exposition is this: whenever one finds in the Ten Commandments a prohibition, one is enjoined to enquire what positive activity is implied for the benefit of the neighbor and the enhancement of his or her life. This is God's "eternal law," the "scheme of equity," the "perpetual rule of love" for the neighbor.[30]

I turn now to Calvin's treatment of three of the commandments; two from the first table, the first commandment and the fourth commandment; and one from the second, the fifth commandment. The first commandment states: "I am Jehovah, your God who brought you out of the Land of Egypt, out of the house of bondage. You shall have no other gods before my face" (Exod 20:2-3). According to Calvin (2.8.13-16), the phrase "I am Jehovah your God" is a preface to the whole law, guaranteeing its majesty. God is the sovereign and free commander who shows himself as the one who has the right to command, as the one to whom obedience is due. The "chosen people" are constrained by the necessity of obeying him; but God also holds out the promise of grace to

---

[30] This point is stated with precision in Little, "Calvin and the Prospect for a Christian Theory of Natural Law."

"draw them by its sweetness to a zeal for holiness." Initially stating the matter in terms of the Old Testament elect people, Calvin can immediately say without the slightest embarrassment that God attracts people to his law with sweetness by declaring himself God of the Church.

Further, the motivation for obeying the law is gratitude: gratitude for the action of God in establishing the chosen people, bringing them out of bondage in Egypt. This gratitude merges imperceptibly with gratitude for the benefits of a good creation. The specification of the commandment in terms of having no other gods before God's face demands that humanity not transfer to another what belongs to God. The self is a "factory of idols" and must constantly be converted to life before God in gratitude.

Not unexpectedly, Calvin lays out the basis of his whole religious and moral system in expounding the first commandment. But quite typically he also articulates a wide range of his preoccupations in dealing with the specific commandment for worship, the fourth commandment. This commandment states: "Remember the sabbath day. Six days you shall labor and do all your work; but the seventh day is a sabbath to Jehovah your God. In it you shall not do any work" (Exod 20:8-10). As read and heard currently in the church according to Calvin (*Institutes* 2.8.33-34), this commandment enjoins a weekly regular celebration of the "Lord's Day." His immediate polemical target is the yearly Roman Catholic liturgical cycle of festivals and saints' days.

Calvin is especially sensitive to the charge that by insisting on celebrating the Lord's Day every seven days, and that exclusively, he is "lapsing into Judaism."[31] Calvin does seem curiously indisposed to make much theological capital out of the linking of the resurrection of Christ with the celebration of the Lord's Day on the first day of the week, as an institution superseding the Jewish celebration of the seventh day.

---

[31] There is no reason to suppose that Calvin escapes from the fundamental Christian teaching, in place since the apologists of the second century, that the church as New Israel supersedes in principle God's *peuple ancien*. Indeed Calvin's French expression *peuple ancien* signifies in certain respects both "the people of the Old Covenant" and "the superseded people." The bafflement about the "persistence of the Jews," however, also remains for Calvin. In connection with the special concerns of this study, it is striking to note that Calvin repeats one of Augustine's theses on the "persistence of the Jews," namely, that the Jews are primarily "book men" preserving independently in the Christian epoch the unadulterated text of Old Testament scripture, a scripture of "the Law and the Prophets" which Jews (no longer) read correctly (*Institutes* 1.8.10).

Calvin insists that, under the Old Covenant and under the New, the fourth commandment points the "people of God" to a day of spiritual rest. Admittedly, the spiritual rest to which the Fathers of the Old Testament explicitly aspire is only a shadow of the final rest that Christians anticipate, secure in their present hope under the kingly rule of Christ. But the people of the New Covenant as well as the Old are enjoined, according to Calvin, to imitate God the Creator, who rested after the work of creation.[32]

Moreover, Calvin insists that the fourth commandment requirement has a specific social-ethical component, the full import of which can be grasped only in the light of a full range of Old Testament legal texts: those who serve under the authority of others are to be given a weekly respite from work.

I turn now to an example of Calvin's interpretation of the "second table of the law," the fifth commandment: "Honor your father and your mother that you may be long-lived in the land which Jehovah your God shall give you" (Exod 20:12). In his exposition of this commandment, Calvin seems strangely attracted from the outset to the fact that God himself is designated as Father, and indeed not merely the gracious Father of Jesus Christ. Calvin's interpretation is controlled by the notion of God the Father as a householder who provides for the maintenance of his whole creaturely "oeconomia." According to Calvin, this maintenance of the "oeconomia" requires the inviolable maintenance of the degrees of pre-eminence established by God. Thus Calvin vindicates the principle of authority in the life of the whole of humanity. The specific commandment "Honor your father and your mother" is a particularization of this principle of authority.

It would be wrong, however, to leave the impression that in Calvin's system as a whole one finds a uniform endorsement of human patriarchal authority. Indeed, in the case of marriage, which is also integral to the functioning of the divine "oeconomia," Calvin stresses elements of mutuality between husband and wife. Admittedly, Calvin says that under the conditions of the fall there is a requirement of the "relative natural law" (in Troeltsch's terms) for subordination of wife to husband. But this subordination is not according to the original creation of humanity in the image of God; in the original creation equality of man and woman prevailed. Nor in the sphere of ultimate salvation is there anything but equality between man and woman. The relative subordination of wife to husband in marriage is, in Calvin's terminology,

---

[32] Calvin here gives independent status to the notion of the "imitation of God," a theme not often adduced in Christian theology, though central to classic rabbinic-Judaic thought.

only a "political" distinction suitable for the condition of fallen humanity.[33]

Thus in the interpretation of both "tables of the law," there is a playing back and forth between knowledge of God (as Creator, Governor, and Redeemer) and knowledge of ourselves.

Concentration on Calvin's interpretation of the Old Testament and the New, coupled with concentration on the moral conscience that is comforted by the message of grace in Christ and empowered to energetic activity, produces a partial account of Calvin's teaching. Taking Gilbert Vincent in tandem with Ernst Troeltsch as principal guides gives one an incomplete tour of the vast territories of Calvin's thought. Is it not possible that, contrary to the impression I have given of Calvin's "scriptural ethical monotheism," Calvin presents an account of a divine will in which there lurks a dark transmoral irrationality? Calvin, in the *Institutes*, seems at one point to be as much debating himself as his opponents when he insists that he does not present two completely divergent wills of God, one secret and utterly impenetrable to human understanding and the other manifest in covenant faithfulness and salvific intent. Have I not, further, underplayed that awesome and tremendous wrath of God exhibited in Calvin's doctrine of penal substitutionary atonement?

Or, to focus on humanity, is not the Calvin I have presented entirely too comforted in conscience, too robustly confident in his moral action? Have I not, so to speak, thrust aside too easily the stunning new portrait by William Bouwsma (1988) of a Calvin riddled with existential anxiety, shut up in the labyrinth of no longer adequate ecclesiastical and social structures yet aghast at the abyss of freedom he sees opening out before him?

Or, to turn to the interaction of God the Governor and humanity the moral actor, even if it is true that Calvin never invokes the doctrine of election in deducing theories or deciding cases in the sphere of ecclesiastical discipline and the interaction of ecclesiastical and political authority, does not the Calvin of the *Institutes* frequently claim to discern with precision the divine punishment of the wicked in history? Does he not presume to identify instances of God's judgment against the moral lapses of nations and individuals?

---

[33] On these questions, see Jane Dempsey Douglass, *Women, Freedom, and Calvin* (Philadelphia: Westminster, 1985) and John L. Thompson, "*Creata ad Imaginem Dei: Licet Secundo Gradu:* Woman as the Image of God According to Calvin," *HTR* 86 (1988) 125-143.

My account is indeed a partial and selective one, but I believe it does give us a Calvin whose religious system shaped a people of God and contributed powerfully to the modern Western ethos. I offer it with respect and affection in honor of Paul Meyer. I first encountered Paul Meyer when I was a doctoral student and he was a professor at Yale University. In more recent years we have been regularly associated in a study group called the Biblical Theologians. This group is dedicated to the proposition that rigorous critical biblical exegesis and sound theology can be amiably associated, albeit not without a certain tension. Calvin believed that and so, I judge, does Paul Meyer.